W9-BXD-786

People Are Talking About

Catholic Social Teaching and Movements

"This book makes a unique contribution to our knowledge of social teaching and movements. Dr. Mich has pulled together not only the teaching but also how it was put into practice by so many heroic people. This is a goldmine of information for anyone who is interested in how the teaching of Jesus Christ should affect our lives and our work."

> Most Rev. Rembert G. Weakland, O.S.B.
> Archbishop of Milwaukee

"This is the only book I know of that tells the story of the Catholic Social Teaching tradition from the 'bottom up' or, in the author's summary, offers an introduction to both parts of the Catholic social tradition—the documents and the movement—in one text. The author calls it a 'risky venture,' but, in my opinion, he has carried it off extremely well.

"It is the best available book of its kind."

> Msgr. George G. Higgins
> The Catholic University of America
> Washington, DC

"This is an extraordinary book. What I found fascinating was that it links the official teaching of Popes and Bishops with the dynamic and self-sacrificing work of the laity in particular, but also of dedicated women religious and clergy, over the last 100 years.

"I could not recommend this study more highly."

> Msgr. John J. Egan
> DePaul University, Chicago

"This is not just another dry listing of authoritative church texts without comment. Rather, it is a very readable and helpful development of thought, reaction, and criticism that situates the reader to move forward on very solid ground. Good historical theology as it should be."

> Richard Rohr, O.F.M.
> Center for Action and Contemplation
> Albuquerque, NM

"This book is both profound and highly readable. It gives us history, philosophy, theology, accuracy, and thoroughness without dullness. I've been reading and writing on the subject for over seventy years and I am impressed."

Msgr. Charles Owen Rice
Social Justice Activist, Journalist, Scholar
Retired working parish priest

"This is a splendid introduction to the development of modern social Catholicism. In my view, no other book provides a better introduction to the prophetic side of the modern Catholic tradition."

Edward 'Joe' Holland, Ph.D.
St. Thomas University
Miami, FL

"What an integration of the theory and practice of Catholic social teaching! On the one hand, I can see this book being used as a basic text for those newly introduced to our church. On the other hand, its breadth and depth will make it something old-timers like myself will return to over and over."

Michael Crosby, OFM Cap.
Corporate Responsibility Program
Milwaukee, WI

"Here Mich offers an attractive exposition of Catholic social thought, linking key encyclicals and their developing themes to contemporary problems such as economic justice, war and peace, liberation theology, race and gender, a consistent ethic of life, and ecology."

Dr. Lisa Sowle Cahill
Boston College

"Can one book give due attention to the social teachings of the church through encyclicals and pastoral letters and yet present the living reality of activists and their creative responses to social needs? Yes and it's this one.

In this much-needed book, Mich demonstrates how church teachings take flesh in movements for peace and social reconstruction, and he writes with verve and clarity."

Eileen Egan, New York City

CATHOLIC SOCIAL TEACHING AND MOVEMENTS

MARVIN L. KRIER MICH

TWENTY-THIRD PUBLICATIONS
Mystic, CT 06355

Twenty-Third Publications
185 Willow Street
P.O. Box 180
Mystic, CT 06355
(860) 536-2611
(800) 321-0411

Copyright © 1998 Marvin L. Krier Mich. All rights reserved. No part of this publication may be reproduced in any manner without prior written permission of the publisher. Write to the Permissions Editor.

ISBN: 0-89622-936-X
Library of Congress Catalog Card Number: 98-60621
Printed in the U.S.A.

The poem on page 100-101 is reprinted with the permission of America Press, Inc. 106 West 56th Street, New York, NY 10019. Phone: 212-581-4640. © 1963 All Rights Reserved.

*To my twin sister, Marilyn Ladwig,
who gracefully taught us about
being connected, joy, and justice
in her living and dying
(1948-1998).*

Table of Contents

Acknowledgments

This work reflects the experience of teaching a course, "The Theology of Social Ministry," at St. Bernard's Institute in Rochester and Albany, New York over the last sixteen years. I am grateful to all the students who have helped me to come to a better appreciation the Catholic social tradition through the discipline of teaching. I am also grateful to the administration and Board of Trustees of St. Bernard's Institute, namely, Father Sebastian Falcone, who as the president of St. Bernard's supported my sabbatical in the Fall of 1991 when the initial research and writing was undertaken. Sister Patricia Schoelles, the current president of the Institute, also supported this project by allowing me to have a lighter teaching load during the Spring semester of 1997.

During the three-month sabbatical in 1991 I was blessed by the hospitality of Father James Lawlor and the staff of St. Mary's parish, Rochester, who provided me with a quiet getaway for writing.

I want to thank my wife, Kristine, and my children, Rachel and Nathaniel, who gracefully shared me with this project. They were supportive and understanding. And thanks, too, to Nathaniel for his help with the indexing.

Finally, I acknowledge the support of the staff at Twenty-Third Publications, especially Neil Kluepfel, who took the risk of publishing a new kind of text on this topic, and Dan Connors, for his careful editing.

CATHOLIC SOCIAL TEACHING AND MOVEMENTS

Introduction

The Roman Catholic church has a rich tradition of social teachings. Some would claim it is "our best kept secret."[1] When Catholics tell the story of our social teachings we tend to focus on the *encyclicals and pastoral letters*. We point with pride to how Pope Leo XIII broke new ground in supporting the workers' right to unions, and we celebrate the breakthroughs of the Second Vatican Council on human rights and religious liberty. What is not often told is the story of Catholic social tradition from the "bottom up," from the perspective of *activists and leaders* who lived out that teaching and, in the process, helped to forge that living tradition.

The purpose of this book is to tell the story of Catholic social tradition "from below" and "from above," from the perspective of the official teachings and the movements that expressed and shaped that teaching. Our story, our history, is more than a collection of official statements, it includes the prophets and activists, thinkers and analysts who wrestled with the meaning of Christian faith amid turbulent social times. My intention is to offer you an introduction to both parts of the Catholic social tradition—the documents and the movements—in one text. I am not aware of any other introductory text that brings together the encyclicals and the activists in the same book, indeed, in each chapter. It is a risky venture. At times it feels like mixing together oil and water, and at other times it fits like a hand in a glove.

The story of Catholic social teaching really begins in the first pages of the Bible when our religious ancestors struggled to follow God's invitation to be a people in covenant. The prophets were sent to help focus the people's attention when they were distracted and sinning. Jesus came to humanity as the justice of God, and he sent his disciples to announce God's liberating and saving message. With the gift of the Spirit the early church continued the work of Jesus. The church wrestled with many social issues—war, wealth, and the use of worldly power—as it spread into the Greco-Roman world. The medieval church emerged with a hierarchical vision of society wherein the church had a role of primacy over other institutions. With the discovery of the New World, another series of questions confronted moralists as did the new religious tensions brought on by the Reformation. The emergence of individual rights in the eighteenth century led to a radically different vision of society and of justice as centered on social contract rather than medieval order, with duty flowing from one's role in society. The political and social unrest that followed reshaped European history with implications for non-European nations as well. It is against this broad backdrop that we take up the story of Catholic social teachings in the modern era.

While there is much to explore in earlier time periods, the modern era holds the greatest interest for us today, for it reveals the church coming to grips with the challenges of industrial capitalism, a challenge that we are still responding to as we move into the third millennium.

The text begins with the Father Emmanuel von Ketteler's Advent sermons in 1848, which were meant to awaken the conscience of German Catholics to the social problems surrounding them. His preaching and writing were sparks that ignited a modest, yet effective, movement in Europe known as the "Social Catholics." The "Social Catholics" had a direct impact on the writing of *Rerum Novarum* in 1891. American Catholics also helped to shape magisterial teaching as they wrestled with the rights of workers in the emerging labor movement (see chapter two).

Chapter three brings us into contact with the vitality of a new breed of Catholics in the United States, people like Dorothy Day and Baroness Catherine de Hueck Doherty who were both radical and Catholic at the same time.

Chapter four looks more closely at the 1950s and 1960s. We examine the contribution of a gifted Jesuit, John Courtney Murray, and the charismatic Pope John XXIII. Both men opened the church to a new understanding of freedom.

In chapter five we examine the revolutionary impact of the Second Vatican Council and the civil rights movement of the late 1960s that unearthed the explicit and implicit racism in society and the church. Chapter six looks at the organizing efforts and spiritual strategies of Cesar Chavez who lived out his religious commitment in working for justice for America's farm workers. His work is contrasted with the global vision of Pope Paul VI's encyclical "On the Development of Peoples," *Populorum Progressio.*

Chapter seven focuses on the "call to action" that was heard throughout the church from the Synod and the taking up of that call by communities of religious men and women who engaged in social analysis and new forms of social ministry that addressed institutional and systemic injustice.

The vision of the "consistent ethic of life" as articulated by grass-roots groups, Cardinal Bernardin, and Pope John Paul II is the focus of chapter eight. The vision of the consistent ethic of life is very much a "work in progress." The next part of the story takes us to Latin America as we examine, in chapter nine, the implications of the Latin American bishops' preferential option for the poor and the movement of liberation theology.

The next three chapters tell of the U.S. bishops' teaching on the morality of nuclear weapons and deterrence, the U.S. economy, and the role of women in society and the church—as the bishops articulated their thinking in the process of writing their pastoral letters. The bishops' efforts are complemented and challenged by the persistent peace movement, a social ministry that goes beyond charity to advocacy, and the feminist movement in the Anglo, Black, and Hispanic communities. The unfinished pastoral letter on the role of women reminds us that the church has a lot more work to do on these issues.

The final chapter takes us beyond the realm of the human to consider the broader community of the biosphere. Here the spirituality, moral reflection, and theology of Catholicism is put in dialogue with the wisdom of the environmental movement found in the traditions of non-Christian cultures and spiritualities. Catholic social teaching is challenged to live up to its name as a theology and a pastoral ministry that is inclusive and universal, that is, truly catholic.

There are a number of reasons for writing a book that covers both the "official" social teaching and the "unofficial" movements and activists. First, we are only telling half of the story if we focus solely on the magisterial documents—as important as these encyclicals are. "...The non-magisterial contribution to the development of the Church's social teaching must be actively embraced. For in truth of fact, Catholic social teachings are not shaped by the magisterium alone. This reality must be acknowledged and celebrated."[2]

A second reason for telling the story of the social activists is to remind us that *we are all responsible* for the shaping of the Catholic social tradition. The church as a whole—activists and theologians, pope and laity, bishops and religious women—is given the task of discerning God's will. As Vatican II proclaimed, "the People of God believes that it is led by the Spirit of the Lord, who fills the earth. Motivated by this faith, it labors to decipher authentic signs of God's presence and purpose in the happenings, needs and desires in which this People has a part along with other men of our age."[3] This task of deciphering God's presence and purpose belongs to the whole church. This book tells the story of some of the men and women in the Catholic community in the last 120 years who have taken up that responsibility in creative and bold ways. It is a summons for the church of the present to continue this holy work.

Third, I believe that knowledge of the past helps us understand the present, and it *opens up the future*. I have been impressed with the work of the Dutch theologian Edward Schillebeeckx, who opened up the history of ministry in the church. His books reveal how the church has been creative in the past in responding to the historical circumstances and reshaping ministry to meets the needs of the day.[4] Knowledge of this history tells us as a church that we can also be creative as we respond to the needs of ministry today. I believe the same can be said in the area of social teachings and social ministry. If we know something of "our collective story" we will be encouraged to respond with the energy of the same Spirit who prompted our predecessors to take bold and innovative steps.

1

"Social Catholics" and *Rerum Novarum*

Part I. Social Catholics in Europe

1848 was a year of revolutions in Europe.

- In January a rebellion broke out in Sicily.

- In Paris the February Revolution broke out and then spread throughout the rest of France.

- A series of revolutions erupted across Europe, especially in Berlin and Vienna.[1]

- as the year unfolded, Karl Marx was about to issue his revolutionary call to workers to throw off their chains in his *Manifesto of the Communist Party*.

5

In 1848 Father Wilhelm Emmanuel von Ketteler of Mainz, Germany, was about to initiate a moral and religious revolution as well. Ketteler's ministry was the beginning of a new way of analyzing and addressing the social and economic devastation caused by the Industrial Revolution. The movement he started is known as "Social Catholicism."

As pastor of the main Catholic church in Berlin he had witnessed the ravages of poverty and the violence it had spawned. He began to pay attention to the social ills around him, especially the subsistence wages of factory workers. "...From 1848 on, it was already clear to him, on the one hand that here lay a great need of the time, an evil to be remedied; and on the other, that the Roman Catholic Church was called upon to make a determined effort in response."[2]

As a parish priest he spoke out on these social ills at the first general assembly of Catholics from all over Germany. This Catholic Assembly (Katholikentag), held in Frankfurt, was made up primarily of the lay Catholic clubs and organizations that were being established everywhere. As a delegate to the assembly Father Ketteler was expected to address one or more of the hot constitutional issues that was on everyone's mind. Instead Father Ketteler directed the attention of the Catholic Assembly to "the social question," by which he meant the gross inequalities of wealth and poverty in Germany and the immense growth of poverty. He believed the church had to address this urgent problem of the age.[3]

Later in that same year Father Ketteler was invited to give the Advent sermons in the cathedral in Mainz. He delivered six powerful sermons that would awaken the social conscience of German Catholics.

In 1850 Father Ketteler became the archbishop of Mainz. He went on to dialogue with proponents of socialism and laissez-faire capitalism in developing a Christian response to the social ills of the day, which he based on Thomas Aquinas. Although his major work, *Die Arbeiterfrage und das Christentum* (The Question of the Worker and Christendom), has yet to be translated into English, he has had an undeniable influence on the shape of Catholic social thought. Later Catholic thinkers in the "Fribourg Union" (see p. 9) would consider Ketteler their spiritual father.

Ketteler, like other Catholic thinkers of the day, condemned the ruthless competition and harsh individualism that typified early capitalism. Building on Aquinas, Ketteler defended private property as a limited right. On the one hand, his position challenged Karl Marx, who had rejected private property, and on the other hand, he challenged the "liberals" of his day who claimed that private property was an absolute right:

> Separated from God, men regard themselves as the exclusive masters of their possessions and look upon them only as a means of satisfying their ever-increasing love of pleasure; separated from God they set up sensual pleasures as the enjoyments of life as the means of attaining this end; and so of necessity a gulf was formed between the rich and the poor.[4]

Archbishop Ketteler not only challenged the socialist and capitalist mindsets of his day, but also offered specific remedies. At an assembly of German bishops on September 5, 1869, he listed the following, which, he maintained, "eliminate or at any rate diminish the evils of our present industrial system":

1) the prohibition of child labor in factories;

2) the limitation of working hours for factory workers;

3) the separation of the sexes in the workshops;

4) the closing of unsanitary workshops;

5) Sunday rest;

6) the obligation to care for workers who are temporarily or permanently disabled;

7) the appointment by the state of factory inspectors.[5]

Ketteler was the forerunner and inspiration of the German Catholic social movement. His influence was "practically dominant in the world of German-speaking social Catholicism; and German-speaking social Catholicism was ahead of social Catholicism elsewhere, in keeping with Germany's industrial development in the latter part of the 19th century."[6] He began a persistent campaign to awaken church and society to the real character of "the social question" in the last half of the nineteenth century.

The roots of *Rerum Novarum* are found in sermons and writings of this parish priest who spoke out and analyzed the poverty and subsistence wages of his community. Forty-three years later, Pope Leo XIII, who studied Ketteler's writing, named Archbishop Ketteler "our great predecessor" in addressing the social question.

LAITY AND CLERGY EXERT LEADERSHIP

A year after Archbishop Ketteler's speech to the German bishops, another series of violent outbreaks in Europe catalyzed Catholic clergy and laity to respond. In 1870 and 1871 Europe witnessed the outbreak of the Franco-Prussian war and the worker insurrection known as the Commune de Paris. According to theologian and historian Normand Paulhus, "both events threatened the stability of Europe and underlined the urgency of rethinking the whole basis of society and of presenting new ways of dealing with the deteriorating condition of a working class rapidly being won over to socialism."[7]

In these worsening conditions, ordained and lay leadership emerged to give direction and focus to the church's social ministry. In France two military officers, Albert de Mun and Rene de La Tour du Pin, who met in a German prisoner of war camp at Aachen (Aix-la-Chapelle) in 1870, were determined to respond to the plight of the working class when they got out of prison. The following year they organized a Catholic Workers' club in Paris, under the name "L'Oeuvre des Cercles Catholiques d'Ouvriers" (Society of Catholic Worker circles). The clubs spread quickly throughout France—by 1884 there were 400 such clubs with 50,000 members.[8] These "circles" or clubs brought together the wealthy and the workers from a given locale for prayer, socializing, and hearing lectures by members of the aristocracy.

De Mun went on to establish the Catholic Association of French Youth in 1886 as a feeder institution for the workers' clubs. The Youth organization eventually attracted over 140,000 members.[9] "Despite its obvious paternalism and its failure to prepare working-class leaders, this movement contributed immensely to the growing social awareness of the aristocracy and the middle class."[10] The "circles" led to a desire for greater understanding and discussion of the issues. Eventually a journal was published, *L'Association Catholique*, which became the primary source of information about the Catholic response to "the social question."

Study groups of "Social Catholics" were started in Italy and Austria as well. Pope Leo XIII established a "Circle of Social and Economic Studies" in Rome. In Austria, Karl von Vogelsang, a convert of Bishop Ketteler, led the German and Austrian study group known as the "Freie Vereinigung katholische Sozialpolitiker" (Catholic Social-Political Free Union). Vogelsang called for the reorganization of society according to professions rather than by classes. These professional associations would be represented in the governing branches of the state, thereby linking together social and political realism. In this way he hoped to overcome both the excessive individualism of capitalism and the collectivism of socialism. "Vogelsang hoped to realize the social ideals of the Middle Ages, not restore its social order."[11]

THE FRIBOURG UNION

One such study group was organized on October 18, 1884 by Prince Karl von Lowenstein and Count Franz Kuefstein of Austria, along with the Marquis Rene de la Tour du Pin and Louis Milcent of France. These four laymen met with the bishop of Lausanne, Gaspard Mermillod, in his residence in Fribourg, Switzerland, and invited other leaders to gather with them forming the "L'Union catholique d'etudes sociales et economiques," or simply the "Fribourg Union."[12]

While Archbishop Ketteler was seen as the spiritual father of these lay and ordained leaders, Bishop Mermillod was their guiding force.

In 1886 Bishop Mermillod challenged the conscience of his people in a speech to the Parisian upper classes. His concern about individualism and poverty caused by unjust social conditions echoes through the century to our times: "The independence of the individual is proclaimed and his solidarity destroyed, man is free, but he is alone...." Having given up nocturnal sleep and Sunday rest to provide the rich with their wealth, he receives in exchange "but a miserable hovel for lodgings and a rare and bitter bread for nourishment."[13]

The "Fribourg Union" met each October from 1885 to 1891. Their intensive days of analysis and discussion began at 9:30 a.m. and concluded at 6:30 p.m. They worked out their ideas in small working groups. After coming to agreement in the small groups they presented their findings to the full body. Attendance at these yearly meetings varied from 20 to 32. Their number included theologians, political leaders, and aristocracy.

The Fribourg Union was predominantly a lay group. This is an important detail, for it shows how clergy and laity can cooperate to shape Catholic social thinking.

These men—unfortunately no women were part of the assembly—came with their own national temperaments and political preferences. Some were more traditional, others were more receptive to the democratic trends of the time—which made for some lively meetings. Despite these differences they shared a common goal of addressing the social cri-

sis of their day out of their faith, in loyalty to the pope, and using the philosophy of Thomas Aquinas. They were committed not only to study and
to presenting papers but also to advocating for changes in international
law that would embody their concern for the worker.

The Fribourg Union was a theological and moral "think tank" of concerned laity and clergy who were committed to shaping attitudes and
public opinion in tumultuous times. In these gatherings Catholics from
different walks of life came together to wrestle with the meaning of their
faith tradition in light of the pressing social and economic problems of
their day. While they did not agree on all issues, they shared common
assumptions that put them at odds with those who wanted capitalism to
remain unfettered.

In the 1880s the thinkers who argued for maximum freedom for business with minimal restraint from the state were known as "economic liberals." The economic liberals favored "laissez-faire capitalism," which
means, literally, "let do," that is, "let people do as they please." The
Fribourg Union argued against laissez-faire capitalism.

Because of conflict with the economic liberal school, Bishop Mermillod
suggested that the members of the Fribourg Union work secretly until a
well-formed body of doctrine could be presented to Leo XIII.

ADDRESSING THE "SOCIAL QUESTION"

In their meetings the Fribourg Union wrestled with "the social question"
of their day. By this term they referred to the tensions between groups in
the industrialized societies. "The social question" referred to the difficulty of reconciling the interests of the new classes of industrial bourgeoisie
with those of industrial workers. It was not just a matter of the tension
between the rich and the poor, but also the question of *the new mode of
production* which, while highly efficient, resulted in a benefit for the few
and the social and economic decline or exploitation of the many.

The Fribourg Union and other "Social Catholics" addressed the *structural and institutional question* of *the morality of the new mode of production,
known as capitalism.* "Social Catholicism" was a unique combination of
progressive and traditional thinking. In general they sought a plan for a
Christian society that avoided the two conflicting ideologies of capitalism and socialism. They rejected the spirit of the French Revolution and
had an unswerving loyalty to the Catholic Church and a firm belief in the
"corporative" vision of society.

CENTRAL THEMES OF THE "SOCIAL CATHOLICS"

The following five themes were central to the discussions and writings of
the Fribourg Union.

1. Charity is not enough

Members of the Fribourg Union realized that the social problems of their
society could not be resolved by charity alone. On this and other points
they collided with the thinking of a group of Catholic economic liberals,
headed by Charles Perin. Some of Perin's followers held that the poverty
of the masses was necessary so that the rich could have the opportunity
to practice the duty of charity.[14] Bishop Mermillod chided this liberal
school of thought, which thought the solution of the day was to be
found in "an individual return to the virtues of Christianity and the
foundation of philanthropic enterprises." Mermillod could be addressing us today when he said, "You have discovered in your theological
sources that it is not enough to alleviate the misery of the poor by your
gifts, but that you must go beyond charity to justice."[15]

2. The just wage

A second area of disagreement with the liberal school was on the crucial
question of wages. The economic liberals saw work as a contract in which
the worker rented out his or her time and was paid accordingly. The just
wage was determined simply by the "freely-accepted" terms of the contract. Nothing else was owed to the worker; other obligations of the owners toward the worker, such as security, coverage for work-related injuries,
and pensions, flowed from the virtue of charity alone.

The Fribourg Union, through the writings of August Lehmkuhl, set
forth basic principles on "work" and wages that shaped Catholic social
thought on this question. First, work must not be seen only as a commodity, but as a personal act of the worker. Second, a just wage is determined by a double criteria, namely, a) the value of human work must
prevail over discussions of wage contracts, and, b) the just wage is determined by the minimum necessary to maintain a family in ordinary circumstances.

3. State intervention

The Social Catholics believed that the intervention of the state was necessary only when the free contracts on wages were oppressive to the worker.
In these circumstances public authorities must intervene to assure that the

workers receive what is necessary for their subsistence. The state's duties are to correct abuses and "to harmonize the activities of private enterprises with the common good while leaving the greatest possible freedom to private initiative."[16] The position of the Social Catholics allowed for greater state intervention than did the position of the economic liberals, but clearly less state intervention than socialists wanted. Pope Leo XIII accepted the Social Catholics' position in its entirety.

4. Private property
On the question of private property the Fribourg Union again walked between the prevailing ideologies of the day, liberal capitalism and socialism. While they defended the right to own private property—against the socialists—they held that the right of private property was a limited right—which the liberals did not accept. The Social Catholics emphasized a prior right ("primordial right"), namely, the right of each person to subsist. This right to subsist limits and tempers the right of private property.

5. "Corporatively organized society"
As the Social Catholics analyzed the situation of their countries they saw a society that was no longer a living organism composed of social cells, each with its own specific role and responsibilities and guided by a distinct authority. They saw a lifeless mechanism, disorganized, lacking an inner harmony and held together solely by a coercive external power. Anonymity and impersonality had become the hallmarks of the economic domain.

Some of the "Social Catholics" wished to return to structures and institutions of precapitalist Europe, but most of them grudgingly accepted that the modern economic system was here to stay. They wished to restore the medieval spirit by proposing a corporative model, not the medieval structures.[17]

The corporative vision of the economy was an "organic" model in which people were to be organized according to their common interests and common social function. For example, in the domain of the arts and crafts workers would move through the three levels of apprentice, journeyman, and master with all three groups working in harmony at a common task. Together they formed a natural grouping, the local corporation. The corporation in this corporative view would try to

- promote a greater "esprit de corps" among its members;

- protect their professional honor;

- increase their material prosperity;

- guarantee the quality of their work;

- oversee the training of apprentices;

- confer certification on those who completed their training success-fully;

- buy raw materials;

- establish steam or electric motors in the workshops; and

- establish stores to sell its products.[18]

The corporative model was also applied to the factory setting. Here they used the metaphor of "family" to describe the relationships between workers and owners. A factory was a professional family focused on a common task in the same place, grouped around its leaders and having common interests. Here we see the desire to restore natural ties and rela-tionships among those working at a common task. The thinkers of the Fribourg Union realized that separate groupings of owners and workers might be necessary in the current situation of antagonism, but this was to be an interim step on the way to a true corporation of uniting both parties into an organic whole.

Building on the "natural relationships and ties" within the factory, the local factory or "professional family" would then be linked with similar fac-tories in the region through a regional council. Membership on this region-al council would include representatives of owners and workers. The own-ers would preside over the council. One of the primary tasks of the council would be to establish, without state interference and with the workers' full participation, the rules governing the profession. The regional council would also establish an endowment to provide for the needs of its mem-bers. This endowment would cover such areas as retirement, insurance, loans, schools, workers' homes, and nursing homes. The endowment would come from membership dues, gifts, and a percentage of the profits. The assumption was that workers, and not just owners, should benefit from the profits of the industry. The Social Catholics created an attractive vision for industry, with collaboration between workers and owners. Unfortunately, it did not mesh well with the economic realities of the day.

The growth of the modern corporation in the nineteenth century was antithetical to the designs and vision of the corporative model. Through the selling of stocks, the modern corporation invests power in owners who are essentially unfamiliar with the industry. The anonymity of the stockholders destroys the personal dimension required in the corporative model. Louis Milcent, a member of the Fribourg Union from France, described the evil of the modern corporation: "...man falls under the yoke of an association which is irresponsible, soulless, without conscience, and without duties; he becomes the instrument of a fictitious being formed by an accumulation of gold and silver, and which is consequently purely material."[19]

The natural ties of a "professional family" were impossible in such a power arrangement. The structure of ownership invested power in the anonymous stockholders. Ownership of the factory by distant stockholders made the relational ties of the "professional family" almost impossible. The corporative model of the Social Catholics was undercut before it could be tested.

SOCIAL CATHOLICS IN RETROSPECT

The Social Catholics believed that the free enterprise system, based on the notion of competition and strife, had transformed the natural human need to associate for the sake of the common good into a selfish search for power for the sake of individual gain. On this point they were generally on target. They traced the economic theory of self-interest to other powerful currents of thought including

- rationalistic philosophies that had eradicated God from society;

- Protestantism, which uprooted the traditional value of authority and had introduced individualism based on excessive freedom; and,

- political philosophies, such as the contract theory of society, which destroyed the basic unity of the medieval world.

As a result of these forces their society had lost its organic unity and was disorganized, anonymous, and impersonal. In their critique of European society they identified many of the forces pulling apart the medieval world. From their vantage point they saw primarily the harm that was being done to society by the forces of individualism and secularization. They did not emphasize the positive contributions of modern thinking, which included granting freedom and dignity to the individual, according respect for dissenting and minority views, and lessening church control over political and social life.

IMPACT OF THE FRIBOURG UNION

These Social Catholics and their Fribourg Union had a clear influence on Pope Leo XIII. As we have already noted above, a number of their positions were adopted by the pope in his encyclical *Rerum Novarum*. In fact, Pope Leo was regularly briefed on the results of the yearly meetings. Bishop Mermillod and several members of the Union met with the pope in 1888, at which time he asked for a copy of all of their work. One of the reasons for the demise of the Fribourg Union was the publication of *Rerum Novarum*, which was seen as a basic confirmation of their positions. Their mission had been accomplished.

The Social Catholics also left a living heritage in the various countries where they were active. This was an emerging tradition of lay and ordained leaders, academic and practical types, that was to continue into the next generation.

Normand Paulhus concludes that "the legacy of the Fribourg Union remains a mixed one." He notes three limitations of its legacy.

- First, their "concrete proposals proved inadequate in the face of the vast changes taking place in industrial society."

- Second, "fascism's use of the organic metaphor to defend totalitarianism further discredited the Social Catholics' efforts to erect a 'corporative system,'" and

- Third, "at times elements of modern liberalism clouded their understanding of Thomas' political theory."[20]

These limitations are understandable. Like all human beings, the Social Catholics were biased and limited in their understanding. We certainly cannot hold them responsible for how their organic thinking was distorted into supporting fascism forty years later. Despite these limitations, the Fribourg Union has "preserved vital elements of the traditional Christian vision of a good society:

- the social purpose of property;

- the positive but limited role of the state;

- the centrality of justice;

- the primacy of duties over rights;

- the principle of subsidiarity, and most important;

- the crucial role of the common good as the unifying force of the political community."[21]

In looking at the Social Catholics, we should also remember that the church was not the first institution to respond to the situation of the workers. The first formal movements for social reform came not from the church but from secular sources that often had an irreligious and even anti-religious character. Both Catholic and Protestant churches had been slow in responding. For decades the Catholic and Protestant churches remained inactive, with near-disastrous consequences.

We also need to remember that the "Social Catholics" were not necessarily representative of the Catholic Church in Europe as a whole. According to the French historian R. Aubert, "The majority of Catholics and the ecclesiastical authorities, till the end of the century, refused to recognize the necessity of the 'reforms of the structure' and considered it very dangerous that the revolutionary forces tried to institutionally modify the workers' conditions."[22] The Catholic Church in the nineteenth century resisted the advances of the French Revolution of 1789 and its Declaration of the Rights of Man. The popes viewed with disapproval the struggles for independence in Latin America. "Certain Catholic circles were haunted by nostalgia for the past.... They believed monarchy to be divinely ordained and continued to proclaim the alliance of throne and altar down to the end of the 19th century."[23]

Social Catholics and economic liberal Catholics in Europe did not agree on how the church's social ethic should be developed in the face of vast social problems and economic unrest. For the conservative Catholics the pope's encyclical was a shock, in that Pope Leo accepted most of the Social Catholics' perspectives.

A number of the Social Catholics' attitudes are not attractive to us today. They were clearly aristocratic and paternalistic as they sought to assist the workers of their time. They also were suspicious of Protestant traditions. They believed that Protestantism uprooted the traditional value of authority and had introduced a rampant individualism based on excessive freedom. This overly individualistic concept of humanity was one of the sources of the society's social ills. Today many social thinkers would agree with the Social Catholics' analysis of the dangers of individualism as a force eroding our social ethic.[24] The responsibility for excessive individualism, however, can no longer be identified with Protestant thinking, because individualism has become a cultural hallmark for Euro-American cultures.

While recognizing that the Social Catholics' paternalism and unecumenical attitudes do not speak to American Catholics today, there is still much in their vision of society that can challenge and awaken us. Many of the questions they wrestled with and resolved in their day are still pertinent for us. Their debates with the economic liberals on questions of private property, the role of the state in the economy, the nature of human work, the necessity of going beyond charity and calling for structural reform—these are all lively issues for our times as well. We can gain insight and perhaps fortitude from dipping into this part of our tradition. They confronted the social issues of their day with the resources of their faith, hard work and long meetings, creativity and dialogue. Those are timeless qualities that would serve us well as we face enormously complex social, political, and economic issues.

AMERICAN CALLS FOR AN ENCYCLICAL

The impact of the Fribourg Union on the writing of *Rerum Novarum* is well established. But the American church also played an important role in shaping the focus and tone of the encyclical. As we shall see in the next chapter, Cardinal James Gibbons of Baltimore was very influential in urging the pope to speak out on behalf of workers. In 1887 he traveled to Rome to urge the pope not to condemn the Knights of Labor, the first American labor union. Gibbons also urged the pope not to condemn the works of Henry George of New York, who as a mayoral candidate urged a single tax on the unearned increment of the value of property as a solution to the nation's social problems. Gibbons argued that, instead of condemnations, the pope should issue an encyclical to address the respective rights and obligations of both capital and labor.[25]

While workers in the United States were experiencing the same harsh social conditions caused by the Industrial Revolution as were the workers in Western Europe, there was one major difference: the workers in the United States generally remained loyal to the church. The success of the Catholic church in the United States in maintaining the loyalty of the working class was "the major influence on Leo's decision to issue an encyclical."[26] While the Europeans were a powerful theoretical influence in shaping the letter, the Americans' practical success was a very important, practical, and positive influence.

From 1887 to 1891, the historian Aaron Abell notes, Leo was

> constantly importuned to elaborate an authoritative statement of principles underlying social thought and action. Beset with controversy involving labor and land issues, American bishops called upon the Holy See for theoretical guidance.... In the hope of putting an end to rifts among American as well as European Catholics, the Pope carefully formulated a social justice program, giving to the world in May 1891 the *Rerum novarum*, a masterly encyclical on the condition of labor.[27]

Part II. *Rerum Novarum*

The future Pope Leo XIII, Vincenzo Gioacchino (Vincent Joachim) Pecci, was born on March 2, 1810, in Carpineto, a small town south of Rome. After his studies at the Roman College (later known as the Gregorian University) he joined the papal service. At this time the Papal States were still under papal control. Father Pecci served as the governor of two Italian regions, Benevento and Perugia, before he was sent as the papal nuncio to Belgium in 1843. During his work as nuncio he made trips to London, Cologne, and Paris, where he came into contact with a more advanced industrialization than in Italy. He also encountered constitutional government. These experiences helped him to be less defensive to modern constitutional democracy than his predecessor, Pius IX. On February 20, 1878, ten days before his 68th birthday, he was elected pope.[28]

FACTORS LEADING TO WRITING *RERUM NOVARUM*

As papal nuncio in Brussels and then as archbishop of Perugia, the future Pope Leo was confronted with the impact of industrial capitalism on the working class. Before his election to the papacy he was familiar with the writings of Archbishop Ketteler. Pope Leo also met with representatives of the Fribourg Union and reviewed their deliberations. Cardinal Gibbons and other American bishops requested his help in addressing the morality of land and labor issues. Other events also played a role in his decision to address the "social question," including:

- contact with the workers on pilgrimage led by the reforming industrialist, Leon Harmel, who brought ten thousand workers to Rome in 1888;

- the public support of Cardinal Manning of London for the striking dockworkers in 1889; and

- the increasingly bitter disagreements between those who argued for some degree of state intervention in economic matters, as espoused by the Fribourg Union, and those who argued to let the market forces be free of government intervention.[29]

The pope had a mixture of motivations that led him to promulgate this letter. His first motivation was theological and moral, namely, that the church as the institution of moral guidance must be part of the solution. The second motivation was a pastoral one. He feared that the church would continue to "lose" the working class to atheistic socialist movements. This, he believed, would put in peril the very salvation of their souls. His third motivation was ecclesial, in that he did not want to see the position of the Catholic church in society weakened any further. Pope Leo did not want the church to be isolated from the lives of the working class, so he confronted the political movements that were eroding the workers' loyalty to the church.

THE MESSAGE OF *RERUM NOVARUM*

Encouraged by the Fribourg Union, Cardinal Gibbons, and the other factors mentioned above, Pope Leo XIII initiated the process of writing an encyclical on "the condition of the worker." The encyclical went through three drafts. The first draft was written by a member of the Roman Curia, Cardinal Tommasso Zigliara, O.P.[30] The final draft was the work of Cardinal Camillo Mazzella, the former dean of Woodstock College in Maryland.

> Mazzella inserted passages more strongly emphasizing the right to private property than earlier versions, probably at the bidding of Archbishop Michael A. Corrigan of New York, who wanted his own position strengthened against the suspected socialism of one of his priests, Edward McGlynn, who had been excommunicated in 1887, in part for his support of Henry George and who, incidentally, was reconciled to the church by [the apostolic delegate Francesco] Satolli on the basis of *Rerum novarum*.[31] [see chapter two, p. 42-46]

Amid all the controversy on the role of labor unions, the popularity of the socialist movement, and the question of whether capitalism was inherently evil, Pope Leo offered his statement on the condition of the worker. He presupposed two realities.

The first reality was that capitalism was here to stay and must be dealt with. There is no turning the clock back to the "good old days," as some romantic Europeans, like Karl von Vogelsang and his followers, hoped for. Historian David O'Brien and theologian Thomas Shannon capture his point succinctly:

> Leo attempted to divert Catholics from a catastrophic stance of an almost utopian vision, which held out for the restoration of medieval guilds and associations at a time when the power and success of capitalism were at their height. Rather, he attempted to nudge Catholics throughout Europe to join with the workers in seeking to alleviate their plight through organized action and social legislation, reforms which required some temporary accommodation to modern society.[32]

Second, Pope Leo assumed that for the majority of people, especially the poor, life was a hard, arduous struggle. Even with the most strenuous efforts one cannot wring from nature much more than the barest necessities of life. For Leo, "a hard and even oppressive way of life for the laborer seemed irremovable. The question, therefore, can only be how to avoid unnecessary hardships...[and] violations of the laborer's human dignity and rights...."[33]

CENTRAL THEMES

1. Suffering of workers

Pope Leo calls attention to the misery and poverty suffered by the workers. While the socialists had been condemning the suffering of the working class for years, the pope finally confronted the church with the reality of the suffering of the masses while others accumulated wealth. By speaking out for the workers he continued the ministry of Bishops Von Ketteler and Mermillod, who had decried these abuses of the workers forty years earlier.

2. Property for workers

Leo condemns the socialist solution to the poverty of the workers, which included the denial of the natural right of private property. He maintains that the solution to the misery of the workers is to enable each person to procure the necessary property to provide for one's needs and dignity so that one would not have to be "wage-dependent."

3. Role of the state

Whenever the general interest or any particular class suffers or is threatened with a harm that can in no other way be met or prevented, the public authority must step in to deal with it. Here, the pope walked between the capitalist and socialist theories of state intervention, the former having a minimalist, the latter a maximalist approach. He also sided with those who believed that the social problem could not be solved by Christian charity but needed state intervention and reform of institutions.

4. Living wage

In justice the worker who contributes to the wealth of the society by his or her labor is entitled to receive a wage that "will enable him, housed, clothed, and secure, to live a life without hardship." While later documents would take up this question in more detail, the basic right is established in this encyclical: the wage is seen as the only way the worker can preserve his or her life, which is a "duty common to all individuals."[34]

5. Right to organize

Leo teaches that workers have a natural right to organize into associations to advance their interests, and that the state must protect that right.[35] Because Leo is addressing a Catholic audience and his political theory insinuates that all citizens are Catholic, some controversy emerged as to whether Catholics could join secular unions. These issues were cleared up later, because of the "regrettable lack" of *Rerum Novarum* on this point.[36]

6. Collaboration rather than class struggle

The pope uses notions of "mutual dependence," friendliness, and neighborliness rather than class struggle. This is in keeping with his organic and harmonious social theory.

7. Role of the church

In that anticlerical era, the pope defends the right of the church to speak on social issues. At times, he exaggerates the church's role. The constructive role of the church is to both educate citizens to act justly and promote social reconciliation.

These seven themes identify the major contributions and strengths of the encyclical. In general the pope brought the church into constructive engagement with the "condition of the worker" of his day. With the benefit of historical perspective we can also identify a few areas that were not adequately addressed in the letter.

CRITICAL REMARKS

This papal letter, like any letter, is addressed to specific communities at a specific time in history. *Rerum Novarum* is very much a product of its times. It reflects the debates and controversies, the strengths and limitations of its times and of the people who wrote it. From the vantage point of history we see some of its limitations. We need to see these limitations, not to be negative about Pope Leo's contribution but to show that the church's social teaching is a dynamic, living tradition that is constantly developing in areas that were ignored or inadequately handled in the past.

1. No positive statement on the meaning of work

Because Leo was confronting the socialists and their theory of social change, the encyclical took on a reactionary tone. Rather than presenting a positive statement about the meaning of human labor, its dignity and value for the individual and for society—all of which were being violated in the abuses of laissez-faire capitalism—the encyclical took on a defensive tone against socialism and its proposed remedy for society. A positive treatment of the meaning of labor was addressed in later papal teachings, especially Pope John Paul II's *Laborem Exercens*.

2. A distorted view of private property

Leo felt that the socialists were a menace to the right ordering of society because they attacked the right of private property, which he held was a prerogative sanctioned by the natural law. "...[T]he human race as a whole, moved in no wise by the dissenting opinion of a few [the socialists], and observing nature carefully, has found in the law of nature itself the basis of the distribution of goods, and, by the practice of the ages, has consecrated private possession as something best adapted to man's nature and to the peaceful and tranquil living together." A few paragraphs later we find: "Let it be regarded, therefore, as established that in seeking help for the masses this principle before all is to be considered basic, namely, that *private ownership must be preserved inviolate*" (par. 24).

It is generally agreed by commentators that Leo's treatment of private property was a distortion of the Thomistic tradition. Father Leo de Sousberghe has pointed out that neither Aquinas nor the other medieval theologians viewed private property as a primary right of the natural law; rather private property was a necessity because of imperfect human nature. In the Thomistic tradition private property is a derived right, not a primary right as Leo taught.

The distortion in *Rerum Novarum* can be traced to the Jesuit theologian Taparelli d'Azeglio, who in 1840 incorporated the thinking of John Locke into the scholastic tradition. Locke had argued that the very act of labor was truly the singular possession of the worker. When a person labored, the fruit of that labor became uniquely his or her own because it came forth from the worker's toil. For another to come and confiscate this "property" was a violation of natural justice, for the laborer was being robbed of the fruits of his or her own labor. In such a case the laborer is being deprived of part of himself or herself.[37] Property that had been earned by labor, in Locke's view, was an extension of the worker. To deny the right of property is to deny the rights of the individual worker. In this view property loses the social context and meaning that the Catholic tradition had always maintained.

The distorted teaching was cleared up in 1931 by Pope Pius XI's encyclical *Quadragesimo Anno* and other subsequent encyclicals. For example, *Mater et Magistra* of Pope John XXIII teaches that the common good and the needs of people take priority over any right to private property.

3. *"Arrogant" role for the church*

Pope Leo, as a teacher of the natural law, maintained that the Roman Catholic Church *alone* could solve social problems. This "alone" had two meanings: 1) that no one else but the church could do it; or 2) that only with the church would a solution be possible; without the contribution of the church no adequate solution would be found.

The first position is "exceedingly arrogant" according to Father Oswald von Nell-Breuning.[38] While Leo's tone was not as defensive as that of his predecessor, Pius IX, this attitude does not completely disappear until the Second Vatican Council. Even the second interpretation— that without the Catholic church no solution can be found—is "claiming too much," according to Nell-Breuning.

The Catholic church believed that its role in addressing the "condition of the worker" was essential because it believed that the disorder in society is at root a moral and religious issue. In paragraph 41 we read, "Wherefore, if human society is to be healed, only a return to Christian life and institutions will heal it." Two years later Leo would write in *Graves de Communi*:

> For it is the opinion of some, which is caught up by the masses, that the social question, as they call it, is merely economic. The precise opposite is the truth. It is first of all moral and religious, and for that reason its solution is to be expected mainly from the moral law and the pronouncements of religion.[39]

TOO BOLD OR TOO TIMID?

As with most ecclesiastical texts, what you see in *Rerum Novarum* depends on where you are standing. In other words, *Rerum Novarum* is open to a variety of interpretations.[40] It can be read as pro-labor and anti-laissez-faire capitalism, and it can be read as anti-socialism and pro-private property. To those who longed for the medieval, pre-capitalist social order this encyclical came as a "bolt of lightning" moving the church into dialogue with the reality of the new economic system. Whereas some Catholic thinkers doubted whether the new economic system of capitalism was permissible, Leo accepted capitalism as part of the reality of his day and set about to tame its immoral aspects.

Leo's acceptance of capitalism can be labeled both "realistic" and implicitly pro-capitalism. This pro-capitalist stance was more the product of being vehemently anti-socialist.

For the conservatives of his day Leo stood out as breaking with the "traditionalist" mentality. Prior to Leo becoming pope in 1878, the official church leadership had been waging a war against the "modern liberties" of the French Revolution. The entire Catholic church had been profoundly shaken by the anticlerical reforms that followed that revolution.[41] The anticlericalism of revolutionary France was temporarily checked during the reign of Napoleon and was almost eliminated in the reaction that followed Napoleon's downfall in 1815. But the liberal, anti-church party kept alive the ideals of the Revolution and gradually returned to power and influence. In order to establish the "modern liberties" of freedom of speech, freedom of the press, and freedom of religion, the liberal party wanted to create a social and political order in which the Christian churches would have no special privileges and no temporal power. Many liberals wanted to eliminate the influence of the

Catholic church completely because they believed it to be incompatible with reason and with social and political progress.[42]

These anticlerical sentiments were translated into severe restrictions of the Catholic church. In the last half of the nineteenth century the governments of Italy, Spain, Belgium, Austria, France, and Germany closed Catholic schools, dissolved monastic orders, deprived clergy of their privileges, and confiscated church property. Mexico, after its break from Spain, enacted some of the most severe anticlerical measures.

When Leo's predecessor, Pius IX, died in 1878, "the Church and its leadership in Rome seemed to be at war against almost every feature of the modern era. Many enemies of the Church confidently predicted that the [Catholic] Church would be destroyed in their life-times."[43] Pope Leo stepped into this conflictual situation. To many it appeared as though the church was fighting for its very survival. The Roman Catholic church was losing its influence in the social, political, and intellectual realms. The Vatican was also literally "losing ground" as it lost most of the papal states in 1860. By 1870 the church's geo-political territory had been reduced to the tiny Vatican city state.

In this "era of negation" the Catholic church fought back by condemning those within the church, both in Europe and in America, who wanted reconciliation with the liberal movements. Pope Pius IX "seemed especially to fear that the spread of liberalism within the Church might lead to a democratization of Church authority itself."[44]

Pius IX gave repeated encouragement to the reactionaries who wished to reverse the trend of the liberal states. In his 1864 encyclical *Quanta Cura* and the accompanying "Syllabus of Errors," Pius detailed the "errors" of modern civilization including almost all of the basic principles of modern liberal democracies. His "Syllabus of Errors" concluded with the harsh dictum: "If anyone thinks that the Roman Pontiff can and should reconcile himself and come to terms with progress, with liberalism, and with modern civilization, let him be anathema."[45]

Against such a negative and defensive backdrop, Leo appears as a reformer, as one who begins to open the church to modern realities. But, if you stand with the radicals of his day, the socialists, the pope appears very traditional. Whereas Pius IX battled the liberals, Leo's prime enemy was the socialists, who denied the right of private property.[46]

For those who were more radical in their social vision, *Rerum Novarum* was too conservative and paternalistic. John Coleman, a Jesuit social ethicist, notes that most of those who influenced the writing of *Rerum Novarum* were counts, marquis, princes, or members of the aristocracy. He asks, "Was it by chance...that no militant union organizer had any impact on the document?"[47]

I would temper Coleman's remark by suggesting that while activists did not have a direct impact on the document they did have an indirect influence on the tone and content of the encyclical. The controversy over Father McGlynn and the controversy around the Knights of Labor, which are discussed in the next chapter, shaped the thinking of progressive bishops whose intervention in Rome did not go unheeded.

LASTING CONTRIBUTION OF *RERUM NOVARUM*

Rerum Novarum was and is read from widely divergent perspectives, and while we will see diverse reactions to the letter, all can agree that the publication of this encyclical has had a lasting impact on the church and the world.

First of all, this letter is the beginning of the official church taking a *less defensive stance* toward modern political thought and the reality of capitalist economies. Leo was not going to continue the reactionary stance of his predecessors. He had seen the negative impact of such attempts to turn back the clock in the mass defection of the French and Italian working classes.

Second, in a very practical way he *legitimated trade unions*. They could no longer be dismissed as revolutionary or socialist. The letter allowed and even encouraged working-class Catholics to join independent trade unions and to work with secular organizations on social reform. The dark cloud hovering over the labor movement was dispersed.

Third, he supported the emerging social conscience of Roman Catholics and offered a fairly coherent *body of moral and social teachings to guide social activism*. These teachings would be developed and adapted by succeeding generations of lay and clerical leaders. A modern legacy of social teachings had begun.

Fourth, with this letter Leo was the first pope to articulate a genuine *recognition of the suffering of the poor* and the working class. Under Pope Leo's leadership the papacy began to break away from its allegiance to the aristocracy. This direction would continue until the bishops of Latin America would endorse a "preferential option for the poor" in 1968.

Leo recognized the wisdom of Cardinal Gibbons' words, "To lose the heart of the people would be a misfortune for which the friendship of the few rich and powerful would be no compensation."[48]

Social ethicist Stephen Pope names this shift very effectively:

> Social Catholicism had flourished in the 19th century, while the highest echelon of the church was recruited from the aristocracy and identified with the forces of reaction, inherited privilege, and the ancien regime. Leo was the first pope to show some grasp of the intolerable suffering of the urban proletariat and to act on this by making the natural rights of the worker official church doctrine. *Rerum novarum* provided a doctrinal *challenge to the apathy and indifference of middle-class and affluent Catholics*, including the clergy, in the face of the widespread misery of the working classes. In issuing this document Leo displayed a degree of human sensitivity, courage, and social imagination absent not only in his 19th-century predecessors but unfortunately also in his immediate successor, Pius X (1903-14), as well.[49]

Finally, the legacy of Leo can be seen in his clear conviction that *human labor cannot be treated simply as a commodity*, because to do so would be a denial of the human dignity of the worker. The pope taught that it was shameful and inhuman to treat people as though they were objects. It was shocking for some and inspiring to others when the pope used this teaching to defend underpaid workers.[50] This message has been repeated again and again in Catholic social thought especially in Pope John Paul II's encyclical on labor, *Laborem Exercens*, and in the U.S. bishops' pastoral letter on the economy, *Economic Justice for All*.

Conclusion

Economic, political, cultural, and social life in Europe and in the U.S. has changed dramatically since the days of Archbishop Ketteler, Cardinal Gibbons, the Marquis Rene de la Tour du Pin, and the writing of *Rerum Novarum*. Yet many of the same moral issues confront us today even though the context may be different. We still wrestle with the meaning of justice and charity in our communities. When facing the question of poverty and the poor, how do we combine the need for structural reform/justice with the need for direct service/charity? These debates, which surfaced during the discussion of welfare reform, echo the discussion the Social Catholics had with their counterparts in the 1880s.

The question of private property is still filled with tension, especially in the U.S., where many citizens place an exaggerated emphasis on private property. The most extreme views are held by the radical militias who arm themselves to protect their property. As we shall see in chapter six, this question surfaced in 1967 with Pope Paul's encyclical *Populorum Progressio*. The Catholic tradition holds that private property is not an absolute right, but is conditioned by the needs of others. Such a view has not found a home in the American consciousness. As we think about the environment, the issue of private property as an absolute right will need to be reevaluated.

The role of the state as an agent of social justice is also an issue that continues to be debated in political and ecclesial circles. The Catholic social tradition has been wrestling with this question for many decades. That tradition steers between the two extremes of the socialist and the laissez-faire capitalist. Eventually, the notion of "subsidiarity" will be added to clarify this complex question.

From the ecclesiological perspective we see the papacy serving the universal church by setting out broad principles in a situation of intense controversy and competing views. Pope Leo made it clear that there was no "going back" to the medieval framework, but the values of those communal days would not be lost. His encyclical did not settle all the controversial questions, but he did give a direction for the Catholic church's social teaching. Yet even in the production of this encyclical we see the importance of the discussion and activism of the laity and church leaders both in Europe and in the United States. The involvement of the whole church in the process of formulating church teaching is a complex issue. It is an ecclesiological question that pervades how the church exercises its teaching function. The Catholic church is not finished with this question and may have a lot to learn from other Christian denominations.

The story of Catholic social teaching and action is a vibrant and dynamic tradition that unfolds anew in each era. Each generation leaves its fingerprints on that story; the graceful and the sinful elements interconnected.

Discussion Questions

1. What do you find in the legacy of the "Fribourg Union" that is relevant for today's debates about social justice?

2. How do you evaluate the central themes of the "Social Catholicism" of the late nineteenth century?

3. What values are evident in the "corporative" model of economic relations? Why was this vision not adopted by business and labor?

4. The right of private property was hotly debated in the late nineteenth century. Evaluate the various positions taken on the question by the socialists, the "Social Catholics," and Pope Leo XIII.

5. How does the legacy of *Rerum Novarum* continue to influence Roman Catholic social thought and action?

2

Social Catholics in the United States

Part I: Catholics and the American Labor Movement

When we open the narrative of the Roman Catholic tradition of social teaching and ministry in the United States we find many similarities with the European story, yet the differences are more striking. The immigrant Catholics brought with them their cultural and ethnic heritage—with all its strengths and weaknesses. These religious, ethnic, and cultural traditions were tested in a new cultural context taking shape—the emerging American culture.

This chapter traces some of the early threads and tensions in the story of the American Catholic tradition of social teaching and action. These threads include three of the major themes that emerge as we focus on the sixty-year period from 1860 to 1920:

- the tension of working out what it means to be Roman Catholic and American;

- the struggle to awaken the church as an advocate for the poor and working classes—this awakening begins with the labor movement, touches some of the priests, and eventually is articulated by the bishops, especially in their 1919 Program of Social Reconstruction;

- the practical and pastoral emphasis of the social thinking, which eventually is articulated with an ethical foundation that speaks to the American setting.

HOW TO BE CATHOLIC AND AMERICAN

By this time, two approaches to the question of how to be American and Catholic had emerged. One approach embraced attitudes identified with modernism, such as historical consciousness, adaptation of religious ideas and structures to the American culture, the belief that God is immanent in cultural development and revealed through it, and that society is moving toward the realization of the kingdom of God. (Many of these ideas were shared by the progressive Protestants, who followed an approach known as the "Social Gospel.") The second approach reflected a defensive, anti-modern stance, typified by Pope Pius IX's condemnation of modern thinking in his "Syllabus of Errors."

A Baptist minister from Rochester, New York, described the two factions as he saw them:

> ...there are two distinct and hostile parties in the Roman Catholic Church in America. One is led by Archbishop Ireland. It stands for Americanism and a larger independence. It is sympathetic with modern thought. It believes that the Roman Catholic Church should take its place in all the great moral reforms. It is small, but progressive, vigorous, and brave. The other party is led by the overwhelming majority of the hierarchy. It is conservative, out of touch with American or modern ideas. It is the old medieval European Church, transplanted into the 19th Century and this country of freedom, interesting as an antique and curiosity, but fast losing its power and consequently, growing in bitterness.[1]

The leaders of the "American Catholicity" included editor and philosopher Orestes Brownson; the Paulist priest Isaac Hecker; Denis O'Connell, the rector of Catholic University; and bishops John Ireland (St. Paul); John Keane (Richmond); and John Spalding (Peoria). Bishops John Carroll (Baltimore) and John England (Charleston) had been leaders of the progressive approach in the previous century.

The leaders of the conservative "party" were Archbishop Michael Corrigan (New York), Bishop Bernard McQuaid (Rochester), most of the German-American hierarchy and clergy, and the Jesuits.[2]

These two groups debated over parochial schools, membership in secret societies, attitudes toward Protestants, and economic and social issues. The tension between these two groups was just below the surface in the controversy with the Knights of Labor, and in Father McGlynn's difficulties with his archbishop. Before we launch into those stories let us briefly consider the context.

THE TIMES

The 1880s and 1890s were tumultuous times, combining economic growth and labor conflicts. The reform movements of the socialists, communists, progressives, and populists were all vying to respond to tremendous social problems. Seen in this context, the liberal-conservative debates within the church were right in step with the turbulent times.

In 1877 the U.S. economy went into a terrible depression. Twenty percent of the nation's workers were unemployed, another forty percent of the workers found work only half the year. Wages were cut, working hours were expanded, people lost their homes, and shantytowns sprang up. The poor took to the streets and chanted, "Bread for the needy, clothing for the naked, and houses for the homeless." This depression was reminiscent of the 1837 depression and the collapse of the economy in 1850. Because the immigrant Catholics were concentrated among the working classes they were hard hit by these social calamities.

The traditional Catholic response to those suffering unemployment and poverty was to appeal to charity. St. Vincent de Paul societies, which assisted the poor, sprang up in the U.S. beginning in 1845. The Catholic "crusades for charity" prior to 1880 aimed at helping the needy physically and spiritually. The role of the church was central in that social evils were seen as the result of Adam's sin. Therefore, according to a priest, "all reform, properly understood, begins with a return to religion and the

Church."[3] Such thinking did not include a vision of social change and reform. Society was envisioned as a static, stratified social system, with each level having its own opportunities and responsibilities. Archbishop John Hughes of New York expressed well this stratified vision of society: "To every class and condition [the church] assigned its own peculiar range of Christian obligations: ...To the rich, moderation in enjoyment and liberality toward the poor. To the poor, patience under their trials and affection toward their wealthier brethren."[4]

Women often took a leadership role in responding to the immediate needs of the poor. As more and more Catholic women of German and Irish descent moved into the middle class, they had the freedom to volunteer in activities outside the home. These women organized citywide charitable organizations to assist the needy among the new immigrants. They started "settlement" houses across the country. In these settlement homes the women lived among the poor, provided education classes for children and adults, and offered health care programs and cooking classes as well as recreation. In cities such as Chicago and New York the houses were serving the Italian and Polish immigrants; in Los Angeles they served the Mexican communities.

As laudable as these efforts were, a minority of Catholics, like their counterparts in France and Germany, came to the conclusion during the 1880s that the times demanded more than charity and mercy. Justice was needed. One catalyst pushing for justice was the American labor movement.

LABOR AS A CATALYST FOR REFORM

The first national labor union was the controversial Knights of Labor. It was founded by Uriah Stephens in Philadelphia in 1869 and grew in numbers and strength until 1886, yielding to the American Federation of Labor, headed by Samuel Gompers. In 1879 Terence Powderly, an Irish Catholic, was the Knights' Grand Master Workman. "One big union," the Knights welcomed everyone into its ranks, men and women of every craft, creed, and color. Unlike the later American Federation of Labor (AFL), which organized only skilled craftsmen, the membership of the Knights was open to all productive workers, skilled and unskilled. Only "nonproducers," such as bankers and stockbrokers, were excluded.[5]

The Knights of Labor was an advocate for the working class and preached a program of social reform. Many Catholics, especially the Irish railroad workers, coal miners, and marble-quarry workers, joined its ranks. As we shall see, these men and women did not always enjoy the support of their church leaders. Women who joined the labor unions had to break through several levels of resistance, including their societally defined gender roles and the conflictual nature of labor organizing.

WOMEN IN THE LABOR MOVEMENT

A number of women rose to leadership roles in the union. Elizabeth Rogers, despite the burden of housework and a growing number of children, became the head of a local chapter of the Knights of Labor in Chicago in 1882. Leonora Barry was a noted organizer in the Knights and a prominent leader in Amsterdam, New York. Mary Kenney O'Sullivan began organizing shirtwaist makers and cabbies in Chicago in the 1880s and served as an organizer for the American Federation of Labor, which emerged in 1891. She was a co-founder of the National Women's Trade Union League in 1903, an active suffragist, prohibitionist, and a member of the Women's International League for Peace—formed after the First World War. O'Sullivan proudly combined motherhood and activism. She picketed for the garment workers and shoe workers while pregnant. Although Mary O'Sullivan was Catholic throughout her life, not all women involved in the labor movement continued to practice their faith, as is evident in the life of Mother Jones.

MOTHER JONES—A FOLK HEROINE

One of the most striking women leaders of the labor movement was Mary Harris Jones, known as "Mother Jones." Mary was born in Monroe, Michigan, in 1830 into a Catholic family. Her brother became a priest, and she taught in a convent school. Although she was a lifelong Catholic she never claimed allegiance to the organized church. As one chronicler put it, "aside from having a few activist priests as friends, she had little patience with religion and often reserved for it her most vehement scorn."[6] This alienation seemed to touch even on her relationship with her younger brother. Rev. William R. Harris was a committed ecclesiastic who served in a number of U.S. and Canadian parishes before becoming dean of the Archdiocese of Toronto. Both Mary and William were prolific writers but scrupulously avoided mention of their family in their writing. There is no indication they met or even corresponded in adulthood.[7] His world was the church and hers was labor and, at least in the Harris family, those two did not mix.

Mary Harris Jones knew the workers' struggles firsthand. Her husband, who was a leader among the workers in Memphis, and four children died in the yellow fever epidemic in Memphis in 1867—all within a week. She recalled,

> One by one, my four little children sickened and died. I washed their little bodies and got them ready for burial. My husband caught the fever and died. I sat alone through nights of grief. No one came to me. No one could. Other homes were as stricken as mine. All day long, all night long, I heard the grating of the wheels of the death cart.[8]

Mary Jones stayed on in Memphis through the epidemic to nurse other victims—about 2,500 were afflicted. Then she moved on to Chicago to take up dressmaking. Mary worked for the wealthy as a seamstress and began to recognize the dichotomy of the haves and have-nots as the promise and price of the growing industrialization.

> We worked for the aristocrats of Chicago, and I had ample opportunity to observe the luxury and extravagance of their lives. Often while sewing for the lords and barons who lived in magnificent houses on the Lake Shore Drive, I would look out of the plate glass windows and see the poor, shivering wretches, jobless and hungry, walking alongside the frozen lake front. The contrast of their condition with that of the tropical comfort of the people for whom I sewed was painful to me. My employers seemed neither to notice nor to care.[9]

In 1871 the Great Fire swept through Chicago. In its wake, Mary was homeless and without possessions except for the clothes she wore. She huddled with other fire victims in the basement of a church. At the age of 41 she had seen more than her share of suffering, but her losses did not crush her. She found her way into a nearby, tumble-down, fire-scorched building where the Noble Order of the Knights of Labor was meeting.

The early Knights of Labor was not so much a union as a fraternal lodge open to skilled and unskilled workers. It was the first large labor organization to admit women on an equal footing with men. Mary began attending gatherings of the Knights every evening, and on Sunday as well, when they often held meetings and picnics in the woods. The ideals and the sense of community of the Knights touched some deep chords in Mary. She was attracted to the speakers and to the vision they offered. Their words touched her heart and sounded for her an undeniable call to work with the poor and oppressed. All of this blended with her deep sense of unionism, which she had learned from her husband. "Coming, as it did, on top of successive personal tragedies, the experience [of the early Knights] forged an amalgam of compassion and fervor which would serve her well in industrial wars over the next half a century."[10] She made her home with the workers in shantytowns near the mills or in tent colonies thrown up near the mines. As she had lost her own family she adopted the workers as her family, and they in turn began to call her "Mother."

The working conditions were harsh for the poor. Mother Jones saw conditions ripe for revolution:

> From 1880 on, I became wholly engrossed in the labor movement. In all the great industrial centers the working class was in rebellion. The enormous immigration from Europe crowded the slums, forced down wages and threatened to destroy the standard of living fought for by American working men. Throughout the country there was business depression and much unemployment. In the cities there was hunger and rags and despair.[11]

Dale Fetherling described the landscape Mother Jones knew so well.

> During the half century when she was most active in the working-men's movement, the country was undergoing a dramatic shift from an agrarian to an industrial nation. The vehicle was corporate capitalism. Small-scale shops gave way to the large. Monopoly often supplanted competition. The nature of work and of workers was altered. Waves of immigrants and displaced farmers dug the nation's coal and forged its steel. All too often, they received in return only starvation wages and nightmarish conditions. Within these men smoldered the sparks of class conflict which Mother Jones would fan for 50 years.[12]

For half a century, from 1877 (in the Pittsburgh labor riots) until 1923 when she was 93 years old (and working with the striking coal miners of West Virginia), Mother Jones appeared wherever labor troubles were acute. She was described as "a little old woman in a black bonnet, with a high falsetto voice and a handsome face framed in curly white hair and lighted by shrewd, kindly gray eyes which could flash defiance from behind their spectacles alike at distant capitalists and at near-by company guards and militia."[13] She organized not only the workers but also their wives, often armed with mops and brooms.

A biographer notes that "she had no consistent philosophy, except altruism and economic betterment. Though she weighed no more than 100 pounds, she didn't hesitate to fight violence with violence, or even incite some on her own." He goes on to say: "Her specialty, aside from violating injunctions and going to jail, was pageants of poverty, processions of the angry and the abused."[14] For example, on September 25, 1900 she assisted in organizing the coal miners' strike near Hazelton, Pennsylvania. She urged the women to "put on their kitchen clothes and bring their mops and brooms with them and a couple of tin pans. We marched over the mountains fifteen miles, beating on the tin pans as if they were cymbals." The all-night march, which included reporters, wagons, and American flags, was intended to elicit support from miners who had not yet joined the strike by catching them early in the morning before they went to work. It is not clear from the reports how much impact this "midnight march" had.[15]

On another occasion, July 7, 1903, she led a band of men, women, and children on a 22-day hike through three states from Philadelphia to President Theodore Roosevelt's home at Oyster Bay on Long Island. The purpose of the march was to promote a reduction in the work week from 60 hours to 55 and to protest the use of child labor, especially in the textile industry. (The textile industry was the largest user of child labor, employing 80,000 children, most of them girls.) Jones considered child labor the worst of industrial sins and was disappointed that the news media did not address the plight of children. When the small band reached Oyster Bay, the president was not at home. Jones had to put her requests in writing, to which Roosevelt responded that, while he sympathized with her cause, it was up to the states to deal with this issue. While Jones saw no immediate response to the plight of children, the march did have an impact in focusing attention on the issue. In 1909 a White House Conference on Children and Youth would be held, and other executive actions began to address the plight of working children. The three states through which they marched did enact stricter laws within a few years of the march. An effective federal child-labor law, however, would not be passed until 1941.[16]

Besides the demonstrations, she was adept at smuggling out "open letters," couched in the most poignant of prose, from the scene of her latest imprisonment. She was noted for her rhetoric. "She was quick to trade barbs with men whose lungs never had sucked in coal dust or whose skin had not felt the heat of a blast furnace." But Mother Jones was more than hyperbole and caustic remarks. Behind the publicity-seeking activism was a woman who spent countless cold nights in miners' hovels, sleeping on a bare floor with her handbag for a pillow.[17]

This fiery agitator had a salty tongue, which she turned on the institutional church and its timid nuns and priests from time to time: "I never saw more moral cowards in my life than those sisters.... They are simply owned body and soul by the Rockefeller interests." She scorned the church when it offered only relief in the next life and did little to lighten the workers' load in the here and now. The relative wealth of the church and its abandonment of what she considered the revolutionary thrust of the Gospel also raised her ire. "Jesus...took twelve men from among the laborers of his time (no college graduates among them) and with them founded an organization that revolutionized the society amid which it arose. Just so in our day the organization of workers must be the first step to the overthrow of capitalism." She believed that the Christian churches should play a liberating role in the here and now, and that with the labor movement the church should "go down and redeem the Israelites that were in bondage," and lead them from the land of bondage and plunder into the land of freedom. She urged workers to "pray for the dead and fight like hell for the living."[18]

"Crusty, ubiquitous Mother Jones," concluded one of her biographers, "was a self-appointed prophet of the nation in a period when introspection was unpopular. She may have been the most spectacular woman the country has produced, and she certainly was the most loved and dramatic female in the nation's labor movement. To millions of men, women, and children she was a profane Joan of Arc...."[19]

Mother Jones returned to the Catholic church, planned her own funeral, received the last sacraments, and died seven months after her 100th birthday. One funeral Mass was held in St. Gabriel's in Washington, D.C. In attendance were dignitaries, including Labor Secretary William Doak, as well as some miners and unemployed workers.

A second liturgy was held in Mt. Olive, Illinois, four days later. Father John Maguire, a labor activist and president of Saint Viator's College in Bourbonnais, Illinois, presided at this liturgy at the Church of the Ascension. The choir at the Mass was composed of miners. In his homily Father Maguire asked, "What weapons had she to fight the fight against oppression of working men?" His answer: "Only a great and burning conviction that oppression must end. Only an eloquent and flaming tongue that won men to her cause. Only a mother's heart torn by the sufferings of the poor. Only a towering courage that made her carry on in the face of insuperable odds. Only a consuming love for the poor."[20]

She was buried in the United Mine Workers' cemetery in Mount Olive, Illinois.

At the end of her life she had received birthday greetings from John D. Rockefeller, Jr., and returned the favor on Rockefeller Senior's birthday, but she told friends, "I wouldn't trade what I've done for what he's done. I've done the best I could to make the world a better place for poor, hard-working people."[21]

The last paragraph of her autobiography gives a sense that she knew things were getting better for the working class—progress that she had helped to bring about:

> In spite of oppressors, in spite of false leaders, in spite of labor's own lack of understanding of its needs, the cause of the worker continues onward. Slowly his hours are shortened, giving him leisure to read and to think. Slowly his standard of living rises to include some of the good and beautiful things of this world. Slowly the cause of his children becomes the cause of all. His boy is taken from the breaker, his girl from the mill. Slowly those who create the wealth of the world are permitted to share it. The future is in labor's strong, rough hands.[22]

I am not attempting to canonize Mother Jones, although in many ways she is one of the "saints" of the labor movement. Her impact is hard to measure. She certainly has not lived on as a social hero in the minds of most Americans. She has not left us an intellectual legacy, or a school of thought or labor union named in her honor. But she made an immeasurable contribution to the men and women struggling in her day. Dale Fetherling says that she brought "the human element, the spirit within the structure. Mother Jones was a necessary third element dimension, a folk heroine whose inspiration reached down to those people who were unimportant in name of wealth or title but all-important" in many other ways.[23]

She brought her passion for justice and her love for workers and their rights and mixed it with her gifts, her personality, and her suffering. Isn't that ministry, isn't that leadership? "In all, she was a benevolent fanatic, a Celtic blend of sentiment and fire, of sweetness and fight, who captured the imagination of the American worker as no other woman—perhaps no other leader—ever has."[24]

TENSION OVER THE KNIGHTS OF LABOR

A good number of Catholics, both laity and clergy, had their misgivings about the labor movement, just as the labor movement—as articulated by Mother Jones—had misgivings about the church. Some of the goals and strategies of the early labor movement alienated leaders in the church. The strategies of secrecy and resorting to violence, and the goal of radical social change, were seen as dangerous by some church people.[25]

In their early days unions needed secrecy to protect their members from the recriminations of owners and managers of industry. The Knights also borrowed trappings from the Masonic tradition. Violence between the unions and the police and industrialists was common—this also alienated the clergy. In the early days the Knights opposed the use of strikes, which they believed were counterproductive to building a cooperative society. They preferred the use of primary and secondary boycotts to obtain their short-range goals of an eight-hour work day and improved working conditions. In 1885 the Knights initiated 196 boycotts, of which 59 were concluded successfully. The Knights came to support strikes very reluctantly. In 1885 they won a major strike against the railroad magnate Jay Gould. With that kind of success their membership blossomed to its high point of over 700,000 members. Just a year later they lost a second strike against Jay Gould. That defeat plus the rising violence of strikes[26] and the creation of the American Federation of Labor signaled the decline of the Knights.

The Knights of Labor had a revolutionary vision of a cooperative society. They were not content to focus only on short-term issues. Rather, they sought to "reform the entire industrial order by ushering in a cooperative society in which the evil of 'wage slavery' would be abolished."[27] Like the Social Catholics in Europe they envisioned a society of small producers organized cooperatively, which, they believed, could resolve most of the problems brought on by the Industrial Revolution.

Despite the Knights' popularity among the workers, many clergy and bishops were suspicious of the organization. A few priests and bishops went so far as to deny the sacraments to the Knights and refuse them the church's burial rites. Archbishop Bayley of Baltimore damned the unions as "communistic"; the nation's first African American bishop, James Healy of Portland, Maine, excommunicated those who joined the Knights; and in 1884, Archbishop Eleazar Taschereau of Quebec secured the Vatican's (Congregation for the Propagation of the Faith) condemnation of the

Knights in the Quebec province.[28] Most U.S. bishops interpreted this condemnation as applying only to Canada and were reluctant to outlaw the Knights in their dioceses. But Archbishop Taschereau was not content with this limited condemnation of the Knights; he asked the Propagation of the Faith to make the condemnation universal.

Some in the hierarchy had a fear of socialism that made them hesitant to support the workers' right to organize and strike. The church was also preoccupied with secret societies since the condemnation of the Freemasons in 1734. It was this ban on secret societies that Taschereau invoked against the Knights.[29]

The issues involved were those mentioned above—secrecy, violence, and radical reform, as well as a concern that Catholic workers would be exposed to danger to their Catholic faith because the Knights accepted workers of all or no religion. The question of collaborating with non-Catholics was an issue in the church until the teaching of John XXIII and Vatican II officially allowed such ecumenical efforts.

The U.S. archbishops met in October, 1886, but only two of the twelve supported the extension of the condemnation of the Knights in the United States.

It was at this point that Archbishop James Gibbons of Baltimore entered the controversy. When in Rome in February 1887 (to receive his cardinal's hat) Gibbons presented to Vatican officials a lengthy statement defending the rights of workers to organize and urging that the Knights of Labor not be condemned. This statement, which had been written by bishops Ireland and Keane and signed by Gibbons, "marked a major turning point in the church's position on labor and social reform."[30]

The statement argued that organizing was the right of workers and their only hope of success against a "mail-clad power which...often refuses them the simple rights of humanity and justice." Yes, Catholics would join trade unions with Protestants and nonbelievers because strictly Catholic unions were not possible.

Gibbons' statement effectively argued that if the condemnation of the Knights was to protect the Catholic faith of the workers, the opposite would likely happen. The consequences of condemnation of the Knights would include:

- the working class would be alienated from the church, their souls surely lost, as had happened in Europe;

- public opinion in the United States would turn against Catholics, who would be labeled as "un-American";

- workers would be hostile to the church;

- the revenues of the church "would suffer immensely," which would be felt in Rome;

- and the Holy See would be looked upon as "a harsh and unjust power."

Finally, Gibbons pointed out that the condemnation would be impractical because of the expectation that the Knights of Labor was not going to last much longer. The emerging American Federation of Labor would take its place on the national scene.

The cardinal's very effectively worded statement did not go unheeded. Immediately the Vatican lifted the penalties that had been imposed on the recalcitrant Knights in Quebec. After a year and a half delay the Vatican ruled that the Knights *could* be tolerated provided that "words which seem to savor of socialism and communism" were removed from its constitution.[31]

The controversy, while a success for the cause of the workers, was personally devastating to Terence Powderly, the Irish Catholic grand master of the Knights. His faith in the church was shaken. This, combined with the decline of membership in the Knights, led him to openly abandon the Catholic church and join the Masons.[32]

Although the Vatican's statement was not a hearty endorsement of labor, Gibbons' defense of the Knights and the Vatican's decision were seen by the American public as a victory for labor. From then on, the leadership of the Catholic church in the United States would officially be on the side of labor. The priests also shifted their support to labor after the Gibbons affair and the pope's endorsement of labor in *Rerum Novarum*. More and more clergy in the 1890s became sympathetic to unions and the struggles of workers against the large monopolies of coal, oil, and steel. Some even became advocates of labor or "labor priests."[33]

"LABOR PRIESTS"

While the bishops were slowly finding their way into the public arena on social reform in the early decades of the twentieth century, many of the clergy were already there. Perhaps it is because the priests' ministry took them into the lives of their working class people that a good number of priests supported their parishioners' struggles. Historian Jay Dolan notes that "some of the priests had worked in the mines themselves and personally understood the workers' grievances." It is understandable, then, that during the coal strike of 1902, "practically all of the priests" in the Pennsylvania mining region "were solidly behind the strike." Father John Curran of Wilkes-Barre, Pennsylvania, stands out as "the miners' friend" as he worked closely with the leadership of the United Mine Workers, even interceding with President Theodore Roosevelt on behalf of the miners. Chicago priests in the stockyard neighborhoods supported their parishioners' strike in 1904. During the steelworkers' strike in 1919, Adelbert Kazincy, a Slovak priest in Braddock, Pennsylvania, lifted the morale of the hundreds of workers who came to his morning Masses and evening talks.

One of the most effective labor priests was Father Peter Yorke of San Francisco. He helped to plan the strike strategy for, and wrote much of the published material on, the 1901 port workers strike in San Francisco. As a gifted orator he "packed the halls" during the strike, giving the admission fee to the strike fund. Yorke used *Rerum Novarum* as his labor bible. He drew on Leo's natural human rights defense of workers' rights to show that organizing unions was not just a pragmatic, expedient strategy for the workers, but also a protection of their dignity and natural human rights. Here, *Rerum Novarum* had provided a needed ethical and intellectual principle for the labor movement.[34] Some of the priests found they were in conflict within their own ethnic communities because of their progressive support of labor.

In the German-American community Father Peter Dietz at first tried to work through the conservative German organization the Central Verein (Central Union). The Verein's social vision was a desire to recapture the attitudes and values of an organic, integrated community reminiscent of the Middle Ages. Dietz's vision conflicted with the Verein in that he focused on the role of labor unions in solving social problems rather than just projecting a nostalgic and utopian vision. Dietz left the Verein and joined the American Federation of Catholic Societies. Under Dietz's leadership the Federation's Committee on Social Reform became a strong advocate of unions. In 1910 he organized that Militia of Christ for Social Service, composed of union workers, to build a bridge between the church and the labor unions.[35]

The Irish-American community was also divided on the labor issue. The middle and upper classes tended to be conservative on social issues, and the working class—the miners, teamsters, meat-cutters, and seamstresses—often sought reform. Even among the workers not all joined the unions. The support for unions was strongest among the more nationalistic segment of the Irish community.[36] The conflict of Father McGlynn with Archbishop Corrigan reflected this division. It also reflected the ongoing controversy between the conservative "Romanists" and the more liberal "Americanists."

DEBATE OVER LAND AND TAXES:
FATHER MCGLYNN VS ARCHBISHOP CORRIGAN

In 1886, the same year that the American bishops met to discuss the Vatican's condemnation of the Knights of Labor, a charismatic priest in New York City was giving expression to a Catholic version of the "Social Gospel"—and being suspended by his bishop, Archbishop Michael Corrigan. Fr. Edward McGlynn became the pastor of St. Stephen's parish, which, with 25,000 members, was the largest parish in New York City. He soon became one of the leaders of a controversial group of clergy who questioned the conservatism of the local church. He supported public schools and was criticized for not building a parochial school in his parish. He was an eloquent preacher and a charming man; as such, his sermons drew large crowds.

In the area of social justice, he subscribed to Henry George's analysis of social ills. In *Progress and Poverty* George painted a compelling portrait of the growing gap between the rich and the poor. He traced the cause of the gap between rich and poor to the wealth earned by the rich in their land speculation. Here was speculative wealth, made without labor, derived from the work of others.[37] George was convinced that this injustice could be remedied by a "single tax" on the land.

McGlynn supported George, who was running in the mayoral election in New York. The priest brought religion into the public arena by describing the struggle for justice as "a religious moment." In his most famous address, "The Cross of the New Crusade" he taught that God had, "by beautiful laws of justice," provided enough for all. All people had a right to the "bounties of nature out of which to make a living."

He supported George's single tax campaign and roused the voters to understand the religious aspects of their struggle for justice. The leader of the Protestant Social Gospel movement, Walter Rauschenbusch, recalled, "how Father McGlynn, speaking at Cooper Union in New York in the first Single Tax campaign in 1886, recited the words, 'Thy Kingdom come! Thy will be done on earth,' and as the great audience realized for the first time the significance of the holy words, it lifted them off their seats with a shout of joy."[38]

Archbishop Corrigan was disturbed by Fr. McGlynn's progressive theology. He also did not share McGlynn's political views. Corrigan was closely tied to the Irish Catholic Tammany Hall political machine, which was opposing Henry George. The George campaign was the centerpiece of a national political effort of labor groups around the country. Corrigan had banned McGlynn from giving political speeches a few years previously. Now McGlynn broke the ban and appeared with George in the campaign. Corrigan responded by suspending McGlynn from exercising his priestly faculties. After the election, which George lost, McGlynn was reinstated and continued his political activity. Corrigan issued a pastoral letter that defended private property. McGlynn was suspended a second time and ordered by Archbishop Corrigan to go to Rome to answer the charges made against him. He refused to go on the grounds that his superiors had no right to question his political activity. Grass-roots support for McGlynn was organized.

In June of 1887, 70,000 people paraded in support of McGlynn. A Father Sylvester Malone, who observed the controversy, wrote to Pope Leo XIII complaining that McGlynn's rights as an American citizen were being infringed upon in the name of ecclesiastical discipline. Archbishop Corrigan used his ultimate spiritual weapon against the recalcitrant Father McGlynn: on July 3, 1887 he excommunicated McGlynn for his refusal to go to Rome. McGlynn, however, would not be stopped. He continued to lecture, now under the auspices of the "Anti-Poverty Society." Corrigan retaliated by declaring that attendance at McGlynn's lectures was a sin for Catholics, absolution for which was reserved to Corrigan himself. Conservatives in the Church were delighted. Bishop McQuaid of Rochester wrote to Corrigan saying, "You can scarcely imagine the excellent effect on the non-Catholic community of this action of the church in setting aside a man of McGlynn's prominence."[39]

While bishops Corrigan and McQuaid tried to have the Vatican put George's book *Progress and Poverty* on the Index, which meant it could not be read by Catholics, Archbishop Gibbons and other progressive bishops cautioned the Vatican on acceding to Corrigan's request. In 1889 the Holy Office tried to keep both sides happy by agreeing that George's positions were deserving of condemnation but the Holy Office would keep its condemnation a secret, that is, it would not issue an official promulgation of condemnation.

In 1893, after six years of excommunication, after the intervention of Gibbons and others, and after four professors at the Catholic University of American found nothing opposed to Catholic doctrine in McGlynn's positions, the excommunication was lifted by the newly appointed apostolic delegate, Francesco Satolli. Satolli did not demand that McGlynn recant his views, and McGlynn did not; he continued to support the "single tax" movement. McQuaid was not happy and reported to his friend Corrigan that "our people are terribly worked up, particularly the better classes. Many say they will not go to church no more."[40] Corrigan moved McGlynn out of the city and assigned him as pastor in the Hudson valley town of Newburgh.

THE BEGINNINGS OF A CATHOLIC
SOCIAL GOSPEL AND SOCIAL ETHIC

It was clear that many causes of strife in the U.S. Catholic church played into the McGlynn-Corrigan confrontation, including the Knights of Labor controversy, the fear of socialism, the status of priests, differences over parochial schools, as well as the question of land and taxes. It is a case study in political controversy, questions of class, and of structural reform. McGlynn's activism and lecturing can be seen as the beginnings of an American Catholic version of the Social Gospel. But unlike their European counterparts, the Social Catholics, the Americans did not have a strongly theoretical and systematic approach to social issues. The pastoral demands of an immigrant church placed the immediate needs of the Catholic community on the front burner. The key players were activists and pastors, not theologians and an intellectual aristocracy. The response of Gibbons and other church leaders to the labor unions was rooted in expediency and pastoral concern rather than in a coherent social ethic. The historian Mel Piehl argues that, "The problem for Protestantism was how to reach a lower class with whom it had little in common; for Catholicism, it was to keep abreast of the pressing demands from a working-class membership eager for its ministrations." He continues:

American Catholicism's encounter with industrialization, therefore, was more institutional and practical than intellectual or moral, more an unconscious necessity than a conscious choice. Its leaders were not a minority of articulate prophets challenging accepted beliefs, but numerous clergy and laypersons who seldom understood or proclaimed their activities as a distinctly religious response to industrialization. Many Catholics, therefore, had a long experience in coping with social problems before they began to reflect on them. [41]

As we shall see in the next section, "reflection" on a deeper level was just around the corner in the work of Msgr. John Ryan, who was able to creatively combine action and reflection in his long ministry.

CHARACTERISTICS OF THE AMERICAN CATHOLIC SOCIAL MOVEMENT

The energies of the Roman Catholic Church in the United States during the last half of the nineteenth century were focused on establishing itself as an immigrant church in a Protestant country. The previous pages give a glimpse of some of the struggles and issues that the leaders of the church faced. In summary we can identify a few dominant characteristics of the American Catholic church's social thinking and ministry.

1. Initiatives for reform "from below"

While we have recognized the leadership of Cardinal Gibbons and his small circle of supporters, by and large the bishops of the Catholic church did not take the initiative for social reform. The initiative came from the people and the labor movement—people like Terence Powderly, Leonora Barry, Mary O'Sullivan, and Mother Jones. Eventually more clergy became involved. One of the "labor priests," Peter Dietz, pointed out to Cardinal Gibbons in 1912 that many of workers who struggled for reform were "discouraged" and "demoralized...because of the lack of moral support by the Church."[42] It was the laity and the priests who worked to bring about social reform. The hierarchy was often seen as conservative on social issues. This would begin to change as the ferment for reform worked its way through the church, "from below." As Jay Dolan summarizes, "Both people and priests provided the initial thrust for reform, and only after this gained headway during the progressive period did the hierarchy unite to support such reform."[43]

2. Pastoral and practical focus

As noted above, the church's social thinking was focused on the immediate and practical problems facing a predominantly immigrant church
trying to establish itself in its new country. A strong theological and theoretical framework for this activism was not present. That theological
and ethical framework was present in the papal encyclical *Rerum
Novarum* and in the writings of European thinkers, but it had not yet
been given an articulation in the American context.

3. Negative and defensive tone

To a great extent the church's social teaching of this era was a reaction
against socialism as it swept through Europe and the United States. In
the battle between Archbishop Corrigan and Father McGlynn we see the
struggle of the antisocialist forces of the church at work. To a lesser
degree, the teaching criticized the excesses of capitalism.

The Catholic church was also defensive in its ecumenical stance; it was
still battling the Protestant Reformation. With the work of Msgr. John Ryan,
a positive and practical program of social reform would be put forward. The
"thawing" of the ecumenical chill would have to wait a few more decades.

4. A limited understanding of Rerum Novarum

Until the 1920s the American church had a limited and distorted view of
Rerum Novarum. Joseph McShane comments, that "American Catholics
were either completely ignorant of the contents of *Rerum novarum* or
chose to construe its message in an exclusively antisocialist way."[44] This
led to a narrow-minded interpretation and application of the encyclical
that crippled efforts to present a positive social stance by the church.

All four of these features of the American church were about to shift
due to the forces for reform at work within the church and society. The
thought and leadership of John Ryan were to play a crucial role in shaping the Catholic church's social vision for the next forty years.

Part II. John Ryan
and Social Reconstruction

The best known and most influential of the Catholic "labor priests" was
John A. Ryan, who taught moral theology at The Catholic University of
America in Washington, D.C., from 1915-1939 and was the director of

the Social Action Department of the Catholic bishops' National Catholic Welfare Conference from 1920-1945. Ryan's draft of social reconstruction became the Catholic bishops' own in their 1919 statement. For three decades he was the foremost "official" Catholic spokesperson for progressive social reform.

The genius of Ryan was his ability to blend Catholic social thought with American perspectives on reform. He drew upon Leo's natural law framework with its insistence on natural human rights and the dignity of the individual person. Ryan insisted that the social and economic problems were essentially moral problems. From this perspective of morality he argued that the church had an important role to play in the reconstruction of the social order. "In an era in which the church's social teaching and policy were too often simply a reaction against socialism, he offered a positive, practical program of social reform that was both Catholic and American."[45]

John was born on May 25, 1865, the oldest of eleven children of William and Mary Ryan. His parents had emigrated from Ireland in the 1850s to escape the potato famine. They settled in the farm community of Vermillion, Minnesota. From a young age John learned firsthand of the economic woes of the farmers: falling grain prices and a monopoly by the railroads that shipped the grain. In his youth Ryan came under the spell of the Populist movement. The Populist orator-agitator Ignatius Donnelly, who had founded the Anti-Monopoly Party, was one of John Ryan's boyhood heroes. Ryan inherited a distaste for monopolies from his father, whom he frequently accompanied to the meetings of the National Farmers' Alliance. "Johnnie rarely missed a chance to hear adult conversation about farmers' grievances. After Mass on Sunday when Hugh McGuire, the town radical...harangued about the railroad monopoly, John was always nearby." If neighbors dropped in to talk over Alliance issues with William Ryan, John was at hand, his mouth sagging as his energy went into keeping his ears open.[46] He also learned of urban conditions by reading a bulky weekly newspaper, *Irish World and Industrial Liberator*. The paper matched the Knights of Labor and later the American Federation of Labor against the large industrial corporations.[47]

As the oldest child, John helped to run the two small farms the family owned, but he also did well in school. In fact, at age eight he hounded his mother, asking "When will it be Monday again so I can go to school?" His intelligence was soon a problem for other parents in the area. They feared that the teachers gave this bright student more than his share of their time. When John's dad heard of the complaints he kept John home from the public school.[48]

The young Ryan eventually went on to St. Thomas Seminary, outside of St. Paul, and was ordained as a diocesan priest on June 4, 1898. While in the seminary he discovered *Rerum Novarum*. It became for him the seminal document: "He would take as his life's work the explanation and adaptation of *Rerum Novarum* to the American situation."[49] Ryan saw some familiar themes in *Rerum Novarum*, such as the condemnation of socialism and the defense of private property, but he also saw some teaching that was revolutionary. Ryan was delighted to see that his own views on the regulation of industry by the state were also taught by the pope. Years later Ryan noted that "the doctrine of state intervention which I had come to accept and which was sometimes denounced as 'socialistic' in those benighted days, I now read in a Papal encyclical... Leo's teaching on the state seemed almost revolutionary." This 28-year-old seminarian also noted with satisfaction that the encyclical defended the notion of a living wage (enough to allow the worker to live in "reasonable and frugal comfort") and that labor unions are legitimate vehicles for defending the workers' rights.

After completing his assignment on *Rerum Novarum* he wrote a letter to the *Northwestern Chronicle* on the right to work. In this article he laid out the heart of his social ethic:

- people have a right to life and the state must protect that right;

- the right to life means the right to work;

- if workers lost the opportunity to find a job, if the state allowed "the greed and usurpation of some other men...to make working impossible," then the state had a positive obligation to find jobs;

- charity and relief were no long lasting solutions—as Henry George had said, "Charity is a poison when taken as a substitute for justice";

- the state's obligation to secure its citizens' welfare was not new; what was new was applying an old principle to new conditions.[50]

After Ryan's ordination Archbishop Ireland sent him to the Catholic University of America (CUA) in Washington, D.C., for doctoral studies to prepare for a teaching career at his diocesan seminary. At CUA Ryan came under the influence of Father Thomas Bouquillon who had been a member of the four-person panel that had defended McGlynn and led to his reinstatement. Both Bouquillon and William Kerby, another professor at CUA, insisted that questions of social morality had to be grounded in precise observations of social reality and not just considered in abstract terms.

Ryan returned to St. Paul in 1902 to begin his teaching career focusing on moral theology and economics. During those years he also helped draft the minimum wage legislation for the state of Minnesota. He worked hard lobbying to get the bill approved. This was a step toward attaining a living wage.

While teaching, Ryan also finished his doctoral dissertation, which was published in 1906 as *A Living Wage: Its Ethical and Economic Aspects.* In his dissertation he argued that each worker had a right to a wage that would allow him to live in a manner in accord with his dignity as a human being. Ryan wasn't afraid of getting specific. He felt that the older formulas about paying the worker the "worth" or "value" of his or her labor needed a more precise formulation adjusted to modern industrial society. Ryan asserted that a family living wage is demanded by justice. "In concrete terms, based on a careful breakdown of living expenses, Ryan suggested $600 a year as the *minimum* acceptable in any American city for decent living. In 1906 the average wage for urban workers (that is, excluding farm labor) was $571; about 60% of America's industrial labor force fell below that acceptable minimum."[51]

In 1914 Ryan was "catapulted into national prominence" when he was invited to join Morris Hillquit, the leading theoretician of the American Socialist Party, in a debate on the question "Socialism: Promise or Menace?" in the pages of *Everybody's Magazine*.[52] While Ryan was no defender of capitalism he also criticized socialism's theory of economic determinism and its antireligious and antimoral tenets. In this debate he pointed to three major evils in the present system: 1) insufficient wages, 2) excessive income for some, and 3) the concentration of capital ownership. He worried about this third evil: "the narrow distribution of capital ownership is more fundamental than the other two evils because it threatens the stability of the whole system." Father John Coleman, a social ethicist, notes, "Because he feared the totalitarian tendency of socialism, Ryan preferred in its stead a widespread people's capitalism embracing industrial democracy and consumer and productive co-operatives." At the same time he urged vigorous governmental intervention through antitrust legislation and the regulation of prices and interest rates.[53] He was developing a social ethic that was able to critique both of the dominant ideologies.

In 1915 John Ryan returned to Washington, D.C., to become a professor of moral theology at The Catholic University of America, where he also offered courses in the department of economics. He taught at the university until 1940. During that time he published his second and last major economic treatise, *Distributive Justice: The Right and Wrong of Our Present Distribution of Wealth*. In this text, which he considered his "most important work," he argued that the present problems were the result of an improper distribution of wealth.[54]

In 1919, in the closing days of World War I, the recently formed National Catholic War Council—the predecessor organization to the National Conference of Catholic Bishops—formed a committee on reconstruction. This committee was asked to produce a program on postwar social reconstruction that would compare favorably with the hundreds of similar programs already before the public. The secretary of the committee, Father John O'Grady, turned to Ryan as the deadline for the document was fast approaching. At first Father Ryan refused the assignment but eventually he gave Father O'Grady a hastily revised speech on reconstruction that he had prepared for delivery at a Knights of Columbus convention in Louisville. Ryan came to realize that this invitation was a great opening for communicating his social vision.

> As time went on, he realized that the bishops' request was the opportunity of a lifetime, for it gave him the chance to produce a document that wedded Leonine Catholic social thought with American Progressivism. In addition, due to the fact that it was published under the bishops' names, it gave him the unparalleled opportunity to present a unified and Progressive Catholic social program to the entire church.[55]

The document, entitled *Social Reconstruction: A General Review of the Problems and Survey of Remedies*, was published on February 12, 1919.

In that same year, Father Ryan was appointed the director of the newly created Social Action Department of the National Catholic Welfare Council. Ryan would serve as its director until 1944. From this position Ryan publicized his notions of social reform. He also sought to educate

American Catholics in the basic tenets of Catholic social teaching. Throughout his long career Ryan was engaged in a wide variety of social issues including child labor, international peace, and civil liberties. In many of these issues Ryan argued for cooperation of Catholics with other non-Catholic and secular organizations to achieve common goals.

His social and economic positions earned him the title of "the Right Reverend New Dealer" from his conservative critic Father Charles E. Coughlin. He had much in common with Franklin D. Roosevelt's political stand even to the point of making a campaign speech for him in 1936. Roosevelt returned the favor by inviting him to give the benediction at his 1937 inauguration—the first Catholic priest to do so.[56]

Ryan's writing, teaching, and activism made a unique contribution to the American Catholic church: "Ryan's approach to the substantive issues in social ethics well exemplifies the best of American Catholic social liberalism with its twin emphasis on economic reform and the basic compatibility between Catholic faith and the American ethos."[57] Ryan also contributed to the development of Catholic social thought on the global scene as well. Theologian Charles Curran writes that

> Ryan's methodological acceptance of distributive justice with its heavy emphasis on the criterion of human needs and his central insistence on the common destiny of the goods of creation are two important foundations for his economic ethics. In these areas Ryan makes a lasting contribution to Roman Catholic social ethics. His position on private property is different from that proposed by Leo XIII and anticipated the approach which would be proposed since the Second Vatican Council with its primary insistence on the common destiny of the goods of creation to serve the needs of all.[58]

Today we see some of the historical limitations of Msgr. Ryan's thought and activism. From our perspective he was not sensitive to the dangers of government centralization. At times he appears naive about economic and political power. Fr. John Coleman notes that "living and writing as he did in the first generation after the rise of the large trusts in America, he still thought their progress could be halted and a people's capitalism of small enterprises instituted." Ryan, like other economists of his day, did not recognize the inherent natural limits to ever-increasing industrial production.[59] Virgil Michel, the Benedictine liturgist we will meet in the next chapter, accused Ryan of a lack of concern for interiority.[60]

Msgr. Ryan's social ethic is not beyond critical evaluation, but on the whole he made an irreplaceable contribution to the development of an American Catholic social ethic—a social ethic that was not merely practical and pragmatic but theoretical, one that was positive as it drew from the best of the Catholic and American traditions, one that began to bridge two realms—"from below" (labor) and "from above" (the hierarchy).

LEADERSHIP "FROM ABOVE"

Historians note that it took a world war to get the American bishops to create an organization that would speak in their name on social issues. Many Catholic organizations were helping in the war effort on various fronts, from providing buildings for recreation and raising money for the war effort, to buying Bibles and Mass outfits for chaplains. The Knights of Columbus were leaders in this regard, raising over $14,000,000. Women took an active role as well:

> Even more impressive was the work of the women's societies.... Catholic women were active in Red Cross work, in chaplain aid, and in the sale of Liberty Bonds and War Saving Stamps. They provided no little housing and protective care for women workers in war industry. In some of the war camps the subcommittee on women's activities established visitors' houses in which nearly a million and a half friends of soldiers were entertained. In order to help meet the desperate need for trained social workers this subcommittee opened the National Catholic Service School for Women at Clifton in the nation's capital.[61]

In fact, there were almost 15,000 Catholic societies at this time, and many of them were engaged in some form of war work. The bishops and the leaders of these lay organizations saw the need to coordinate all of these efforts. "In order to meet the many heavy and ever changing demands for aid and counsel an organization broadly representative of the whole Catholic body was deemed necessary."[62] Three Cardinals—Gibbons, Farley, and O'Connell—called for a General Convention of Catholic societies to meet at Catholic University of America in Washington, D.C., on August 11-12, 1917. Sixty-eight dioceses were represented, along with twenty-seven national lay organizations and the Catholic press. From this convention the National Catholic War Council (NCWC) was established "to study, coordinate, unify, and put in operation all Catholic activities incidental to the war."[63] At first the executive committee of the NCWC was to include the heads of the American Federation of Catholic Societies, the Knights of Columbus, and an ordained and lay appointee of each of the fourteen archdioceses. But a few months later, in November 1917, the fourteen archbishops, sensing that the executive committee was unwieldy and inefficient, constituted themselves as the NCWC and asked four bishops who had been identified with the lay organizations to serve as the executive committee.[64]

BISHOPS' PROGRAM OF SOCIAL RECONSTRUCTION OF 1919

The four member Administrative Council of the National Catholic War Council accepted a draft paper on social reconstruction made by Fr. Ryan (see above, page 52) and made it their own. These four were bishops Peter Muldoon, chairperson, from Rockford, Joseph Schrembs of Toledo, Patrick Hayes of New York, and Bishop William Russell of Charleston. The document notes in the opening sentences that "the ending of the Great War has brought peace. But the only safeguard of peace is social justice and a contented people." The bishops realized that not everyone would agree with their specific proposals; at the same time, they rooted these reforms in the principles of Catholic social teaching that must be given serious attention. "Its practical applications are of course subject to discussion but all its essential declarations are based upon the principles of charity and justice that have always been held and taught by the Catholic Church, while its practical proposals are merely an adaptation of those principles and that traditional teaching to the social and industrial conditions and needs of our own time."[65]

The document had three parts: a brief introductory essay; a survey of other reconstruction proposals, both foreign and domestic; and a series of programmatic proposals for change. Part three is where "the rubber hits the road" in that specific proposals are suggested as a way of "translating our faith into works." These proposals were not seen as revolutionary by Ryan or the bishops, but were "desirable and also obtainable within a reasonable time."[66] The recommendations of the statement can be divided into short-term and long-term reforms. Under the category of *short-term proposals* we find the following:

1. a call for minimum wage legislation;

2. a call for social insurance to protect workers in cases of industrial accidents and unemployment;

3.child labor laws;

4.the recognition of labor's right to organize and bargain collectively;

5.the continuation of the National War Labor Board to mediate labor disputes;

6.public housing for the urban poor;

7.the creation of a national employment service;

8.progressive taxation;

9.the regulation of monopolies;

10. government control of utilities;

11. a land colonization program for returning soldiers; and,

12. replace women in their wartime employment.

The statement had two *long-range proposals*, which were more radical in nature: a call for the formation of workers' cooperatives, and the realignment of industry so as to foster co-partnership in industry.

Regarding "co-partnership" Ryan and the bishops suggested that workers be given a say in determining their wages and their working conditions and also be given a say in the management of the entire industrial enterprise.[67]

It is interesting to read how the document addresses the role of women in its proposals for social reconstruction. By today's standards some sections have a paternalistic or sexist tone as it recommends that "no female worker should remain in any occupation that is harmful to health or morals. Women should disappear as quickly as possible from such tasks as conducting and guarding street cars, cleaning locomotives, and a great number of other activities for which conditions of work and their physique render them unfit." Other sections of the document are clearly egalitarian: "Those women who are engaged at the same tasks as men should receive equal pay for equal amounts and qualities of work."[68]

RESPONSE TO THE DOCUMENT

Ryan had maintained that the above proposals were both traditional and conservative. By that he meant that they were rooted in the thought of Leo

XIII. Those who read the bishops' statement thought that these proposals were innovative and radical. The liberals and labor leaders greeted the program with "incredulous delight," but some conservatives and members of the business community were hostile. One group of Catholic critics sought to undermine its binding authority by questioning the NCWC's canonical standing. They believed the NCWC had no clearly defined authoritative position as part of the church's teaching office.[69]

Joseph McShane argues that "the charges of radicalism and novelty leveled against [the bishops' statement] obliquely testified to the fact that nearly thirty years after its publication most American Catholics still did not understand *Rerum Novarum.*"[70] It is no doubt true that many Catholics were not informed about the teachings of *Rerum Novarum*, but the novelty that is noted is not only *what* was said, but *who* said it. Prior to World War I the American church—the hierarchy in particular—was seen as a conservative player on the American landscape, often caught up only in internal parochial affairs. Now the bishops in an organized way had inserted themselves into the American body politic. This was a novelty—even if people had heard of *Rerum Novarum.*

"The confused and hostile reaction given the document, however, was strangely fortuitous."[71] For it gave the bishops and the newly renamed National Catholic Welfare Council a clear agenda. Cardinal Gibbons put it in these terms:

> First, the presentation, definite, clear and forceful, of Catholic social principles. Second, more knowledge as to the best methods of Catholic social and charitable work. Third, a more general impulse to put our social principles and methods into practice.... Too often, we must admit, our principles, the principles of the Gospel, have been hidden in our theologies, so much so that the recent pamphlet on Social Reconstruction appears to many as a complete novelty. The Church has a great work of social education and social welfare lying before it. Here, again, the Hierarchy must take the lead.[72]

We see in his words the call to his fellow bishops to take the lead in educating the people about the church's social principles. The educational task identified by the reaction to the bishops' Program of Social Reconstruction was addressed on two levels:

1. First, the NCWC had to articulate a short-term explanation and defense of the bishops' program. On this point, Ryan and other like-minded social thinkers took up the charge. Ryan explained how the bishops' proposals

could be rooted in *Rerum Novarum*. In addressing some of the proposals Ryan had to freely and creatively adapt Pope Leo's writing.[73]

2.The second level of the educational task called for a structure within the church to explicitly tackle the challenge of educating American Catholics in the social thought of the church. To respond to these educational needs the NCWC issued a pastoral letter in the Spring of 1919 defending the Program of Reconstruction—this was the bishops' first pastoral letter since 1884. The bishops also established the Social Action Department with a threefold charge:

1.to produce educational programs in Catholic social thought;

2.to engage in ongoing analysis of social conditions in the United States; and,

3.to bring Catholic influence to bear on social legislation before Congress.

Under the leadership of John Ryan the Social Action Department tackled these tasks with special attention to defending the rights of labor and the necessity of using state intervention to promote social justice in society.

IMPACT OF THE PROGRAM OF SOCIAL RECONSTRUCTION

The bishops' 1919 Program of Social Reconstruction caused a considerable reaction. In responding to that reaction the bishops put in place a structural response to make the church's social teaching a force within the American context. Joseph McShane summarizes the impact of this letter for the American Catholic church by noting its three contributions.

> First, it represented a step forward in the attempts to retrieve the full critical potential of *Rerum novarum* and to apply its central insights to concrete local circumstances.

> Second, on the basis of a perception of a shared natural-law basis, it sought to effect a reconciliation between the American and Catholic traditions of social criticism.

> Finally, in that it gave impetus to the founding of the Social Action Department, it marked the beginning of the church's institutionalized and ongoing ministry of social criticism in the United States, a ministry that continues to the present day.[74]

While we can name these "successful" outcomes of the bishops within the church community, on the legislative level the impact of the document was not as successful in the short-term. The optimism of the pre-war era was fading. The nation was heading into a decade when, as John Ryan noted, "social thinking and social action were chilled and stifled in an atmosphere of pseudo prosperity and thinly disguised materialism."[75] Jay Dolan continues,

> During the 1920s the vitality of the progressive movement died out; the bishops, like most Americans, lost interest in plans for social reconstruction. Conservatism, rather than progressivism, characterized the spirit of the times, and social reform became a victim of the age. Nevertheless, American Catholicism had taken an important step forward in the development of a social-gospel tradition. Further development of this impulse would have to wait until another time.[76]

Better days for social reform would come. In fact, the decade of the 1930s proved to be a time of social reform and activism, as we shall see in the next chapter. By 1939, the bishops were able to claim in the preface of the twentieth anniversary of their *Program on Social Reconstruction* that, of the twelve proposals, all but one had been either wholly of partially translated into reality.[77]

Conclusion

The four characteristics of the American Catholic social movement discussed earlier in the chapter have taken on a different color and texture as we weave in the life and work of John Ryan and the impact of the bishops' *Program on Social Reconstruction*.

The emerging leadership of the bishops begins to complement the work of the laity and clergy in the labor movement. The negative and defensive tone is still present in some quarters but a positive framework of concrete proposals is presented and promoted. This is rooted in an ongoing educational effort to inform the Catholic community of the principles of *Rerum Novarum* as they could be applied to the American situation. Finally, the practical and pastoral focus of the church's ministry is now undergirded by an emerging ethical and theological reflection rooted in the Catholic tradition yet articulated in a creative and responsive fashion. The Catholic church is ready for the renaissance of social activism blended with spirituality and liturgical participation that will unfold in the 1930s.

Discussion Questions

1. What did the Knights of Labor stand for, and why were some church officials opposed to their efforts and strategies?

2. How do you see the tension between the two groups of U.S. bishops discussed in this chapter as an ongoing tension in the American church?

3. Why did the social activists discussed in this chapter, especially Mother Jones and Father McGlynn, have difficulties with some of the leadership of the church?

4. In what ways does the writing of Father John Ryan open a new chapter in Roman Catholic social thought in the the United States?

5. Why is the relatively brief *1919 Statement on Social Reconstruction* by the U.S. bishops an important milestone in American Catholic social thought and action?

3

The 1930s:
Hope Amid Cynicism
and Disillusionment

After World War I a type of conservatism and cynicism was evident in the church and society. As I stated at the end of chapter 2, John Ryan noted that "social thinking and social action were chilled and stifled in an atmosphere of pseudo prosperity and thinly guised materialism." The historian Jay Dolan also laments that "during the 1920s, the vitality of the progressive movement died out; the bishops, like most Americans, lost interest in plans for social reconstruction. Conservatism, rather than progressivism, characterized the spirit of the times, and social reform became a victim of the age."[1] Fellow historian James Hennesey calls the 1920s and 1930s a time of "cultural and political disillusionment and cynicism."[2]

In the midst of such social and ecclesial disillusionment we discover the voices, the vision, and the lives of Christians who stand against the cultural attitudes, witness to hope, and commit themselves to social reform. They are shoots of green life amid the desert of disillusionment and materialism.

Part I: Lay Movements, Spirituality and Liturgy

As we discussed in the previous chapter the work of Msgr. John Ryan was foundational and formative of the American Catholic tradition of social ethics. Yet, his work, as brilliant as it was, did not cover all the needs of a Catholic social tradition. It did not focus on the interior life, the spiritual life, nor did he bridge disciplines to connect his thinking with the church's liturgical life. The linkage of liturgy and social justice was forged by another man from Minnesota, Virgil Michel, a Benedictine priest.

In the 1930s Michel, who was teaching at St. John's University in Collegeville, Minnesota, traced the social implications of liturgy for an integral and revitalized Catholic living. He did his most original thinking in this area and made a specific contribution to American Catholic social thought. In explaining the linkage of liturgy to social issues, Michel was ahead of his European counterparts in the liturgical movement who were primarily focused on the dogmatic, archaeological, and historical aspects of liturgy. Even though the liturgical renewal began in Germany, Switzerland, Belgium, and France, it was in the United States that liturgy was linked with social justice.[3]

Michel used the symbol of the Mystical Body of Christ, the community of Christ's Body on earth, as the heart of his socio-liturgical vision. He reasoned that centuries of individualism had eroded the corporate mentality of Christians and, as a result, left them with a weak sense of community and oneness in Christ. Christian liturgy is the place where this sense of community and oneness in Christ can be learned so that it penetrates all areas of life. In recovering the essential communitarian nature of Christian life, Michel believed that Christians would have to become not only apostle-conscious, conscious of one's apostolate in the world, but also culture-conscious, to be discerning of harmful aspects of one's culture. He presented four features of a healthy culture and suggested the threats to these values:

1) cooperation—threatened by rugged individualism and competition;

2) freedom of the creative spirit—threatened by totalitarian regimes, as were emerging in Germany and Italy;

3) coordination of the material and spiritual needs of people—threatened by the one-sided pursuit of wealth and possessions;

4) balance of all integral human elements, the rational, sensual, affective, physical, etc.—threatened by a sensuous culture that overshadows the other elements of humanity.[4]

For Dom Michel the Christian faith as expressed in its worship was a resource for shaping a *sensus catholicus*, a Catholic communitarian ethos. He believed and hoped that the reform of Catholic worship that encouraged the active participation of the laity would help to overcome the dichotomy between worship and work and would lead to a continuous living out of the Christ-life in one unceasing act of worship.[5]

Virgil Michel and others were reacting to the fractured state of Catholic life. They turned to the eucharistic liturgy as the central religious and cultural symbol for the Catholic community. The Mass was symbolic of the integration of the various fractured dimensions of Christian life. Through the liturgical movement Michel and others promoted the integration of areas of life that seemed cut off from other areas, for example, the fracture between:

- the spiritual life and social reform,

- the individual and the community,

- subjective personal piety and the "objective" piety of the liturgy.

The reformers' "emphasis on baptism and the ecclesiology of the Body of Christ pushed toward the democratization of the priesthood of Christ and the creation of an active and free lay Catholic community."[6]

Father Michel believed the enemy to be confronted was the Christian's surrender to individualism and materialism, which led to a destructive social apathy. Michel believed that the way out of this social morass would be found in active participation in the community's worship, in the development of a spirit of love and mutual sacrifice rooted in a personal commitment, and in the free giving of oneself to others.

Active participation, for Michel, meant not only singing with gusto but engaging the whole person in the mystery of Christian redemption reenacted in the liturgy. "By means of actions and gestures, signs and symbols, creeds and narratives, sights and sounds and smells, the liturgy also engages the passions and the will and thus provides the inspiration and the power that enables Christians to give themselves over to the mystery of Christ in their midst."[7] As Father Michel noted, the liturgy's "appeal is not abstract but concrete, and is brought out in terms of past human achievement and present possibilities—it addresses and inspires the human person to a maximum of the Christ-life both in regard to prayer and to the service of God in the daily occupations and work."[8]

Virgil Michel believed that true society is grounded in the Christ-life and that this "grounding" occurs in local settings—parishes, houses of hospitality, and worker co-ops where the works of mercy and justice are practiced and where they find their source and summit in the Eucharist. This vision was especially attractive to other social activists, such as Dorothy Day.[9]

SPIRITUALITY AND SOCIAL JUSTICE: THREE MOVEMENTS

The liturgical movement, along with Catholic Action, which encouraged laypeople to become active apostles in society to advance God's kingdom on earth, as well as the "Catholic Revival," which was "a resurgence of Catholic thought and belief brought about by a brilliant crowd of novelists, poets, dramatists, historians, philosophers, biographers, and theologians," all converged to foster a new generation of Catholics. This "new breed" of Catholics had a heightened sense of social responsibility and "broke down a strong strain of individualism nurtured by the immigrant Catholic ethos."[10]

An important part of this "revival" was its spirituality. By the 1930s it was apparent that the church's efforts to train social workers and administer relief to the poor did not go far enough. Among a number of educated middle-class Catholics there emerged a need for a deeper sense of solidarity, commitment, and lay spirituality.

Three lay grass-roots movements responded to this yearning for an integration of spirituality and social concern. These movements were led by women—the Catholic Worker, Friendship House, and the Grail—and they transformed the social vision of the American Catholic church. Without explicitly criticizing "the spiritual and social limitations of the hierarchy's centralized efforts at social reform, all three movements pointed the way to an alternative vision based upon the conviction that the spiritual solidarity that bound together members of the Mystical Body of Christ had radical social implications that could only be realized in small communities." Here we see the influence of the liturgical movement and the impact of Virgil Michel's focus of the image of the Mystical Body of Christ—along with others of his day. Historian Debra Campbell notes that "these three movements represent a clear departure from turn-of-the-century Catholic reform and mark the emergence of a distinctive form of Catholic social activism."[11]

1. The Catholic Worker

One of the lay reform movements born in this time of Catholic vitality and resurgence was led by a striking woman, Dorothy Day (1897-1980). Day, although confirmed in the Episcopal church, became a socialist agnostic in 1915 while at the University of Illinois. Conversion to Roman Catholicism came through ironic circumstances. She lived, she said, with an atheist whose "ardent love of creation brought me to the Creator of all things."[12] After becoming pregnant and giving birth to a girl, she committed herself to the Roman Catholic church. Speaking of her daughter, Dorothy wrote, "I am not going to have her floundering through many years as I had done, doubting, undisciplined and amoral. For myself I prayed for the gift of faith." It came. In 1927 she left her common law husband and was baptized. From 1927 to 1933 she had a variety of jobs, including writing for *Commonweal* and *America*. She longed for some way to apply her faith to helping the poor. In the depths of the Depression she met a wandering French philosopher-laborer named Peter Maurin. On May Day 1933, to challenge the Catholic church's social conservatism, they launched the monthly newspaper, *The Catholic Worker*.

It is hard to capture the theology and ethics of the Catholic Worker, for neither Day nor Maurin were systematic theologians.[13] They were activists and journalists. Their social philosophy was neither Communist nor capitalist—nor was it overly lucid. The Catholic Worker philosophy included a rigid pacifism, opposition to the revolutionary class struggle, acceptance of private property but with industry owned by workers, and, generally, the less government the better.

Maurin brought with him a "gentle personalism," which was a Catholic radicalism based on the literal interpretation of the Beatitudes. He rejected the liberal institutions of capitalism and the modern state and their faith in material progress and technology. He replaced all that with a personal commitment to love and an eschatological vision of the Christian mission. He proposed a radical imitation of the gospel life of voluntary poverty in solidarity with the weak, the poor, the sick, and the alienated.

The Catholic Worker movement's consistent intellectual position was based on a radical interpretation of the Sermon on the Mount and on papal social encyclicals. In this way the Worker used the New Testament as a primary source for its ethical guidance, something that set off the Worker from the official Catholic social thought of the time.

The Catholic Worker was founded to serve the poor and needy in "a radical personalist action" and to join "with the worker in his struggle for recognition as a man and not as a chattel."[14] To accomplish these goals Day formed lecture groups, opened houses of hospitality, and edited the newspaper. The circulation of *The Catholic Worker* rose to 200,000 in a few years. The Worker was also committed to racial equality and featured articles attacking lynching and denouncing racism. Day also fought against the growing anti-Semitism of the 1930s and denounced the Jew-baiting of Father Charles Coughlin, a popular radio personality. The movement became a prophetic voice calling for nonviolent revolution against capitalism.

The Worker encouraged communal living, ecumenism, and the concept of laypeople as missionaries. The movement is best known for its "direct action" on behalf of the poor. They started Houses of Hospitality, imitating the medieval hospice. These were soup kitchens, meeting rooms, clothing centers, and places of reflection. By 1941 there were 41 such houses.

They also started rural communes. In 1936 a twenty-eight acre farm was established and soon eleven other farming communes were set up. According to Maurin, a return to the farm was one of the solutions to the crisis of modern industrial society. These communes struggled because many of the families or single people who came to live and work on the farms knew little about farming. Mark and Louise Zwick, who founded the Catholic Worker House for immigrants in Houston, point out that "the agronomic universities were perhaps the least successful of the Catholic Worker projects, but they put flesh on the distributist economics embraced by the Worker. There are several Catholic Worker farms in existence today."[15] While the communal farms were not entirely successful they did help to attract families to the movement and served as rural retreat centers, halfway houses, and suppliers of produce to the urban houses.

Dorothy Day was not only an activist; she was also a woman of prayer, worship, and spirituality. From the earliest days of the Catholic Worker Day felt that the spirituality of laypeople had been neglected. She lamented, "So little is expected of laypeople, the moral theology we are taught is to get us into heaven with scorched behinds. What kind of an unwilling, ungenerous love of God is this? We do little enough, and when we try to do more we are lectured on Jansenism! I don't even know what it is. I only know that I am self-indulgent."[16]

Dorothy held a higher standard for the laity. She believed that the evangelical counsels to perfection, namely, poverty, chastity, and obedience, were norms of Christian conduct for laity and religious alike. She thought it was sad that only the minimum was expected of laypeople. Vatican II would endorse Day's position in calling all Christians to holiness and "the perfection of charity."[17]

Dorothy Day was committed to the importance of the eucharistic liturgy. In the early 1940s she urged "would-be Catholic Workers" that all their activities were first to be offered and united with the sacrifice of Christ on the cross and on the altar. She believed that "all life flowed from worship, only thus would their work be a success, irrespective of its external attainment."[18] The liturgical movement led by Virgil Michel and others, which emphasized the Body of Christ, brought a wholeness to Dorothy's faith and worship. She joined forces with Father Michel and those who wanted to bring the liturgy to the people, through their participation. Already in the 1930s she participated in dialogue Masses.

Dorothy Day, Peter Maurin, and others in the Catholic Worker movement became friends with Father Michel. From their diverse perspectives they worked to bring together the social teaching of the church, the liturgy, and their understanding of the Mystical Body of Christ. It was a natural fit.

> Benedictine spirituality was a natural connection with the Catholic Worker, where hospitality and the Mass were emphasized. Fr. Michel had the inimitable skill of connecting social consciousness with the social nature of worship, especially the liturgy of the Eucharist. He believed that our responsibility for our neighbor, believer or not, flowed from the fact that we were connected to one

> another in the Body of Christ and the Eucharist.... Fr. Michel's writings were published in *The Catholic Worker* and Dorothy wrote in *Orate Fratres*, edited by Fr. Michel.... [M]uch of the heart of the Worker was related to Benedictine spirituality.[19]

Dorothy Day died as she had lived, in Maryhouse, a residence for the destitute on New York City's lower East Side, in a room next to a bag lady. This was on Nov. 29, 1980, when she was 83 years old. At her funeral when Cardinal Cooke was blessing the plain pine coffin outside the church of the Nativity, where she had worshiped daily for years, a drifter, who gave his name as Lazarus, said with tears oozing down his seamed cheeks, "That fine lady gave me love."[20]

Dorothy Day was the heart and soul of the Catholic Worker. Because of her unique charisma and the movement's appeal numerous men and women joined the Catholic Worker. Many of them moved on to other ministries, bringing the spirit of the Catholic Worker with them. Patrick Jordan, who lived at the Catholic Worker from 1969 until 1975, recalls her charisma.

> For me, Dorothy Day was the most engaging and engaged person I have ever met. Even now seventeen years after her death in 1980, I think of her almost daily, with deep affection.... In person, even in her seventies, Day was physically striking: tall, lean, her pale blue eyes keen but not intrusive. In the ideal movie of Dorothy's life, Jessica Lange would be cast in the part. Dorothy was one of those individuals whose presence can affect the tone of whole gatherings. When she entered a crowded room, people with their backs to the door would turn spontaneously. Yet she was unfailingly modest, and almost painfully shy in public.[21]

In the 1930s and '40s Dorothy Day and the Catholic Worker movement attracted followers across the country. "The mixture of radicalism and Catholicism had an obvious appeal to people who had grown tired of the old immigrant church and sought something new and challenging."[22] One could be a radical and a Catholic at the same time. It also was not controlled by the clergy. The clergy could join as fellow workers, but the laypeople ran the show, which was something unusual for Catholic and Protestant churches of the 1930s.

The Catholic Worker movement still permeates the church. Patrick Jordan points out that, "On the hundredth anniversary of her birth

[November 8, 1897], her spirit is alive in the Catholic Worker movement she and Peter Maurin founded in 1933." He said that "the movement is still building, a rather remarkable feat in the history of American religious communities, now with over 125 houses and farming communes in the United States and in seven other countries."[23]

In a number of ways the radical vision of the Catholic Worker challenged the ethos of the culture, but it also challenged the Catholic church itself. This challenge was never confrontational, as in the case of Father McGlynn in the 1880s, yet Dorothy Day always lived "in a state of permanent dissatisfaction with the Church."[24] Her challenge was to its leaders, the priests and bishops, as well to its way of doing social ethics. Although she was clearly orthodox in her theology and not a feminist in the contemporary sense of the term, she was not afraid to disagree with the hierarchy (namely, Cardinal Spellman) on social issues, such as the morality of war and the gravediggers strike in 1949. Her positions, moral influence, and following made her a visible countervailing force within the Catholic community and part of its "unofficial" social tradition.

A Lasting Legacy

Dorothy Day has left a lasting legacy in the Catholic social tradition. She has inspired activists and the magisterium alike. Daniel Berrigan, S.J., credits Dorothy with breaking new ground and opening new trails that he and others followed.

> Without Dorothy, without that exemplary patience, courage, moral modesty, without this woman pounding at the locked door behind which the powerful mock the powerless with games of triage, without her, the resistance we offered would have been simply unthinkable. She urged our consciences off the beaten track; she made the impossible (in our case) probable and then actual. She did this first of all, by living as though the Truth were true.[25]

Dorothy Day was effective because she lived out what she believed: "It was not what Dorothy Day wrote that was extraordinary, nor even what she believed, but the fact that there was absolutely no distinction between what she believed, what she wrote, and the manner in which she lived."[26]

During the Second Vatican Council Dorothy lobbied the bishops to include nonviolence as an essential element of living the Gospel. *The Catholic Worker* under her guidance prepared a special edition on peace and the moral problems of modern warfare, which she airmailed the bishops gathered in Rome.[27] In that issue she wrote,

> One of our Catholic pacifists asked me to write a clear, theoretical, logical pacifist manifesto, and he added so far in these thirty-two years of the Catholic Worker, none had appeared from my pen.
>
> I can write no other than this: unless we use the weapons of the spirit, denying ourselves and taking up our cross and following Jesus, dying with Him and rising with Him, men will go on fighting, and often from the highest motives, believing that they are fighting defensive wars for justice and in self-defense against present or future aggression.[28]

Dorothy followed up the airmailed copy of *The Catholic Worker* by traveling to Rome with a group in order to be a physical presence during the Council. She met with many people, including bishops, and she fasted with other women so that their message of nonviolence would be heard in the Council sessions. While the text of *Gaudium et Spes* did not meet all the expectations of the pacifists, it did praise those who, like the Catholic Worker movement, "renounce the use of violence in the vindication of their rights" (par. 78) and it called government officials to "make humane provisions for the case of those who for reasons of conscience refuse to bear arms" (par. 79). The council fathers recognized that in the nuclear age "the horror and perversity of war are immensely magnified by the multiplication of scientific weapons" (par. 80). Because of these new circumstances the bishops felt compelled to "undertake an evaluation of war with an entirely new attitude." They continued,

> With these truths in mind, this most holy Synod makes its own the condemnations of total war already pronounced by recent Popes, and issues the following declaration:
>
> Any act of war aimed indiscriminately at the destruction of entire cities or of extensive areas along with their population is a crime against God and man himself. It merits unequivocal and unhesitating condemnation. (par. 80)

The witness of Dorothy Day's life was recognized by the bishops of the United States as they crafted their pastoral letter *The Challenge of Peace* three years after her death.

In the twentieth century, prescinding from the non-Christian witness of a Mahatma Gandhi and its worldwide impact, the non-violent witness of such figures as Dorothy Day and Martin Luther King
had a profound impact upon the life of the Church in the United
States. (par. 117)

Dorothy Day has helped the church focus on real problems in society.
In 1968 she complained that the Catholic press in the United States was
too much concerned with problems of authority, birth control, and
celibacy, whereas the real problems were "war, race, poverty and wealth,
violence, sex, and drugs."[29]

In concluding his reflections on this woman for whom he had great
affection, Patrick Jordan recalls the author George Bernanos.

Without the saints, Bernanos said fifty years ago, the church is only
dead stones: Without them, the very grace lying within the church's
institutional and sacramental forms remains fallow. Despite the
unparalleled upheavals of our times, grace has not remained hidden. We have seen its appealing power.[30]

2. Friendship Houses

In 1939 when Dorothy Day was organizing the Committee of Catholics to
fight Anti-Semitism she was assisted by another woman already renowned
for her commitment to social justice and minority rights, Baroness
Catherine de Hueck (1900-1985). As part of the Russian nobility de Hueck
and her husband had fled Russia to escape the Bolshevist purge and settled
in Canada. In Toronto in 1930 she established Friendship House as an
interracial residence for the poor. In 1938, at the request of New York clergy, she opened a storefront office and community center in Harlem. There
with a staff of nine and forty volunteers, de Hueck lived a life of poverty
while serving the needs of the poor.

The center became a source of emergency assistance for the poor, a
recreational place for young people, a meeting place to discuss Catholic
social thought, and a place where the community of the liturgy became
a lived reality. Friendship Houses were started in Ottawa and Hamilton,
Ontario; Chicago, Illinois; Washington, D.C.; Portland, Oregon; and
Shreveport, Louisiana. The movement, like the Catholic Worker, invited
middle-class men and women to move beyond discussion groups and
reading circles to live out the solidarity and spirituality of the option for

the poor. Some members of Friendship House made a full-time commitment to this social-spiritual apostolate, like the Brooklyn schoolteacher Ann Harrigan, who left teaching to work full-time in the Chicago House, and Monica Durkin, who sold her Cleveland insurance firm to run the Friendship House Farm, intending to integrate blacks and whites in rural Wisconsin.[31] They realized the wisdom of de Hueck's words, "In order to make the 'masses' listen, a new way had to be found. It was not a part-time job! Nor would one be listened to if he or she came from a comfortable neighborhood or from a secure job and gave only an hour or two. No, that would not do."[32]

The Friendship House movement sought the transformation of American society by communal efforts to combat racism. Located in the African American ghetto, it tried to rouse the consciences of Americans to the social sin of racism. The very structure of the movement identified itself with the marginal and insecure by refusing financial support from the church or community funding, rather relying on the contributions of interested individuals.

Few social activists at that time were addressing the question of racism; in fact most social activists were preoccupied with the rights of workers and were blind to the issues of race. That is why the work of de Hueck and a few others stands out as the exception.[33] De Hueck played an important role in focusing on the racism within the church and within the society. Through its periodical, *The Catholic Interracialist*, and the "outer circle" of supporters, the impact of Friendship House helped to prepare Catholics for the civil rights movement of the 1950s and '60s. Only in the 1950s did Catholics begin to turn their attention to racial justice.[34]

Catherine de Hueck returned to Canada in 1947 with her second husband, Eddie Doherty. (Eddie was a reporter who was assigned to write a series on Harlem. After meeting de Hueck he volunteered for Friendship House, and they got married in 1943.) There she began another apostolate known as Madonna House, a rural community where laity and priests share life and prayer as they prepare for lay ministry. She continued writing books on lay spirituality until her death in 1985.

3. The Grail
The third grass-roots movement of this period led by women was the Grail. The beginning of the Grail is traced to two Dutch laywomen,

Lydwine van Kersbergen and Joan Overboss, who transplanted the movement from its roots in the Netherlands. In 1921 the Society of the Women of Nazareth had been established by Jacques Van Ginneken, S.J., to "...counteract in the world all masculine hardness, all the angles of the masculine character, all cruelty, all the results of alcoholism and prostitution and sin and capitalism, which are ultramasculine, and to Christianize that with a womanly charity."[35]

From its new headquarters on a farm known as Grailville, outside of Loveland, Ohio, the Grail sponsored courses and retreats to emphasize the link between involvement in the liturgy and the lay apostolate in the world. The chief features of this movement were hard work and a daily routine centered in the liturgy, with elaborate celebration of feast days, deep asceticism, and an eagerness to convert the world from secularism to Christian humanism. By the 1950s the center was "bursting at the seams" as Janet Kalven, a leader in the movement, recalls,

> Every summer, carloads came from the cities to Grailville for week-long or summer-long courses, some staying on for the full year. Grailville burst at its seams, all the barns becoming sleeping places, the dining rooms spilling over to the porch and lawns. As strange as the lay apostolate, the liturgical movement, and social action were to most Catholics, the momentum was gaining on all fronts, a quiet revolution, for new life in the church.[36]

By 1962 the Grail had had a small but significant impact in that 14,000 women had participated in its programs, 600 women were active members, and its core group of lifetime, celibate members numbered close to 100.

These three movements were not confined to official expectations and definitions of lay Catholic Social Action. The official definition articulated by Pope Pius XI in 1929 was as follows.

> There is a need for elect groups of men, both of the secular and regular clergy, who shall act as faithful dispensers of the mysteries of God. In addition to these we must have compact companies of pious laymen, who united to the Apostolic Hierarchy by close bonds of charity, will actively aid this by devoting themselves to the manifold works and labors of Catholic Action.[37]

It is significant that the three movements discussed above operated

outside of this definition of Catholic Action. They had good relationships with the hierarchical church but also enjoyed a healthy autonomy
and self-direction.[38]

Young Catholics were also energized by the activism of the 1930s.
They were attracted to the Cardijn method of social analysis and action.
This method was named after a Belgian priest, Joseph Cardijn. His
approach suggested that small groups of laity would meet weekly to systematically

a) observe and discuss their environment,

b) judge the situation in light of the gospel, and then

c) act.

 The thrust was clearly on action. Each week the group would conclude its meeting with a decision to act. This was not a study-club
approach.

In 1938 Rev. Donald Kanaly, who had studied in Louvain, Belgium,
introduced the Cardijn method in Chicago at a clergy summer school for
social action. According to historian Jay Dolan, "It was like throwing a
match into a puddle of gasoline."[39] Chicago and Notre Dame became
two centers of this modified Catholic Action. Two groups emerged: the
Young Christian Workers, which spread to 35 cities, and the Young
Christian Students, which was established in a number of colleges and
high schools. They tried to effect change in their schools or places of
work through specific action programs. At schools like Notre Dame they
did have an impact in opening the school to African Americans, and in
establishing a college press and courses on marriage. At work, it meant
promoting unions and encouraging a strong spiritual life. The clergy who
were involved encouraged lay ownership and responsibility and tried to
keep the movement as far removed as possible from the hierarchy and
official church bureaucracy.[40]

As these students and young workers moved into the next phases of
their lives they took with them the lessons learned in these movements.
In 1949 the Christian Family Movement (CFM) was started by a married
couple, Pat and Patty Crowley. CFM moved beyond the traditional
framework of Catholic Action in a number of ways: it emphasized
Catholic involvement with non-Catholics in working for social justice for
the sake of the family; it promoted lay leadership; the clergy were in an

advisory role; and, finally, it encouraged women to function as equal partners in the movement. In an age of social activism, the CFM flourished, reaching a membership of 30,000 couples by 1958.[41]

WRAP UP

The 1930s was a decade of great vitality and creativity among Roman Catholics on many fronts, not the least of which was their focus on the church's social ministry. We see not only activists who had a strong commitment to action and practical solutions, but we see a growing academic and theoretical articulation of church teaching and worship as it related to current social concerns. At the same time, Pope Pius XI brought the weight of his office to analyze the current scene in light of the Catholic social tradition.

Part II. Pope Pius XI—His Social Vision

Pope Pius XI came from a sedate life as a librarian in Milan to become "an activist pope." Ambrogio Damiano Achille Ratti was born near Milan, studied in Rome, taught in the Milan seminary, and then served as librarian for 20 years both in Milan and in the Vatican. By profession he was a paleontologist, but by avocation he was a mountain climber who dreamed of exploring the polar regions.[42] He succeeded Pope Benedict XV as pope on February 6, 1922, after serving as the Cardinal of Milan for one year. During his 17-year papacy (1922-1939) he faced turbulent times including the ongoing world economic crisis marked by famine in Russia, financial collapse in Germany, the stock market crash, and worldwide economic depression.

Pius XI broke the self-imposed papal isolation of his four immediate predecessors with his public ministry. His motto as pope was "the peace of Christ in the Kingdom of Christ." By this he meant to communicate his vision that the solution to world problems was to be found in religious renewal, namely the restoration of all things in Christ. Only the church offered a "true community of nations"—in contrast to the League of Nations and the "illusory peace" on which it was based. He established the feast of Christ the King in 1925 as a way of projecting his vision of religious renewal through Christ.

In his encyclical *Ubi Arcano* he called for the participation of the laity in the work of the hierarchy and under its guidance and direction. Prior to this time most of the social justice movements were directed by lay-led societies.[43]

As mentioned above, Pius XI did not give in to the spirit of the times. In the face of the cultural and political disillusionment Pius was "unabashedly authoritarian, energetic, and decisive."[44] He took the offensive as he addressed the social dilemmas of his time and injected the church with his social vision rooted in a confident Catholic faith.

Three of his encyclicals addressed socioeconomic questions:

- *Quadragesimo anno* (May 15, 1931);

- *Nova impendet* (October 2, 1931), which discussed the unemployment crisis and the arms race; and,

- *Caritate Christi* (May 3, 1932), which stressed Pius' call for religious renewal, in that the answer to the world crisis was a religious solution that included a call for love, prayer, penance, and devotion to the Sacred Heart of Jesus.

Pope Pius used all the instruments of the papacy to insert the church as an actor on the global scene, always stressing the moral and religious contribution of the church.

THE CONTEXT FOR *QUADRAGESIMO ANNO*

As discussed in chapter one, the Social Catholics proposed a corporative vision for society as a third way between capitalism and socialism. "Corporatism" referred to a model of society that would restructure the economy around vocational or occupational groups of trades and employers. Such groups were intended to revive the spirit and relationships that were found in the guilds of the Middle Ages, which had gone into decline and had been suppressed during the French Revolution.[45]

Extreme forms of corporatist thinking were emerging in Italy and Austria in the 1930s. In Austria the democratic constitution was overthrown in 1933, and corporatist ideals were established. Fascist Italy revamped its entire economic and social structure, claiming to follow the Catholic corporatist model. Portugal and Spain also showed the influence of corporatist thinking. Yet in reality, none of these models followed the principles of the "corporatist regime" developed in the nineteenth century, even though many Catholics thought they did. "In almost all cases, 'corporatism' was only a facade concealing the domination of a centralized, totalitarian state and therefore was contrary to the dreams of most of the original corporatist theorists."[46]

The major problem of these totalitarian expressions of corporatist thinking was the control of the worker-employer association by the state. This lack of liberty was clearly rejected by the pope, though in principle he was too conciliatory toward these fascist governments, especially that of Mussolini.[47] Pius also disagreed with the extreme corporatist followers of Karl von Vogelsang, who hated the property holding system of modern capitalism; in this the "corporatists" sounded very much like the socialists. Even though Pius was a conservative corporatist, he rejected, as did Leo, the corporatists' extreme restriction on the use of property by the individual.

Pope Pius XI had turned to a few German Jesuits to assist him in writing the encyclical *Quadragesimo Anno*, primarily Oswald von Nell-Breuning and Gustav Gundlach. Indirectly he was turning to a third German Jesuit, Heinrich Pesch, who had been the teacher to both Nell-Breuning and Gundlach. Pesch had died in 1926 but his influence was felt through his students and through his writings, the five-volume, 3,900 page work, *Lehrbuch der Nationalökonomie* (Textbook of National Economics) and shorter *Ethik und Volkswirtschaft* (Ethics and the National Economy).[48]

Pesch's version of the vertically integrated economy was known as solidarism. In brief, solidarism was an organic view of society and the economy in which the prosperity of the entire nation was accomplished through the harmonious cooperation and interdependence of all the segments of the economy and society. All individual and group activity was subordinated to the common good of social prosperity. The cooperation of all was seen as a duty, not as something voluntary. Pesch's theory of solidarism attempted to safeguard the individual and the social dimensions of the human community; it avoided the individualism of capitalism and the class war of collectivism.[49] It is no wonder that the pope and other Catholic social thinkers found this "middle way" attractive.

It is clear that the social vision of Pesch permeated the thinking of the consultants who were to draft the papal encyclical. Pesch's teaching also influenced other theologians and activists both in Europe and in the United States.[50]

AN ENCYCLICAL WRITTEN IN SECRECY

Pius enlisted Nell-Breuning's help. The forty-year-old Nell-Breuning, who had earned his doctorate in 1928 with a dissertation on the morality of the stock exchange, was not allowed to consult others. According to Nell-Breuning he was most influenced by the social philosophy of solidarism and especially by the work of Gustav Gundlach.[51] Pius met with Nell-Breuning only once at the beginning of the project. Toward the end of the writing Nell-Breuning received the sections on the controversial sections on Italian fascism, which Pius had been dealing with. These paragraphs (91-96) were written by the pope himself.[52]

Forty years later Father Nell-Breuning criticized the secretive process wherein one individual carries the full burden of writing the social encyclical:

> Formally, the whole responsibility lay with Fr. Ledochowski, though in fact he depended on me in technical questions. When I think back on it today [1971], *it seems to me that such a procedure that allowed the whole bearing of an official document to be determined by a consultant...without establishing any counter check worth mentioning, seems frighteningly irresponsible. ...*

> Today, people expect that announcements of the highest Church authorities—on questions in which the profane sciences also have a voice—be on just as high a level as that of scientific statements of the most qualified international bodies. This presumes that an international group of recognized specialists in the science participate in the elaboration and assume the technical scientific responsibility for such new announcements.[53]

Father Nell-Breuning was to work in strictest secrecy. Not even the superior of his house nor the provincial superior of the Jesuits knew what he was working on for Fr. Ledochowski, the Superior General, and for the pope. Yet, even in this secretive atmosphere the author sought out the insight of the specialists of his day without their knowing it. As he attended the meetings of the Konigswinter Group—a group of specialists meeting in Konigswinter, a Rhine town in Germany—he would surreptitiously bring up points for discussion that he would then incorporate into the draft of the encyclical. "So later, the Group noticed to their astonishment how many of their stock of ideas reappeared in the encyclical."[54]

THE CONTENT

The content of the encyclical can be summarized as follows. Pius XI continued the direction taken by Leo XIII, but clarified and corrected a few points. The letter emphasized the common good of society and the responsibility of the state to promote the well-being of every segment of society. The principle of intervention by the state in the economic arena was balanced by the principle of subsidiarity. Social justice was presented as the virtue, with social charity, that is essential for the reconstruction of society. In place of class conflict, Pius XI urged cooperation between workers and managers. To this end he suggested "employer-worker councils" that would reorganize all industries and professions along vertical lines rather than along horizontal class lines. He also recommended some form of partnership contract whereby workers would share in ownership or management as well as profits. Finally, he gave support to the lay apostolate as a means of restoring the social order. Of all the ideas presented in the encyclical I will comment on four: social charity, social justice, subsidiarity, and employer-worker councils.

1. Social Charity

According to Pius XI, social justice and social charity are the principles that must govern and penetrate the fabric of society. The "economic dictatorship" of his time was "a headstrong power and a violent energy that, to benefit people, needs to be strongly curbed and wisely ruled. But it cannot curb and rule itself." The principles of social justice and charity must be used to govern this "economic dictatorship." "To that end all the institutions of public and social life must be imbued with the spirit of justice, and this justice must above all be truly operative. It must build up a juridical and social order able to pervade all economic activity. Social charity should be, as it were, the soul of this order."[55]

Both of these notions beg for further clarification. Father John Cronin, who worked for many years with the U.S. bishops' conference and wrote extensively on social ethics, tries to unravel the two in this manner:

> The distinction between social justice and social charity is not easy to express, since both incline the individual to seek the common good. Justice emphasizes what is due to another. This aspect of "otherness" and "debt" is a necessary emphasis,...but at the same time, it is vital to stress the "oneness" of mankind. In seeking the common good, under social justice, we are also working for those bound to us in the

charity of Christ. Social charity, as generous concern for the good of the community, is a unifying principle over and above the organizing force of social justice. For this reason, the task of rebuilding the social order cannot be accomplished by justice alone.[56]

"Social charity" is a term used by Pius XI that is distinct from the general understanding of charity, that is, giving aid to the poor. Almsgiving is one form of charity that could be labeled "individual charity." *Social charity has structural and institutional dimensions.* It means putting policies and structures in place that help to achieve the harmony and "oneness" that may not be achieved through fighting for justice. Whereas the struggle for justice may polarize and lead to class conflict, social charity seeks to overcome those divisions and identify and draw upon the basic bonds of unity within the human family. Whereas social justice may be seen as each receiving their "due" and paying their "debt," social charity emphasizes a more positive orientation of benevolence, of wishing another well, not simply that they receive their "due." The pope's motivation in coining the phrase "social charity" was to keep love, *caritas*, as the central moral virtue in Catholic social teaching, but not let it be reduced to almsgiving.

2. Social Justice

The meaning of "social justice" is also complex and confusing. While the term is commonly used today it has only been part of the ethicists' vocabulary since the early 1840s and part of official church teaching since 1905. It was Pius XI who used the term with some frequency and gave it a specific meaning. In *Quadragesimo Anno* Pius XI used the term eight times. Six years later, he gave his most explicit definition of social justice:

> It is of the very essence of social justice to demand from each individual all that is necessary for the common good.... [I]t is impossible to care for the social organism and the good of society as a unit unless each single part and each individual member... is supplied with all that is necessary for the exercise of his social functions. [57]

Before Pius, the term "social" justice had been introduced in Catholic social ethics by the Italian theologian Father Luigi Taparelli d'Azeglio. It was introduced as a replacement for what Thomas Aquinas had called general justice or legal justice.

Confusion and disagreement arose as some thinkers held that the new term should continue to be an equivalent for general justice and others argued that it had a meaning distinct from that older term.[58] Because the notion of law had shifted away from the Thomistic meaning and had come to be identified with the legal system of the emerging nation state, the notion of legal justice was seen by some as the wrong term for their contemporaries. They chose instead the term social justice, which brought with it its own connotations and shifted the meaning of justice. At the same time, others argued to retain and restore the traditional language of legal justice.[59] A third group, under the influence of individualist and liberal philosophies, restricted the meaning of justice to commutative justice. Commutative justice is that part of justice that is concerned with the equity of reciprocal repayments, for example, labor contracts or buyer's contracts. In this narrow perspective of justice (which is very prevalent in the United States today), obligations of justice are restricted to implicit and explicit *contracts* between individuals and between individuals and corporations.[60] Everything else, including the needs of the common good, is a matter of charity.

Pius XI intervened in these discussions to emphasize that *justice is much more than commutative justice, or individual justice.* He used the term *social* justice to recall the traditional teaching that there can be no justice in the full meaning of the word without an awareness that the good of the individual is part of the common good.

3. Subsidiarity

According to Pius XI's reading of the situation, nineteenth-century economic and political liberalism led to a situation where, for the most part, society was composed of only individuals and the state. "...Things have come to such a pass that the highly developed social life, which once flourished in a variety of prosperous and interdependent institutions, has been damaged and all but ruined, leaving only individuals and the State, with no little harm to the latter" (par. 78). The intermediate bodies or associations, such as the guilds, were lacking. As a result either the pure economic forces of the marketplace prevailed or the state itself had to continually intervene.

In this situation Pius enunciated a traditional principle that was found in Pope Leo's writing and in Thomistic thought on the nature of the state, but to which Pius gave a specific description: the principle of subsidiarity. The principle is rooted in the role of assistance, and help, in Latin *subsidium*, that intermediate groups should provide for individuals:

> Just as it is gravely wrong to take from individuals what they can accomplish by their own initiative and industry and give it to the community, so also it is an injustice and at the same time a grave evil and disturbance of right order to assign to a greater and higher association what lesser and subordinate organizations can do. For every social activity ought of its very nature to furnish help [subsidium] to the members of the body social, and never destroy and absorb them. (par. 79)

This principle takes on specific definition in Pius' call for vocational groups or employer-employee councils. He calls for a restoration of "that rich social life which was once highly developed through associations of various kinds" (par. 79).

The principle of subsidiarity calls for the establishment of *intermediary groups* between individuals and the state, and means that the higher levels (the state) should never intervene when economic and political realities can be handled adequately on the local level.

Many debates have emerged on the correct interpretation of subsidiarity. Some commentators, like Michael Novak, argue for a minimalist role for the higher levels, trusting the market forces to adequately fulfill the needs of individual and common good.[61] Here the state plays only a negative role of protecting threatened individual rights. Others, like David Hollenbach, argue that the Catholic tradition has seen a positive role for higher levels of the state in promoting the common good in the economic and political arenas.[62] This interpretation leads to a more activist role for government in economic issues.

The complexity of the issue, or shall we say the ambiguity of the principle, can be seen in the question of nationalization. Nationalization, in general, violates the principle of subsidiarity, because it claims for the state the right to manage economic enterprises that should be left to intermediary groups. In specific circumstances, however, when a particular private enterprise is detrimental to the common good, then nationalization can be in keeping with the principle of subsidiarity. Each case must be argued in light of the specifics of its situation and the full complement of social principles.

4. Employer-worker councils

In paragraph 83 we find Pius XI's prescription for owner-worker councils.

> But complete cure will not come until this opposition [of workers

and capitalists] has been abolished and well-ordered members of the social body—industries and professions—are constituted in which men may have their place, not according to the position each has in the labor market but according to the respective social functions which each performs. For under nature's guidance it has come to pass that just as those who are joined together by nearness of habitation establish towns, so those who follow the same industry or profession—whether in the economic or other field—form guilds or associations, so that many are wont to consider these self-governing organizations, is not essential, at least natural to civil society.

In order to promote social justice, whose goal is the common good of society, Pius XI urged that the direction of economic life be assigned to "vocational groups," one for each trade, profession, or industry. Here he is following the lead of Leo, the Social Catholics, and the solidarism of Pesch. In these vocational groups, employer and employees would "join forces to produce goods and give service." These groups would be "autonomous," that is, self-governing bodies, with power to set prices, determine wage scales, and in general to control and regulate industrial conditions. The role of the state—a crucial difference with Italian and Austrian models—would assist, not dominate, the process, imposing restraints only when necessary to adjust unresolved differences or to safeguard the interest of consumers and the general public. In his vision the state would be more activist than a "free market" model would suggest, but less activist than the socialist model would suggest. At work here is the principle of subsidiarity.

The pope held that bringing employers and employees into the same organization would put an end to class conflict and bind men together "not according to the position each has in the labor market but according to the respective social functions which each performs."

This vision of the employer-employee councils has an idealistic ring to it. Its vision of social harmony and interdependence is attractive, yet it does not deal with the realistic questions of power and conflict. Yes, the state will intervene when there are conflicts, but where does the state generally put its weight? Also it seems that shared ownership of the industry would be necessary so that the business is not controlled by the board of directors who are beholden to the stockholders. The pope urged that workers become property owners and have some share in the ownership. But how is this to happen, especially if you have poor, semi-skilled workers who earn a minimum wage? They have no capital to buy into the corporation. These are some of the details that needed to be worked out in each country and segment of the economy.[63]

In the United States the pope's advocacy of joint employer-worker councils was considered the central point in Catholic social teaching at this time.[64] It came to be known as the "industry council." In 1940 the new president of the CIO, Philip Murray, proposed the "Industry Council Plan." According to this plan, each defense industry would set up an industry council to introduce more efficient methods of production and encourage union-management cooperation. Each local council would have equal representation from labor and management. On the national level a representative of the government would sit on the board. The tasks of coordination would be handled by a National Board Review with equal representation of management, labor, and government.[65]

Murray claimed that his industry council plan contained the essential ingredients of the "vocational group system" suggested by Pius XI. Yet a major difference was that Murray's industry council was in essence an agency of management and labor in which these two interest groups held all the power. The papal vision, by contrast, subordinated the interests of labor and management to a broader societal structure that strove to serve the common good and not just the interests of labor and management.

The industry council system was not adopted. The plan did not suit well the needs of a wartime economy. Historian Aaron Abell argues that "the plan lacked sufficient power and scope to insure total industrial mobilization following Pearl Harbor." He also points out that "in the unexpected economic prosperity which continued after the war, neither management nor labor saw any advantage in integrated industry, being able to pass on the cost of increased profits and wages to the public through higher prices."[66]

The lack of implementation of Pius XI's plan of vocational or functional groups does not mean the idea was unsound. The vertical cooperation among the various levels of the corporation in some companies today, which is touted as a breakthrough for labor and management, sounds very similar to the vision of the encyclical.

THE ENCYCLICAL TODAY

The social vision of Pope Pius XI offers a jewel of an insight. That jewel, however, is set in a brooch that is not appealing to our modern eye. We need to reset his vision in a contemporary setting to appreciate its value. The language of Pius is paternalistic and slightly arrogant, and this may distract us from hearing the truth of his letter. Some may see Pius' teaching as an expression of nostalgia for the social order of medieval times—and there is some truth in that. But there is something in this older, pre-capitalist, pre-modernist view of society that compels a second look. Just as we "look back" to the words of the Bible, so we look back to the words of Nell-Breuning and Pius XI to let their social vision reshape our own.

Andrew Greeley contrasts the social vision of *Quadragesimo Anno* with the modern theory of society this way.

> Instead of looking forward to the efficient, rational, mechanistic, atomized society, it looks backward to an organic, "corporative" society in which the intermediate networks between the individuals and the mass society (or the state) were respected, honored and invested not only with the informal power they always had, but also with formal political and social authority.[67]

Greeley also summarizes the insights of this older, pre-capitalist social vision.

> More concretely, the Catholic social insight is that individuals are integrated into a larger society not as isolated units over against a massive and perhaps highly structured whole, but rather as social actors in a dense, overlapping, interlocking, organic network of relationships in which the individual is integrated more or less painlessly into the social whole, which is not, indeed, a massive collectivity but something that is rather little more than a congeries of more intimate, diffuse, overlapping relationships. In this picture society is not a collection of atomized individuals but, to quote William James, "a buzzing, teeming pluralism" of messy, confused, uncertain and unpredictable network of relationships.[68]

A new appreciation of the "solidaristic system" of Catholic social teaching is evident not only from Greeley, a Roman Catholic social commentator, but also from Protestant theologians and economists, namely the process theologian John Cobb and his co-author, economist Herman E. Daly. In their book, *For the Common Good,* they claim that

> this interest in a third model based on concern for human community is not new. It was vigorously pursued by the Roman Catholic Church in the nineteenth century. The Catholic critique of both cap-

italism and socialism is quite similar to our own..... The emphasis
on community was important when Pesch was writing sixty years
ago. Today it has become urgent.[69]

Although we may sense a certain "musty odor" to the "corporative" view
of Pius XI and his predecessors, there is something in their social vision that
was unmistakably cogent for their time and even more so for our "post-
industrial era." That insight is the necessity for individuals in the modern
society to belong to affective and effective intermediary associations and
that the very structure of our economic and political lives should respect the
reality and the importance of "intermediary groupings" or networks.

This tenet of social organization is linked with the governing principle
of subsidiarity, which strives to keep ownership as close to the people
and their networks as possible. In the days of transnational corporations
and mergers, these words sound quaint and perhaps naive. Yet they
touch on a foundational truth of human sociality, which if ignored, may
lead to profits and wealth for some, but does not lead to integral human
happiness and well-being.

THE TEACHING'S IMPACT

Pope Pius XI expected that Catholics would implement his teaching. He
especially favored "Catholic Action" as an educational program that would
train Catholic leaders—all under the watchful eye of the hierarchy. As the
first part of this chapter reveals, "Catholic Action" in a broad sense was alive
and well in the United States, but not exactly in the form that Pius expected. "Catholic Action" in the United States meant a lot of different expressions of Catholics putting their faith into action: worker priests, liturgy and
social justice, *The Catholic Worker*, the Grail, CFM, and more. Many of these
were not directed by the hierarchy but by laywomen and men.

In a narrow sense, the encyclical did not have much of an impact.
Although it was printed in full in the *New York Times* it "failed to generate
wide reaction among U.S. Catholics."[70] Most papal encyclicals don't cause
much reaction among the faithful. But in the broader sense, the encyclical helped to energize those involved in social ministry and in some areas
of the country helped to shape the education of priests. For example, in
the Archdiocese of Chicago Reynold Hillenbrand, the rector of St. Mary of
the Lake seminary at Mundelein, educated "a generation of Chicago
priests to a sense of liturgy, community, and social involvement."[71]

In the United States some Catholics used the encyclical to support the

New Deal of President Franklin Roosevelt. One of the president's advisors, Henry A. Wallace, compared Roosevelt's programs with the suggestions found in the papal encyclicals. President Roosevelt himself declared in Detroit on October 2, 1932 that *Quadragesimo Anno*, which he had just quoted, was "as radical as I am…" and was "one of the greatest documents of modern times."[72]

In Europe and Latin America, Catholic political parties used the encyclical to advocate for more restrictions on capitalism and protection of workers. In the United States the letter was seen as a vindication of the work of Msgr. John Ryan who had been discussing many of the issues found in the encyclical, including distributive justice and a living wage. For the minority of priests and laity involved in social justice and labor issues, "*Quadragesimo Anno* justified their work and kept alive their hope in a church that cared for justice and for the poor."[73]

Conclusion

This chapter surfaced a number of dynamic grass-roots movements during the 1930s as well as the ongoing refinement of papal teaching on economic issues. A number of features of this era should be highlighted as we conclude this chapter. These are areas that are still part of the ferment within the church as it seeks to fulfill its mission in the world.

The Initiative of Women
In chapter 2 we discussed the role of women in establishing Settlement Houses to serve the direct needs of the immigrant communities. By the 1930s we see women in social justice ministry moving into new arenas. They did not wait for the hierarchy to take the lead; rather they responded to their own Christian calling and to the needs of the poor.

Spirituality and Social Transformation
Dorothy Day, Catherine de Hueck, and the Grail all were rooted in a spirituality that served as a resource for the vision of social transformation. This spirituality carried with it a powerful vision of a society transformed by social justice. Here activism and a deep prayer life were intertwined: contemplation and transforming action.

Liturgy and Social Justice

The social vision and spirituality of these movements were rooted in the liturgical life of the church as well. It was in worship that the community expressed communal character amid an individualistic culture. It was in worship that the people enacted and celebrated their oneness in the "body of Christ." The eucharistic liturgy is a breaking open of the Word and the "bread of life" for the life of the world. Pope Pius XI also stressed the importance of the liturgy as a force for social vision and transformation. He established the feast of Christ the King to focus and celebrate the implications of the Catholic faith for the social and political order. While today we might choose other images of Christ, the intention is the same: to connect our liturgical and prayer life with the social concerns of the day.

Tension with the Institutional Church

At the same time there were tensions with the hierarchical church—not as explosive as the Father McGlynn story described in chapter two, but still present. Dorothy Day articulated this tension most succinctly in saying that she lived in a state of "permanent dissatisfaction with the church." It is the tension of the prophetic presence judging the institutional church, which so often takes on the ways of the world, rather than the way of Jesus. By their lives and their ministry these men and women were a voice of challenge to the institutional church—a church they loved but also sought to transform. Pius XI tried to extend the authority and leadership of the hierarchy through his understanding of "Catholic Action." His teaching on this can only be understood in light of the struggle he was having with Mussolini.

Confronting Cynicism and Disillusionment

Amid the cultural and political disillusionment and cynicism of the 1920s and 1930s we hear the voices and see the actions of the men and women—journalists and popes, seminary professors and school teachers who found creative energy and meaning in the Catholic tradition and forged a new spirituality that confronted the Zeitgeist of their time. Their lives brought hope and meaning to a world being pulled by materialism, poverty, and emerging fascism. And it made a difference. It made a difference to those who came to be fed at the soup kitchens, to those who came to be nourished by the prayer and study of their faith, and it made a difference to those in the pews.

The Boston social activist and editor Francis P. Lally claimed the 1930s were the first decade when "we can really speak in realistic terms of a widespread Catholic social consciousness and with it a willingness not simply to adapt to the community life but also to work to transform it."[74] That is the powerful legacy that Dorothy Day, Catherine de Hueck, Virgil Michel, John Ryan, Pius XI, and many others have left us. They lived lives of hope amid cultural and ecclesial cynicism. They found hope and energy in the Gospel, in the Catholic social, liturgical, and spiritual tradition, and in the Spirit's prompting in their lives.

Discussion Questions

1. Father Virgil Michel broke new ground in the 1930s when he linked liturgical renewal with a concern about social issues and the common good of society. In what ways is his message appropriate for today?

2. The Catholic Worker movement is still alive in many American cities. How do you evaluate its prophetic contribution to the larger society and to the Catholic community?

3. Why was Father Cardijn's method of social analysis so attractive to activist Catholics?

4. Do you agree with Father Nell-Breuning's assessment that the method of one consultant writing an encyclical "seems frighteningly irresponsible"? What are more responsible ways for the church to develop its official teaching on complex social questions?

5. Why did Roman Catholic ethicists replace the Thomistic term "legal" justice with the term "social" justice?

6. Explain the notion of "subsidiarity." What role should it play in society and in the church?

7. What values should be salvaged from the "solidarism" of Father Pesch and the idea of "employer-worker councils" of Pope Pius XI?

4

Focus on Freedom: Pope John XXIII and John Courtney Murray

AWAKENING FROM "THEOLOGICAL HIBERNATION"

By the late 1950s the Roman Catholic church in the United States had established itself as an institution whose theology and tone were generally introspective, defensive, and self-righteous toward "the world," including Protestants, non-Christians, Communists, and all others who were "in error." The prosperity of the times had dulled a sense of urgency about social issues and undercut earlier efforts of social activism and reform. "But overall the continuing preoccupation with internal discipline of a clerically dominated church, and the persistent fascination with the corporatist views of the encyclical [*Quadragesimo Anno*] reflected the poverty of Catholic social thought and the lack of imagination among leaders of the Catholic social movement. In fact, even the most

90

basic principles of Catholic social teaching remained almost unknown to most Catholics."[1]

There was some energy and vitality accompanying the Bishop Fulton Sheen spirituality, which blended conservative piety, anti-communism, and concern for the poor. Lay-led organizations such as Cana Conference for married couples, Christian Family Movement (CFM), and the Catholic Youth Organization (CYO) flourished in some dioceses.[2] As a whole, however, the American Catholic community had "slipped more or less peaceably into a half-century's theological hibernation."[3]

The period of hibernation was just about over. A Spring-like thawing of attitudes was coming. The Catholic church's stance toward "the world," and toward Protestants and others "in error," was to make a historic and dramatic shift. At the center of the vortex of change was the unassuming, rotund cardinal of Venice, Angelo Guiseppe Roncalli, the soon-to-be Pope John XXIII, and an American Jesuit, John Courtney Murray.

While both men were rooted in tradition they were not afraid to move beyond the traditional answers. They responded to the needs of the times with creativity and optimism. They opened up the Catholic church—its theology and pastoral attitudes—to a refreshing dialogue, "freeing Catholicism from the harmful baggage of past centuries."[4] It is also true that as they opened a new chapter in the church's social ethics, their work also signaled the end of an era—the era of thinking that had lasted too many centuries, which held that "error has no rights." Such thinking had led to the atrocities of the Inquisition, unproductive condemnations of Protestant thought, suspicion of secular movements for liberty and human rights, and other unevangelical policies and behavior within the church.

Part I. Pope John XXIII

John XXIII served the church as bishop of Rome for only five years, 1958 to 1963. In that short time he left his mark of openness and freedom not only on Catholic social teachings but also on the self-understanding of the Catholic church and its relationship with other churches and the contemporary society. John's *aggiornamento* (updating) of the church brought the official church into a new relationship with contemporary society. Pope John did not give in to the fear, suspicion, and defensiveness of those around him. His opening address at the Second Vatican

Council, entitled "Mother Church Rejoices" (*Gaudet mater ecclesia*), on October 11, 1962, signaled his hopeful and positive attitude:

> In the daily exercise of our pastoral office, we sometimes have to listen, much to our regret, to the voices of persons who, though burning with zeal, are not endowed with too much sense of discretion or measure. In these modern times they can see nothing but prevarication and ruin.... We feel we must disagree with those prophets of gloom, who are always forecasting disaster, as though the end of the world were at hand. In the present order of things, Divine Providence is leading us to a new order of human relations which, by men's own efforts and even beyond their expectations, are directed toward the fulfillment of God's superior and inscrutable designs. And everything, even human differences, leads to the greater good of the Church.[5]

In these few words Pope John summarized his vision and the heart of his social teachings. His vision, as Donal Dorr describes it,

> represents a new theology of the world. It would perhaps be more accurate to speak of a new *spirituality of commitment to the world*, a spirituality that contains the seed of a new theology.... The new spirituality can be detected mostly as a difference of tone;... What comes through is the fact that he is not afraid that commitment to the world and its values will cause people to neglect the highest spiritual values.[6]

Pope John's optimism and openness to "the world" were much needed by the tradition-laden, institutional church. As we shall see in this chapter, Pope John's work tried to maintain a balance of optimism without becoming naive or blind to the damaging power of sin in the world. The dialogue with the world would also have to avoid accommodating the church's central values and beliefs. The *aggiornamento* is more than dressing up traditional teaching in contemporary garb. *Aggiornamento* requires a genuine dialogue in which the church does not presume it has the higher moral ground. Rather the church's role is "essentially a receptive one in recognizing and promoting the modern world's positive value and interpretation of structures as its own in the perspective of the gospel."[7] Topics for this dialogue would be freedom of religion and freedom of thought, the relationship with democracy and constitutional governments, and human rights. In these dialogues Pope John XXIII (and John Courtney Murray) would prove to be highly successful participants.

Two social encyclicals punctuate his five-year papacy. The first, *Mater et Magistra*, in 1961, commemorated the 70th anniversary of *Rerum Novarum*; the second *Pacem in Terris*, in 1963, addressed the question of peace in the aftermath of the Cuban missile crisis.

MATER ET MAGISTRA

To prepare the commemorative text for the 70th anniversary of *Rerum Novarum*, Pope John invited a fellow short and unassuming Italian, Msgr. Pietro Pavan, to be his primary consultant. Professor Pavan had earned two doctorates, one in theology and a second in social sciences, and since 1948 had served as professor of social economy at the Lateran University in Rome.[8] Pavan has never formally acknowledged his role in the encyclical, as the straightforward German Oswald von Nell-Breuning had for *Quadragesimo Anno*. Yet when I visited Msgr. Pavan in retirement outside Rome in 1979 with Msgr. George Higgins, he came very close to admitting to us that he was the author of the encyclical. His sly smile confirmed the common assumption.

While a key role was played by Pavan, the influence of German and French thinking is also evident. Part of the encyclical, the section on "socialization," was originally written in German. Here as in other places the echoes of Pesch, Nell-Breuning, and Gundlach are still heard. The French influence is from the Dominican school of *Economie et Humanisme*, especially the writings of François Perroux and Andre Piettre. The pope was also influenced by the conclusions of the 47th Congress of the Semaines Sociales de France, which met in Grenoble in July, 1960, to discuss the theme, "Socialisation et Personne humaine" (Socialization and the Human Person).[9]

The Tone and Content

When interpreting documents it is important to attend not only to what is said, but also to how it is said. Donald Campion, who studied 200 commentaries on the letter, noted the "constant refrain in comments issuing from different nations referred to the encyclical's manifestly modern tone."[10] The openness and optimism of Pope John is obvious in this letter: "the style of the present pope is characterized by its direct, familiar tone; by its concrete, realistic, positive approach to problems; by a preoccupation less with discussing doctrinal and theoretical matters than with outlining practical directives."[11] The French-Canadian Cardinal Leger captured something of Pope John's spirit: "It is a youthful spirit of confidence in the future, without yearning for the past; one that strives instead to make the best use of the opportunities of the present moment." Others too noted the lack of nostalgia and the realistic tone of the letter. "What strikes one even on a first reading," noted the Belgian Jesuit Jules De Meij, "is the open, appreciative reception John XXIII accords to modern society. Nowhere does one encounter the nostalgia for outdated structures that has characterized the thinking of some Catholics in the past."[12]

Father Nell-Breuning said it succinctly. The encyclical "has finally rid the Church of 'romantic' images of society and of the economy, which formerly held it prisoner."[13]

The encyclical begins with a review and an updating of his predecessors' writings, especially *Rerum Novarum*. It then moves on to identify "new aspects of the social question," including a lengthy discussion of agricultural issues, issues of less developed areas, population and development, and international cooperation. The final section addresses the application of these principles through educational efforts, the lay apostolate, and the renewed dedication of all as the body of Christ.

Three questions will be discussed in more detail: the controversial question of "socialization," agriculture, and concerns of developing nations. The question of the papal "authority" to write on complex social and economic questions will be examined, because it was raised by various critics of the encyclical.

Socialization

One of the most complicated terms used in the encyclical is "socialization." It is also seen as the central theme of the encyclical and its distinctive contribution to the development of Catholic social thought.[14] The term has a variety of meanings in different disciplines. For economists, especially British and American economists, it is synonymous with nationalization, that is, the public control and ownership of production and distribution of goods and services. In psychology and sociology, the term refers to the process by which a child gradually learns to live in society.

In previous papal teachings the term had been identified with socialism. Pope Leo had condemned the "socialization" of private property. Pope John's immediate predecessor, Pius XII, had used the term nine years earlier in a pejorative sense when he warned the Austrian Catholics that "the person and the family must be saved from falling into the abyss into which an all-embracing socialization tends to lead them, a socialization at the end of which the terrifying image of the leviathan would become a horrible reality."[15] Pope Pius XII used the term to connote the nationalization that is part of socialism. Obviously, Pope John is not using the term as his predecessor did.

For Pope John the term "socialization" is descriptive without negative moral overtones. He describes the reality of socialization this way: "one of the principal characteristics of our time is the multiplication of social relationships, that is, a daily more complex interdependence of citizens, introducing into their lives and activities many and varied forms of association, recognized for the most part in private and even in public law"(no. 59-60). In paragraphs 60-67 he offers an evaluation of this process pointing out that, first of all, this reality is "a serious moment and not without danger" because public authorities are involved in the more "intimate aspects of personal life," such as health care, education of the young, choosing one's career, and more. There is a tendency for a restriction of human freedom as the "rules and laws controlling and determining relationships of citizens are multiplied."

The associations in their diversity are to strive to be true communities in which members of the group are encouraged to participate. The freedom of the group and of individuals to act autonomously is to be protected. The state is to foster and regulate the undertakings of individuals and groups, guided by a correct understanding of the common good. If these principles are kept in mind, the complexity of social life "will lead to an appropriate structuring of the human community."

On this question, as on other controversial issues in modern society, Pope John does not fall into the pattern of condemning societal trends but rather invites Catholics "to abandon an attitude of passive defense in the face of growing socialization for a buoyant acceptance of the latter as a social and historical fact, and a willingness to work along with it."[16] As the French Dominican Jean Thomas remarks, "Instead of preaching an 'ostrich' policy, it [the church] finds that 'socialization' can and ought to be achieved in such a way as to enhance its advantages...."[17]

Agriculture
Pope John addresses the problems of agriculture in part III of the encyclical, which is entitled "New Aspects of the Social Question." By this we see

that he is broadening the focus of Catholic social thought from the problems of workers in the industrial setting to include the problems of farmers. Although long overdue, the analysis and recommendation of the section are seen by the British philosopher Douglas Hyde as "down-to-earth" and as "a charter for rural life."[18] The encyclical urges state assistance in addressing the concerns of farmers. The role of the government, while essential, does not obviate the other basic levels of voluntary organizations and the farmers' own individual initiatives. All three levels must play their part, in keeping with the principle of subsidiarity.

While not ruling out large agro-business farms, the letter has a clear preference for family-type farms that model a community of persons. (This same approach will be recommended by the U.S. bishops twenty-six years later in their pastoral letter on the economy.)

Less Developed Nations

Another sign of the broader vision of Pope John is the attention he gives to the issues of the developing nations. Joseph Joblin, S.J., of the International Labor Organization in Geneva, suggests that "some of the most original thoughts contained in *Mater et Magistra* concern the demands of justice and the common good in the relations between nations at different stages of economic development."[19]

The letter warns against providing aid to developing nations as a form of domination or as a way of imposing one nation's culture on another people. Pope Paul VI would devote more attention to these questions in his encyclical *Populorum Progressio (On the Development of Peoples)*, but Pope John paved the way by his remarks in this letter.

Authority of the Encyclical

Critics challenged not only the specific content of Pope John's encyclical, but also the very authority of the pope to write on economic and social issues. Philip Land, S.J., who spent three months lecturing on the encyclical in U.S. cities from coast to coast, repeatedly heard the question, "What right has the pope to talk about social questions?" and "Why doesn't the pope just stick to what's in the Gospels?"[20] According to Father Land many of these disgruntled Catholics were avid readers of William Buckley's journal *National Review,* which had criticized the encyclical in its July 29, 1961 editorial, calling it "a venture in triviality" and "like Pius XI's *Syllabus of Errors* it may become the source of embarrassed explanations."[21] A few weeks later Buckley quipped, "Mater Si, Magister No"—"Mother Yes, Teacher No."[22]

What Father Land found ironic was that this rejection of the papal authority to teach on social matters came from the conservative side of the American church, while in Europe rejection of the pope's teaching authority came from left-wing Catholics. The European left-wingers said, "Let the church confine her exhortations to the Gospels and to the law of love. These are things of the spirit, and it is only things of the spirit that are or should be properly the concern of the church. The task of civilization is purely temporal, wholly secular, and the church has nothing at all to say about it."[23] Europe had a long history of the church dominating its cultural development. These critics were fearful of efforts to restore "Christendom."

We can not enter into a complete discussion of this topic of the church's right to speak on economic and political issues. I will only offer a few brief reflections.

First, the separation of the spiritual from the temporal, of faith from everyday life, is described by the Second Vatican Council as one of the "more serious errors of our age."[24] A Christian cannot separate faith from social and economic realities. Life "under God" is "of a piece," it cannot be fragmented into unconnected areas.

Second, since New Testament times theologians and church leaders have been wrestling with the implications of the Christian faith for all areas of our lives. Some of the strongest statements on these issues are found in the writings of the early church.[25] Informed conservatives would be familiar with this long-standing tradition, which the popes see themselves as interpreting for the contemporary society.

The question raised by Buckley and others, then, should be stated not as, "What right has the pope to talk about social matters?" but, "How should we express our disagreement with papal teachings?" or "What are the conditions for public and private dissent from official church teaching?" The question of dissent affects all in the church, conservatives and liberals, lay and ordained, whenever we find it difficult to assent to an official teaching.

Without going into a full-fledged discussion of this complex issue, I would simply make three points.

First, disagreement, opposition, and dissent from church teaching are to be expected, as the U.S. bishops recognized in their 1919 *Program of Reconstruction* and the 1986 pastoral letter, *Economic Justice for All*. "We expect and welcome debate on our specific policy recommendations.... We believe that differences on complex economic questions should be expressed in a spirit of mutual respect and open dialogue."[26]

Second, such dissent is healthy for the church if carried out in a respectful manner by both sides. Vatican II teaches that "an individual layman, by reason of the knowledge, competence, or outstanding ability which he may enjoy, is permitted and sometimes even obliged to express his opinion on things which concern the good of the church."[27]

Third, the church needs to look at its inconsistency in moral teachings. On the social and economic issues the official teaching does not present its teaching as moral absolutes as it does in the area of sexual ethics. (This question will be examined in more detail in the chapter on the consistent ethic of life.)

Work and Spirituality

Msgr. Pietro Pavan, Pope John's chief consultant for this encyclical, identified its underlying motivation. The encyclical was to shore up our personal human dignity by linking our work with our spirituality.

> The fundamental motive of the encyclical, ever present in the solution of these problems, can be found in the fact that we live in an age when a host of factors contribute to undermine, in man's minds, the consciousness of his own dignity as a person. For this reason, it is of primary importance that the economic world be constructed and function in such a way that men do not run the risk of sacrificing what they are to what they do; they must be inspired to live their work as a means of achieving spiritual enrichment and perfection.

Pavan then refers us to paragraph 256 of the encyclical:

> That a man should develop and perfect himself through his daily work...is perfectly in keeping with the plan of divine Providence....
> In concluding their human affairs to the best of their ability, they [the laity] must recognize that they are doing a service to humanity, in intimate union with God through Christ, and to God's greater glory. And St. Paul insisted: "Whether you eat or drink, or whatever else you do, do all for the glory of God" (I Cor. 10:13).[28]

In these few lines Pope John dissolves the walls between the secular and the spiritual. Here is an integrating perspective that views our labor as enhancing personal dignity, serving the needs of the community, and essential to our spiritual journey toward God. Pope John XXIII's encyclical signals a dramatic shift of spirituality and moral teaching for official Catholic church social teachings.

The church's motivation is no longer a fear of "losing" the workers to anticlerical social movements. Faith and work are no longer seen as in competition for the soul of the worker. According to Pope John, Catholics are now to see their workplace as their way of serving God and community as they spiritually enrich themselves. While it may strike us as a bit idealistic, it nonetheless symbolizes the historic opening of papal thought, and the structures of the entire Catholic church, to a new relationship with secular realities. This was the legacy of Pope John and the Second Vatican Council.

Two years after *Mater et Magistra*, between the first and second session of the Second Vatican Council, Pope John issued his second encyclical on economic, political, and moral issues, *Pacem in Terris*. In this letter he continued the social vision of *Mater et Magistra*.

PACEM IN TERRIS

The world seemed ready for a message on peace. The Korean War was a recent and painful memory, the Berlin Wall—the symbol of the Cold War—was in place, the Cuban missile crisis had brought the two superpowers to the brink of war, and the United States was involved in the war in Vietnam.

While the content of the encyclical is consistent with the previous social encyclicals, the style and manner of presentation are new.[29] There is no lengthy summary of previous encyclicals. The style is taut, succinct, concise; its statements and arguments are presented clearly and effectively with little elaboration. It has no lengthy and flowing sentences. In short, it has a more contemporary style, even if the content and methodology are traditional.

This is the first encyclical to be addressed to all people of goodwill and not solely to the Catholic community. Here we see Pope John's ecumenical thrust.

A number of consultants were used in the writing of this encyclical. The one most often named is Pietro Pavan.[30]

The Reaction to Pacem in Terris

The letter was generally well received. *L'Espresso*, Rome's anticlerical magazine, noted the new stage in church teaching.

> By the encyclical of Holy Thursday, 1963, the Church has entered on a new stage of life. No matter what may happen, no one can ever take the credit away from papa Roncalli for having signed this gen-

uine edict of freedom and for having again turned his faithful subjects into citizens of the world.[31]

John Courtney Murray recalled the letter's general appeal: "It was publicly praised by the President of the United States and the Secretary
General of the United Nations; it was quoted with approval in the
Communist Press. Such a universal consensus might appear nigh mirac-
ulous."[32] Perhaps its natural law basis had hit on some common aspirations and needs.

A number of Protestant and Jewish leaders praised the encyclical. Rev.
J. Irwin Miller, president of the National Council of Churches, said
Protestants "welcome the historic encyclical" and are "gratified at the
growing areas of agreement among leaders.... We find remarkable similarities in this statement between Roman Catholic thought and that in
our own constituency." Rabbi Julius Mark, president of the Synagogue
Council of America, said the encyclical's reference to religious liberty was
"exceedingly refreshing."[33]

Professor John C. Bennett, a noted Protestant theologian, commented
on the new attitude toward communism, which "may prove momen-
tous." He went on to note:

> *Pacem in Terris* may be the most powerful healing word that has
> come from any source during the Cold War. We cannot predict its
> effect with Communist nations, but it is significant that in at least
> some of them it is being taken seriously. It calls Christians in the
> West away from the kind of anti-communism by which they have
> often been obsessed.[34]

Pacem in Terris, like all texts, is susceptible to selective citation. John
Cogley penned the following lines on this problem, entitled, "Poems on
Postcards: How to Read an Encyclical":

> David Lawrence read it Right
> Lippman saw a liberal light
> William Buckley sounded coolish
> Pearson's line was mostly foolish
> Courtney Murray wasn't certain
> (We haven't heard from Thomas Merton)
> *Nation*-readers learned to hope
> That J.F.K. would heed his Pope
> Welch saw Red, red redder than titian

As Rome fell under Birch suspicion
Time caressed each Lucid text
While *Playboy* found it undersexed
Pravda praised the portions peacenik
(No comment on the UN policenik)
The Dept. of State was terribly kind
The Pope, it said, had us in mind
By now we know the simple trick
Of how to read Pope John's encyc
To play the game, you choose your snippet
Of *Peace on Earth* and boldly clip it.[35]

Main Themes

Our survey will touch on five important themes in Pope John's second encyclical: justice as the basis for peace, freedom, a new attitude toward communism, disarmament, and human rights.

Justice as the basis for peace

Pope John used the moral framework of the natural law as the foundation for peace. Peace is possible only "if the order set down by God be dutifully observed" (par. 1). From this framework he set out the rights and duties of persons, public authorities, states, and world community. He included economic, political, and religious rights, immigration rights, and the mutual responsibilities of citizens.

The natural law approach, while it can be rightly criticized, provided a context for talking about the only lasting basis for peace, namely justice. John Courtney Murray noted, "The quality and virtue emphasized is justice. If justice means giving to a man what is his due, then the mind of Pope John is that the ideas and principles he is outlining are what is due to man because of his natural dignity as a person, and therefore what is owed to him in justice."[36] Justice is the foundation that is necessary if the world is to experience genuine peace. In this regard *Pacem in Terris* can be seen as "a 'resume' of traditional Catholic teaching on human relations." Murray calls it "The Statesman's Handbook," a "succinct and admirable vade-mecum for sane thought and action."[37]

Freedom

Since the French Revolution the official teachings of the Catholic church have been suspicious of the modern concepts of freedom and liberty. It was only now in the era of the Second Vatican Council that freedom, especially religious freedom, was accepted within the official teaching. The breakthrough in this area is credited to the work and influence of a few Americans at the Council. (We will pick up this discussion when we present the work of John Courtney Murray.) Up until this time the papal pronouncements on political and social order were rooted in the concepts of truth, justice, and charity. According to Murray, "a fourth word is added...freedom." Murray continues: "Freedom is a basic principle of political order; its also the political method. The whole burden of the encyclical is that the order for which the postmodern world is looking cannot be an other that is imposed by force, or sustained by coercion, or based on fear...."[38] The freedom that John speaks of is a "freedom under law" which is a creative force in human affairs. The order that is the basis of peace, "if it is to be qualified as reasonable and humane must be 'founded on truth, built according to justice, vivified and integrated by charity, and put into practice in freedom.'"[39]

New attitude toward communism

Pope John offered a more nuanced stance toward communism. In paragraphs 159-160 he distinguished between false philosophical teachings and historical movements that are constantly changing. While not accepting the false philosophical teachings, he asked, "Who can deny that those movements, in so far as they conform to the dictates of right reason and are interpreters of the lawful aspirations of the human person, contain elements that are positive and deserving of approval?" This reference to communism effectively replaced Pius IX's condemnation of collaboration with communists. Pope John cautioned that such collaboration must be approached "with the virtue of prudence."

Disarmament

Pope John called for the end of the arms race and the banning of nuclear weapons:

> Justice, right reason and humanity, therefore, urgently demand that the arms race should cease; that the stockpiles which exist in various countries should be reduced equally and simultaneously by the parties concerned; that nuclear weapons should be banned; and that a general agreement should eventually be reached about progressive disarmament and an effective method of control.[40]

He maintained that true peace depends on "mutual trust" not on the "equality of arms."

Human rights
According to Pope John, if societies want peace they must respect "the order laid down by God" (par. 1). The first principle of this well-ordered and productive society must be

> that every human being is a person, that is, his nature is endowed with intelligence and free will. By virtue of this, he has rights and duties of his own, flowing directly and simultaneously from his very nature. And as these rights and obligations are universal and inviolable so they cannot in any way be surrendered. (par. 9)

When the pope goes on to specify these rights he begins with the social and economic rights:

> Beginning our discussion of the rights of man, we see that every man has the right to life, to bodily integrity, and to the means which are necessary and suitable for the proper development of life. These means are primarily food, clothing, shelter, rest, medical care, and finally the necessary social services. Therefore, a human being also has the right to security in cases of sickness, inability to work, widowhood, old age, unemployment, or in any other case in which he is deprived of the means of subsistence through no fault of his own. (par. 11)

In subsequent paragraphs (12 through 27) Pope John discusses a complex network of rights, such as:

- rights concerning moral and cultural values (right to education, art),

- respect for one's person and one's good reputation,

- religious rights,

- family life rights (to choose to set up a family, right of parents to educate their children, equal rights for men and women),

- economic rights (right to work, right to human working conditions, to appropriate participation in management),

- political rights (rights of assembly and association, right to participate in public affairs), and,

- rights of freedom of movement and migration.

The strength of this listing is that Pope John offers "a systematic reca-
pitulation of the rights claims made by the tradition since Leo XIII."[41]
This is why Murray refers to *Pacem in Terris* as a resume of the major
social encyclicals.

Criticisms of Pacem in Terris

Even his admirer John Courtney Murray realized that Pope John's optimism may not have taken sufficient account of the reality of the tension
between the two dominant ideologies. He cordially challenged the pope's
lack of realism: "...there may be some warrant for the thought that the spirit of confident hope which the Pontiff courageously embraces fails to take
realistic account of the fundamental schism in the world today."[42]

Murray was echoing the concern of many other Americans who found
the pope's new understanding of communist movements, his trust in a
more powerful U.N., and his belief in mutual trust rather than arms as
the basis of peace to be in "rather sharp contrast" with their own assumptions. William O'Brien of Georgetown University summarized how
Pacem in Terris challenged American Catholics' basic assumptions.

> ...few American Catholics would have guessed that the very ground
> on which most of them stood in the debate on the nuclear dilem-
> mas would be shaken, not by the latest findings of a nuclear scien-
> tist, defense analyst or Kremlinologist, but by the Sovereign Pontiff
> of the Catholic Church himself![43]

Protestant theologians, as should be expected, were not so impressed
with Pope John's trust of human reason and spirit of optimism. Reinhold
Niebuhr found its reasoning "breathing a Pelagian, rather than an
Augustinian, spirit."[44] The encyclical was also criticized because it lacked
a sustained moral analysis of the reality of power in the world. This is an
ongoing weakness of Catholic social teaching.[45]

The Debate About Human Rights

Pacem in Terris addresses the need to protect both civil and political rights
and economic and social rights. The drawback to these overlapping lists
of rights is that there is no priority given to all these rights. The letter
"gives no direction as to which rights are the most important should a
conflict arise between rights." Social ethicist Darryl Trimiew goes on to
argue that "where the category of economic rights is too broad, it is
counter-productive to the very concept of economic rights."[46]

In the discussion of human rights in the international community the complex listing of rights is grouped into two sets according to the two Covenants of Human Rights of the United Nations: a) the Covenant of Civil and Political Rights and b) the Covenant on Economic, Social, and Cultural Rights. The first set of rights, the civil and political rights, are generally given priority in the U.S. setting and have been enshrined in the Bill of Rights; the second set of the rights, the economic and social rights, are emphasized in socialist countries.

There is significant debate over the status of the two sets of rights both within the church and in the political community. Philosophers like Michael Novak argue that the economic rights are not properly rights but "'goods' indispensable to a full human life."[47] This follows from his conviction that "positive rights," that is, rights that require the provision of goods and or services to carry them out, do not qualify as real rights. Only "negative rights," such as civil and political rights, that is, those that the state is asked to protect through its laws and institutions, are true rights in Novak's understanding. Novak prefers to speak of civil rights in the economic realm rather than straightforward economic rights. The closest he comes to accepting economic rights is in his later works where he concedes a conditional right to an economic entitlement. As Trimiew explains, "this concession is, however, only for those individuals who have basic needs to be met that they have not been able to meet despite their best efforts." These are the "deserving poor" rather than the "lazy poor." Therefore, Novak interprets *Pacem in Terris* as a document that, while it (1) affirms civil rights in the economic realm, (2) misleadingly describes in rights language certain social goals concerning material welfare.[48]

David Hollenbach and others have no trouble accepting the concept of economic rights. Therefore Hollenbach, in contrast to Novak, interprets *Pacem in Terris* as a document that "goes beyond prior Catholic social teaching to unambiguously affirm the recognition of specifically economic rights to be religiously and politically mandatory."[49] (The debate around economic rights would emerge during the drafting of the U.S. bishops' pastoral letter on the U.S. economy, *Economic Justice for All*, starting in 1984. We will pick up this discussion in that chapter.)

Michael Novak maintains that "one can meet all the 'basic needs' of all Americans without confusing 'welfare rights' in the Catholic sense (*Pacem in Terris*, par. 11) with the political, civil, and economic rights (*Pacem in Terris*, par. 18-22) already recognized in the U.S. Constitution and in the U.S. legal tradition." Novak does not unconditionally accept what he calls the "welfare rights" of *Pacem in Terris*, par. 11. "The 'economic rights' properly so called (*Pacem in Terris*, par. 18-22) need to be carefully distinguished from 'welfare rights' (*Pacem in Terris*, par. 11). The conditional nature of the latter needs to be emphasized in order to defend human responsibility, which is the fundamental ground of human dignity."[50]

These differences are not just the "stuff" of academic journals; they have an impact in the political arena. Michael Novak, a resident scholar at the American Enterprise Institute, served as the chair of the U.S. delegation to the United Nations Human Rights Conference in Geneva during the Reagan Administration. He also worked with Alexander Haig and Jeanne Kirkpatrick in an effort to reverse many of President Carter's policies on human rights and all of Carter's policies on economic rights.[51]

Thirty years earlier when the international community was seriously debating economic rights, a number of Catholic theologians were influential in shaping the discussion about the U.N.'s "Universal Declaration of Human Rights" in 1948. Jacques Maritain was one of the chief authors of the Declaration, and Angelo Guiseppe Roncalli was involved in the discussions. Ten years later Roncalli took the name of John XXIII.[52]

The human rights debate has an impact on many areas of our communal life. The right to work and the right to health care and the government's role in achieving these rights are often debated in our society. The American bishops continued the tradition of *Pacem in Terris* in stating in 1991 that "adequate health care is a basic human right. Access to appropriate health care must be guaranteed for all people without regard to economic, social or legal status."[53]

Part II. John Courtney Murray

In the debates about economic rights and about the Catholic tradition on war and peace both sides have substantiated their positions by turning to the ground-breaking work of John Courtney Murray. This man's thought continues to influence and shape Roman Catholic social ethics in the United States and beyond.[54] We could not write a survey of Catholic social thought without acknowledging Murray, whose "creative genius has made him the most outstanding Catholic theologian in the United States in this century."[55]

As is true with so many creative thinkers, John Murray found himself embroiled in the middle of controversy and was silenced for a time by the church, but eventually he was recognized as a first-rate theologian by theologians and hierarchy alike. His contribution (unlike that of John Ryan, the other major Catholic social ethicist of the century) was not in the area of economic justice, but in political ethics. Murray was basically positive about the U.S. economy. He is remembered also for his significant contribution to the formulation of the Catholic church's new stance on religious liberty during the Second Vatican Council.

In this brief discussion of Murray I will (1) outline his conflict with Cardinal Alfredo Ottaviani of the Holy Office, (2) summarize his main themes, 3) note his influence on John XXIII and Vatican II, and, finally, 4) identify some areas in need of further development.

1) FROM SILENCE TO CENTER STAGE

Murray was ordained in the Society of Jesus in 1933, earned a doctorate in theology at the Gregorian University in Rome, and began a thirty-year teaching career at Woodstock College in Maryland that lasted until his death in 1967. It was his writings on the relationship of church and state in the 1950s that brought him into conflict with other theologians and Cardinal Alfredo Ottaviani of the Holy Office (now called the Congregation for the Doctrine of the Faith). The persistent question facing the hierarchy and theologians in the U.S. (and other countries) was how the church should relate to the state. This question had plagued the American Catholic church since the days of Bishop John Carroll. The debate resurfaced in the 1940s and 1950s under the heading of "religious liberty." Some bishops urged a conciliatory attitude toward the American system, which guaranteed religious liberty to all religions and did not give a preferred status to Roman Catholicism. For example, Archbishop John McNichols of Cincinnati who was the chairman of the National Catholic Welfare Conference Administrative Board, issued a statement in early 1948 that fully endorsed the American system guaranteeing religious freedom. He wrote, "If tomorrow Catholics constitute a majority in our country, they would not seek a union of church and state. They would then, as now, uphold the Constitution and all its Amendments...."[56] Murray had worked with the NCWC on this sensitive question.

The other side in the debate was led by Father Francis J. Connell (a Redemptorist priest and the nation's foremost Catholic moral theologian), and Father Joseph Clifford Fenton (the dean of the School of Theology at Catholic University and editor of the *American Ecclesiastical Review*). Connell and Fenton held to the theory of the "Catholic state" in which the activities of non-Catholic religions were restricted, as they were in some "Catholic countries" such as Italy and Spain. (For example, in Italy no Protestant church can have a door opening on a main street, nor can any non-Catholic church, temple, or mosque have a building taller than St. Peter's Basilica.)

In January 1953 Pope Pius XII named Alfredo Ottaviani a cardinal and appointed him the prefect of the Holy Office. In March of that year Cardinal Ottaviani lectured at Rome's Lateran Seminary, where he argued that when Catholics are in the majority, they must create a confessional state in which only the Catholic religion is legally protected. Cardinal Ottaviani was not consistent, for he held that when Catholics are in the minority, the Catholic Church has the right to be tolerated on an equal basis with other religious groups. He claimed this double standard was justified, because, as he put it, there is "one [standard] for truth, the other [standard] for error." In this talk he referred to the controversy between Fenton and Murray in the U.S., and he came down firmly on Fenton's side.[57]

Murray did have some support from Roman officials. In 1950 he went to Rome and received encouragement in his work on the church-state question from Monsignor Giovanni Battista Montini, the substitute secretary of state. Thirteen years later in June of 1963, Msgr. Montini would be elected pope and take the name Paul VI, and he would intervene in the controversy between Ottaviani and Murray—but we are getting ahead of the story.

Six months after Ottaviani's address, on December 6, 1953, Pope Pius XII spoke to the Italian jurists on the question. This talk, entitled *Ci riesce*, seemed to modify Ottaviani's position in that the pope recognized religious pluralism as a fact not only between states but also among them. A few months later Father Murray, in an address at The Catholic University of America, argued that Pius' allocution laid to rest the ideal of the Catholic state in favor of religious pluralism. Murray suggested that Ottaviani's position on church and state was not in accord with the thinking of the pope. As Richard McBrien notes " from that point on the cardinal sought to have Murray silenced."[58]

In July 1955 Murray was silenced by Rome through his Jesuit superiors and forbidden to write on the topic of church and state because his position was in sharp contrast to that of Ottaviani, who championed the traditional nostalgic view of the union of church and state. Murray was crushed, but complied with the directives. He canceled a contract for a book on church and state and symbolically removed books on the subject from his room and concentrated on other issues including the school question and the ethics of national security policy. His biographer, Donald E. Pelotte, S.S.S., notes that, "defeated on the Church-State issue, Murray did not completely give up writing or lecturing."[59] "Defeated" is an overstatement. Murray lost the first battle, but as we shall see, he eventually won the war.

Three years later, in 1958, he tried again by submitting an article to his Roman superiors, hoping it could be published in Rome. The answer was "no." But a few months later there was a new pope, John XXIII, and the beginning of a new era in the church. This time his book on these controversial issues, *We Hold These Truths*, was approved and published in 1960—just as another Catholic named John was moving toward the White House. It earned Murray considerable attention including his picture on the cover of *Time* magazine.

In 1962 as the Second Vatican Council began, Murray was "uninvited" from attending the first session. But in April of 1963 at Cardinal Spellman's request, Pope John XXIII named Murray a *peritus*, or official theological expert, at Vatican II.[60] Spellman and other bishops wanted Murray's help in presenting an American perspective on religious liberty. Even though they had not defended him earlier, they now hoped that his sophisticated defense of religious liberty would be heard.

When Murray arrived in Rome he learned that the subject of religious freedom had been dropped from the agenda. Murray was instrumental in persuading the American bishops, with Cardinal Spellman leading them, to demand its restoration. Murray wrote a four-page memo for the American bishops, stating the reasons why the topic of religious liberty should be restored. And even though the president of the Council, Cardinal Cicognani, had canceled discussion of the topic from the agenda, the American bishops sent a letter to Cicognani and to the four moderators demanding the issue be discussed. The bishops' request had also been passed on to Pope Paul VI by Cardinal Spellman. Paul VI is said to have ordered Cardinal Ottaviani to call a meeting of the Theological Commission to discuss the topic of religious liberty.[61] Pope Paul respected the request of the American bishops, and he trusted the work of the American theologian whom he had encouraged in 1950.

The drama of the two worldviews clashing can be felt in Murray's recollection of the two-day meeting to discuss religious liberty.

> A personal high moment was the meeting of the full Commission on Faith and Morals on November 11. They (i.e., Ottaviani) had claimed the right to review the Secretariat text. There was a big battle over this, but in the end the Secretariat had to give in. I was invited by Card. Leger. Card. Browne, Archb. Parente, and two others spoke strongly against our text. Bishop Charue of Namur, after speaking strongly for it, suggested that the periti be heard beginning with me. Ottaviani, however, called first on Rahner, then on one or two others. Bishop Wright introduced my name again, amid other murmurs of approval and invitation, and I got to make my speech— face to face with Ottaviani, with Msgr. Fenton at the end of the periti table. The final vote was 18-5—a glorious victory for the Good Guys. The meeting lasted from 4:30 to 7:00. And it was pretty tense from the beginning to end. We had a big party at the Hilton later in the week to celebrate the occasion.[62]

The historical account is clear that "had it not been for the American intervention, the topic would have been discarded."[63] John Courtney Murray was the primary theological consultant behind the U.S. bishops' intervention.

Murray eventually became the "first scribe" or the primary author of the third draft of what was to become the Declaration on Religious Freedom (*Dignitatis Humanae*). Changes were made to appease the conservative minority but the document was overwhelmingly approved by the council. John Courtney Murray had moved from silence to center stage.

Following the council's conclusion Murray returned to Woodstock, Maryland, where he returned to other topics of personal interest, including freedom *within* the Church, the development of doctrine, and the problem of contemporary atheism. In the Spring of 1966 he was appointed director of the John LaFarge Institute, which had been established in 1964 by the editors of *America*. The Institute gathered leaders from many areas of life for off-the-record discussions of social issues. Through the Institute Murray was able to dedicate the last years of his life to ecumenical and racial problems. His biographer notes that

> he applied his theological principle of freedom to the critical...issues of the late 1960s. In every discussion, he always brought with him the conviction that freedom was "the first truth

about man, a positive value, both personal and social, to be respected even when it involves man in error and evil."[64]

In the last few years of his life he was plagued by heart problems and hospitalized a number of times. In June of 1967 he suffered a new and serious heart attack. After taking some rest he attempted to go back to work. He died in a taxi cab on August 16 while traveling to the John LaFarge Institute.

His contribution was recognized by president and pope alike. President Lyndon Johnson said that his life "transcended the barriers of nation, race, and creed." Speaking for Pope Paul, Archbishop Benelli noted that "his humble yet precious theological contributions will be his monument and a guide to others."

Fellow Jesuit and confidant, Walter Burghardt, who preached at his funeral, said that Murray's name was synonymous with "the man of freedom."

Unborn millions will never know how much their freedom is tied to this man whose pen was a powerful protest, a dramatic march, against injustice and inequality, whose research sparked and terminated in the ringing affirmation of an ecumenical council. "The right to religious freedom has its foundations" not in the church, not in the society or state, not even in objective truth, but "in the dignity of the human person."[65]

2) A SUMMARY OF HIS THOUGHT

Murray began in the 1940s with the question of cooperation among Christians—intercredal cooperation. In this he anticipated the openness of the Second Vatican Council by some twenty years. Murray held that in order to bring about social justice and peace, especially in the war-torn era of the 1940s, organized cooperation among all people, especially Christians, was necessary. He realized that individual efforts alone would not bring about the needed changes in society. This organized cooperation would be headed by laypeople and would not come under the direct control or authority of the hierarchy. Individual Catholics are still responsible to their bishops but the organization of ecumenical cooperation would be interconfessional. This cooperation would be a blending of civic and religious realms: it pursues the civic goal of the common good in the social, economic, and political arena based on the religious motivations of faith in God and love of God's law.

As mentioned above, a number of theologians challenged Murray's thinking, including two faculty members at the Catholic University of America, Francis J. Connell, professor of moral theology, and Paul Hanly Furfey, professor of sociology. Connell was a conservative who feared Murray's thought would lead to indifferentism, Furfey was a radical who feared that cooperation would weaken the distinctively Catholic spirituality of social justice, namely being rooted in the Eucharist.

In the late 1940s and early 1950s Murray elaborated his theory of the relationship of the church and state. In his writing he drew upon the theory of medieval theologians, such as John of Paris, who held a middle position between the curialists, who stressed the primacy of church, and the regalists, who emphasized the primacy of the state.[66]

Murray also applied a historical hermeneutic to the writings of Pope Leo XIII to distinguish what was permanently valid and what was historically and polemically conditioned. From 1952 to 1954 Murray published five articles in *Theological Studies*, the Jesuit theological journal, of which he was the editor, in which he dealt with the teachings of Leo XIII. The sixth article was at the printer and already in galley form when he was silenced.[67] In these articles Murray was able to justify Leo's acceptance of the ethical primacy of the church over the state, the confessional state, due to the historical conditions. But Father Murray went on to call for new understanding of the church-state relationship because of the new historical conditions 60 years after *Rerum Novarum*, which included increased literacy rates and heightened personal and political consciousness, which resulted in limited constitutional governments.[68]

To get to this conclusion of accepting the role of a limited constitutional government that guarantees the freedom of religion, not just for Catholics but for all citizens, Murray built his case on four basic principles:

1) The distinction between the sacred and the secular orders. Human existence includes both realms, and the institutions that represent each order—church and state—must respect each other without attempting to dominate the other. The church has in history dominated the temporal realm, just as the state in continental liberalism wrongly claims the omnicompetence of the state and the autonomy of individual reason. Both of these situations should be avoided.

2) The distinction between society and the state. Murray distinguished four concepts: civil society, political society, the state, and government. For Murray civil society refers to the total complex of organized relationships on the temporal plane, which arise either from nature or from choice. Political society refers to civil society as it is politically organized. The state is not the political society but the particular, subsidiary, functional organization of the political society. The state is a set of institutions of which government is a part whose functions are not coextensive with the functions of society.

With these distinctions in place, Murray held that the functions of society are much broader than the functions of the state. The state, because of its limited function, has no competence in the area of faith and religion. The functions of the state are limited to the fact that it is only one, although the highest, subsidiary function of society. Murray teaches the maxim: "As much state as necessary, as much freedom as possible."[69]

3) The distinction between the common good and the public order. The common good includes all the social, moral, spiritual, and material goods that human beings pursue. Public order, in the society of limited constitutional government, includes the goods of public peace, public morality, and justice. These goods are the responsibility of the state to promote and protect. Promoting and protecting *public order* is the criterion that controls and justifies the intervention of the state in all matters including the area of religion.

4) The principle of freedom under the law. Murray stressed the importance of freedom as the goal of society and the political method par excellence. It is not the absolute freedom of liberalism in nineteenth-century Europe but a freedom within the context of the common good and public order of twentieth-century constitutional government.

From these principles he argued for the limited but interrelated roles of both church and state in an era of constitutional government. He rejected the curialist position of church-state union as well as the Enlightenment position wherein religion and church are reduced to the private realm. In this framework he was able to demonstrate the possibility and necessity of religious liberty as a basic human right. While at first rejected, his approach was very influential in shaping *Dignitatis Humanae*, the Vatican II document on religious freedom.

3) AMERICAN AND CATHOLIC

John Courtney Murray elaborated an American political ethic that was not only compatible with Catholic social tradition and natural law but also audaciously claimed that the Catholic social vision, rooted in the natural law, was necessary to rebuild and articulate the lost consensus of the founding fathers. Murray attempted to show the compatibility of the Roman Catholic social tradition with the American ethos as expressed in the consensus of the founding fathers and enshrined in the sacred texts of the country—the Declaration of Independence, the Constitution, and the Bill of Rights. His creativity and insight enabled him to negotiate some very controversial issues that the American Catholic church had been wrestling with since the time of Bishop John Carroll.

The creativity and the vision of three men named John came together in the early 1960s as a turning point in the American Catholic community: John Courtney Murray's ground-breaking thought on intercredal cooperation and religious liberty was given ecclesial endorsement in principle by documents of Vatican II, a council called by Pope John, and the compatibility of American and Catholic political ethics was given concrete expression when John Kennedy became the first Roman Catholic to be elected to the office of the President of the United States. Murray's role in bringing about this change of vision within the Catholic church cannot be denied. Charles Curran summarizes his achievement.

> He stands at the apex of that long line of predecessors who tried to show that Catholicism and the American political ethos are compatible. Without a doubt, Murray was the most significant single voice in the development of Catholic teaching on religious liberty. Murray's apology for full Catholic acceptance and participation in the American political system received a sympathetic hearing not only from many Catholics but also from many other Americans.[70]

John Courtney Murray taught the Catholic church that there is no necessary contradiction between being American and being a Roman Catholic. This was a mixed blessing for the church. On the one hand, it helped Catholics to appreciate the form of government they lived under and the importance of religious freedom for all religious groups—in other words, that pluralism was not a threat to the Catholic church. On the other hand, by accommodating American political realities to Catholic social theology he softened the edges between the Catholic faith and the American political situation. In a distorted way some have claimed that Murray's work blesses the American form of constitutional government. From such an accommodating position it is harder to be critical of U.S. political realities.

Social commentator George Weigel takes such an interpretation of

Murray's work, and on that basis he criticizes the U.S. bishops' pastoral letter *The Challenge of Peace*. Weigel accused the American bishops of "abandoning the traditional heritage" of social teaching as developed through the time of Murray.[71]

Father David Hollenbach responds to Weigel's charge.

> He [Murray] was too critical a theologian and observer of history, however, to affirm the ideal type of a synthesist view of Christianity and American culture in an unambiguous way. The completion of Murray's "grand project" will therefore demand that the tensions Murray acknowledged between Christ and the historical American achievement be given greater weight than Weigel seems prepared to do. It is a serious distortion to charge all those who adopt a more critical approach than does Weigel with abandoning Murray's legacy.[72]

4) LIMITATIONS

The debate between George Weigel and David Hollenbach on how to interpret Murray's thought reminds us that his work was controversial in his lifetime and continues to be controversial over thirty years later. The task of interpreting Murray for today is complicated by the fact that his own thinking changed throughout his life. As J. Leon Hooper, S.J., a theologian who has extensively studied Murray's work, notes, Murray

> discovered that many of the definitions with which he initially worked were inadequate to the reality in which he lived: definitions of the state, the church, of human cognition.... He had to recast some of those definitions, and adopt terms and definitions that had earlier not even occurred to him or to the school out of which he developed.[73]

Murray had the courage to change as old definitions and methods were seen to be morally inadequate. This means that his early and later writings are not necessarily consistent. Social ethicists who draw on Murray can misinterpret him if they do not follow the development of his thought.

As theologians and moralists continue to work on Murray's thought, a number of limitations have been identified. These are limitations that Murray himself would most likely agree with if he were alive today.

First, his work, in stressing the primacy of conscience, can be read in a highly individualistic way. Murray's writing fails to give enough attention to the communitarian side of human nature. His stress is on "liberty," which has an individualistic ring, and in the process the emphasis on social justice is weaker.

Second, in presenting a theory of church-state relation, Murray does not discuss the role of religion as a *cause* of social conflict, intolerance, and injustice. As theologian Father John Pawlikowski notes,

> No complete assessment of Church-state relations can ignore this dimension. It is inaccurate, and highly dangerous on the basis of historical experience (including that of the present day), to assume in principle that the introduction of "religion" into the social sphere will foster the social good. It may do just the opposite.[74]

Third, Murray's thought does not recognize the importance of the nonrational dimensions of the human person. His approach is overly rationalistic. The affections, emotions, arts, and common culture all shape ethical behavior—along with cognitive analysis.

A fourth limitation that a number of Murray analysts have named is his use of language. Murray used "secular" language rather than drawing upon the richer language of his faith tradition. "His clear preference for the 'ascetic' language of the Enlightenment, for example, leaves him with a rather 'thin' set of social symbols that lack the power to generate commitments."[75] Murray's "secular" language falls short in its ability "to stir human hearts and minds to sacrifice, service, and deep love of the community."[76] Hooper puts it this way:

> By muzzling his faith, Murray helped rob our public conversation of the one, and perhaps the only, language we have for effectively escaping the individualism, superficiality, and materialism that seem to be so much of our national, can-do, pragmatic ethos. The language that he left us, namely that of natural law, has proven much too thin to encourage the rich discussion of the values that might ground our living with one another.[77]

A fifth limitation of John Courtney Murray's work is that he does not come to grips with the prophetic dimension of Christian faith. John Pawlikowski asks, "In what way can Churches 'intrude,' as it were, into the public realm when they judge the social fabric as seriously bereft of justice and dignity?" How can the Catholic church maintain a prophetic voice in society in the Murray framework?[78]

These five areas call for serious refinements of the Murray project.

Conclusion

As we draw this chapter to a close, a few insights emerge that call for ongoing reflection.

Openness to criticism

A critical discussion of Murray's work as outlined above does not diminish the enormous contribution of his thought for American Catholic social thinking. Murray would not be afraid of these constructive criticisms, he would welcome them. This is one of the lasting legacies of both John Courtney Murray and Pope John XXIII. They were not afraid to be open to self-criticism. John Pawlikowski says,

> Walking with Murray then means that the Church must also pay special attention to the importance of speaking the truth. This involves in part the willingness of the Church to engage in constructive self-criticism regarding its activities in societies. It cannot put forth the contention that as an institution it has always stood on the side of human dignity. History clearly shows that is not the case. To the extent that "speaking the truth" is seen as an essential trait of a sound pluralistic society, the Church cannot expect to be a major force in the shaping of society unless it adopts self-criticism as a cardinal principle.[79]

While Pawlikowski was speaking of Murray, the same could be applied to Pope John XXIII.

This is a hard lesson to learn, especially when many in the church assume that its authority would be undermined by changing its position, or being self-critical. Pope John XXIII, by calling the council, helped the church to see itself in a new way—no longer as a "perfect society" but as the "people of God," a people who are both faithful and unfaithful to the God they worship.

Men of Freedom

John Courtney Murray's lasting legacy is identified with his groundbreaking work on freedom. Freedom was the hallmark of his vision. It was at the end of his life that he offered this description of freedom:

> Freedom therefore is authenticity, truthfulness, fidelity to the pursuit of the truth and to the truth when found.... Freedom is experienced as duty, as responsibility—as a response to the claims of justice, to the

demands of rightful law, to the governance and guidance of legitimate authority. In its intimately Christian sense, however, freedom has a higher meaning than all this. Freedom, in the deepest experience of it, is love, to be free is to be-for-others. The Christian call to freedom is inherently a call to community, a summons out of isolation, an invitation to be-with-the-others, an impulse to service of others.[80]

As I mentioned at the beginning of this chapter, Pope John XXIII and John Courtney Murray helped the church take on a new identity. Accepting a new identity means letting go of the old secure and familiar identity. One of the most significant pieces of this new identity is to finally let go of the old Catholic notion that "error has no rights" and the Catholic ideal of the church dominating the social order. In these areas, and in many others, Pope John and John Courtney Murray helped Roman Catholics take on a new identity. They helped to free Catholicism from the harmful baggage of past centuries. Truly, they put the focus on freedom.

Discussion Questions

1. *Mater et Magistra* takes a less nostalgic view of outdated economic structures, and the document sees a positive role for "socialization" on the national level. How do you evaluate this contribution of Pope John XXIII's encyclical?

2. How do you evaluate William Buckley's criticism of *Mater et Magistra*—"Mater si, magister no"?

3. Why is *Pacem in Terris'* notion of economic rights controversial? How do you reconcile this tension?

4. John Courtney Murray addressed the question of religious liberty in a pluralist society. This is reminiscent of the debates among American bishops in the previous century. Why do you believe a breakthrough was made on the question at the Council?

5. How do you evaluate the interrelationship and the double challenge of being both Catholic and a citizen of the United States? Does the work of John Courtney Murray help resolve the dilemma? If so, explain.

5

Ecclesial and Racial Revolutions: *Gaudium et Spes* and Racism

The 1960s were tumultuous times in American society. The Vietnam War and the civil rights movement were powerful forces reshaping American attitudes toward authority, race, and national identity. Through the civil rights movement with its sporadic outbursts of violence in white communities and riots in the black communities, along with the Black Power movement and the articulation of black theology, the African American community was redefining itself vis-à-vis the dominant white society. The American society was forced to recognize its systemic racism, its institutionalized violence toward people of color. It was during these turbulent times that the black activist H. Rap Brown named the reality that violence is "as American as apple pie."[1] With violent and nonviolent means, the African American community "challenged the dominant ethos and pattern of accommodation to segregation."[2]

During this same period within Roman Catholicism a quiet revolution was underway—an ecclesial revolution that changed the way Roman Catholics defined themselves, their church, and the way they related to other religious groups and the world. The documents and the spirit of Vatican II initiated radical changes in the Roman Catholic church that continued through the Medellín Conference of Latin American Bishops in 1968 and the synod of bishops in 1971.

This chapter will examine the main themes of these turbulent times in society and in the church—the ecclesial and racial revolutions within the Roman Catholic church and within the African American community.

Part I. *Gaudium et Spes*—A New Approach

The Second Vatican Council was an event and a process that redefined the Roman Catholic church's self-identity and its relationship with contemporary societies. Fifteen of the sixteen documents of the council focused primarily on the *internal issues* of the church, such as liturgy, priestly formation, and the role of the laity. Only one document, *Gaudium et Spes*, the *Pastoral Constitution on the Church in the Modern World*, focused on the church's *external* relationship with contemporary society. The external focus is seen in the fact that *Gaudium et Spes* was the first document of any council to be addressed to the people of the world.

The very idea of such a document did not emerge until after the council was already in session. Pope John had called for the council on January 25, 1959. From that time until the opening of the council on October 11, 1962, 70 *schemata* (draft documents) were prepared by the various preparatory commissions. One of these 70 schemata, No. 7, which was prepared by a subcommission of the Theological Commission, was on the topic of "social order." This document was distributed to the bishops a month before the opening of the council and dealt with some of the topics that would end up in the pastoral constitution but with a classical tone emphasizing the objective character of the moral order.

A second preparatory text on social action was being prepared by the Preparatory Commission for the Apostolate of the Laity. This text was more concerned with practical matters. It is interesting to note that Msgr. Pietro Pavan was a member of both subcommissions.

The impetus to move beyond the internal issues of the church surfaced during the first session of the council. It was a small, but charismatic auxiliary bishop of Rio de Janeiro, Dom Helder Camara, "who gave the impulse which led to the decision to produce a schema on the Church in the world." Camara "constantly discussed with visitors the problems of the Third World. He kept asking 'What ought we to do now?'... Are we to spend our whole time discussing internal Church problems while two-thirds of mankind is dying of hunger? Will the council express its concern about the great problems of mankind?'" In a lecture in Rome he said: "Is shortage of priests the greatest problem of Latin America? No! Underdevelopment."[3] Other bishops were also concerned about the questions that Camara was raising, including cardinals Suenens of Belgium, Lercaro of Bologna, Leger of Montreal, and Montini of Milan, who became Pope Paul VI.

In early December these men spoke out on the need to deal with more than just *internal* ecclesial issues, and to address the needs of the poor. In light of this initiative a coordinating commission was established to address the new agenda item. Members of the previously mentioned commissions were combined into what was called the mixed commission, which now totaled 60 members.

At first no laity were involved in the process of the mixed commission. Finally, in April of 1964, twenty-three lay*men* were invited, fourteen of whom were able to attend. Three others were invited as observers, one of them a woman from Australia, Miss R. Goldie. They were invited to advise the bishops on the practical sections; the dogmatic chapter was not given to them and was discussed by the clerical theologians alone.[4]

The drafting process went through a torturous process of six drafts. Even the sixth version had about 20,000 amendments that the mixed commission had to deal with. Three issues in the final draft were hotly debated: 1) the discussion of atheism, 2) birth control, and 3) war.

A number of bishops wanted condemnations of communistic atheism. After various maneuvers and petitions the intention of both Pope John and Pope Paul, that the council not engage in sterile condemnation or vindictive name-calling, won the day. Only a footnote was added to reference previous papal condemnations of communism.

The debate over birth control was considered by some moderate members of the mixed commission as the most serious crisis of the council.[5] Conservative members wanted a clear condemnation of birth control in the text. They encouraged the ambivalent Pope Paul to support four *modi* (amendments) to the text that, according to the chronicler of the council "Xavier Rynne," would "explode" the idea "that conjugal love enjoyed equal status with procreation as one of the ends of marriage and reasserting Pius XI's doctrine of *Casti connubii* banning all and every type of artificial contraception unequivocally." Rynne estimated the damage of such a stance: "At one fell swoop not only would the work of the council so far be compromised, but the Special Papal Commission entrusted with the whole matter of demographic study and family planning by the Pope himself would be rendered useless."[6] The moral theologian Bernard Häring, who helped to write this section of the schema, noted that the "acceptance of the modi would either have made the Council, and especially the relevant commission, quite unconvincing, or would have provoked a massive *"non placet"* ["no" vote] from the open-minded majority of the Council."[7]

The conservatives countered by claiming the *modi* came from the pope himself and therefore should be accepted without discussion "in holy obedience." This tactic did not work, because it was discovered that the pope had not intended these changes without discussion.[8] Pope Paul accepted the commission's wording of the controversial point, which was subsequently modified slightly and approved by the full council.

A third issue that threatened the passage of Schema 13 was the question of the morality of war and the possession of nuclear weapons. This time the charge was led by an American, the newly appointed archbishop of New Orleans, Philip Hannan, who was a former paratrooper chaplain. Five days before the final vote on the text Hannan distributed three amendments to the council fathers. He also persuaded ten bishops including Spellman of New York, Shehan of Baltimore, O'Boyle of Washington, D.C., and Hurley of Durban, South Africa, to sign his petition, which called for a rejection of the proposed text. His three points were:

1) He disapproved of paragraph 80, which stated that the possession of nuclear weapons can lead to use of such weapons. He countered by saying that the possession of nuclear weapons had preserved freedom and has been a great service.

2) He challenged the claim that total war had been condemned by recent popes. Where are the sources?

3) The council should not vote on this matter when there was neither consensus among theologians nor among other specialists on this question.

The chairman of the subcommission of this chapter, Bishop Schroffer, and the general editor, Archbishop Marie Garrone, responded point by point to Archbishop Hannan's petition. They explained that Hannan had misinterpreted the text. With this explanation Cardinal Spellman and Hannan withdrew their support of the petition. With these clarifications the negative votes shrank from 483 on December 2, the date of Hannan's petition, to 251 after Schroffer's explanation, to 75 on December 7, the final vote, a day before the closing of the council.[9] Historian Willem Schuijt bluntly concludes that "The American bishops and their supporters...had little understanding of Chapter V, but when a decision had to be taken, they voted loyally and collegially out of respect for the majority, the Pope and the historical solemnity of the hour."[10]

Pope Paul's leadership on the question of the morality of modern warfare cannot be denied. Two months before the vote on the final version of *Gaudium et Spes* the pope had addressed the General Assembly of the United Nations in New York City and proclaimed the message of peace: "No more war, war never again. Peace, it is peace which must guide the destinies of peoples and of all mankind."[11] It is clear that the "prudent and realistic and at the same time more prophetic tone of the definitive text" of *Gaudium et Spes* "on this delicate point derives in part from Paul VI's speech before the United Nations."[12]

These questions on the morality of war in a nuclear age and nuclear deterrence would be debated again by the American bishops in 1980-1983 when they would draft their own pastoral letter on these issues. Archbishop Hannan would be heard from again during those debates.

MOTIVATION AND TONE

The three issues discussed above, while they may have added a bit of drama to council proceedings, by no means summarize the rich and diverse scope of the pastoral constitution. Some of the most notable dimensions of the document are its motivation, scope, and tone.

The council fathers, having addressed the internal questions of the vision, identity, and structure of the Catholic church for itself, now yearned "to explain how it conceives of the presence and activity of the Church in the world of today"(par. 2). The motivation is not to define new doctrine but to explain the church's social teaching in a way that *invites dialogue and cooperation* with those in the human family who are not part of the Roman Catholic community.

The desire for conversation and dialogue with the human family dictated the tone of the document as well. A defensive or pessimistic tone would not be very inviting. The majority of the council fathers did not feel threatened (as Pius IX and Leo XIII did) by the political and social movements of their time. The only condemnation in the text is reserved for the "abomination" of indiscriminate bombing of civilian populations in paragraph 80. The pastoral constitution reaffirmed the Catholic church's positions on current issues but did so in a way that invited reflection and dialogue in a *positive and hopeful* context.

The scope of *Gaudium et Spes* is comprehensive. It includes a reading of the contemporary situation in the introduction, and then it moves on in Part I to develop foundational notions of the centrality of human dignity, social relations and interdependence, the meaning of human activity, and the role of the church in the contemporary setting. The second part focuses on "problems of special urgency," including marriage and family, cultural diversity and cultural development, economic injustice, the political realm, war and the arms race, international cooperation, and the role of individual believers and the diocesan churches.

The positive and inviting tone of *Gaudium et Spes* is one of its most important contributions. It continued the spirit of openness breathed into the Catholic church by Pope John XXIII. While rooted in the tradition, it consciously maintained a positive approach that was intentionally more Christocentric and more biblically informed. This stance of openness and willingness to dialogue on behalf of the hierarchy of the Catholic church is a significant contribution of the Second Vatican Council in general and the pastoral constitution in particular. Such an attitude was in sharp contrast to the declarations of the previous Vatican council ninety years earlier.

An important dimension of the church's open and nontriumphal attitude is seen in the recognition that the church itself must bear some responsibility for the present plight of the world. The council fathers acknowledged that, regarding atheism, "believers themselves frequently bear some responsibility for this situation." Since atheism often arises in reaction to deficiencies in the "religious, moral or social life" of believers, the latter "have more than a little to do with the birth of atheism"(par. 19). *Gaudium et Spes* acknowledged the errors of the church: "The Church... is very well aware that among her members, both clerical and lay, some have been unfaithful to the Spirit of God during the course of many centuries.

In the present age, too, it does not escape the Church how great a distance lies between the message she offers and the human failings of those to whom the gospel is entrusted" (par. 43). The church comes to the world not in judgment or triumphalism, but as Christ came, to serve (par. 3).

METHODOLOGY

Gaudium et Spes proposed as its methodology an examination of social, cultural, and political realities "in the light of the gospel and human experience" (par. 46). The bishops noted that the world has passed from "a static concept of reality to a more dynamic evolutionary one" (par. 5), and this document reflected that shift as well. Theologian Lois Lorentzen notes that "by analyzing the signs of the time rather than by exploring abstract ideas of church and the common good suggests a *methodological change from classicism to a historically conscious approach.*"[13] The shift to a historically conscious approach means that history is seen as the place of ongoing revelation, where the Spirit of God is present and not merely as the locus for applying universal principles. The increased historical sensitivity translated into a decreased reliance on the philosophical structure of the natural law. This shift also led to more reliance on the insights of the human sciences. In paragraph 62 the bishops recognized the importance of the dialogue between religion and the insights of the human sciences.

> ...it is sometimes difficult to harmonize culture with Christian teaching. These difficulties do not necessarily harm the life of faith. Indeed they can stimulate the mind to a more accurate and penetrating grasp of the faith. For recent studies and the findings of science, history, and philosophy raise new questions which influence life and demand new theological investigations.... In pastoral care, appropriate use must be made not only of theological principles, but also of the findings of the secular sciences, especially of psychology and sociology.... Through a sharing of resources and points of view, let those who teach in seminaries, colleges and universities try to collaborate with men well versed in the other sciences.[14]

In the historically conscious approach the focus shifts from the objective moral order to the subjective realm, the realm of the person. Personalism pervades the document: in the section on politics the person is viewed as the link between the church and society (par. 76). In the section on marriage the document teaches that the moral character of behavior is determined by objective criteria "based on the nature of the human person and his acts" (par. 51). The official commentary states that acts are to be judged not by "merely biological aspects, but insofar as they refer to the human person integrally and adequately considered."[15] This means that morality is based on considering all the human person's essential aspects, including personal conscience, embodiment in the material world, sociality, developing life stages, equality, and the call to worship God. Louis Janssens, a Belgian moral theologian, refers to this approach to morality as an "ethic of responsibility on a personalistic foundation."[16]

CONTENT

Gaudium et Spes begins with a *cultural analysis* in nontechnical language that it refers to as reading the "signs of the times." The council fathers intentionally begin with a description of the historical reality, as they see it, before unfolding the church's social teaching—this reveals their historically conscious methodology. The next section presents the church's understanding of the dignity of the human person—endowed with freedom, intelligence, and moral sensitivity. Human dignity and human nature are essentially social: "by their innermost nature persons are social beings and unless they relate themselves to others they can neither live nor develop their potential" (par. 12). The bishops draw out the implications of this vision of the human person:

> ...whatever insults human dignity, such as subhuman living conditions, arbitrary imprisonment, deportation, slavery, prostitution, the selling of women and children; as well as disgraceful working conditions, where men are treated as mere tools for profit, rather than as free and responsible persons; all these things and others of their like are infamies indeed. They poison human society, but they do more harm to those who practice them than those who suffer from the injury. Moreover, they are a supreme dishonor to the Creator. (par. 27)

The bishops explain that "the basic equality of all must receive increasingly greater recognition" and "with respect to the fundamental rights of the person, every type of discrimination, whether based on sex, race, color, social condition, language, or religion, is to be overcome and eradicated as contrary to God's intent" (par. 29). This is a clear denunciation of racism and sexism as contrary to God's will. (These two topics will be developed in subsequent chapters of this book.)

In Part II the bishops address "some problems of special urgency" in five chapters. Again, these chapters begin with a historical approach rather than an abstract account of the situation. The first chapter discusses marriage and family and reflects the competing visions of marriage—the traditional canonical view and the contemporary, personalist view. The discussion of these issues generated some of the more heated debates of the council. Evidence of both approaches is found in the text, but the language used to define marriage, says Lois Lorentzen, "signals major shifts in the church's understanding of the marital relationship." The constitution, says Lorentzen, "places conjugal love and covenantal relationship at the heart of its formulation, using personalist language to move marriage beyond the earlier legalistic framework."[17] Marriage is described as a "community of love," an intimate partnership of married life and love," which is rooted in the conjugal covenant of irrevocable personal consent" (pars. 47, 48).

In the next chapter the bishops address the development of culture. They strike a positive approach to culture, noting that the church exists in a reciprocal relationship with the culture of the community, mutually requiring each other. In order to understand God's activity in the world, the bishops remind the church that it must understand its own "specific historical environment" (par. 53).

In chapters III, IV, and V the bishops continue the development of Catholic social teaching on socioeconomic issues. In the positive spirit of Vatican II the document affirms industrial development, global expansion and growth, and technological advances. The text is not blind to the injustices that afflict the poor as it:

- contrasts the plight of the poor with the life of the wealthy (par. 63);

- condemns the injustice in international trade (par. 83);

- reiterates the common purpose of created things (par. 69);

- relativizes the right of private property (par. 69);

- maintains that labor is superior to other elements in economic life (par. 67);

- defends the rights of minorities (par. 73);

- calls for a reevaluation of war with an entirely new attitude (par. 80); and

- defends the rights of conscientious objectors (par. 79).

Gaudium et Spes, in tone, orientation, methodology, and content, set the agenda for a new era in Catholic social teaching. The highlights of its positive impact include 1) its attitude of "walking with humanity," 2) its historically conscious method, and 3) that it opened the doors to new directions in Roman Catholic theology and ministry. I will comment briefly on these three positive aspects.

POSITIVE IMPACT

By the time the council fathers came to writing *Gaudium et Spes* any vestiges of the old triumphalism of the past were drummed out by the powerfully humble stance of Popes John XXIII and Paul VI. Pope John XXIII set the tone for the council, which was not to offer condemnations or harsh judgments, but to *"walk with humanity."* The opening line of the document says it all: "the joys and hopes, the griefs and the anxieties of the men of this age, especially those who are poor or in any way afflicted, these too are the joys and hope, the griefs and anxieties of the followers of Christ." The church is part of the world; the church identifies with the suffering of the men and women of our time. Later, the council fathers note the diaconal focus of the church; like Christ, the church is to be of service: "Inspired by no earthly ambition, the Church seeks but a solitary goal: to carry forward the work of Christ Himself under the lead of the befriending Spirit. And Christ entered this world to give witness to the truth, to rescue and not to sit in judgment, to serve and not to be served" (par. 3). These quotes capture the nonjudgmental, nontriumphal approach of *Gaudium et Spes*. The attitudes about theology and ministry of many bishops, clergy, religious, and laity were redirected by this refreshing servant orientation.

One of the lasting legacies of *Gaudium et Spes* is that it brought a contemporary, *historical and personalist theological methodology* into the church's official social teachings. This was in contrast to the deductive natural law methodology of previous social documents. There was a notable absence of the natural law language that was so evident only a few years earlier in *Pacem in Terris*—the best of the old. *Gaudium et Spes* legitimated an inductive and historical approach to social issues that would reach its high point a few years later in Pope Paul's 1971 letter *Octogesima Adveniens*. The pastoral con-

stitution begins with the current situation and then turns to the Christian tradition for direction, rather than articulating moral principles in an *a priori*
fashion and then applying them to the contemporary scene.

A third positive contribution of *Gaudium et Spes* is that its central theological affirmations, such as the equality of all persons and the dynamic historical consciousness, *opened the doors for further exploration of
Catholic theology in a new key.* This new approach included:

- theology done from below, theology done from the perspective of
  the poor (Manuel Velasquez argues that "the most significant contribution of *Gaudium et Spes* was the impetus it gave to the liberationist themes that emerged in church documents in the late six-
  ties and early seventies."[18]);

- from the perspective of women (Anne Patrick, a moral theologian,
  makes the argument that the pastoral constitution was responsible in
  part for the growth of Catholic feminist theology. The council fathers
  did not realize how women who read *Gaudium et Spes* would "move
  by a logic implicit in the text from affirmation of women's rights in
  society to affirmation of women's rights in the church"[19]); and

- theology from the perspective of race (Shawn Copeland, an
  African American theologian, argues that the changes of Vatican II
  overlapped with the civil rights movement, and that this convergence of ecclesial and social change was a kairotic moment—a
  time of grace, a time of kairos[20]).

These movements would break onto the Catholic theological and pastoral landscape in the late 1960s and 1970s because of the new orientation taken by *Gaudium et Spes*.

WEAKNESSES

As good as it is, the pastoral constitution has a few weaknesses. For example, while the document succeeds in avoiding any defensive or judgmen-
tal stance toward the contemporary world, its receptive and optimistic
tone struck others as naive. "They decry inequality (29, 66) and call for
social change (26, 42, 66, 85, 86). However, the persistent emphasis on
the person throughout the document yields a weak analysis of structural
realities and of social sin."[21]

In setting a positive and optimistic tone, *Gaudium et Spes* may have been *too uncritical* of the world and of the tension between the gospel and the world's agenda. Robert McAfee Brown, a Protestant observer at the council, noted the "temptation throughout the document to assume that the gospel crowns the life of natural man, rather than being, as well, a challenge to, and judgment upon, that life. The document minimizes the degree to which the gospel is also a scandal and a stumbling block, by which men can be offended as well as uplifted."[22]

While the pastoral constitution opened the door for future theological reflections that takes women's experience seriously, Lois Lorentzen notes that it also "contains serious problems for a feminist perspective. Explicit *concern for women rarely appears* in the constitution." The document's "limited analysis provides little insight into the concrete situations of women, demonstrating a blindness to rape, domestic violence, poverty, excessive workload, and so forth. It also does not offer an internal criticism of the church's own structures and ways in which the institutional church might not affirm the full personhood of women."[23]

While *Gaudium et Spes* reveals "traces" of a Third World perspective, its orientation is dominated by First World concerns. There is scant attention to the issues of the developing nations. For instance, the section on private property reveals an explicit openness to communitarian patterns of ownership as found in some parts of Africa and Asia (par. 69). Here the drafters of the document responded to the sharp criticisms voiced in the council that the tone and outlook of the earlier drafts was overly Europeanized. The issue of land reform reflects the input of the Third World voices (par. 71). But in general, the text is dominated by the concerns of Europe and North America.

Two priests who work among the base communities and the poor in Brazil point out that the ideal of a Vatican II renewed morality is a First World perspective that

> addressed a type of man and woman who enjoys a privileged position in the economic, social, cultural and religious spheres.... The ideal it puts forward in family terms presupposes adequate income, a house with several rooms, good health, emotional stability and a lot of free time. The families of the impoverished have no hope of achieving any of these things.[24]

The Irish moral theologian Enda McDonagh notes

the absence of the cross from the gospel reflections: social sin, mass oppression, a sheer conspiracy of evil needed to explain so much of human history, all that is largely absent. The world it portrays is one needing development rather than liberation. It is one whose problems seem rather easily resolvable with a bit of goodwill and a renewal of Christian idealism. And this from a dominantly European-American gathering whose members had been through two world wars in this century and still had to live with the responsibility of the Holocaust. This sense of the tragic is largely missing from its world-view as the cross is from its theology.[25]

Although the document clearly contained the seeds for later developments in liberation theology, its critics claimed that it too easily adopted First World "liberal" values. The Canadian sociologist Gregory Baum noted, "This liberal notion of the self-development of persons corresponded to the aspirations of the Western middle class, but did not shed light on the emancipatory struggles of people, including the working class, who were structurally oppressed."[26] A shift in perspective would be evident after the 1968 meeting of the Latin American bishops in Medellín, Colombia, and the gathering of bishops for the 1971 Synod. Both of these events revealed that the Roman Catholic church's official documents were beginning to give serious attention to the perspectives of the Third World.

THE REFORM CONTINUES

While the official deliberations of the Second Vatican Council concluded on December 8, 1965, the impact of the council will echo through the church for generations. That impact is evident in the vision of the council, which continues to permeate the church. The reform of Vatican II is also evident in the revision of church structures and procedures during and after the council. Some of those structural changes were:

- The Curial Offices were reformulated, new departments were added, others revamped. One of the new departments, alluded to in paragraph 90 of *Gaudium et Spes,* is the Pontifical Commission on Justice and Peace, *Iustitia et Pax.*[27]

- The process of revising the Code of Canon Law was also initiated to reflect the theology of the Second Vatican Council. The new Code of Canon Law was promulgated in 1983.

- A final structural change was the establishment of an international synod to meet regularly to provide for an ongoing collegial forum for the bishops to discuss theological and pastoral issues. The Third International Synod met in 1971 and produced a significant document, *Justice in the World*, which will be discussed in the next chapter.

RACISM—ALMOST OVERLOOKED

As the reform started by Vatican II continued, church leaders and laity began to realize that the church had not given adequate attention to the evil of racism. There are only a few references to racism in the sixteen documents of the council:

- *Gaudium et Spes* speaks of the "right of all men to a human and civic culture favorable to personal dignity and free from any discrimination on the grounds of race, sex, nationality, religious, or social conditions" (par. 60) and

- the *Declaration on Non-Christian Religions* (*Nostra Aetate*) declares that "the Church rejects, as foreign to the mind of Christ, any discrimination against men or harassment of them because of their race, color, conditions of life, or religion" (par. 5).

These minimal references to racism at the council reflected where the Roman Catholic church was on the question in 1965. Racism was not seen as a major moral and social issue. In Pope Paul's social encyclical *Populorum Progressio*, issued in 1967, we find only two brief references to the question of race.[28] The white church of Europe and North America was not aware of its own racism. It was only after the racial violence of 1968 and the assassination of Dr. Martin Luther King, Jr., that the Catholic church directly and actively addressed the question of racism.

To be fair, we should note that the Roman Catholic bishops of the United States had issued a statement on *Discrimination and the Christian Conscience* in 1958, which condemned racism in all its forms. But it wasn't until *after* the death of Dr. King that the bishops labeled racism as a "national crisis." In their statement issued three weeks after Dr. King's death they acknowledged that there was "unfinished business" in the Catholic religious community: "First among these is the total eradication of any elements of discrimination in our parishes, schools, hospitals, homes for the aged, and similar institutions" (par. 10).[29]

During the 1971 synod a number of African bishops addressed the great injustice of racism on the global scene. Archbishop Yougbare from Upper Volta addressed the injustices experienced by the black community: "The Negro is continually detested, despised, and maltreated. Must we wait until we get to heaven to be rid of separate compartments for black and white?" Bishop Lamont of Rhodesia condemned racial discrimination as a denial of the solidarity of the human race.[30]

Cardinal Carberry of St. Louis also addressed the issue of racism, which had become very volatile in the U.S. "...Very grave injustices have been frequently committed through discrimination of race, as is found in the United States of America and other regions of the world.... The laws and the court decisions and the patterns of behavior that favor an unjust segregation must be abolished." He recognized the contribution that minorities can make. "Help must be provided for the various minority peoples so that each group will not merely acquire for itself that dignity and equal status in social life which is its due, but also will be able to enrich the other groups by the contribution of the riches that are inherent in its own character and culture."[31]

The Catholic church was finally turning its attention to the question of racism both in society and within the church—a challenge that is ongoing.

Part II. The Catholic Church and Racism

Too long the assumption has been that American Catholicism is a white, European phenomenon. It never was. Blacks seem to emerge in the most unlikely places throughout the history of Catholic America, exerting either a pronounced or a passive influence in the Church on behalf of their fellow black Catholics. Too long has this history of African Americans been buried; it must be rediscovered.[32]

The white European-American church has not told the story of our black sisters and brothers. This is part of the implicit and explicit racism of the American society in general and of the American Catholic church in particular.

It is important to tell the story of racism in the Catholic church. We begin with naming the experience of African American Catholics and a brief history of racism in America. Accusing the Catholic church of racism may strike some ears as a harsh judgment. The stereotypical image of the racist is a hate-filled member of the Ku Klux Klan. That image of racism is *dominative racism*. While it is the most dramatic example of racial hatred, it is by no means the only or most predominant expression of racism. The cool racism of the *aversive racist* is more subtle and genteel and therefore more elusive and insidious.[33]

OVERT AND COVERT CATHOLIC RACISM

"The history of the American church in its relationships with black people is the history of the theological sin of scandal and the triumph of prejudice." These words of Robert Robinson, the coordinator of the National Black Catholic Lay Caucus in 1980, capture the sad story of Catholic racism. He speaks from his own experience.

> When I was a child in Washington, D.C., because of the color of my skin I was admitted only to the balcony of the church, while my sister, whose skin was much lighter, was assumed to be white and was allowed to sit with the congregation on the main floor of the church. As I gazed down upon my fortunate sister, I often wondered who was passing—my sister as white or her fellow parishioners as Catholics.

> Priests truly did publicly wash their hands to reassure white Catholics that priestly hands had not touched black lips immediately before serving them the Lord's Supper.

> So churches were segregated and unfriendly. Schools were segregated and unfriendly. Bishops were segregationists and unfriendly. Active racism was rampant among white lay people, the clergy, sisters and the hierarchy. The church, supposed to be the living witness of the meaning of the Body of Christ, instead reflected the dominant white society's narrow and racist cultural and spiritual values.

Robinson recognizes that some white priests, nuns, and laity were working to change the prejudicial attitudes in the church and in society. He admits that the overt racism of his youth has disappeared but the scandal of racism is still present: "It is with sorrow that I tell you that racism in the church is not getting any better; it is only swept under the rich red robes of bishops and cardinals, and under the rich red carpets of diocesan chanceries."[34]

Many others could attest to the reality of racism in the Catholic church, in parishes, in religious communities, in seminaries, and in our diocesan offices. For example, Sister Francesca Thompson tells of a racist reverend mother of a large white community that wasn't in the South. The mother superior asked Sister Francesca, "Sister, would you mind being invested [into the community] in the sacristy instead of on the high altar with the other sisters? We just can't afford to irritate the white parents of the other postulants."[35]

RACISM—THE LEGACY OF SLAVERY

"Twentieth-century institutional racism is the immoral and independent child of institutionalized slavery."[36] On the question of slavery the Catholic church in the United States reflected the attitudes of the larger society. Prior to the twentieth century the common Catholic teaching held that the social, economic, and legal institution of slavery was morally legitimate as long as slaves were properly cared for materially and spiritually.[37] As a consequence it was common for Catholic laity, bishops, priests, and religious orders to be slaveholders. During the colonial period slavery was viewed exclusively as a legal or political issue. Not all African Americans were slaves but the majority of black Catholics in seventeenth-, eighteenth-, and nineteenth-century America were found in the Catholic regions of Maryland and Louisiana. They often were the slaves of Catholics, including the Catholic clergy and religious communities. For example, the Jesuits had African slaves working on their four plantations in Maryland until 1837. Other male and female religious orders owned slaves. It was accepted that some women entering the convent would bring a slave as part of their dowry.[38] The Capuchins and Ursulines also used slaves as servants or laborers on their plantations. Bishop John Carroll had two black servants—one free and one a slave.[39]

The Catholic church was racist in "the overwhelming refusal of Catholic bishops and seminaries in the United States to accept Black men for study for the priesthood." Diana Hayes, an African American theologian, points out that "only a very few Blacks were able to enter foreign seminaries."[40] Women did not fare much better, "until the present century...religious vocations, for men and women, were also actively discouraged."[41]

The church reflected the implicit and explicit racism of the American society. Rev. George Cummings sees this racism as a "denying of the basic humanity of black people":

...Black people are unique among oppressed peoples in western civilization in that they have not only suffered imperialist and class
exploitation (and black women sexual oppression), but have also
had to endure racial oppression which takes the form of *denying the
basic humanity of black people, a continual and systematic denial of black
membership in the human family.* The "authority" of this denial is
unprecedented in western civilization. It has been supported and
promoted for over two centuries in the academy, in scientific institutions, projects and books, popular folklore, national institutions,
legal documents, encyclopedias, film, television, radio and in
churches. No other oppressed people in western civilization has had
their humanity attacked and assaulted to this extent. In this regard,
the plight of black people symbolizes the very worst and most inhumane aspects of capitalist civilization.[42]

Professor Diana Hayes tones down the language but not the sentiment
in her summary of the endemic racism in the American Catholic church
over the last four hundred years.

Looking at a Church in which they have been a part for over four
hundred years, they [black Catholics] see an institution which has
tolerated their presence but not encouraged it, an institution which
has required that they give up much of what was naturally and legitimately theirs in order to become part of an often sterile and
oppressive system in which many have never felt fully at home. Yet,
they have persevered.[43]

CATHOLICS AND ABOLITION

It is true that the slave trade had been condemned by Pope Urban VIII in
1639. But this declaration did not stop the lucrative trade. Two hundred
years later Pope Gregory XVI repeated the condemnation of the slave
trade. Northern and Southern Catholic bishops such as John England in
Charleston, South Carolina, argued that Pope Gregory's letter condemned only the slave trade and not slavery itself. "Slavery...is regarded
by the Church, of which the Pope is the presiding officer, not to be
incompatible with the practice of the natural law, to have been established by human legislation and, when the dominion of the slave is justly acquired by the master, to be lawful not only in the sight of human tri-
bunal, but also in the eyes of Heaven."[44]

Archbishop John Hughes of New York City did not support the abolition of slavery because of his concern for Irish immigrants who would have to compete with emancipated slaves for jobs. Hughes acknowledged that the Catholic church taught the equality and freedom of all human beings and that the church had condemned the slave trade as a crime against humanity, yet Hughes maintained that once slaves had been introduced to a country, the church did not require that they be freed. Rather, the master should treat the slave with humanity and the slave should "bear his lot and be faithful to the master."[45]

Prior to the Civil War

> most Catholics—including most bishops—viewed abolitionists, who proclaimed that holding slaves was "a sin against God," as insurrectionists who were a threat to the "safety of the country." Their ideas were thought to be in conflict with the basic ideals of Catholic ethics. Abolitionists, in turn, were publicly anti-Catholic. They generally looked upon Catholics as ignorant, pro-slavery foreigners at odds with the ideal of social equality.[46]

Most Catholics were intent on proving themselves "patriotic" because they were viewed and treated by the dominant Protestant society as immigrants who owed allegiance to a foreign power—the pope. In an effort to demonstrate their patriotism and to protect their jobs, "Catholics were generally hostile to the insurrectionist cries of the abolitionists against slavery."[47]

Racism was evident in church customs after the Civil War. The 100,000 African American Catholics—less than 1.5% of the total Catholics in 1900—were treated in the same racist way in both the North and the South:

> In southern communities black Catholics attended segregated churches and schools or found themselves relegated to church galleries. They approached the communion rail after whites and confessed their sins in segregated confessionals. Some of the external signs of discrimination were missing in the North, but there the realities of Catholic life for black people were in many cases even less pleasant.[48]

Pope Leo XIII decried slavery in 1888 and 1890, but the American Catholic church was not eager to embrace racial equality. Sister Jamie Phelps argues that in accepting slavery damage was done to the Catholic soul. "Having accepted and given theological legitimation to a moral compromise with the dehumanizing brutality of slavery, Catholics—bishops, priests, religious and laity—had infected their minds and hearts with erroneous justifications and racial attitudes that would have a more deleterious effect on their moral integrity."[49]

EARLY BLACK CATHOLIC ACTIVISM—LED BY THE LAITY

Black Catholics have confronted the pervasive racism in the U.S. in various ways. Two black Catholic movements, in 1889 and 1916 respectively, addressed the concerns of a black minority in the immigrant, white Catholic church. During the era of the "Social Catholics," five *Black Catholic Congresses* signaled a new consciousness and a new determination among black Catholics. Between 1889 and 1894 five congresses were organized by Daniel Rudd of Cincinnati. Rudd, the son of slave parents, was the editor of the *American Catholic Tribune*, a paper published by and for African American Catholics. These meetings were held in Washington, D.C., Cincinnati, Philadelphia, Chicago, and Baltimore. The congresses served as "a forum for Black opinion, they voiced the desires and hopes for the spread of Catholicism within the African American community and sounded a clarion call to the American Church to change the racist policies so prevalent on the local level in the American Catholic Church of that day."[50]

The participants of these lay congresses recognized that they shared common concerns with the immigrant Catholic community, as they put it, "our brethren of the Emerald Isle, who, like ourselves are struggling for justice." They asked for schools, institutions, and societies for African Americans, as well as help in addressing racial discrimination by labor unions, employers, landlords, and real estate agents. The last congress in 1894 again focused on the racial discrimination in the hiring practices of the unions.[51] (It would be 93 years before the next National Black Catholic Congress would be held. In 1987 the congresses would be reestablished to continue the work of the addressing racism and celebrating Black Catholic identity. The VI Congress in 1987 developed *The National Black Catholic Pastoral Plan*.[52] Congresses were planned for every five years with the VII held in 1992 and the VIII Congress held in Baltimore, August 28-31, 1997. Five thousand people attended the 1997 Congress from 49 states, Africa, and several Caribbean islands; they came together to "share their pride, renew their roots, and fortify their spiritual wings."[53])

The African American historian Cyprian Davis gives a positive interpretation to the work of the first five congresses even though they faded away for almost a century.

> The black lay Catholic congresses were not a failure. In fact, they achieved what Rudd set out to do in calling the first congress. They demonstrated beyond a doubt not only that a black Catholic community existed but that it was active, devoted, articulate and proud. It also demonstrated that given the opportunity, there was real leadership within the black community.

Here Davis touches on the ongoing need in the black community— the lack of a black clergy, which was the result of the racism of the churches and seminaries.

> Other ethnic groups had their clergy who could speak on their behalf. Black Catholics lacked a body of black priests who commanded respect on a national scale. *From the beginning a black laity had to take charge. Strong lay leadership would remain a constant characteristic of African American Catholicism.* Furthermore, this leadership involved men who were authentic leaders within the black community and men who were also strong Catholics despite many rebuffs.[54]

According to Brother Cyprian Rowe, the director of the National Office of Black Catholics, support for the Black Lay Congresses waned because the attitude of the participants was seen as "militant."

> Even in the euphoria that followed the first congress, there were the seeds of its destruction. That blacks were speaking for themselves, that they were calling the total Catholic community to just behavior, earned for them the epithet "militant." Support dwindled. Rudd was pressured to move his paper to the East, where he could work under ecclesiastical supervision. When he tacitly refused to do so, another black Catholic paper was established. Both failed. The movement died, in a sense, but it addressed the critical issues and planted necessary seeds.[55]

Cyprian Davis considers the work of these congresses, especially the address of the IV Black Catholic Congress published in the *Boston Pilot* on September 23, 1893, as a *"foundation ... of Black Catholic theology."* He lifts up their sense of social mission, the focus on human rights, a theology of the priesthood of the faithful, and their rootedness in the African origins of the church.[56]

The second major movement of black Catholics emerged in 1916, twenty-three years after the last Black Congress. Dr. William S. Lofton, a prominent Washington dentist who had served as the president of the fifth Black Congress was joined by Dr. Thomas Wyatt Turner, a professor at Howard University. They initiated the *Committee for the Advancement of Colored Catholics*. The goals of their movement included improving social services to black military people serving in World War I, calling the church to end all discrimination, to end segregation in Catholic schools and organizations, and to encourage an indigenous African American clergy.

Dr. Turner knew that the development of black ordained leadership was essential for the black community *and* for the good of the broader white church. In an exchange with the rector of a seminary Turner discovered the deep-rooted racism that was typical of the Catholic church in those days. The rector wrote to Dr. Turner that he did not think it advisable to bring in blacks because if they were brought in, ordained, and sent to parishes, the people of those parishes would, in effect, be forced out. "Their distaste for such a priest would cause their spiritual needs to go unfulfilled."[57] This rector blatantly acknowledged the racism of the white Catholic community, and yet he appeared not to be offended by it.

In 1924 the Committee for the Advancement of Colored Catholics evolved into a new organization known as the *Federated Colored Catholics*. The thrust of the new movement was "to be an action group led by black Catholics and for black Catholics that would ensure that the black Catholic community take a responsible and leadership role in American Catholicism and American society."[58] The Federated held national meetings in Washington, D.C., in 1925, New York in 1927, and in Cincinnati, Baltimore, Detroit, St. Louis, and New York in successive years.

In 1932 a split in the leadership emerged. Rev. John LaFarge, a white Jesuit who had assisted Dr. Turner, now felt that the future of the movement lay in the direction of interracial councils. According to Cyprian Rowe "their differences ultimately caused ecclesiastical supports to be pulled away from the Federated Colored Catholics, which was finally supplanted by the *Catholic Interracial Council....*" Rowe goes on to note that "it is clear that *black Catholics* did not look on the C.I.C. [Catholic Interracial Council] as *their organization*, though they may have seen it as the only viable structure concerned with the advancement of racial justice within the church."[59]

What is striking about these early black movements is that they were started by *lay leaders* in the black community. This showed, paradoxically, both the strength and the institutional weakness of these movements. The strength is evident in that black laity took up the challenge of confronting the racism in the church. They did not wait to be led by the bishops and the clergy. For this they should be recognized for their heroic effort in a hierarchical church that was uneasy with laity in leadership roles. In a church where ecclesiastical power is clearly related to ordination, however, the black community had a serious disadvantage. Brother Rowe concludes that "there is little doubt that the Afro-American Catholic Congress and the Federated Colored Catholic movements both suffered from the absence of an indigenous black clergy."[60] The leaders of both movements, Rudd and Turner, recognized this weakness and tried to address it with the limited power they had. Blacks had almost no access to the seminaries. They had to study in Africa or in a seminary for black seminarians that opened in 1920 in Bay St. Louis, Mississippi. Because of this exclusion from seminaries, "blacks were always on the outside and powerless."[61]

The *Interracial Councils* blossomed around the country under the inspiration of Father John LaFarge. By 1958 there were approximately 40 councils that tried to cooperate with other local groups in combating racial discrimination in the church and society. LaFarge believed that education was the most important prescription for addressing the needs of the black community. Hence he established the Cardinal Gibbons Institute in southern Maryland in 1922. He also believed that educating whites was crucial to eliminating racism. He focused on institutionalized racism, especially the racism in labor unions and banking practices.[62]

Father LaFarge was also asked by Pope Pius XI to help write an encyclical on racism. The pope wanted to address not only the white racism in the United States, but also the anti-Semitic racism that was gaining momentum in Europe. In the summer of 1938 LaFarge and two other Jesuits from Europe, Gustav Gundlach and Gustav Desbuquois, produced an encyclical in two months. The document was held up by the Jesuit superior general, Wlodimir Ledochowski, who claimed the encyclical was "too strong and provoking." Ledochowski was a Polish count with, some said, anti-Semitic inclinations of his own. The pope finally received the document on January 21 1939, but he died on February 10 before he could promulgate it.[63] Pope Pius XII did not follow through on his predecessor's initiative. In hindsight we can see that this was a major missed opportunity for the church to confront the vicious racism that was emerging in the late 1930s.

Despite the good work of Father LaFarge, the desire in the black community was for an organization that would reflect black goals and aspi-rations and that would be led by *black* clergy and laity. It wasn't until 1970 that such a committee, the National Office of Black Catholics, was established within the hierarchical structure.

Prior to the civil rights movement most social activists were preoccupied with the rights of workers and were blind to the issues of race. Only in the 1950s did Catholics begin to turn their attention to racial justice.[64] This "blindness" to race is also a form of latent racism in the white Catholic church. Sociologist Joel Kovel's description of the "aversive" racist could fit the behavior of many American Catholics. "The aversive racist is the type who believes in white race superiority and is more or less aware of it but does nothing overt about it. He *tries to ignore the existence of black people*, tries to avoid contact with them, and at most tries to be polite, correct, and cold in whatever dealings are necessary between the races."[65]

The dramatic events of the civil rights movement and the reactionary racism in the North and the South challenged black and white Catholics to examine their relationship to the racism of their country and their church. Shawn Copeland notes the fortunate convergence of the two movements of social and ecclesial change—a time of grace, a *kairos.*

> The civil rights movement challenged the dominant ethos and pattern of accommodation to segregation; the Second Vatican Council chal-lenged the historic intellectual, theological, and cultural insularity of the Catholic Church. Change in the social mood without change in the ecclesial mood might have forced Black Catholics in the United States to abandon their centuries-old religious tradition; change in the ecclesial mood without change in the social mood might have com-pelled them to barter their racial-cultural heritage for silver. There was a propitiousness to these times. This was God's time, this was *kairos.*[66]

THE CIVIL RIGHTS MOVEMENT

In the early days of the civil rights movement Roman Catholics, black or white, were generally *not* in the forefront. It is true that some courageous laywomen and men, sisters, and priests marched at Selma, and the bish-ops had denounced the sin of racism. But, as Sister Copeland notes, "as a whole, as an institution, the Catholic church in the United States made no significant contribution to the civil rights movement."[67] Father Jerome LeDoux, a black scholar, declared the failure of the church at this crucial moment as one of the "most shameful scandals of modern

Christianity; the damning exposure of the Church as the tail-light in matters of justice where the civil courts did not hesitate to be a head-light."[68]

Black priests, unlike many black Protestant clergy, were not in the vanguard of grass-roots leadership that supported Martin Luther King, Jr. Cyprian Davis explained this lack by pointing out that few black priests were in leadership roles of any kind in the early 1960s and that the black priests shared the bias of other Catholics that it was unseemly for either clergy or religious to engage in public spectacles like demonstrations. This resistance began to break down after Martin Luther King's call to the nation's clergy to come to Selma, Alabama, to support the civil rights movement.[69]

In some cities reaction to racism was expressed in the frustration and desperation of riots and burning. Some black leaders, such as Malcolm X, stressed a militant "Black Power" approach rooted in a new sense of black nationalism. In places like Milwaukee where Father James Groppi led marches into the white neighborhoods, the racism of the white community was exposed in the anger and resentment of the heavily Catholic neighborhoods. On April 4, 1968 Dr. King was assassinated in Memphis. Again, riots broke out in areas already ravaged by fire and in cities as yet untouched by black frustration and anger.

Twelve days after the King assassination some sixty Roman Catholic priests met in caucus as part of the Catholic Clergy Conference on the Interracial Apostolate held in Detroit. Father Herman Port, an African American priest from Rockford, Illinois, and the vice-president of the organization, had invited all the black priests in the country to this special caucus. The invitation was in response to the crisis of racism and in particular the police order to "shoot to kill" all those engaged in looting issued by Chicago's mayor Richard J. Daley. Cyprian Davis, who participated in the meeting recalls:

> In that meeting, which went on through that day and night, black priests of all ages and backgrounds dealt with the question of their personal and corporate responsibility in a time of racial crisis. In order to determine such responsibility, the individual priests had to look at their respective sense of racial identity. Ultimately, this meant a look by each one at his own personal history as an African American cleric in the American Catholic church. For many it was a time of painful discovery and sometimes bitter revelation. For all it was a time of anger or of deep-seated unease.[70]

The Black Catholic Clergy Caucus decided to do two things: 1) to write a statement to the American Catholic bishops informing them of the seriousness of the situation facing the church in the black community, and 2) to form an organization for black priests, permanent deacons, and religious brothers. A strongly worded statement was agreed upon after prolonged discussion and argument. The priests "were pulled between a real sense of loyalty to the church and a sense of responsibility to the black community in a time of struggle and increasing militancy."[71]

This group of black priests "stunned the white Catholic hierarchy by publicly and collectively naming their church as 'primarily a white racist institution.'"[72] The Caucus called for greater control by blacks themselves of the Catholic institutions in the black community, and warned that the church "is seriously dying in the black community.... In many areas there is a serious defecting... on the part of black Catholic youth... The black community no longer looks to the Catholic church with hope."

The black priests made nine demands of the American bishops, including that black priests be placed in decision-making positions in their dioceses and in the black community; that greater efforts be made to recruit black men for the priesthood and permanent diaconate; that a department for the affairs of African Americans be established in the United States Catholic Conference under black leadership; and that each diocese set aside funds for leadership training of black laypersons.[73]

Davis notes the historic importance of this gathering of the Black Catholic Clergy Caucus in April 1968, calling it "a milestone in the history of the black Catholic community. It created a solidarity among the black Catholic clergy that had never previously existed. It was a return to the tradition of black Catholic initiative that had marked the black Catholic lay congresses and the Federated Colored Catholics."

From his perspective, Davis points to the positive results of the statement, claiming that the demands of the caucus were and are being implemented. Furthermore, it served as the catalyst that initiated

> a change of direction on the part of the American Catholic church. No matter how one may view the assertion that the Catholic church in the United States was "a white racist institution," it is remarkable that the church as an institution opened itself with a minimum of resistance to the needs of its black members in most areas.[74]

Catholic black religious women were also coming together in solidarity. In August 1968 the first meeting of the National Black Sisters'

Conference was held in Pittsburgh. This association is "the first vehicle through which black religious women have dealt critically and creatively with reality in such a way as to discover their desire and make their choice to participate in the transformation of their black world."[75]

Two years later in 1970 the National Office for Black Catholics was established with the support of the United States Catholic Conference to address racism within the church, to speak for black Catholics, and to facilitate the growth of the black Catholic church by providing programs and resources. In the following years diocesan offices of black Catholics were organized in various dioceses, the first two being Detroit, Michigan, and Rochester, New York, in 1971 and 1972.

In August of 1970 two other black Catholic organizations were established: 1) the National Black Catholic Lay Caucus, "to bring about a genuine black control and authentic decision-making in the black Catholic community both in matters pertaining to the Church and with broader society [and] to bring the years of accumulated resources of the Church to foster development of the black community," and 2) the National Black Seminarians' Association, which addressed the concern that the white seminary was not preparing anyone to serve in the black community.[76]

In reflecting on these new organizations from within the black community, Professor Copeland notes that the "contemporary movement among Black Catholics was not without dissension and conflict." She claims that "Black Catholics were never in complete accord over the function and organizational structure of the NOBC [National Office of Black Catholics]." The role of the laity was also problematic:

> the clergy, sisters, and brothers were well-schooled in ecclesiastical protocol; at times they used this to disadvantage the laity. The new emphasis on lay leadership was no less threatening to Black clerics and religious, than it was to their white colleagues. Long denied pastorates and other appropriate outlets for their talent, they were not always eager to share leadership with the laity.[77]

According to Copeland each of these movements made an important and complementary contribution to confronting racism.

> The Black Catholic Clergy Caucus always has formed a visible and vigorous vanguard confronting ecclesiastical racism at every turn, collectively offering Black Catholics and our activities an offensive and defensive pastorate, and initiating communication with our

> counterparts in Africa.... But it was the establishment and staffing of
> the various national offices, especially those of the National Office
> for Black Catholics and the National Black Sisters' Conference, that
> *put teeth and soul into the shaping of a distinctive African American*
> *Catholicism.* These two organizations carved out space for the devel-
> opment of leadership, for study, for spiritual and psychological for-
> mation, for the creative intellectual and pastoral interpretation of
> the Black Catholic experience in the United States.[78]

The newly emerging national church organizations in the 1970s are evidence of the awakening and revolution underway within the black community. The explosion of organizations reflected the creativity and sense of solidarity that was evident as African Americans continued to confront the racism that was part of their church and their society.

BLACK CATHOLIC THEOLOGY

As we have noted, the leaders of the civil rights movement were pre-dominantly Protestant, as were most black theologians. Professor Diana Hayes explains that "Catholicism, because of its hierarchical and institu-tional structures, did not, prior to Vatican II, lend itself to the develop-ment of new ways of theologizing, especially by a people who played (or were allowed to play) only a marginal role in the Church." She is cau-tiously optimistic about the future: "This, however, is changing, slowly, but, I believe, inevitably."[79]

As a Protestant theologian, James Cone is less optimistic about the freedom of black Catholics within the Catholic church as they try to chal-lenge the Catholic tradition and remain members of the Catholic com-munity. He commented in 1984 that

> Although black Catholics challenge the racist character of the
> Catholic Church in the U.S.A., they have not made a significant aca-
> demic contribution in the field of black theology, and the reasons
> are at least partly obvious. The white power structure in the Catholic
> Church is so restrictive on what blacks can do or say that it is almost
> impossible to think creatively.... It will take a little more time, and
> the Catholic hierarchy will have to become a little more flexible in
> what it defines as theology and dogma, before a genuine black the-
> ology can emerge in the Catholic Church.[80]

Later, Cone reflects that "as a black Protestant who looks at the Catholic Church from the outside, the immensity of the task of trying to challenge the tradition of Catholic theology *and* also remain inside the church is so great that it overwhelms me."[81]

Professor Copeland, as a Roman Catholic, responded to Cone's critique by arguing that he is correct "insofar as theology has been a privileged meta-language to which African Catholics only recently have had full access." But, she counters, "his comments neither sufficiently appreciate the ways in which Black Catholic organizations have functioned over the past twenty years to provide occasions for leadership, fellowship, collaboration, and criticism; nor do they acknowledge the fidelity of Black Catholics to their own best interests. Moreover, we are not overwhelmed; this is precisely how we perceive our sacred task."

Copeland sees strength and solidarity in the Catholic church's global reality: "[Cone's] assessment also fails to situate Black Catholic thinkers within the larger international context of Catholic theologians, church scholars, and pastoral ministers who are women and men of color." But she agrees that the Catholic African American theological contribution is in its early stages. "...Given the dearth of formal-academically trained African American Catholic theologians, our intellectual appropriation and particular contribution to the ongoing development of Black theology await maturity. But some beginnings have been made."[82]

SPIRITUALITY

The Roman Catholic tradition has traditionally been more explicitly attentive to the question of spirituality than most Protestant traditions. While all Christian traditions have a spirituality, Roman Catholics have been more intentional about this area of theology and pastoral ministry. Because of this tradition of spirituality, black Catholics may be able to contribute to the development of black theology by linking spirituality with social ethics and systematic theology. The black Roman Catholic bishops began that process in their pastoral letter of 1984, *What We Have Seen and Heard.* In this letter they speak of four major characteristics of black spirituality that they identify as contemplative, holistic, joyful, and communitarian. Such a spirituality can enrich both black theology and white theology and spirituality.[83]

TO SERVE AS A BRIDGE

Diana Hayes uses the image of a "bridge" to speak of the role of black Catholic theology. Black Catholic theology can help break down the denominational boundaries that separate black Catholics and black Protestants. It can serve as a bridge between the two groups by "reminding them of their shared histories, recalling their shared heritage." She goes on to say that black Catholic theology can also serve as a bridge between the larger communities of American Protestants and Catholics, "because they share a heritage as Christians seeking to live up to the ideals first set forth in our earliest beginnings that 'all are created equal and are endowed by their creator with certain unalienable rights,' including life, liberty and the pursuit of happiness." Hayes suggests that "after continued development and dialogue, it [black Catholic theology] can be a bridge between other religious faiths as well."

The final linking role of black Catholic theology: "Most important, it can be a door open to understanding for all Catholics of the true catholicity of their faith. And in its vision of a more just social order, it can catalyze the most creative elements of the religiosity of the poor."[84]

WORSHIP AND LITURGY

Father Clarence Rivers identifies the liturgical challenge for black Catholics: "The Catholic church will remain religiously ineffective in the black community unless it can effectively syncretize African culture with Catholic worship, just as the black Protestant church two centuries ago syncretized African culture and Biblical religion."[85] Rivers led the way in the late 1960s and '70s as he "single-handedly revolutionized the hymnody, the ritual form, the symbols, the mood and the atmosphere" of African American worship. Even before Vatican II Father Rivers had begun to compose, perform, and lecture on Catholic church music in a black cultural style. Shawn Copeland notes that "Black Catholics dove into the treasure chest of African American sacred music lifting up the spirituals, plundering the Baptist hymnal, tracking down organists competent in the Black musical genre and idiom—often from the Baptist congregation across town!"[86] Other changes gradually took place: the nationalist colors—red, black, and green—along with traditional African styles, patterns, and weaves were employed in the design of vestments and stoles. Crucifixes and statues of the mother of Jesus with African features began to appear. It was not long before hand-clapping, call and response, the shout, the tambourine, and the drum sounded in U.S. Catholic churches. Sister Shawn Copeland notes that this transformation of the European Roman liturgy into worship reflecting African cultural symbols began a process of "psychic healing."[87]

Brother Cyprian Rowe saw this process of acculturation as overcoming cultural ignorance and imperialism.

> Catholics of African descent have suffered intensely from the sterility of liturgical rites, because they have somewhere in their bones a tradition of worship in which the sung and spoken word have been fused into celebrations of joy. Afro-Americans are therefore among the first to realize that it is a certain cultural ignorance, and even cultural imperialism, that have resulted in their almost total exclusion from worship, except as spectators.[88]

The recovery of the African American heritage includes a recovery and an inculturation of black ritual, song, and dance. This process is filled with tension and conflict as well as joy and appreciation. Despite the conflicts the process of cultural adaptation of the liturgy must continue, for "African American Catholics are refusing to remain in the shadows, as strangers in a strange land, mouthing words and phrases that do not speak of their experience with the Church...."[89]

As a liturgist, Bishop Wilton Gregory defends the right of African Americans to "affirm ourselves and exalt our heritage." He addressed his fellow African Americans with confidence: "Jealously and unashamedly, we have seized the challenge and the opportunity to affirm ourselves and exalt our heritage with a resultant impatience with individuals or institutions that curtail, critique, or even question either these processes or their tentative conclusions." He warns against the danger of "cultural solipsism, the unfortunate situation where a culture cannot benefit from the legitimate and healthy exchange between itself and other cultures."[90] This danger is present for both the African Americans and the Euro-Americans. The challenge in the cultural adaptations of worship is how to encourage worship and rites that are culturally diverse and at the same time maintain a sense of unity. Because the Roman Catholic church is so clearly a church rooted in many cultures, it could and should help to lead the way in gracefully encouraging diverse cultural expression within the one community of the church.

STILL A "BLATANTLY RACIST SOCIETY"

In 1979 the bishops of the American Catholic church admitted that "racism is an evil which endures in our society and in our church."[91] On the tenth anniversary of their pastoral letter on racism, *Brothers and Sisters to Us*, the bishops reflected on the intransigence of racism: "The question of why we have receded into a blatantly racist society this late in the twentieth century looms larger than life itself. Why has the Church been so vocal nationally and so silent locally? A part of the answer relates to racism in the Church itself, as well as in other society institutions."[92]

A sanguine and almost angry tone is struck in this anniversary document—an anniversary with very little to celebrate. "In spite of all that has been said and written about racism in the last twenty years, very little—if anything at all—has been done in Catholic education; such as it was yesterday, it is today."[93]

In 1992 the diocese of Rochester, New York, named its own racist practices and policies in the report of its Task Force on Societal Injustice. The headlines read, "Study finds racist attitudes in Catholic diocese" and the story continued, "The Roman Catholic Diocese of Rochester is guilty of the same kind of institutional racism that some say contributed to the Los Angeles riots, according to a task force appointed by the bishop. Racism exists in its practices and policies, having to do with everything from hiring to worship...."[94]

In 1997 the Catholic Archdiocese of Chicago was forced to face the lethal racism in its midst. Three white teenage boys who attended or graduated from Catholic high schools mercilessly beat a 13-year-old African American teenager, Lenard Clark. Clark was in a coma for a week. How do we explain such racist behavior from students in the Catholic community?

Professor Diana Hayes of Georgetown University responds that

> In many ways, the situation for Blacks in the Catholic Church in the United States has not changed. Despite papal and other documents which have allegedly opened doors to new forms of expression in the Church and new ways of "being" Church together across racial, class, and gender lines, in actuality the unique contribution of a people, forged in slavery and oppression, yet full of hope and love, is still ignored or condemned as inappropriate.[95]

Some would even question if a people "full of hope and love" reflects the black community today. That hope and love have been destroyed by powerful personal and systemic forces in the community. Some even use the word "nihilism" to describe the loss of hope and love in the black community.

A LACK OF HOPE?

The insightful social philosopher Cornel West does *not* paint a picture of the black community that is full of hope and love. As an African American he sees signs of just the opposite. The "most basic issue now

facing black America: *the nihilistic threat to its very existence."* He goes on
to explain, "This threat is not simply a matter of relative economic depri-
vation and political powerlessness—though economic well-being and
political clout are requisites for meaningful black progress. It's primarily
a question of speaking to the profound sense of psychological depression, personal worthlessness, and social despair so widespread in black
America."[96] A few pages later he explains that nihilism in the black community is not a philosophical doctrine, rather, "it is, far more, the lived
experience of coping with a life of horrifying meaninglessness, hopelessness, and (most important) lovelessness." This nihilism has devastating
results: "The frightening result is a numbing detachment from others and
a self-destructive disposition toward the world. Life without meaning,
hope, and love breeds a cold-hearted, mean-spirited outlook that
destroys both the individual and others."[97]

Cornel West sees two reasons why the threat of hopelessness and lovelessness is so powerful in the black community: (1) "the saturation of
market forces and market moralities in black life," and (2), the present
crisis in black leadership."[98]

West believes that "the recent market-driven shattering of black civil
society—black families, neighborhoods, schools, churches, mosques—
leaves more and more black people vulnerable to daily lives endured with
little sense of self and fragile existential moorings."[99] Whites and blacks are
both affected by the damaging impact of market morality—a morality that
focuses on pleasure, comfort, convenience, and sexual stimulation. In this
market morality people are turned into objects for personal pleasure.

> Like all Americans, African-Americans are influenced greatly by the
> images of comfort, convenience, machismo, femininity, violence, and
> sexual stimulation that bombard consumers. These seductive images
> contribute to the predominance of the market-inspired way of life over
> all others and thereby edge out nonmarket values—love, care, service to
> others—handed down by preceding generations. The predominance of
> this way of life among those living in poverty-ridden conditions, with a
> limited capacity to ward off self-contempt and self-hatred, results in the
> possible triumph of the nihilistic threat in black America.[100]

Within the *market morality* is a destructive racism: "Under these circumstances black existential angst derives from the lived experience of
ontological wounds and emotional scars inflicted by white supremacist
beliefs and images permeating U.S. society and culture. These beliefs and

images attack black intelligence, black ability, black beauty, and black character daily in subtle and not-so-subtle ways."[101]

West points to the *underlying anger and pessimism* that racist attitudes have caused in the black community.

> The accumulated effect of the black wounds and scars suffered in a white-dominated society is a deep-seated anger, a boiling sense of rage, and passionate pessimism regarding America's will to justice.... Sadly, the combination of the market way of life, poverty-ridden conditions, black existential angst, and the lessening of fear of white authorities has directed most of the anger, rage, and despair toward fellow black citizens, especially toward black women, who are the most vulnerable in our society and in black communities.[102]

West does not leave us without hope. The response to this devastating nihilism is what he calls a "politics of conversion" that focuses on new models of leadership and an *ethic of love and care*.

> New models of collective black leadership must promote a version of this politics. Like alcoholism and drug addiction, nihilism is a disease of the soul. It can never be completely cured, and there is always the possibility of relapse. But there is always a chance for conversion—a chance for people to believe that there is hope for the future and a meaning to struggle. This chance rests neither on an agreement about what justice consists of nor on an analysis of how racism, sexism, or class subordination operate. Such arguments and analyses are indispensable. But a politics of conversion requires more. Nihilism is not overcome by arguments or analyses; it's tamed by love and care. Any disease of the soul must be conquered by a turning of one's soul. This turning is done through one's own affirmation of one's worth— and affirmation fueled by the concern of others. A love ethic must be at the center of a politics of conversion.[103]

Is not the "politics of conversion" another way of speaking about the church's mission to announce the reign of God? If the churches do not take up their role in addressing this "disease of the soul," who will? The credibility of the church is on the line. If the church does not root out the sin of racism it will be an obstacle to the reign of God and the Good News of liberation, and the white church will be depriving itself of the richness of becoming a truly "catholic" community.

Conclusion

The 1960s were a time of revolution; a revolution against racism, a revolution against authoritarianism and the misguided war in Southeast Asia. These societal revolutions hit the streets and cities of the United States. A less violent revolution erupted within the tradition-bound halls of the Roman Catholic church.

In the Second Vatican Council, the Roman church *began* to hear the voices from the Third World, and the church *began* to identify with the poor and suffering in a new way. This shifting of attention from Europe to the Third World would continue into the next decades with the emergence of liberation theology—filled with controversy and struggle. The Roman Catholic church also had to confront persistent racism in society and in the church. Important changes have taken place within the church and society to dismantle personal, institutional, and cultural racism. But racism continues to weave its insidious poison in our institutions and our cultural attitudes. The revolutions that erupted in the 1960s have cooled, and yet the conversion they envisioned has yet to be fully realized.

Discussion Questions

1. *Gaudium et Spes* was the first document of any ecumenical council to be addressed to the people of the entire world. What does that reveal about the shift in tone, focus, and methodology of the social teachings of the Catholic church?

2. In reading this chapter did you learn something about racism within the Catholic church that you did not know before? What does that tell you about the church's attention or lack of attention to this issue?

3. Evaluate and discuss the strengths and weaknesses of the early organizations within Catholicism that addressed racism, including the Black Catholic Congresses, Federated Colored Catholics, and the Catholic Interracial Council.

4. Why is it so important for African American Catholics to have priests who are African Americans?

5. How does black Catholic theology confront the lack of hope in the black community described by Professor Cornel West?

6

Challenging Structures: *Populorum Progressio* and the Labor Organizing of Cesar Chavez

For many U.S. Roman Catholics Pope Paul VI is best remembered for his controversial encyclical on birth control, *Humanae Vitae,* issued on July 25, 1968. While it is true that the debate about birth control lingered like a dark cloud over his papacy he also made an immense contribution to the unfolding of Catholic social teaching during his fifteen years (1963-1978) as bishop of Rome.

Giovanni Montini brought to the papacy a long-standing concern for social justice and the active role of the church in addressing these concerns. As archbishop of Milan he was nicknamed "the red Cardinal" because of his advocacy of the church's "social engagement."[1] He also was one of the bishops in the first session of Vatican II who called for a document to address the church's role in the world—along with Dom Helder Camara, Suenens, and others.

About the same time in the San Joaquin valley of California, a 26-year-old Mexican American, Cesar Chavez, began organizing farm workers. Chavez, as we shall see, was a charismatic and effective labor organizer in the best of the Catholic tradition. Although these two men lived in worlds apart, they both contributed in significant ways to the unfolding of the Catholic social tradition—a tradition effective in word and deed.

Part I. Pope Paul VI and *Populorum Progressio*

In 1963, the first year of his papacy, while the commissions of the Council were beginning their work on *Gaudium et Spes*, Pope Paul began the process of drafting his first social encyclical. The two documents, *Gaudium et Spes* and *Populorum Progressio*, are linked by more than just chronology.[2] In *Populorum Progressio* Pope Paul was clearly carrying out the vision of Vatican II, which sought to be in dialogue with the world, as church and society addressed current social issues.

Pope Paul had four specific motivations for writing *Populorum Progressio*. First, he wanted to emphasize the problem of development in language that was more direct, spontaneous, vigorous, and even more personal that the conciliar text, which was a "compromise" document written by a committee to achieve unanimity. Second, while the council discussed problems familiar to the authors of the document, the majority of whom were from the "developed" countries, Pope Paul wanted to stress plans for the "developing countries." Third, he wished to continue his series of personal denunciations of injustice as he had done on his trip to Bombay in December 1964 and in his address to the United Nations in October 1965. Finally, Pope Paul wanted to emphasize the connection between development and peace, as summarized in his belief that "development is the new name for peace" (par. 86).[3]

During the early 1960s there were competing notions of development, including the "American" emphasis on growth in the Gross National Product, the U.N.'s approach of economic growth and social change, and the "French school," which discussed development as integral, that is, including growth in spiritual values.[4] Because he was something of a Francophile already, it wasn't hard for Pope Paul to side with the French school. So he asked the French Dominican economist Louis Lebret, O.P., to be the primary editor. Lebret served admirably in that capacity until his untimely death in 1966. Msgr. Paul Poupard, another Frenchman picked up the reins and brought the process to its conclusion.

In commenting on the "behind the scenes" work on the text Poupard explained that the pope wanted a letter that would be conclusive and energetic in orienting the church and public opinion toward development. The authors drew upon a variety of sources including the letters and documents of bishops and the curial resources of the Vatican. In addition, theologians, economists, statespeople, and internationally known persons were consulted. The working language of the drafting process was French, although other languages were used in the drafts as they were sent out for evaluation by the various consultants. The encyclical went through seven editions; the first was dated September 1964, and the last, February 16, 1967. The pope read and annotated these drafts, as did other experts and consultants from various countries. On February 20, 1967, the pope approved the final draft with the words "sta tutto bene" (everything is fine). The text was then translated into various languages, indexed, and printed for promulgation on Easter Sunday, March 26, 1967.[5]

CONTEXT

"Development" was the watchword of the day in the mid-1960s for the reform-minded; "revolution" was the goal of the radicals; and "liberation" was beginning to emerge as a dominant perspective for many Christians, especially in Latin America. The United Nations was in the midst of its "Second Development Decade"; the two superpowers, the U.S. and the U.S.S.R., were using development and military aid to line up allies in the Third World. Military interventions were used to try to control the destiny of the "less developed" nations: President Johnson had sent 14,000 troops into the Dominican Republic when a leftist president, Juan Bosch, was elected; he had also escalated the U.S. commitment in South Vietnam to 400,000 troops.

Radical priests like Camilo Torres in Colombia left the security of the sanctuary and took up arms with revolutionary forces. Torres was killed by the Colombian military. The American Maryknoll missionaries Thomas and Marjorie Melville were expelled from Guatemala for being critical of the government. Father Gustavo Gutiérrez, shaken by the events in Latin America, was giving shape to a new perspective in theological reflection that would be called "liberation theology." Racial unrest continued in the United States with the civil rights movement in full swing, as well as riots in the hot summer of 1967 in Newark and Detroit.

In 1967 the newly formed United Farm Workers Union (UFW), was in the midst of a five-year strike of the grape growers in California. In the previous spring Cesar Chavez had led a 300-mile pilgrimage from Delano to the state capitol in Sacramento to recommit the UFW movement to nonviolent change in the midst of the persecution and violent tactics of some of the growers.

Into this world Pope Paul VI added his word and social vision for full and integral human development. While the Catholic community was still reeling from the changes of Vatican II, the pope did not want the church to focus all of its energies on the internal issues of change, but sought to address the problems of human and economic development, primarily in the poorer nations.

CONTENT

In the section entitled "The Data of the Problem" (par. 6-11), the pope described a series of problems that, if not addressed, could lead to "being swept away toward types of messianism...violent popular reactions, agitation toward insurrection, and a drifting towards totalitarian ideologies." He named:

- frustrated aspirations, that is, the rightful aspirations of freedom from misery, finding adequate subsistence, health, unemployment, education, and freedom from violence to human dignity—all these are frustrated by the poverty and violence of the real conditions;

- the legacy of colonialism with its inadequate economic structures;

- the widening gap between rich and poor: "The imbalance is on the increase: some produce a surplus of foodstuffs, others cruelly lack them and see their exports made uncertain";

- the "scandal of glaring inequalities not merely in the enjoyment of possessions but even more in the exercise of power";

- and the conflict between traditional civilizations and elements of the industrial society that destroy traditional social patterns and frameworks.

If these issues were not addressed the pope believed that "the very life of the poor nations, civil peace in developing countries, and world peace itself are at stake." These injustices threaten "so many innocent children...the peace of the world and the future of civilization" (par. 80).

In the face of these problems and temptations to violence Pope Paul offered a social vision of "authentic development" that promoted the good of every person and the whole person (par. 14). This is not just economic development; but "the transition from less human conditions to those which are more human" (par. 20), physically, socially, and spiritually.

To begin the process of integral development the pope preached the following duties, which are made explicit in concrete strategies:

- human solidarity, which is made real in "the aid that rich nations must give to the developing countries";

- social justice, which is expressed in "the rectification of inequitable trade relations between powerful and weak nations" (par. 44);

- universal charity, which includes welcoming emigrant workers, treating others across national boundaries as equals and as brothers and sisters (par. 66-75).

The pope's encyclical caused quite a reaction, especially the sections on private property and expropriation or nationalization of unused lands (par. 23-24), capitalism (par. 26), and the discussion of revolution (par. 31). Let me explain.

Private Property

Pope Paul placed significant restrictions on private property. Theologian John Pawlikowski notes that "he goes well beyond the positions of Leo XIII, Pius XI, and even John XXIII."[6] The encyclical first noted the long-standing teaching of St. Ambrose, "'You are not making a gift of our possessions to the poor person. You are handing over to him what is his. For what has been given in common for the use of all, you have arrogated to yourself. The world is given to all, and not only to the rich." Then the pope elaborated, using quotes from his 1965 letter to the 52nd Session of the French Social Weeks.

> ...private property does not constitute for anyone an absolute and unconditioned right. No one is justified in keeping for his exclusive use what he does not need, when others lack necessities. In a word,

> "according to the traditional doctrine as found in the Fathers of the
> Church and the great theologians, the right to property must never
> be exercised to the detriment of the common good." (par. 23)

The pope then applied this teaching to today's situation and the possibility of expropriation. "If certain landed estates impede the general prosperity because they are extensive, unused, or poorly used, or because they bring hardship to peoples or are detrimental to the interests of the country, *the common good sometimes demands their expropriation*" [emphasis added]. He also condemned the rich who transfer their wealth to another country "purely for their own advantage, without care for the manifest wrong they inflict on their country by doing this" (par. 24). These are strong words that clearly challenge those who see the rights to private property as an absolute right.

Denunciation of the Abuses of Capitalism
In paragraph 26 Pope Paul VI went on to criticize unrestrained capitalism and profit as a key motive:

> But it is unfortunate that on these new conditions of society a system
> has been constructed which considers profit as the key motive for eco-
> nomic progress, competition as the supreme law of economics, and
> private ownership of the means of production as an absolute right
> that has no limits and carries no corresponding social obligation. This
> unchecked liberalism leads to dictatorship rightly denounced by Pius
> XI as producing "the international imperialism of money." One can-
> not condemn such abuses too strongly by solemnly recalling once
> again that the economy is at the service of man.

These words caused a reaction among some Americans and Europeans in the business community. They were so concerned that they flew to Rome for a three-day meeting to discuss the consequences of the encyclical in developing countries, especially in Latin America. Participants included Mr. George Moore, president of the First National Bank (U.S.A), Mr. Peterson, President of the Bank of America, U.S. Senator Farley, Signor Agnelli, president of FIAT, Don Alfonso Siervo, president of Banco Iberico, and members of the hierarchy.

In reporting on the meeting, *The Tablet* from London noted that

> The repercussions of the encyclical had been enormous, and the
> American representatives had come to Rome with the distinct pur-

pose of ensuring the openness of discussions and of qualifying various objections and difficulties that had arisen over the interpretation of the encyclical—in particular par. 26, where the Latin and English texts differed.[7]

The primary concern was whether the pope in referring to capitalism could have been applying a condemnation of all forms of capitalism or a condemnation of any one particular form. The group felt the need to clarify this point to avoid misinterpretation by the Latin American countries was well as by the enemies of the church. The main conclusion reached was that "if the pope was condemning any aspect of capitalism, he was condemning its abuse."[8] Such was the diplomatic solution. Pope Paul met with the group but only commended them for their study of the encyclical.[9]

The encyclical must have been hitting some nerves if it caused such a reaction in the business community. They were afraid that the document would be used by those critical of capitalism in developing countries, and that the church would be lending moral support to such efforts.

Revolution

Pope Paul urged nonviolent means of social change. But he did leave the door open to a justified revolution where there is long-standing tyranny that denies human rights and harms the common good. He wrote:

> There are certainly situations whose injustice cries to heaven. When whole populations destitute of necessities live in a state of dependence barring them from all initiative and responsibility, and all opportunity to advance culturally and share in social and political life. Recourse to violence, as a means to right these wrongs to human dignity, is a grave temptation. (par. 30)

The next paragraph reads:

> We know, however, that a revolutionary uprising—save where there is manifest, long-standing tyranny which would do great damage to fundamental personal rights and dangerous harm to the common good of the country—produces new injustices, throws more elements out of balance and brings on new disasters. A real evil should not be fought against at the cost of greater misery.

The phrase between the dashes shows that, according to the church's moral teaching, there may be times when a violent revolution may be morally permissible. This teaching is more than an abstract ethical discussion. It would be used in various Latin American countries to justify a violent overthrow of the government. For instance, many in the Nicaraguan church came to this conclusion after fifty years of the Somoza family dictatorship. Another case where a revolution was also deemed justifiable was in the Philippines.

The use of violence in a revolutionary situation is a complex question. The pope stated his preference for nonviolent means, but he did not say that revolutionary violence is to be rejected in every situation.

EVALUATION

In evaluating the encyclical, I would identify three strengths and one major weakness.[10] The strengths are a) a critique of capitalism when it does not serve the common good, b) a rejection of "trickle down" development, and c) his ecumenical leadership in word and deed.

After the positive and optimistic thrust of *Gaudium et Spes*, Pope Paul's encyclical returned to a stance that is positive yet critical of capitalism. The response of the businessmen who flew to Rome to clarify *Populorum Progressio*'s teaching shows that they realized that the pope was raising many questions about "business as usual." The "values" of the capitalist marketplace—competition, profit, private ownership of the means of production—are identified as leading to an abusive situation wherein the economy is not serving people (par. 26). The commitment to the common good leads the pope to be critical of policies, practices, and institutions that thwart the development of the whole person and every person. This communitarian social vision challenges those in the business community whose only goal is profit.

Second, the encyclical did not follow the predominant theory of development in the West, which held that the developing nations would follow the "stages of growth" of the advanced nations and that the wealth created in the process would inevitably trickle down until it reached the poorest persons. The "stages of growth" approach to "modernization" was challenged by various Third World ethicists and social scientists, claiming that it really creates a cycle of dependency. These analyses would provide the foundation for liberation theologies that challenged the various cycles of dependency (as we shall see in the chapter on liberation theology). By not accepting the "trickle down" approach, the pope situated church teaching between the two approaches. These debates would emerge in the 1970s and 1980s. Pope Paul clearly avoided endorsing the myth that all developing nations would simply have to pass through "stages of economic growth" as did the U.S. and northern Europe.[11] This model of development was very popular in the 1960s, but the encyclical offered a broader and more comprehensive vision of human and economic development.

A third contribution of *Populorum Progressio* was to provide leadership in the ecumenical community in addressing the concerns of the developing nations both in word and in deed. Many of the other Christian churches and the World Council of Churches were also involved in issues of Third World development. This encyclical provided the social vision and motivation that put the Catholic church on the front lines of human and economic development in the poorer nations. Robert McAfee Brown noted that "...On the front of common concern for mankind, Pope Paul is taking vigorous and dynamic leadership, and that in this increasingly central part of the ecumenical task, non-Catholics will have to scramble simply to keep up with him."[12]

The pope wanted his support of integral development to be more than simply verbal and moral. After his visit to Medellín, Colombia, in 1968 the pope established the *"Populorum Progressio* Fund" in that country. The million dollars for the fund came from the sale of Vatican property in Paris and was used to resettle 847 poor Colombian families on 44,000 acres near Popayan, Colombia. After ten years the small project had exceeded expectations: 57 community businesses were established, 6,602 family members had benefited from the schools, health center, new homes, and the agro-businesses that were established.[13]

Another concrete sign of concern for development in the ecumenical era of the Second Vatican Council was the establishment of a jointly sponsored office of the World Council of Churches and the Pontifical Commission *Iustitia et Pax* known as the Society for Development and Peace (Sodepax). In 1968 this semi-independent agency was established in Geneva with an American, George Dunne, S.J., as the first director. The agency sponsored a number of successful international conferences and published a journal, *Church Alert,* to promote ecumenical understanding and cooperation in efforts of development and peace. This was the first agency sponsored by the Vatican and the World Council of Churches and seemed to augur continued collaboration and the possibility of the Catholic church joining the World Council of Churches. But in the early 1970s the momentum shifted and the activities of Sodepax were curtailed because of Vatican politics between the pontifical commission *Iustitia et Pax* and the secretary of state. Sodepax was allowed to die in 1980 with no institutional replacement.[14]

Despite its relatively brief life Sodepax is the kind of cooperation for development initiated by the vision of *Populorum Progressio,* and the project in Colombia is a down-to-earth example of what is possible when the church, government, and private initiatives cooperate to improve the lives of the poor. This is part of the legacy of *Populorum Progressio.* As we shall see, the organizing of Cesar Chavez was another example of the encyclical's moral and spiritual vision.

A Weakness: Lack of Analysis of Power

While *Populorum Progressio* does support the right of people to be agents of their own development (par. 15), the overwhelming thrust of the letter is addressed to the rich and powerful to change their values and institutional arrangements (such as trade policies) to assist the poorer nations. In effect, the letter is an *appeal to the altruism of the wealthy nations* to respond to the needs of the developing nations. The duties of the "better-off nations" are solidarity, justice, and universal charity, which are rooted in "brotherhood" (par. 44ff.).

While we need a social vision of the common humanity of all peoples, as a strategy for social change the call to altruism does not fully face the underlying reality of power and the empowerment of the poor. Appeals to altruism alone are naive and may often support the continued domination by the powerful and reinforce an attitude of paternalism toward the poor.

The Catholic "optimism" about appealing to altruism needs to be challenged by the "realism" of the Protestant theologian Reinhold Niebuhr. Niebuhr was one of the first to chastise educators and preachers who believed that appeals to love would bring about social change. Niebuhr held that such approaches

> ...completely disregard the political necessities in the struggle for justice in human society by failing to recognize those elements in man's collective behavior which belong to the order of nature and can never be brought completely under the dominion of reason or conscience. They do not recognize that when collective power... exploits weakness, it can never be dislodged unless power is raised against it.[15]

While I support the social vision of the encyclical, I find the means of achieving the vision problematic. The political strategy of the encyclical is rooted in a harmonious social vision that relies on the goodwill and largess of the rich and powerful and is generally not attentive to strategies that empower the poor classes. As François Perroux, a French social ethicist, has said,

> Never in the course of the history of the West have we seen a class or a nation give up its own well-being for the benefit of a disadvantaged group. Effective altruism—exceptional enough with individuals—is never found in organized groups. Our societies are plutocracies...they tend to shape technocratic and political power groups to their own interests.[16]

A specific example of the problem of this lack of a power analysis in the letter can be seen in the question of land expropriation discussed in paragraphs 23 and 24. The encyclical teaches that it is the responsibility of public authorities to settle conflicts between the needs of the common good and the claims of the private landowners, and that, at times, the private lands may be taken over by the public authorities. While this may be sound moral reasoning, it is faulty political analysis, for we know that in most developing countries the "public authorities" are controlled by the interests of the wealthy landowners. The struggle for land reform in Brazil and other Latin American countries reveals that often the "public authorities" are part of the problem rather than part of the solution. The encyclical naively and idealistically implies that the public authorities are independent of these power relationships and are oriented to serving the common good.

The focus on power analysis and the need for empowerment emerged in various communities during the 1960s. Black power and the civil rights movement were expressions of this in the African American community. In the Hispanic community Cesar Chavez led the effort to empower farmer workers through labor organizing efforts. Various urban churches were joining neighborhood community organizations to coalesce power to effect change in their neighborhoods. The American bishops were also initiating an empowerment program in November of 1969, known as the Campaign for Human Development. But this awareness is not evident in the papal encyclical.

Pope Paul's encyclical, along with all other papal documents, is rooted in the classical Catholic social vision that views political power in an idealistic way. According to this vision of society, the purpose of the state is to serve the common good. The Catholic social tradition views political power "from the top down," rather than from the "bottom up." In *Populorum Progressio* political power is viewed as the responsibility and prerogative of those in leadership roles in the community—in business, government, education, and church. It is their duty and responsibility to care for the needs of the poor. Only in later documents do we begin to see the awareness that the poor themselves must become agents of change, that is, exercise political power through "empowerment." While the church's social tradition has supported the importance of workers organizing through unions, the Catholic church has been very slow in applying this strategy for empowerment on the global scene.

While official church documents have been slow to analyze the reality of political power, there were and are groups of church people who are confronting the issues of political and economic power through church-sponsored community organizations. Central to the purpose of a community organization or a union is the question of *power*. Generally the members of these organizations have experienced the reality of being "powerless" to effect change. "The whole purpose of a people's organization is to bring about change through the use of power. Those in the establishment who have power will naturally resist very strongly any attempt to change the power structure."[17] To be effective "people power" must be coalesced and organized. That is where the need for an "organization" and an organizer is apparent. As Gregory Pierce notes in his book *Activism That Makes Sense: Congregations and Community Organizations*, "Even congregations that decide to seek power as the means to defend their families and communities often do not know how to get it. Power is obtained through organization."[18]

In the next section we will look at a Catholic activist who was rooted in the Catholic social tradition and understood the importance of power analysis and empowerment.

Part II. Cesar Chavez—An Activist Rooted in Catholic Social Tradition

It is difficult to create an organization of poor, migrant farm workers who are empowered to speak for themselves rather than depend on the goodwill of those in power. Cesar Chavez was willing to tackle this very difficult task, but then he knew what a life of struggle was all about. As a Mexican American from the farms of Gila Valley (near Yuma), Arizona,

Cesar had known the poverty, despair, and discrimination that went with being a migrant worker. In 1949 when Chavez was 22, he was married and living in a barrio of San Jose, California, called "Sal Si Puede" (meaning "leave if you can").

MORAL AND SPIRITUAL VISION

In 1949 Chavez met a priest from San Francisco, Donald McDonnell, who was ministering to the farm workers. McDonnell began to tell Chavez about labor organizing during their late-night visits. Chavez recalled,

> He told me about social justice and the Church's stand on farm labor and *reading from the encyclicals of Pope Leo XIII,* in which he upheld labor unions. I would do anything to get the Father to tell me more about labor history. I began going to the Bracero camps with him to help with the Mass, to the city jail with him to talk to the prisoners, anything to be with him....[19]

The young Chavez was being shaped by his own experience of poverty and despair, but also by the vision and moral principles of Catholic social thought. *Rerum Novarum* and the Roman Catholic tradition were not distant, dusty principles for Chavez, but rather the building blocks for his emerging social, moral, and spiritual identity. But Cesar Chavez needed more than Catholic social principles and a vision, he needed the skills and training to learn how to organize and empower his people. These skills came through training in community organizing.

In 1952 Father McDonnell recommended Chavez as a potential leader to community organizer Fred Ross, who had come to the barrio to set up a local chapter of the Community Service Organization (CSO). At first Chavez was distrustful of this "gringo," but Ross earned his trust not only because of Ross' sincerity but by his vision "of a method through which Chavez, his friends in San Jose, and Chicanos across California could gain the power to change their lives." Chavez recalled that: "He did such a good job of explaining how poor people could build power that I could even taste it, I could feel it."[20] Chavez would discover a way to respond to his own deep feelings regarding the pain of racial discrimination and the immorality of the economic arrangements that had kept his family poor despite long hours of work in the hot sun.

Ross helped Chavez gain the skills and strategies of community organizing, which he combined with his own sense of social justice and spirituality. Fred Ross had been trained in the community organizing method of Saul Alinsky, who set up the Industrial Areas Foundation in Chicago. His approach included listening to the needs of the people, identifying the issues and grass-roots leaders, training the leaders, doing research on the issue, staging "actions" that bring attention to the issue and galvanize the people, reflection and evaluation, and continued strategies and "actions" until the goals are accomplished. Outside organizers are hired to serve as consultants and guides in this complex and conflictual process. Fred Ross was the organizer who brought these skills to San Jose.[21]

For ten years Chavez, Ross, and others worked to organize the Mexican Americans in California through the CSO. They made significant progress in exposing and fighting police brutality, school and job discrimination, and inadequate housing. They also sponsored successful citizenship classes and voter registration campaigns.

Chavez had hoped that the CSO would become a base from which to organize farm workers, but this was not to be. In the early 1960s CSO was attracting more middle class Chicanos—owners of small businesses, teachers, politicians, a few lawyers—who did not have the concerns of the poor and the migrant farm workers as their highest priority. The split along class lines was a source of frustration to Chavez as he wished to empower the poorer class of Mexican Americans. At the annual Community Service Organization convention in March 1962 Chavez shocked nearly everyone by resigning from CSO. As he reflected later his reasons were very straightforward: "I worked with CSO for ten years—they taught me how to organize. Then they got pretty middle class, didn't want to go into the fields. So I left."[22] He could have had a secure life as an organizer with CSO but Chavez remembered his roots and the needs of the workers in the fields. He took on the almost impossible task of organizing poor farm workers.

THE STRIKE

In the Spring of 1962 Chavez began building an organization of farm workers. He visited every farming community in the San Joaquin Valley inviting workers to join his militant and democratic association of farm workers.

> Having studied the history of farm worker strikes and feeling ebullient and strengthened by his success in the CSO, Chavez vowed to avoid some of the fatal mistakes of his predecessors. By using the techniques which he and Ross had learned in the CSO, Chavez

began organizing hundreds of house meetings—a Ross device—where he encouraged the farm workers to talk about their many problems. During these discussions he would suggest the possibility of working together to form an association in which they could resolve some of the mutual concerns. Carefully, he avoided alarming those who might fear a union because of previous bad experiences with organizers.[23]

The association would be led and paid for by the workers out of their subsistence wages. He asked $3.50 a month and promised no quick fixes, rather hard work and real risks. Chavez himself lived sacrificially. He took no salary but continued, when he had time, to work in the fields with his wife, Helen, to support their family.

By the fall of 1962—just as the Second Vatican Council was beginning—Cesar Chavez was able to call together a few hundred workers—men, women, and children—to the founding convention of the National Farm Workers Association on September 30. This small group of migrants met in a dusty, abandoned theater in Fresno under the leadership of Chavez and two other organizers, Dolores Hertz and Antonio Ordain. This new association was a sign of hope for the farm workers, who faced immense odds.

The veteran organizer Saul Alinsky doubted that Chavez would be able to organize a large mass of farm workers into a union. Chavez himself realized the powers amassed against their fledgling union: "The power of the growers was backed by the political power of the police, the courts, the state and the federal laws and by the financial power of the big corporations, the banks and utilities."[24] But Chavez and the farmworkers found ways to be effective against these established power structures. Their success was due to skillful and persistent organizing, support from the churches and the depth of his spirituality and social commitment. Chavez would employ the traditional strategy of unionists, the strike. He also used the boycott, pilgrimage, and fasting. All of these strategies were used as nonviolent means of empowering his people and addressing the consciences of the growers and the larger community. This is how Chavez revealed his charismatic leadership, which combined organizing "know how" with a solid Catholic spirituality rooted in his Hispanic culture.

In September 1965 the members of the National Farm Workers Association, NFWA, were asked to join a strike started by another farm workers union, the Agricultural Workers Organizing Committee, AWOC, of the AFL-CIO against the table grape growers in the southern San Joaquin valley around Delano, California. On September 8 about 700 workers, mostly Filipino, walked out of the vineyards at the urging of AWOC. Although Chavez did not yet believe his union was strong enough to maintain a successful strike he was committed to the right of the workers to speak on their own behalf. The 1200 members of the union voted in favor of the strike; a mandate that Chavez accepted. But he quickly called for a second vote—that the workers commit themselves to maintain nonviolent tactics during the strike. They committed themselves to the principle of nonviolence from the beginning.[25]

In 1966 the NFWA and the AWOC merged to form the United Farm Workers Union, UFW, with Cesar Chavez as the director and AWOC's Larry Itliong as the associate director. The strike, *la huelga*, which began in September 1965, lasted for five years before contracts were signed with 140 grape growers and the United Farm Workers. During this time many church people and college students joined the strikers and supported the call for a national table grape boycott. But at the heart of the effort was Cesar Chavez: "With dogged persistence the union pursued its goals under the profound spiritual motivation of Chavez' leadership, which gave his *huelgistas* the backbone to persevere. It was this spiritual leadership, more than any other factor, which allowed this strike eventually to succeed where others, throughout history, had failed."[26]

The United Farm Workers Union–AFL/CIO under Chavez's direction was an atypical labor union. Chavez drew upon Mexican American culture and religious traditions to shape a union that was as religiously expressive as it was politically savvy. Here was a union that was not only committed to nonviolence, its leadership was in solidarity with the workers and shared their life-style. This union had a unique integrity and spirituality. And because of this, it attracted widespread support among the middle class, other trade unions—even international unions—and the support of the Catholic, Protestant, and Jewish religious communities.

THE BOYCOTT

In addition to the strike Chavez used three other means of organizing support for the farm workers' cause. The first was the boycott. The boycott called on consumers not to buy table grapes and not to shop at stores, especially the giant chain stores (e.g., Safeway in the western states), that sold nonunion grapes. The grape boycott helped to focus nationwide attention on the farm worker movement. Churches all over the country began responding to the call to boycott table grapes. The grape boycott and strike were successfully concluded in 1970 after 140 grape growers signed contracts with the UFW. Subsequently a lettuce boycott was called in 1970 to bring the lettuce growers to the bargaining table. The lettuce growers tried to undercut the UFW by establishing contracts with the Teamsters' Union. The Teamsters' Union did not really represent the farm workers but was in collusion with the growers. These contracts with the Teamsters' Union were called "sweetheart contracts" because the two parties—the growers and the union—were really partners or "sweethearts" in their common effort to subvert the legitimate organizing efforts of the UFW. In 1973 when the grape contracts expired the grape growers also signed sweetheart contracts with the Teamsters, so a second grape boycott was called. In 1974 a boycott was called of Gallo wines, which were made from California grapes.

Chavez sent farm workers to major cities in the U.S. and in Canada to urge people to support the boycotts. This was a difficult mission for these unsophisticated farm workers, many of whom knew little English and were intimidated by the large urban centers. But their message was heard, and they returned home telling how they had gained self-esteem and confidence.[27]

LA PEREGRINACIO—THE PILGRIMAGE

The second strategy used by Chavez was the pilgrimage, la Peregrinacio. The pilgrimage is a time-honored religious custom of traveling to a sacred location. For Mexicans the tradition of pilgrimage to the shrine of Our Lady of Guadalupe in Mexico City, often traveling the last mile on their knees, is part of their spiritual heritage.

Chavez announced a pilgrimage from Delano to the steps of the state capitol in Sacramento in 1966 after the Schenley Company "accidentally" sprayed, from the air, some union pickets with a poisonous pesticide. The 300-mile pilgrimage, a dramatic response to this heinous act, was chosen because of its potential impact on the public conscience, but also as a way for the farm workers to renew their commitment to nonviolence in the midst of persecution and violence.

Chavez incorporated civic and religious symbols in the pilgrimage. Here is how he described the first day, March 16:

> At the front we had the American flag, the Mexican flag, the flag
> from the Philippines and the banner of Our Lady of Guadalupe.
> People wore hats bearing the union's red hatbands with the black
> eagle, and many of the strikers wore red armbands with the black
> eagle and carried the *huelga* flags. Out in the country it was a thin,
> serpentine line inching its way along the flat valley with lots of red
> flags silhouetted against the blue sky. The first day there were more
> than a hundred marching as some of the wives and kids had come.
> There were about 70 who planned to walk all the way.[28]

On Easter Sunday a crowd of about 8,000 was waiting to welcome the
marchers as they approached the capitol building. The pilgrimage was an
organizing and spiritual success. During the march relations with the
AFL/CIO were strengthened as the AFL/CIO's national director of organizing, William Kircher, came to march with Chavez. By the time the
marchers reached Stockton Chavez received a call from Schenley's legal
counsel offering to recognize the union and sign a contract.

For Chavez the spiritual value of the pilgrimage was important. The
discipline of the march had tested the strikers' endurance for the long
hard struggle ahead. The pilgrimage gave the workers an opportunity to
demonstrate nonviolent action and to build public support.

THE FAST

The fast grew out of Cesar's religious and cultural background and was
used both for his own spirit and for the spiritual needs of his followers.
The fast came when Chavez felt the nonviolent commitment of union
members had weakened. Some the strikers, due to attacks and harassment from the growers and their hired thugs, wanted to strike back and
show their machismo—their "manly courage."

Cesar Chavez undertook a fast of water only on February 15, 1968,
which he maintained for 25 days. Each night, Father Mark Day would preside over a eucharistic liturgy in a warehouse near the room where Chavez
was fasting. Hundreds of people would gather for the liturgy, and then a
number of them would take turns visiting their union leader as he lay in
bed. On March 10th more than 4,000 people gathered in a Delano public park to celebrate a Mass and mark the end of the fast. Senator Robert
Kennedy sat next to the feeble Chavez. He had lost 35 pounds and would
suffer from the debilitating effects of the fast for many months. During

the offertory a United Auto Worker official came forward with a $50,000 check given by the auto workers to support the young union.[29]

While some growers and others were cynical of the fast and called it a publicity stunt, Chavez defended the deeper meaning of the fast.

> The fast is a very personal spiritual thing, and it is not done out of recklessness. It's not done out of a desire to destroy myself but is done out of a deep conviction that we can communicate to people, either those who are against us or for us, faster and more effectively, spiritually, than we can in any other way.[30]

Chavez fasted a number of times in the following years; sometimes others joined him. Although he suffered from the fasting he felt it was a necessary part of the struggle. It is clear that the social transformation Chavez was trying to effect was linked to and rooted in his deep spirituality.

HIS LEGACY
LINKING SPIRITUALITY AND SOCIAL TRANSFORMATION

Chavez began one last fast in April 1993. Now he was battling agribusiness, not in the fields but in the courtroom. Lawsuits were draining the UFW's monetary resources as well as Chavez's physical and emotional resources. In 1991 the union lost a $2.4 million suit. In April of 1993 he was back in Yuma, Arizona, where he had grown up, contesting a $5.4 million dollar judgment against his union. The suit was brought to court by Bruce Church Inc., a multi-million dollar agribusiness with vast land holdings in Arizona and California. Church Inc. had sued for damages done by a UFW boycott and had won. Chavez was back in court giving testimony as part of the appeal.

He was on an eight-day fast until the night before his death. Friends persuaded him to break his fast because they were concerned about his health. He ate a vegetarian meal, but he did not rise the next morning. David Martinez, the UFW secretary-treasurer found him lying on the bed, dressed, with court papers around him. By Chavez family standards, he died young at age 66—his father lived to 101 and his mother to 99.[31] The fasting and the 41-year struggle to organize farm workers had taken their toll on his body and spirit.

Cesar Chavez led a very unique labor organizing effort. He combined the best of his Saul Alinsky training with the faith and spirituality of his Roman Catholic tradition. While often being in the spotlight, his goal was always to empower in a nonviolent way his fellow farm workers in their struggle to overcome the injustice and discrimination in their lives. He once said, "The greatest tragedy is not to live and die—as we all must. The greatest tragedy is for a person to live and die without knowing the satisfaction of giving life to others."[32] Cesar Chavez was clearly one who consistently gave life to others.

CONVERGENCE AND DIVERGENCE

Both Pope Paul VI and Cesar Chavez have made historic contributions to the story of Catholic social teaching and activism, each in his own sphere of activity: one as a pastor and teacher, the other as a community organizer rooted in faith and his Hispanic spirituality. They shared common ground in their diverse ministry, and they also made distinctive contributions that at times complemented the other and, at other times, were unique and even contradictory. I would like to point out five areas of convergence and a few areas of divergence.

Convergence

1. Pope Paul VI and Cesar Chavez shared the same Roman Catholic *communitarian grounding*. Their commitment was to the common good of the entire society. This common good is jeopardized when the wealthy and powerful hoard the resources that were meant for all humanity. From the perspective of the common good Pope Paul was not afraid to challenge capitalism and the sacred cow of private property when it legitimizes drastic inequalities among the rich and the poor. For his part, Chavez worked to empower the voiceless, for without their active participation in the economic and political process, the common good is not served.

2. This activist and this bishop of Rome shared a *sacramental worldview* with a *spirituality that is rooted in commitment to social justice* and a faith that is lived out in the world. Pope Paul wove his concern about the poor throughout his ministry. It was not restricted to one or two encyclicals. His care for the poor and all of God's people was rooted in Catholic identity and was nourished by his personal spirituality and ministry. Chavez's convictions, perseverance, and choice of strategies were rooted in his faith and in his Mexican American culture. Faith is linked to the struggle for empowerment. In this struggle the sacramentals of one's religious faith—the pilgrimage, the fast, the liturgy—became the symbols of a deep faith and a longing for social justice.

3. In diverse ways, both leaders shared a conviction about *nonviolence as the way to bring about social change*. Chavez repeatedly called his union members not to retaliate when attacked physically and verbally by the growers' agents. When the farm workers were attacked, Chavez used the fast and the pilgrimage to focus their energy and transform their anger. Pope Paul urged nations and peoples to seek nonviolent ways of social change, but he did leave the door open to a "justified revolution" when the common good is threatened by the tyranny of the powerful.

4. Both the pope and this Mexican American organizer were *committed to the marginalized* of the earth. Pope Paul's vision is global: he pointed to the poor of the developing nations. Chavez focused on the marginalized farm workers within the most "developed" nation. While their strategies for change were diverse, their intended audience was the same: those whose basic needs were not being met.

5. Finally, these two men were committed to the *development of the whole person*, not just the economic needs of the person—as important as those are. Chavez and Paul VI were both deeply concerned about the moral and spiritual needs of the community.

Divergence

1. The most obvious difference for our two leaders was their starting point and who they saw as the primary *agent of change*. Cesar Chavez's starting point was rooted in the experience of the struggle of organizing farm workers. He was rooted in the day-to-day struggle of keeping a union together against immense odds and powerful forces. Cesar Chavez worked "from the bottom up" by organizing workers who were the primary agents of change. Pope Paul VI, on the other hand, stands as a teacher and moral leader trying to bend the Catholic moral tradition toward the needs of the poor in the developing nations. He appealed to those with power in the First World to respond out of altruism and Christian love to the needs of the poor. The thrust of the encyclical is generally "from the top down."

2. The question of *power* was handled differently by Pope Paul and Cesar Chavez. As discussed above, the papal teaching is predominantly focused on calling for an altruistic response on the part of those with resources to help those in need of economic development. While Chavez draws on the altruism of others who supported the fledgling union and its boycott, the centerpiece of his effort was to *organize the workers' power*. Chavez could not

avoid the question of political and economic power. He explicitly analyzed these issues as he galvanized countervailing power to bring about change.

Conclusion

The struggle of the farm workers continues in many areas of our country. Their struggle is less visible without a galvanizing and charismatic leader like Cesar Chavez. The power of the large agribusinesses seems to have drained the fiscal resources of the union. The expensive lawsuits have also drained its energy and focus. The mood of the country is also less supportive of unions and more suspicious of migrant farm workers— many of whom are immigrants. More recently, others have noted a resurgence of the UFW in the years since Chavez's death. Sal Alvarez who has worked with the farm workers for 32 years, and is a permanent deacon and director of the Interfaith Support Committee, sees a "resurgence of a coalition between church and labor."[33] Membership in the UFW has increased in recent years after dipping to a low of 21,000; it was 26,000 in April 1998. Union membership was at its peak in the early 1970s when 80,000 farm workers were part of the UFW. The most recent target is the working conditions of strawberry workers. In this struggle they have received the support of the U.S. Catholic Conference as well as almost every religious leader in California including Jewish and Protestant leaders.[34]

This chapter clearly shows the strength and richness of the Catholic legacy, which includes moral teachings and social activism rooted in a deep faith and spirituality. Pope and organizer gave hope to the marginalized and challenged the apathy of the comfortable. That prophetic challenge is still needed in society and the church.

The late 1960s was a vibrant time in Catholic social thought and action, as this chapter documents. While the catchword "development" may be outmoded by today's vocabulary, the vision painted by *Populorum Progressio* is compelling for every generation. The Catholic community is challenged today by its holistic vision of meeting the needs of the whole person. The community today is also challenged by the legacy of Cesar Chavez who creatively combined his concern for his fellow farm workers with his deep faith and culturally conditioned spirituality. He is one of the social saints of our time. His legacy and that of the leadership of Pope

Paul VI can encourage and awaken in us that same desire for justice and the development of all people—especially the poor.

Questions for Discussion

1. Pope Paul VI taught that private property is not an absolute and unconditional right for anyone. How does that teaching play out in concrete terms, and how do you think it would be received by most Americans?

2. *Populorum Progressio* leaves the door open to a justified revolution. What circumstances does Pope Paul say justify such an uprising? How do you evaluate that teaching?

3. In 1968 Pope Paul gave $1,000,000 to resettle 847 poor Colombian families. What is the role of such a "gesture"? What does it mean for your local Catholic community?

4. Cesar Chavez combined the social teaching of the church with the organizing skills of the Industrial Areas Foundation (Saul Alinsky). What does this tell us about effective social action?

5. Why is a lived spirituality so important for people like Cesar Chavez who work with the powerless for social justice?

7

Calls for Action: *Octogesima Adveniens, Justice in the World,* and Centers for Analysis and Advocacy

The effect of the Second Vatican Council's turning toward the world with a new attitude was permeating the worldwide church. Pope Paul VI give a new impetus to the church's concern about social issues with his powerful encyclical on the development of peoples—*Populorum Progressio*. The Latin American bishops met in Medellín, Colombia to examine the poverty of their countries in light of the theology of Vatican II. The pace continued with Pope Paul's 1971 apostolic letter, *Octogesima Adveniens* (*A Call to Action*). The 1971 synod of bishops meeting would bring attention to structural injustice and the need for action as a constitutive component of preaching the Gospel. The synod's statement is called *Justice in the World*. Catholics around the world would take up this call to action in the establishment of a variety of educational efforts, programs, and peace and justice centers. This chapter will examine the two remarkable documents associated with the 1971 synod, *Octogesima Adveniens* and *Justice in the World*, along with how a variety of social justice ministries helped to carry out that synod's vision. The Center of Concern, Woodstock Theological Center, Network, and Corporate Responsibility were the work of American religious orders committed to social justice as a "constitutive dimension of preaching the Gospel."

Part I. *Octogesima Adveniens*

Octogesima Adveniens, as the Latin title suggests (the "Coming Eightieth"), was the commemoration of the 80th anniversary of *Rerum Novarum.* The pope's letter was sent to Cardinal Roy, the chair of two recently formed Pontifical Commissions—on the Laity, and Justice and Peace (*Iustitia et Pax*)—on May 14, 1971, to call attention to the topic of the synod, "Justice in the World," which would begin on October 22, 1971. This papal letter was not meant to curtail the bishops' deliberations at the synod, but to serve as an "authoritative and comprehensive guide" for them.[1]

A CHURCH OF SERVICE

Following the lead of *Gaudium et Spes* Pope Paul painted a role of service for the church, not the defensive, arrogant, and triumphalistic stance found in earlier documents. We find phrases like, "The Church, in fact, travels with humanity and shares its lot in the setting of history" (par. 1) and "a renewed consciousness of the demands of the Gospel makes it the Church's duty to put herself at the service of all..." (par. 5).

The heart of the document focuses on current social issues that "must in years to come take first place among the preoccupations of Christians." In this regard the letter mentions the problems "created by the modern economy" including "human conditions of production, fairness in the exchange of goods and in the division of wealth, the significance of increased needs of consumption and the sharing of responsibility" (par. 7).

The pope then discussed a variety of issues, including urbanization, the role of women, youth, workers, victims of change, discrimination, emigration, creating employment, the media, and the environment. Members of the church, including the hierarchy, according to the pope, will need to recognize the importance of these issues of social morality and no longer be preoccupied with the traditional area of Catholic morality, namely, sexuality.

SIX IMPORTANT THEMES

Pope Paul's *A Call to Action* "carves out an enduring mark upon the development of Catholic social thought."[2] Its lasting imprint is evident in six areas:

- a new methodology for social teachings and analysis;

- its emphasis on participation;

- the preferential respect due to the poor;

- the need to move from economics to politics;

- the recognition of a plurality of options; and

- a vibrant call to action.

With these themes Pope Paul broke new ground in the development of Catholic social teaching. These themes will serve as the outline for discussing the content of *Octogesima Adveniens.*

1. A New Way of Developing Social Teachings

What stands out in this letter is its open-ended methodology and its modest assessment of the pope's role in offering solutions. The pope has no intention of proclaiming specific solutions to the problems of social justice in various national settings: "In the face of such widely varying situations it is difficult for us to utter a unified message and to put forward a solution which has universal validity." He doesn't see this as his responsibility even if it were possible. "Such is not our ambition, nor is it our mission." Rather, it is the task of Christians in each country to come up with solutions appropriate for their situation.

To discern the proper solutions, the pope offered the following method of analysis and reflection.

- First, "to analyze with objectivity the situation" in their own country. In other words, Christian communities are to engage in social analysis.

- Second, "to shed on it [their situation] the light of the Gospel's unalterable words and to draw principles of reflection, norms of judgment and directives for action from the social teaching of the Church."

- Finally, "It is up to these Christian communities, with the help of the Holy Spirit, in communion with the bishops...and in dialogue with other Christian brethren and all men of goodwill, to discern the options and commitments which are called for..."(par. 4).

This methodology gives responsibility to the Christian community in every country to engage in theological reflection and discernment of the proper strategies and social ministry. This approach was started when Vatican II called for a reading of the "signs of the times," but Pope Paul developed that historically conscious methodology to a more detailed and nuanced level. In the early 1970s Catholics around the world were ready for this responsibility, and they took up the challenge.

Pope Paul clearly shifted away from the static, ahistorical worldview of some of his predecessors. He initiated a fresh approach that trusts the work of the church in each locale to do its own homework as it responds to the social and human problems of its society. No longer is there the assumption that "one size fits all"; rather the church's social teaching and social ministry will reflect the diversity of the local church. This methodology overturns any vestiges of the static, natural law approach employed in earlier social teachings.[3] *Octogesima Adveniens* could truly be called "a document of freedom."[4]

Father Philip Land sees this approach as a dramatic departure from the approach of previous papal documents. He believes Pope Paul is giving up the Roman practice of "handing down solutions to specific questions." The French Dominican Father Marie-Dominique Chenu concurs with Father Land that the pope has made a truly radical change. "Formerly there was a deductive method by which a universally valid 'social doctrine' was applied to changing circumstances, but now there is an inductive method in which the different situations are themselves the primary location from which theology springs, through a discernment of 'the signs of the times.'"[5]

This historically conscious methodology has implications both for the role of the pope as a moral teacher and for how Catholic social teaching evolves. Irish theologian Donal Dorr explains: "As a moral teacher the pope cannot hope to be familiar with situations all over the world; so *he must respect the discernment done at local or regional levels.*" The implications for Catholic social teachings are also revolutionary: it means "accepting that if one is to discover universal principles about social morality one must start from the variety of cultural and geographical situations in which moral issues arise."[6]

2. Participation

Pope Paul recognizes the growing importance of two fundamental aspirations in society: the desire for *equality and participation*. He calls these two aspirations "two forms of man's dignity and freedom" (par. 22). By associating equality and participation with human dignity the pope is establishing these as "fundamental rights to which every member of the human community may lay claim." According to theologian Bernard Evans, "this is a major step in the Catholic human rights tradition. No previous document had granted the status of a human right to this notion of participation. No teaching prior to this letter had so strongly insisted that every person has a right to be actively involved in all decision-making processes that affect their lives—economic, cultural, educational, political." The consequence of these yearnings for equality and participation is that people will "seek to promote a democratic type of society."

Pope Paul's endorsement of equality and participation is a stark reversal of the church's teaching some 80 years earlier, which held that *inequality* was an essential aspect of society because it was rooted in nature itself. In 1884 Pope Leo XIII had rejected the claim that people are created equal. Leo and his successors argued that inequality was a fact of nature in that God had created people with unequal abilities, intelligence, and energy. These natural inequalities lead to social and political inequalities as well. They believed that God established a hierarchical order in society where there are rulers and subjects, employers and workers, rich and poor. This was the way God created the world and this was how God wanted the world to continue. Pope Leo argued in *Rerum Novarum* (par. 26) that struggling against the inequality of nature was in vain.

Pope Leo XIII and his immediate successors were primarily concerned with maintaining political stability. They feared the revolutionary instinct of people who were discontented with "their God-given lot in life." They viewed the social and political conflict that followed from the desire for equality as a major evil of modern society because it disrupted the harmony, stability, and order of society. These early popes could not embrace equality or participation.

Finally in 1971, after Vatican II, Pope Paul embraced the basic human desires for equality and participation. The U.S. Catholic bishops would build on this notion of participation in their letter on the economy (*Economic Justice for All*, par. 77) where they would say that participation is another way of talking about justice. We are treating people with justice when they can participate in the economic, social, and cultural life of society. If people are excluded from participating, this is a destructive injustice.

3. Preferential Respect Due to the Poor

In paragraph 23 Pope Paul reminded Christians that "the Gospel instructs us in the preferential respect due to the poor and the special situation they have in society: the more fortunate should renounce some of their rights so as to place their goods more generously at the service of the poor." This is a powerful statement that continues the lifting up of the poor discussed in the previous theme. The poor are people who desire equality and participation because of their basic human dignity. Now the pope interprets the Gospel as requiring Christians to give "preferential respect" to the poor and that "the more fortunate should renounce some of their rights" so that the needs of the poor may be served.

This text addresses both the poor and the more fortunate, tying the two together. One commentator responded:

> What a remarkable development this statement brings to Catholic social teaching regarding people who are poor and those who are not! No longer are the poor exhorted to practice patience, or to offer earnest prayers to God, or to await their reward in heaven. No longer is it sufficient to the more affluent to give to the poor out of their surplus goods (*Rerum Novarum* 36; *Quadragesimo Anno* 50) or even out of their abundance (*Gaudium et Spes* 69). Now much more is required.[7]

The theme of a "preferential respect for the poor" would be developed extensively by liberation theologians, and the U.S. bishops would make it a central moral theme in their *Economic Justice for All.*

4. From Economics to Politics

While previous documents recognized that there were political dimensions to socioeconomic problems, Pope Paul, "in notable contrast to papal tradition," recognized "that most social problems are at bottom political problems."[8] The breakthrough in *Octogesima Adveniens* is found in the extent to which it intentionally focuses on the political problems involved in creating a more just order in society. In light of the structural changes that must be realized, the pope stated that it is necessary to move beyond the economic realm to the political arena. He admitted the limitation of a primarily economic approach: "It [economic activity] runs the risk of taking up too much strength and freedom.[9] That is why the need is felt to pass from economics to politics" (par. 46).

While Pope John XXIII's *Mater et Magistra* stressed how important sharing responsibility was in the economic arena, Pope Paul saw a need to move beyond the economic arenas: "Today the field is wider, and extends to the social and political sphere in which a *reasonable sharing in responsibility and in decisions must be established and strengthened*" (par. 47, emphasis mine).

Pope Paul believed that political control must be exercised over economic activity through *new forms of democracy*. "In order to counterbalance increasing technology, modern forms of democracy must be devised, not only making it possible for each man to become informed and to express himself, but also by involving him in a shared responsibility" (par. 47). If such forms of democracy are created, "human groups will gradually begin to share and to live as communities," and human freedom will be seen in a new light. "Thus freedom, which too often asserts itself as a claim for autonomy by opposing the freedom of others, will develop in its deepest human reality: to involve itself and to spend itself in building up active and lived solidarity" (par. 47).

5. Plurality of Options

As mentioned above, Pope Paul recognized that in the face of "widely varying situations" it was difficult for him "to utter a unified message and to put forward a solution which has universal validity." In fact, he bluntly admitted that "such is not our ambition, nor is it our mission." In the famous paragraph 4 he put the burden on Christians in the situation to analyze the situation in light of the Gospel and come up with appropriate political solutions.

Pope Paul continued this openness to a plurality of options when he evaluated the dominant ideologies of the time: Marxist socialism and capitalism. In evaluating Marxist socialism the letter distinguishes between the various levels of the socialist and Marxist movements. Pope Paul noted the difference between 1) class struggle as the heart of Marxism, 2) a single party exercising political and economic power, 3) an ideology of historical materialism, and 4) Marxism as type of social analysis.

We find no blanket condemnation of Marxism and socialism in their diverse expressions; in fact, the pope even recognized positive dimensions of these historical movements. "In so far as they conform to the dictates of right reason and are interpreters of the lawful aspirations of the human person, [these movements] contain elements that are positive and deserving of approval" (par. 30). That is a far cry from the condemnations of socialism by Pope Paul's predecessors. This nuanced teaching means that Catholics are not forbidden from cooperating with Marxist-inspired movements or parties.

The U.S. Catholic bishops employed this teaching on cooperation a year later when they were challenged for funding certain groups through the Campaign for Human Development. Some of these groups did not always agree with Catholic moral teachings. Archbishop Krol, on behalf of the United States Catholic Conference's Administrative Board, rejected the position of those who

> espouse the principle that CHD [Campaign for Human Development] should give no money to any project, no matter how worthy, if it is sponsored by an organization which also has some involvement, however small, in other activities unacceptable to the Church. Such a principle, applied across the board, would presumably rule out the financial assistance given to by the Holy See over the years to international agencies whose programs included population control activities. It would presumably rule out payment by Catholics of local, state, and federal taxes, since many local, state, and federal agencies have population-related programs. No principle of Catholic moral theology requires or supports such a course of action.[10]

In treating capitalism, Pope Paul recognized the values of the capitalist ideology, which include economic efficiency and the defense of the individual against totalitarian tendencies, but he also reminded the faithful that "at the very root of philosophical liberalism is an erroneous affirmation of the autonomy of the individual..." (par. 35). The Christian is to exercise careful discernment to avoid an uncritical allegiance to any ideology—socialist, Marxist, or capitalist.

In asking Christians to be discerning in their particular political and economic situation, the letter teaches that in whatever system a Christian lives he or she needs to be aware of its distortions and abuses of the economic and political system. The Christian is to draw strength from the Gospel and the Church's tradition as the church seeks to be a transformative influence in every social setting. The political systems and ideologies that dominate the world are judged by how well they promote human dignity, especially in terms of recognizing the equality of all, and extending participation and responsibility as far as possible.

6. A Call to Action

The letter concludes with a call to action, echoing the words of *Gaudium et Spes*, which urges the laity to take the lead in bringing their faith to bear on their institutions, structures, and culture. "It belongs to the laity, without waiting passively for orders and directives, *to take the initiative freely* and to infuse a Christian spirit into the mentality, customs, laws, and structures of the community in which they live" (par. 48, emphasis mine). The laity are accorded a freedom and a responsibility for taking the initiative not found in the church in the days of Pius XI's version of Catholic Action.

Pope Paul reminded the church that "it is not enough to recall principles, state intentions, point to crying injustices and utter prophetic denunciations." Proclaiming the Gospel will not be effective unless it is "accompanied by the witness of the Holy Spirit, working within the *action of Christians in the service of their brother*" (par. 51). In these words, Pope Paul anticipated the words of his fellow bishops who would gather in synod within a few months. He reminded the church that Christian faith demands "a just and consequently necessary transformation of society."

EVALUATION
THE ROLE OF THE REGIONAL CHURCH

As is evident from the six points presented above, *Octogesima Adveniens* is a major contribution to the development of Catholic social teaching in terms of methodology and content. The letter teaches that a discernment of "the signs of the times," which the Second Vatican Council began, is best carried out at a regional or national level. This is exactly what the Assembly of Latin American Bishops accomplished at their Medellín Conference in 1968. Donal Dorr concludes that "*Octogesima Adveniens* really offers very solid support to the Medellín conclusions—not so much because the pope agrees with the details of the evaluation as because he recognizes the right and duty to make the kind of moral evaluation which the Latin American bishops undertook there."[11]

Because each region undertakes its own analysis and theological reflection, one region cannot simply transplant its insights to another setting. Each region will have to go through its own process of discernment. There are no easy answers for every situation. The church of each region will have to engage in its own pastoral and theological reflection in light of its particular circumstances. The church cannot generalize or universalize these particular teachings and options.

The bishops' conferences around the world have been following the lead of the Latin American bishops with the encouragement offered by Pope Paul in this letter:

- the bishops of the United States have undertaken that reflection in their pastoral letters on nuclear weapons and the U.S. economy;
- the bishops of the Philippines have issued pastoral letters on their situation under the dictator Ferdinand Marcos and on ecology;
- the Polish hierarchy has offered pastoral guidance to its people in their transition from communism to capitalism.

Father J. Bryan Hehir notes that Pope Paul was not afraid to invite the local churches to

> become active agents of social teaching, to be sources of insight, the author of ideas which could move from the edge of the church to the center. The invitation was accepted: the Brazilian hierarchy's human rights ministry in the 1960s and 1970s, the emergence of the theology of liberation throughout Latin America in the same period, and the development of the pastoral letters of the 1980s *all testified to the potential of the local churches to be teachers in the social ministry.*[12]

In truth, both the local church and the papal magisterium have distinct roles to play in the development of Catholic social teachings. The local church by reason of its structure and experience can offer insight to the wider church and to the bishop of Rome. The local church has the advantage and the capacity to engage the specifics of a social question. "Specificity here means the ability to enter the concrete complexity of a problem, and to engage the public discussion by which social policies are shaped and influenced."[13]

The teaching of the papal magisterium is necessarily cast at a general level that will be applicable to a variety of settings. While papal teaching loses something because of its generic tone it also makes a distinctive and irreplaceable contribution. As Father Hehir points out, "Its strength lies in its ability to project a vision, to protect principles and values of abiding moral significance and to call the community of the faithful to forms of service and witness in the social arena." The generic orientation of papal teaching reveals its strength and its weakness:

> Precisely as a universal message it stresses the catholicity of the church and it defines values and principles to be held by all. But the generality of the teaching leaves it open to either remaining isolated from the places and points of decision in society, or being manipulated by multiple parties claiming legitimation for opposing positions.[14]

Many local churches took up Pope Paul's invitation, from bishops' conferences to diocesan structures to religious orders establishing social justice think tanks and centers of advocacy. *Octogesima Adveniens* bore much fruit in the local churches.

ONGOING QUESTIONS

A number of issues raised in the letter beg for further reflection and development. For example, how does the letter understand political power? How is its teaching on equality and participation to be lived out *within the church?*

First, although the letter notes the importance of political power, its treatment of that category is idealistic and inadequate (par. 46). Statements like "It [political power] always intervenes with care for justice and with devotion to the common good, for which it holds final responsibility" are idealistic and theoretical. The reality of political power is often just the opposite. Here, as in *Gaudium et Spes,* the seamy and sinful side of life is overlooked in an effort to paint a positive social vision. Further reflection is needed on the move from "economics to politics." Of course the church must pay attention to the political arena and promote needed and effective forms of democracy that gives genuine space for participation and equality, but the letter does not give enough attention to linkage between the political and the economic spheres. As we know from our experience of electing our political leaders and the problem of campaign financing, those with economic power often wield political power as well. Some would argue that the state, while speaking about the rights of all, often shows by its actions that it is beholden to the wealthy. The collusion of political and economic power is a little-examined issue in Roman Catholic social teachings. It is a topic that could benefit from some frank analysis.

A second question is the perennial concern about how these teachings in the social realm are to be implemented within the church itself. In other words, how do Roman Catholic church structures, laws, and customs recognize the aspirations of equality and participation? How are the laity, and especially women, experiencing the establishment and strengthening of sharing in responsibility and decision making within the church? The 1971 synod began a reflection on this question, which must be continued at every level of the church and whenever a new document is being formulated.

A DISTORTION OF *OCTOGESIMA ADVENIENS*?

A final concern is how the papal magisterium since Pope Paul VI has been interpreting and possibly distorting the historically conscious methodology of *Octogesima Adveniens*. Sister Mary Elsbernd, who teaches at Loyola University in Chicago, put the question this way, "What ever happened to *Octogesima Adveniens*?"[15] Her contention is that Pope John Paul II has *not* continued the methodology of Paul VI, which gave immense responsibility to the local community to analyze their own situation and to help shape the church's unfolding social tradition. Recall that paragraph 4 said,

> It is up to the Christian communities to analyze with objectivity the situation which is proper to their own country, to shed on it the light of the Gospel's unalterable words and to draw principles of reflection, norms of judgment and directives for action from the social teaching of the church. This social teaching has been worked out in the course of history.

Sister Elsbernd's critique is that the vision of *Octogesima Adveniens* has been reinterpreted and distorted by Pope John Paul II and the Congregation for the Doctrine of the Faith by taking it out of context. The proper context is "where both the activity of the local church and the nature of social teaching are viewed as historically constituted."[16] In its place Pope John Paul II has emphasized a "transcendental or Thomistic personalism as the basis of universal and absolute norms transcending all historical contingency."[17]

The vision of *Octogesima Adveniens* is one where the social teaching of the church is worked out in the course of history with the help of the Spirit *in the community and with broad consultation*. Pope John Paul II has shifted the

process to one in which the Spirit is linked to the magisterium, and the discernment by the local community is limited only to the *application* of social
doctrine to the situation. The drawing of principles of reflection and norms
of discernment is no longer the prerogative of the local communities but is
the special reserve of the magisterium. Pope John Paul II reasserts the doctrinal role of the magisterium in an ahistorical fashion, which is a distortion
of the orientation and vision of Vatican II and *Octogesima Adveniens.*

Perhaps a future pope will rediscover the historically conscious
method of *Octogesima Adveniens* and once again invite local communities
to participate in the shaping of Catholic social teaching and the application of that teaching to their specific situation as Pope Paul VI did in this
magnificent document. It is, no doubt, difficult to hold the role of the
papal magisterium and the role of the local church in a beneficial balance without denying the contribution of either.

Part II. 1971 Synod: *Justice in the World*

The practice of holding a world synod every few years was established
after the Second Vatican Council to continue the reform of the church
initiated by the council. They were also to be vehicles of collegial reflection by the Roman Catholic bishops on issues facing the church. The
synod is considered a consultative body and not a deliberative body. This
distinction was clarified only two days before the end of the 1971 synod.
From that time on the synod would *not* speak on its own behalf by issuing public documents. The report of the synod would be an *internal document,* sent to the pope and appropriate curial offices. This shift of procedures brought the synod more under the control of the Roman bureaucracy and weakened it as a vehicle for continuing the collegial spirit of
the Second Vatican Council.

Pope Paul asked the synod for guidance in better articulating and promoting the church's engagement in the cause of global justice. Published
on November 30, 1971, with the pope's approval, the synod document
Justice in the World was both "a response to his request and a personal
appeal of the world's bishops to the people of God to become actively
involved in the work of justice. It is very much a 'call to action' rather
than a doctrinal statement."[18]

BACKGROUND PREPARATION

The background preparation and methodology for the synod reflected the inductive and historically conscious approach recognized and initiated by *Gaudium et Spes* and evident in *Octogesima Adveniens*. As professor Ron Hamel notes, it was a "more consultative, dialogical, inductive, culturally sensitive approach."[19] Prior to the synod gathering, the local episcopal conferences met to discuss a set of guideline questions prepared by the council of the synod. Sixty reports from these discussions were sent to the planning committee of the synod. These reports reflected a "surprising convergence of views. There was strong agreement, for example, on the appropriateness of denouncing global injustice and addressing justice within the church itself, on the theology that should ground the church's involvement in social justice, and on the need for new approaches to education for justice."

Professor Hamel reflects that "this remarkable convergence can be attributed to the influence of the social teaching of the previous decade"[20] [*Mater et Magistra*, 1961; *Pacem in Terris*, 1963; *Gaudium et Spes*, 1965; *Populorum Progressio*, 1967; and *Octogesima Adveniens*, 1971], as well as the documents from the Second General Conference of Latin American bishops held at Medellín, Colombia, in 1968. The newly formed Pontifical Commission *Iustitia et Pax* had sent all the episcopal conferences the major statements on social justice from the national and regional episcopal conferences of Asia, Africa, and Latin America, along with other pertinent papers dealing with social justice and development. All of these materials helped prepare the representatives at the synod. They came prepared and ready to work and dialogue in the synod's twelve work groups and plenary sessions.

The 1971 synod had two distinct topics to address: first, the discussion of priesthood and celibacy and, second, the question of "Justice in the World." Many participants at the synod felt that the order should have been reversed. "Sober consideration of world problems might well have changed the context of the debate on priesthood for the better. It would have been profitable to see the Church putting the good of mankind before its own domestic anxieties."[21]

MINIMAL LAY INVOLVEMENT

From October 22 until November 6, 1971, 190 bishops (140 representing the various local episcopal conferences [four were from the United States], 14 oriental patriarchates, 19 curial prefects, plus 15 appointed by the pope), and the ten superiors generals of male orders discussed and voted on the synod position papers.[22]

The bishops were assisted by ten *periti* (experts), of whom six where laity, four were women.[23] The voices of three lay experts, Lady Jackson (Barbara Ward), Dr. Candido Mendes (Rector of the faculty of Social Sciences in the University of Rio de Janeiro) and Dr. Kinhide Mushakoji (a Japanese expert on peace and disarmament) were especially helpful in shaping the direction of the discussion both in plenary sessions and in the working groups.

Lady Jackson, the first woman to address the synod, spoke on "Structures for World Justice," in which she analyzed the growing gap between the rich one-third and the poor two-thirds of the world. She urged Catholics to reconsider social structures and personal living standards, and she asked the bishops to ensure that the church itself conduct its own affairs "in the strict spirit of justice and poverty."

Dr. Mendes discussed the problem of "Structural Marginality," which refers to the obstacles, the vicious circles, the distortions, the interactions that prevent whole classes of people from enjoying their fair share of economic, social, and cultural benefits. He noted that nations themselves become "marginal" or "non-viable" through dependence on outside agencies.

Dr. Mushakoji spoke on "The Universal Aspiration to Participation" that is painfully emerging in the world as societies move from immature authoritarian exercise of authority based on inequality between the powerful and the weak toward a new participatory society wherein all persons achieve a greater share in responsibility and decision making.[24] As one reads the final text of the synod, it is obvious that the bishops incorporated the thinking of these three lay consultants.

THIRD WORLD PERSPECTIVES

The voices of the poor nations were heard not only in the analysis of Dr. Mendes but in the majority representation from the Third World—over half the bishops of the 1971 synod were from the Third World. Msgr. Gremillion recalled that "during the prior decade most of them had become well 'conscientized' about these political-economic systems, national and global, which radically affect their people."[25] Not only had the bishops from Latin America experienced the Second Vatican Council with its stance of dialogue and openness, they had also interpreted the meaning of the Christian faith for their continent in the 1968 meeting of

Latin American bishops at Medellín, Colombia. This had been an eye-opening experience for many of them regarding the poverty and dependence of their people. The momentum of these important turning points continued to influence the tenor of the synod.

While the bishops of the Third World were heard from in an unprecedented proportion, they did not all speak with one voice. For instance, the conservative hierarchies of Colombia, Venezuela, and Argentina favored a "top-down" approach to structural reform, summarized in the words of Cardinal de Araujo Sales: "Let us not forget that those in power are the ones who can change structures. Let us preserve our contacts with them. Let us also in the Church avoid all appearances of class warfare." The progressives, including the majority of the Brazilian bishops, the Chileans, and others, were equally convinced that radical changes in social structures were necessary and that the old methods of working through the aristocracy would work no better in the present than they had in the past.

Despite the diversity of voices a common message was emerging from many bishops of the Third World: "Both Africans and Latin Americans clearly revealed how they chafe under the servitude of outside influences, whether political or commercial, and how closely they are identified with their people's desire for genuine independence and development."[26] Professor Hamel concludes: "...This is not a First World document. The influence of the African, Asian, and Latin American churches, and particularly of the Medellín bishops present, is unmistakable, especially in the analysis of global injustice and in some of the dominant themes."[27]

CONTRIBUTIONS OF *JUSTICE IN THE WORLD*

While *Justice in the World* reveals some of the above tension of perspectives, and while some amendments that were tabled would have given it a more practical tone, it is nonetheless a strong document. One significant breakthrough was that the document stated in plain language that *"action on behalf of justice...fully appear to us as a constitutive dimension of preaching the Gospel..."*(par. 6, emphasis added). This is a powerful statement that implies that action on behalf of justice is an essential part of the mission of the church in preaching the gospel. The phrase became a point of debate at the 1974 synod, which focused on the topic of "evangelization." Some argued that the words of the 1971 synod should be understood as saying that action on behalf of justice is integral to preaching the gospel, that is, it is but one and only one dimension of preaching. Others challenged this "softer" interpretation. The author of these words, Vincent Cosmao, O.P., a French member of the Pontifical Commission *Iustitia et Pax*, claimed that the word "constitutive" was used "to make engagement for justice not merely an ethical deduction from faith but a very condition for the truth of faith."[28]

Msgr. Charles Murphy, who has studied this question, sees the disagreement stemming from differing notions of justice present in current Catholic social teachings: natural law justice or biblical justice.

> If justice is conceived exclusively on the plan of the natural, human virtue of justice as explained in classical philosophical treatises, then such justice can only be conceived as an integral but nonessential part of preaching of the gospel. But if justice is conceived in the biblical sense of God's liberating action which demands a necessary human response—a concept of justice which is far closer to agape than to justice in the classical philosophical sense—then justice must be defined as of the essence of the gospel itself.[29]

This simple sentence on "action on behalf of justice" captured "the heart of the synod's message: the church must be engaged in this world to bring about justice for all." Hamel notes that "by using the term 'constitutive,' the synod underscores the centrality and indispensability of the work of justice in the preaching and living out of the gospel and in the church's mission. Without it, the church would not be true to itself or to its vocation."[30]

The document's teaching that action on behalf of justice is constitutive of preaching the gospel has had a powerful impact within developing countries. Father Cosmao notes that "the militant Churches in the Third World have recognized themselves in this phrase." Gustavo Gutiérrez, a Peruvian liberation theologian, places the issue in its concrete, Third World setting: "How are we to preach the Gospel with any credibility to that two-thirds of humanity which goes to bed each night hungry, ill-housed, chronically ill and without hope for the political and material improvement of their lives?"[31] Action on behalf of biblical justice, then, should be seen as the pre-condition and the consequence of preaching the gospel.[32]

A second significant contribution of *Justice in the World* is its social analysis, which acknowledged and named *structural injustice*. According to the synod, injustice is due not only to human sinfulness but to the way society has organized and structured its economic, social, cultural, and political life.

The bishops "perceive the serious injustices which are building around the world of men a network of domination, oppression and abuses which stifle freedom..." (par. 3). They recognize the "stifling oppressions" of "marginal" persons on the fringes of the urban centers, "ill-fed, inhumanely housed, illiterate and deprived of political power as well as of the suitable means of acquiring responsibility and moral dignity"(par. 10).

The synod bishops made a more sanguine assessment of the extent of the suffering and injustice in the world than we find in the Vatican Council's optimistic outlook. They recognized that the hope of economic growth and eliminating world hunger "has proved a vain hope in underdeveloped areas and in pockets of poverty in wealthier areas..." (par. 10). Optimism is tempered by the realities of seemingly intransigent structural injustice.

Third, the synod did not offer ready-made answers drawn from Catholic natural law tradition but issued an invitation to listen to what God is speaking today: "In the face of the present-day situation of the world, marked as it is by the grave sin of injustice, we recognize both our responsibility and our inability to overcome it by our own strength. Such a situation urges us to listen with a humble and open heart to the word of God, as he shows us new paths towards action in the cause of justice in the world" (par. 29). The proper Christian response is found in listening and developing an action plan with God's help.

The synod itself offered that opportunity to listen and be taught. "Despite its appalling disorganization the synod was confirmed as an embryo assembly in which the bishops both teach and learn."[33]

Fourth, the synod participants, reflecting the wish of their fellow bishops, stressed that action on behalf of justice must begin at home, within the church: "While the Church is bound to give witness to justice, she recognizes that anyone who ventures to speak to people about justice must first be just in their eyes. Hence we must undertake an examination of the modes of acting and of the possessions and life style found within the Church herself" (par. 40). They go on to talk about "rights within the Church," participation of women in the church, a sparingness in lifestyle for clergy and laity (par. 41-48).

A fifth contribution of the synod was to energize the call for effective education for justice. Education in the past was seen as training in and acceptance of traditional values. The synod urged a new "conscientizing" education that will awaken a critical sense, which will lead us to reflect on the society in which we live and on its values; it will make men ready to renounce these values when they cease to promote justice for all men. In developing countries, the principal aim of this education for justice consists in an attempt to awaken consciences to a knowledge of the concrete situation and in a call to secure a total improvement; by these means the transformation of this world has already begun. (par. 51)

Education for justice should be promoted through the episcopal conferences and dioceses "by setting up centers of social and theological research" (par. 72). Many dioceses and religious communities took the suggestion seriously and formed "Justice and Peace" centers to educate their constituencies.

In a rather brief document the synod brought together challenging ideas for their fellow bishops to reflect on. The document was sent on to Pope Paul as a consultative document. He instructed that it be made public so that the entire church would benefit from its hard-hitting message.

CONCLUSION: A VIBRANT LEGACY

1971 was an important year in the history of Roman Catholic social teachings—with publication of Pope Paul's Apostolic Letter *Octogesima Adveniens* and the international synod's statement on *Justice in the World*. More than any previous church writings, these two relatively brief documents were a *catalyst* for the local churches to "get off the dime" on social justice ministry. The documents by themselves did not bring about a renewed activism, rather it was the attitude of openness and fresh beginnings initiated by the remarkable achievements of the Second Vatican Council that brought about a convergence of vision, creativity, and energy that led to a new level of commitment to social justice ministry.

Looking back at 1971 from the 1990s, it is clear that these two documents were Catholic milestones. With the synod's declaration that "justice is a constitutive dimension of the preaching of the Gospel" Catholics were challenged to realize that justice was neither an option nor a postscript to the gospel: it was its very essence. This insight had a great impact on the church.

For many religious, this was revolutionary. It drove them out of big, barracks-like institutions toward specialized service of the poor, the marginalized, the victims of injustice. It led others deeper still, toward living among the poor as one of them. Still others set out to examine the causes of injustice. It was no longer a matter of serving the poor from the outside but of identifying with them from within.[34]

Justice in the World and *Octogesima Adveniens* were set against the backdrop of *Gaudium et Spes'* opening line, which proclaimed that "the joys and hopes, the griefs and anxieties of the men of this age, especially those who are poor or in any way afflicted, these too are the joys and hopes, the griefs and anxieties of the followers of Christ." Many Catholic followers of Christ took these words to heart, and it was revolutionary.

Sister Helen Prejean is an example of the kind of revolution that took place in the lives of many religious. In her book *Dead Man Walking*, she tells of the transformation that was going on in her religious community and in her life.

> I came to St. Thomas [a New Orleans housing project of poor blacks] as part of a reform movement in the Catholic Church, seeking to harness religious faith to social justice. In 1971, the worldwide synod of bishops had declared justice a "constitutive" part of the Christian gospel.... My religious community, the Sisters of St. Joseph of Medaille, had made a commitment to "stand on the side of the poor."[35]

Part III. Centers of Advocacy and Justice Education

As we have seen from the methodology of *Octogesima Adveniens*, Pope Paul VI realized he could not offer solutions to every area of the world; rather it was up to Christians in those areas to take up the task. This is exactly what happened in response to the papal "call for action." Dioceses and parishes established social ministry committees, and religious orders set up justice and peace centers and social "think tank" centers, as well as centers for action and advocacy. Some of these were focused on educating their Catholic constituents, others were ecumenical and interfaith in orientation. These new efforts were to complement the traditional Catholic "works of mercy," which addressed the needs of the poor and needy.

With the multiplication of social ministry efforts at all levels in the 1970s it is important to clarify the diverse approaches taken by these groups. I generally divide social ministry into five approaches.

TYPES OF SOCIAL MINISTRY

While there is no definitive classification of social ministry, I find the following five categories helpful.

1. Direct Service

Direct service is the time-honored tradition of responding to the immediate needs of a person or a group, whether that be in terms of emergency, food, shelter, health care, clothing, or counseling. The Christian churches have long traditions of such care rooted in the Judeo-Christian tradition of caring for the widow, the orphan, the stranger. This is the work of Mother Teresa, Catholic Relief Services, food baskets, clothing cupboards, and Christmas "giving trees."

2. Parallel Institutions

When direct service is structured in a way that it becomes an institution, some people refer to it as a parallel institution. Catholic hospitals, hospices, nursing homes, orphanages, credit unions, and schools are examples of direct service taking on a long-term response. These parallel institutions have the advantage of caring for the needy in an atmosphere of Christian values.

3. Advocacy

Advocacy is that form of social ministry that goes beyond the direct handout to give voice to the needy in terms of changing public policy and legislation. Often the person in need or whose rights are denied must rely on the voice and power of others to address these needs. Immigrants, farm workers, prisoners, and many others in society need others to be their advocate to fight an injustice. The rights of the unborn and children are also addressed by advocates because they are not yet able to speak for themselves. Groups like Right to Life, Bread for the World, Amnesty International, and environmental groups, "speak for" others whose rights are being ignored or denied.

4. Empowerment

The term empowerment is used in many ways. I am referring to a narrow understanding of the term, as social ministry whose intent is to enable others to speak for themselves and not be dependent on others to speak for them. The work of Cesar Chavez and the United Farm Workers is the ministry of empowerment—farm workers are organized to speak for themselves through their union. Community organizations in which citizens develop their leadership skills and organize their neighbors to address their own concerns are engaged in the social ministry of empowerment. As we have seen in the chapters on the Knights of Labor and the United Farm Workers, empowerment often involves conflict and controversy. As we shall see the U.S. Bishops' Campaign for Human Development is specifically focused on empowering the poor.

5. Justice Education

Some groups and programs focus primarily on educating their constituents and the public on current social issues with a variety of books, pamphlets, posters, workshops, lectures, web pages, videos, journals, art, music, and drama. Oftentimes a social ministry will include a justice education component as part of its empowerment or advocacy work. For example the Campaign for Human Development carries on a justice education effort along with its funding of empowerment groups.

The above categories are not watertight divisions; many groups may employ one or more of these strategies in addressing particular social issues. But these types of social ministry are distinct in their orientation, methods, and goals.

The groundswell of movements and programs in the early 1970s was to give heightened attention to advocacy, empowerment, and justice education. Direct service and parallel institutions had already been well established within the Catholic church. The next section gives a glimpse of a few organized efforts that responded to the call for action on behalf of justice articulated by *Justice in the World*.

CENTER OF CONCERN

The Jesuit community heard the "call to action" issued by Pope Paul VI in 1971. Pedro Arrupe, the Superior General of the Jesuits, urged the Society of Jesus to take up the challenge of reflecting theologically and acting on the human problems of the day.[36] Father Arrupe asked an American, William F. Ryan, S.J., to assist in the establishment of an international center to study issues relating to development, justice, and peace from a Christian perspective. Ryan had solid credentials to undertake this task: he had attended the 1971 synod and was serving as the co-director of the Social Action Department of the Canadian Catholic

Conference. The proposed center was to be a joint venture of the United States Catholic Conference and the Society of Jesus and at the same time was to be an independent organization.

On May 4, 1971, the founding of the Center of Concern was formally announced by Father Arrupe and Bishop Joseph Bernardin, the General Secretary of the United States Catholic Conference. While the Center was to be located in Washington, D.C., the announcement of its beginning was made at a meeting with United Nations Secretary General U Thant in his New York office. "The setting was strategic: from its inception, the Center would have a global perspective."[37]

Throughout its three decades of service the Center has been faithful to that global perspective. *"The Center's overriding goal today, as it was in the early seventies, is to enable all people to realize that humanity is united in a common destiny, and to assist them to exercise their common responsibility to shape that destiny."*[38]

The Center of Concern (which describes itself as "an independent, interdisciplinary team engaged in social analysis, religious reflection, policy advocacy, and public education around questions of social justice"[39]) has taken on national as well as international issues. The Center has participated in many United Nations conferences on issues of population, food, women's rights, trade, development, and unemployment. The Center is involved in both advocacy and justice education with its outreach into the policy-making, religious, and civic communities. It also conducts a variety of workshops and institutes on themes linking faith and justice.

Over the years the Center of Concern has shifted its focus. In the 1970s it attended to the United Nations agenda, which included the call for a new international economic order and a series of world conferences that addressed global issues such as population, environment, habitat, science and technology, and women. During the 1980s, the Center shifted from a primary focus on institutions to participate in social movements, including the peace movement, the women's movement, and the labor movement. The Center's work moved to linking global issues with local issues as it continued to study the process of development, especially as it impacted the poor and women. During this period the Center was helpful in the shaping of the U.S. bishops' pastoral letters on racism, peace, and the U.S. economy. In fact, the Center was recognized by many as "the most influential single 'outside group' shaping the Church's important pastoral letters on nuclear arms and the economy."[40]

In the 1990s the Center of Concern has pressed for greater cooperation among nongovernmental organizations as an alternative approach in working for global justice. The Center believes that the model of development that has governed the programs of the international financial institutions has outlived its usefulness. Instead, a more just world order must be built on community-centered, local, and grass-roots efforts linked together in global networks.

One of the Center's most effective educational tools has been the publication of the brief book *Social Analysis: Linking Faith and Justice* by Joe Holland and Peter Henriot, S.J. This text describes how to move below the surface in analyzing complex social problems from a faith perspective. This text has sold over 75,000 copies in the United States with translations available in five languages. The linkage with *Octogesima Adveniens* is undeniable. Inside the front cover the authors quote from the famous paragraph 4 of *Octogesima Adveniens*: "It is up to Christian communities to analyze with objectivity the situation which is proper to their own country, to shed on it the light of the Gospel's unalterable words, and to draw principles of reflection, norms of judgment, and directives of action from the social teaching of the Church." Their book is a direct response to that invitation by Pope Paul VI.

The Center of Concern has a number of other helpful texts and videos that address the questions of social analysis, justice, spirituality, social teaching, and peace-building. They offer a free bi-monthly newsletter, *Center Focus*, which presents social analyses and religious reflections on global and domestic issues. Their mailing list includes 5000 names.

In September 1996 the *National Catholic Reporter* commended the 25-year history of the Center with these words:

> A quarter century after its birth, the center continues to show impressive leadership and continues to shape Catholic understanding of Catholic social teachings. The center's mission was sound when it set out to work 25 years ago. It remains sound today. Its work, meanwhile, is all the more vital in a justice-starved world. The entire church is indebted to the Center of Concern. Thanks for 25 years.[41]

NETWORK

Ten years *before* the Second Vatican Council began, religious women in the United States had initiated a process for critiquing social changes occurring in the church and society. This process was known as the Sister

Formation Movement, which was organized in 1952. The religious women in this movement rallied to the call of Vatican II to "read the signs of the times" in light of recent Catholic social teachings. The *Call to Action* of Pope Paul and the synod document *Justice in the World* motivated the sisters to intensify their social analysis. Many of the women had wrestled with complex social issues in their ministry. Sister Maureen Kelleher noted that sisters who were working in urban ministry felt they were

> running around stamping out brush fires as one tries to help prevent a gang war or counsel a drug addict. After reflecting on the causes of the gang war and the amount of available drugs, sisters want to address themselves to action on the causes of these problems, causes which relate to unemployment, crowded housing and corruption in high places. And so this combination of study and experience has brought them to a new consciousness leading to a new response—organizing for social impact.[42]

Their years of experience and study brought the sisters to recognize the need to take their ministry to a new level of sophistication and advocacy to achieve greater social impact. In December of 1971 47 sisters from 21 states and 30 cities met at Trinity College in Washington, D.C., and committed themselves to a ministry of structural change. On December 19 the sisters agreed to a resolution to "form a political action network of information and communication" known as NETWORK.

This resolution to form a political action network resonated with communities of religious who were searching for ways to transform unjust structures through political action. The Conference of Major Superiors of Women invited the first executive director of NETWORK, Sister Carol Coston, to present NETWORK to the one hundred superiors gathered at their 1972 assembly. The assembly supported NETWORK "in its efforts for social justice by letters of support, by financial contributions, and by encouraging other sisters to become active members."[43] The resolution by the superiors was effective in building support for the new project.

NETWORK grew from 47 supporters in 1971 to 8000 by 1987 and 10,000 in 1997.[44]

The purpose of NETWORK as stated on its letterhead: is to be "A National Catholic Social Justice Lobby." Its mission is "to courageously move forward in faith and determination to lobby for policies on the federal level that reflect the truest values of this nation."

NETWORK's mission statement includes the following eight themes:

Empowerment of the Poor
NETWORK analyzes public policy issues primarily from the perspective of how the poor and vulnerable are affected, asking what the policy does to and for the poor and what it enables them to do for themselves.

Church and Gospel Values
NETWORK roots its vision of the good society in the tradition of Catholic social teaching and Gospel values as expressed in the principles articulated in church documents and the reflections of the Christian community.

Systemic Change
NETWORK works through the political process to change societal structures which violate people's dignity, the common good, and ecological sustainability.

Active Citizenship
NETWORK seeks to build political will among active and committed citizens who work against unjust public policy and for creative alternatives that foster social justice.

Eco-Justice
NETWORK seeks policies which foster conservation and enhancement of global resources and ecosystems now and in the future in ways that develop a more just, participatory, and sustainable world community.

Integration
NETWORK takes a holistic view of human needs—physical and spiritual, personal and social—and of human rights—economic, social and cultural, as well as civil and political.

Mutuality
NETWORK seeks a world where relationships between persons and among nations are based on equality and mutual respect, where all patterns of domination and submission rooted in sexism, racism, classism, and ethnocentrism will be rejected.

Solidarity
NETWORK seeks a world in which people everywhere work co-responsi-

bly for the universal common good, collaborating as sisters and brothers for a world in which all can live in dignity and peace.[45]

To carry out its vision NETWORK is committed to:

• developing a value-based vision of justice and peace,

• lobbying and organizing for just federal legislation, and

• educating about legislative issues.[46]

In 1997, for example, during the first session of the 105th Congress, NETWORK focused its energies on lobbying federal legislative issues as diverse as campaign finance reform, death of the balanced budget amendment, affordable housing, closing of the School of the Americas (a training center that teaches "counter-subversive" tactics for the Latin American military, including torture and assassination), and reform of the social welfare system. Its justice education and advocacy efforts use a variety of formats, including briefings and testimony with senators and congresspeople. It applies pressure on the legislators through "action alerts" and gives "phone alerts" to its membership. Its bimonthly magazine, *NETWORK Connection*, provides an analysis of current issues and updates on legislation and grass-roots organizing. It offers an annual report that gives the voting record of representatives and senators, and it offers a variety of education programs with well-researched materials, workshops, and programs to enhance the voter's knowledge and skills for political action.

NETWORK is highly regarded as an organization that "does its homework" as it carries out its ministry of justice education and advocacy on a national level.

CORPORATE RESPONSIBILITY

Roman Catholic priests were not far behind the religious women in calling for organized efforts on behalf of justice. One expression of this concern was seen in the National Federation of Priests' Councils (NFPC) resolution on March 15, 1972, "to determine guidelines and criteria based on the Church's social justice teaching for examining Catholic Church investments."[47] Guidelines were developed and distributed to affiliated councils in November 1972, under the title *Exploitation or Liberation: Ethics for Investors*. This document pointed out the various strategies the church can use to influence a corporation that is "deemed to be acting in ways contrary to the norms of the Gospel and church social doctrine." They offered different levels of interaction to encourage the corporation to change its policy, beginning with:

1. church representatives making contact in letter or in person to explain the church's concern;

2. if the private conversation is effective, the church could make its concern public, perhaps at the annual stockholders' meeting;

3. a stockholder resolution calling for change in the corporate policy or practice is the next avenue to pursue;

4. if the church does not own stock in the corporation under consideration it could purchase some to be part of the shareholder resolution;

5. the church could also bring suit, or join others in litigation, against a corporation for violation of laws dealing with human rights or safety; and finally,

6. the church might employ a variety of means of public pressure such as boycotts and seeking support from other groups and churches.

The 1972 guidelines discouraged disinvestment as a strategy:

> An option for action which does not appear to be an effective means for influencing corporate change is disinvestment or "cleaning up the portfolio." This approach does not recognize the immensely complex character of present-day corporate enterprise, and the many variables that must be considered in making moral judgments about the activities of corporations. A truly "clean" portfolio is simply not achievable. More often than not, "cleaning up the portfolio" serves to remove the investor from the arena of controversy and difficult dialogue, an abdication of responsibility, rather than an embracing of it.

The priests did not feel that the church should avoid controversy and difficult dialogue. "Staying in the thick of things" is the church's moral responsibility and a more effective strategy in the long run:

> Even when not practiced as a means of avoiding controversy, divestment would not seem to be an effective form of action for corporate change. If anything, the corporation probably will welcome the

relief from critical review which divestment offers it. The opportunities afforded by stock ownership for access to corporate management and for moral leadership within the corporation far outweigh the questionable influential power of disinvestment.[48]

A number of religious communities picked up this initiative to be vigilant about their investments. They realized they needed to work together to have a greater impact on the corporate world. On January 29, 1973, representatives from diverse church organizations met in Chicago to discuss the feasibility of Catholic institutional involvement in corporate responsibility. The National Federation of Priests' Councils, which had done some initial work in this area, called the meeting. The following individuals and organizations participated:

- Sisters Ethne Kennedy and Marjorie Tuite of the National Assembly of Women Religious;

- Sister Jacqueline Jelly of the Catholic Committee on Urban Ministry;

- Sister Mary Assunta Stang of the Leadership Conference of Women Religious;

- Rev. Jerome McKenna of the Conference of Major Superiors of Men;

- Sister Joyce Williams of the National Catholic Conference on Interracial Justice;

- Robert Aldrige of the National Association of the Laity;

- Rev. William Moore of the Task Force on Corporate Review in St. Paul, Minnesota;

- Rev. Dale Olen of the Capuchin Office of Justice and Peace in Milwaukee;

- Rev. Eugene Boyle of the National Federation of Priests' Councils;

- Rev. Joseph Burke from the newly formed Corporate Information Center; and,

- the National Association of Religious Brothers.

The nine sponsoring organizations established the National Catholic
Coalition for Responsible Investment (NCCRI). Father Gene Boyle of
San Francisco was named the first coordinator of NCCRI.

The coalition decided to put on symposia on corporate responsibility
around the country to educate Catholic orders, dioceses, health care centers, parishes, and other institutions on the need for corporate responsibility. The goals of these symposia would be:

1. to understand the role and influence of corporate involvement in
   the contemporary world;

2. to raise theological and ethical questions related to investments;

3. to determine criteria for ethical church investment;

4. to present action options for achieving effective change in corporation decisions, practices, and policies;

5. to lead a firm commitment for a practical local program of social
   responsibility; and,

6. to connect the local programs with the national effort.[49]

While these symposia were being planned, the National Federation of
Priests' Councils met on March 18-22, 1973 and approved the pamphlet
Exploitation or Liberation: Ethics for Investors, and recommended it to its
local members for discussion and action. The NFPC put their own words
into action by deciding to purchase one share of General Electric stock
and vote it in support of a Clergy and Laity Concerned resolution against
the production of the B-1 bomber. This was the first case of a Catholic
organization becoming involved in a shareholder action in the history of
the American Roman Catholic church.[50]

The first symposium on corporate responsibility took place in
Milwaukee on May 1-2, 1973, with 56 participants. Subsequent workshops were held in Adrian, Michigan, and Nazareth, Kentucky, during
the Fall of 1973. Seven more workshops were held in the following year.
The organization established a position of Project Coordinator and invited Father Michael H. Crosby, a Capuchin in Milwaukee, to serve in that
capacity. He has served the church in that role as an advocate of social
justice and social responsibility since then.

Between May 1973 and April 1976, NCCRI, under the leadership of
Father Crosby, held a total of fifteen symposia around the country. Most of

these symposia led to the organization of regional coalitions of religious groups. By the end of 1978 NCCRI had grown from the nine sponsoring organizations to over 190 members. In 1998, twenty-five years after the founding of NCCRI, approximately 250 Catholic organizations are connected with the coalition. To be more effective many of these Catholic orders and institutions have joined the more inclusive Interfaith Center on Corporate Responsibility (ICCR) located in New York.[51] ICCR has become the active coalition of corporate responsibility for Catholic, Protestant, and Jewish institutions. Because of this shift toward the interfaith coalition, Fr. Crosby notes that NCCRI is now in a dormant phase as a separate Catholic organization. "While NCCRI is on the back burner right now, the coalition could be activated if it was necessary." At the same time "the regional sections of the National Catholic Coalition for Responsible Investment are still active."[52] The Roman Catholic presence in the Interfaith Center on Corporate Responsibility is so strong in terms of members and money that a separate coalition of Catholics is not necessary.

ICCR has grown to include twenty-two Protestant denominations and agencies, two Jewish groups, and over 250 Roman Catholic orders, dioceses, health systems, and other groups. The member groups represent over $80 billion in investment.[53] In 1996 Timothy Smith, the Executive Director of ICCR looked back over its 25-year history:

> ICCR's twenty-fifth anniversary is a rich opportunity for reflection on what has been a prophetic ministry for faith communities. ICCR has assembled the beliefs and power of its 275 Protestant, Roman Catholic and Jewish members who have had tangible impact on countless corporate decisions. Some companies will never give credit to the ideas of the religious corporate responsibility movement, but others like General Motors, candidly declare that ICCR has been a social and environmental early warning system for them and others.[54]

The religious corporate responsibility movement has tackled many social problems, from apartheid in South Africa to the infant formula controversy. It will continue to underscore the important message that "corporate decisions must serve the social as well as the financial bottom line."[55]

Pope Paul VI's call to action has been heard in dioceses and religious orders as they began to use their corporate wealth on behalf of social justice and the needs of the poor.

WOODSTOCK THEOLOGICAL CENTER

This third center was established in Washington, D.C., a few years after NET-WORK and the Center of Concern. The Woodstock Theological Center describes itself as a nonprofit research institute at Georgetown University, established in 1974 by the Maryland and New York Provinces of the Society of Jesus. "Drawing on the Roman Catholic tradition, the Woodstock Center is ecumenically open, multi-disciplinary, and collaborative with others." It aims to "be attentive to Scripture's concern for the poor and the powerless. Its work is a particular instance of the contemporary mission of the Society of Jesus: the service of faith through the promotion of justice."[56] To accomplish this goal the Center offers research, forums, and publications on such issues as church and society, business ethics, international development, technology and culture, public philosophy, and religion and politics.

The Woodstock Center has a number of very effective programs that would generally be considered as "justice education and transformation," including the very popular "Preaching the Just Word" Retreat. This retreat/workshop, which is co-directed by Walter Burghardt and Father Raymond Kemp, helps priests and other preachers refresh their knowledge of Catholic social teaching and enables them to preach the Scripture as "the Just Word of God." As of 1997 2,500 preachers had participated in this retreat experience.[57]

Conclusion

Pope Paul VI invited Catholics around the world to engage in transforming action on behalf of justice and to discern the principles of reflection and the norms of judgment. The synod document strengthened that invitation by naming action on behalf of justice as an essential component of preaching the Gospel. As the final part of this chapter reveals, many Roman Catholics in the United States in general, and a number of religious orders in particular, took that invitation seriously as they established centers and structures to carry out the church's social ministry. The work of these and many other centers continues to enrich the church and influence the shaping of public policy.

The tension identified when discussing *Octogesima Adveniens*— between the role of the papal magisterium and the role of the local church in the articulation of social teaching is a healthy and necessary tension. Both the local church and papal magisterium have an important and irreplaceable role to play as the church struggles to live out its own social vision. That vision is one in which the dignity of each person is recognized and protected in the basic equality of all and in the promotion of participation in all areas of life. The church universal and local, has made strides toward recognizing the need for equality and participation not only within society but also within the church. But the job is not finished. The "call to action" is needed in every decade, just as it was minded and acted upon in the 1970s.

Discussion Questions

1. Pope Paul VI's *Octogesima Adveniens* broke new ground in a number of areas. How do you evaluate those breakthroughs at this point in the development of Catholic social thought and activism?

2. The methodology of *Octogesima Adveniens* taught that it was up to Christians in the situation to analyze, reflect, and choose the appropriate option for action. Does this appear too open-ended, or is it the most realistic approach to follow? How do the churches in various countries have a sense that they are part of a united Catholic church?

3. The synod document *Justice in the World* taught that work on behalf of justice is constitutive of preaching the gospel. How is this evident in your faith community?

4. The movements discussed in this chapter—NETWORK, Center of Concern, NCCRI, and the Woodstock Theological Center—are advocates of institutional reform. Discuss how these and similar groups have affected your life.

5. How is your diocese, parish, or school committed to corporate responsibility?

8

The Consistent Ethic of Life and the "Gospel of Life"

A LACK OF CONSISTENCY

In 1971 a young Catholic journalist, Margaret O'Brien Steinfels, was sitting at her kitchen table reading the newspaper. "The inconsistency of the Catholic church's pro-life position is about to hit [her]."[1]

On the front page of the newspaper is a photograph of New York's Cardinal Terence Cooke wearing a pilot's helmet as he sits in a jet bomber in Vietnam. His presence is an implicit blessing on the war in Vietnam—a war in which the Mylai massacre of women and children had already taken place, a war that was proving to be a moral nightmare, for it seemed to violate every principle of the church's just war teaching.

Steinfels felt an intense inconsistency and anger.

> I was appalled and outraged, the more so because the previous Sunday a letter from Cardinal Cooke was read from the pulpit. He wrote opposing New York's reform law permitting abortion on demand through the twenty-fourth week. In his letter he urged New York Catholics to work to "stop this slaughter of the innocent unborn." Where was his concern, I asked myself, for the innocent Vietnamese, born and unborn—and yes, for the American soldiers being maimed or slaughtered in an unjust and useless war?[2]

Margaret O'Brien Steinfels had put her finger on the need to link the pro-life concern for the unborn with a concern for the victims of war. She felt a lack of consistency and a lack of moral leadership from her bishops. She recalled,

> Well, I wrote him off, and with him most of the other American bishops. Lean, mean and twenty-nine, I dashed off a column.... "The day has long since passed when one expected moral leadership from one's bishop. But it is never too late for them to join their fellow Christians in deploring not only the immorality of abortion, but the immorality of Mylai and, if their vision prove large enough, the immorality of the Indochinese war."[3]

This chapter tells the story of the American bishops and laity articulating a consistent ethic of life that addresses all the life issues. After a brief survey of the beginnings of the consistent ethic of life movement in the United States, initiated by the laity, and the pastoral vision of Cardinal Joseph Bernardin, the chapter presents Pope John Paul II's teaching in his encyclical *Evangelium Vitae* (The Gospel of Life). The chapter concludes with a few evaluative reflections on the moral vision of the consistent ethic of life and some "resources" for responding to our "culture of violence."

Part I. An Emerging Movement

The consistent ethic of life was articulated almost simultaneously in different places by very different people: an Irish peace activist, an archbishop in Boston, and two pro-life women in Columbus, Ohio. These people, with many others, gave shape and form to the emerging movement.[4]

Eileen Egan, a pacifist, who, as a member of the Catholic Worker movement, was wrestling with how to link these life issues. She recalled that in early 1971 she was being interviewed by the British journalist

Malcolm Muggeridge. He was asking her about her views on war, capital punishment, and abortion. Ms. Egan came up with the image of "the seamless garment" as a way of picturing the linkage between these diverse issues. The life issues are threads that are woven together into a seamless garment. Malcolm Muggeridge disagreed with her connecting these issues but the image stayed with Eileen and eventually became the symbol for those concerned about being consistently "pro-life."[5]

In 1971 another Catholic leader felt the discrepancy in Roman Catholic teachings on life that Margaret Steinfels had named. *Archbishop Humberto Medeiros* of Boston gave an address entitled "A Call for a Consistent Ethic of Life and the Law." Richard McCormick, a noted moral theologian, called it "one of the finest social statements I have seen from an American prelate."

Archbishop Medeiros suggested that if the church wanted to appeal to the conscience of contemporary men and women it must have an ethic that is both "comprehensive in scope and *consistent* in substance." As Father McCormick noted "the remarkable aspect of the archbishop's text is its repeated emphasis on the fact that consistency in an ethic of life demands a strong stand on issues touching the quality of life." Medeiros said, "if we support the right of every fetus to be born, consistency demands that we equally support every man's continuing right to a truly human existence." Medeiros applied this down the line to problems of housing, education, welfare, race, warfare, etc., where the quality of life is continually threatened. McCormick thought it was "an excellent example of a truly holistic perspective."[6]

At about the same time in Columbus, Ohio, a member of the National Organization for Women (NOW) was disappointed and frustrated by the feminist movement's carte blanche acceptance of abortion. As a member of the Columbus chapter of NOW, *Pat Goltz* actively objected to NOW's decision to promote the legalization and acceptance of abortion as a primary goal for feminism. Pat declared, "They can't do that to my movement!" She valiantly tried to persuade NOW not to embrace abortion, arguing that accepting abortion as the solution for all the problems of womankind was a lethal virus that would eventually destroy feminism. The next step was not too difficult to predict. NOW not only rejected Pat's opinion, it rejected her. She was expelled in 1974 because of her pro-life views.

But Ms. Goltz was not the type of person who was intimidated by these difficulties. She used her frustration to energize a search for a better response. In the process she connected with *Catherine Callaghan* who also saw abortion as an abhorrent aberration for a movement committed to equality for women. "Half of all abortions kill our sisters!" they exclaimed. The two women decided to establish an organization for pro-life feminists, firmly believing that "we can't be the only ones!"[7]

FEMINISTS FOR LIFE

Pat and Cathy started to attend meetings of the Ohio Right to Life group, whose more conservative members initially assumed that they were spies from the liberal NOW organization. Once the pro-lifers realized the integrity of Pat and Cathy the Ohio Right to Life members enthusiastically supported the fledgling Feminists for Life (FFL). Pat recalls that the Ohio Pro-life group referred many pro-lifers with "latent feminist tendencies" to the new organization. FFL received good publicity: Pat was in demand as a public speaker at conventions and debates for radio and television talk shows. The group started a newsletter, called the *Feminist for Life Journal*, which was later changed to *Sisterlife* and finally to *The American Feminist*.

According to Pat, most of the earliest members of FFL were basically conservatives. In 1976 when Pat moved to Arizona she turned the administration of the organization over to the Wisconsin chapter, at which point the organization assumed a more liberal tone through the 1980s and early 1990s. Rosemary Bottcher, the president in 1997, claimed that as of that year the membership covered the entire political and ideological spectrum.[8]

The mission of Feminists for Life is "dedicated to securing through nonviolent means basic human rights for all people, especially women and children, from conception until the natural end of life."[9] As a non-sectarian, grass-roots organization FFL opposes "all forms of violence, including abortion, euthanasia and capital punishment, as they are inconsistent with the core feminist principles of justice, non-violence and non-discrimination."[10]

To carry out this mission the organization focuses its efforts on "education, outreach and advocacy, as well as facilitating practical resources and support for women in need." The national office, now in Washington, D.C., prepares the newsletter, educational programs (such as the effective "College Outreach Kits," a public education campaign for abortion survivors), publicity materials, bumper stickers, and other materials.

The structure tends to be grounded in the local level: a great amount of responsibility rests with the grass-roots leaders in each state. The ideas and concerns of these leaders are addressed at a general assembly held each spring in Washington, D.C. The state chapter presidents are also responsible for electing national officers and the board of directors, as well as helping to define the direction of the organization. The annual assembly also serves as a forum for the exchange of ideas, projects, and experiences of the state leaders, which is intended to assist the chapters in promoting the mission and goals of FFL.[11]

The Feminists for Life organization is connected with other groups with similar goals including the National Women's Coalition for Life, the Seamless Garment Network, the National Coalition to Abolish the Death Penalty, and the Coalition for a Caring Society. In its advocacy role Feminists for Life will, at times, join forces with pro-choice groups on particular issues. For instance in 1994 Feminists for Life joined in an unprecedented coalition with such long-established pro-choice groups as Planned Parenthood, the National Organization for Women, the National Abortion Rights Action League, and the ACLU to fight the "child exclusion provision" in the welfare plan proposed by President Clinton. The provision would allow states to cut off any additional benefits to women who have more children while receiving welfare.[12]

Although their organization was started in 1972, Feminists for Life claim Elizabeth Cady Stanton, who organized the first women's rights meeting in 1848, as one of their foremothers. "When we consider that women are treated as property," Stanton said, "it is degrading to women that we should treat our children as property to be disposed of as we see fit."[13]

FFL has grown to a membership of 5,000 with a presence in 32 states, two student chapters, and contacts in Canada and Australia.[14] It is a small but rather vocal group that is helping women and men see the linkage between these life issues.[15] Their statement in 1978 captures something of their vision and energy.

> We, as pro-life feminists, offer a return to the roots of feminism in this country, a feminism which is a loving, nurturing response to any human suffering...be it the suffering of a woman, a man, or an unborn child. We reject the violence which is the world's way. We believe that our non-violence and our embracing of life where we find it must extend to the entire human family, and beyond the narrow confines of our biological families. We proclaim that we are homemakers—that the world is our home and we make it—loving, nurturing and pro-life.[16]

SEAMLESS GARMENT NETWORK

A second grass-roots movement was started by Juli Loesch in 1979 for the purpose of linking opposition to abortion with opposition to nuclear weapons. This group was called Prolifers for Survival. (Four years later Cardinal Bernardin would make the same connection between abortion and nuclear weapons.) In 1987 Prolifers for Survival decided to move beyond the two issues of abortion and war. At a three-day conference held in March in Chapel Hill, North Carolina, Prolifers for Survival brought together representatives of more than a dozen religious, pro-life, peace, and social justice organizations in order "to explore avenues for consistently promoting the sanctity and protection of life." Faye and Jeff Kunce, members of Prolifers for Survival, recall that "the participants developed the Seamless Garment Network as a means for mutual support toward these ideals."[17]

With the birth of the Seamless Garment Network (SGN), the parent organization, Prolifers for Survival, decided to cease as a separate organization. The Prolifers decided to fold the organization in order to focus the development of the consistent life ethic beyond the two issues of war and abortion, to include poverty and capital punishment. After a few years euthanasia and racism would be added to the list.

The Seamless Garment Network was set up with two major functions in mind. First, to serve as a clearing house for audiovisuals and print resources, and, second, to be a prophetic voice proclaiming the sacredness of life. The clearing house function enables organizations and individuals involved in specific areas of concern to connect and to learn from others working on other issues and forming a communications system for mutual support. The prophetic aspect was envisioned to take the form of a publication dedicated to exploring and expanding both direct and indirect connections between issues threatening life today, and "challenging readers to cooperate in their different approaches to protecting the unprotected." The Seamless Garment Network did establish a periodical known as *Harmony: Voices for a Just Future*. The first edition appeared in September 1987. *Harmony*, which is published bimonthly, describes itself as offering "news, events and innovative thinking about the growing, changing consistent ethic movement."[18]

In addition to publishing their periodical the Seamless Garment Network set about to publicize its mission statement in order to attract more groups and individuals into the Network. Their mission statement reads,

> We the undersigned are committed to the protection of life, which is threatened in today's world by war, abortion, poverty, racism, the arms race, the death penalty and euthanasia.
>
> We believe that these issues are linked under a consistent ethic of life.
>
> We challenge those working on all or some of these issues to maintain a cooperative spirit of peace, reconciliation and respect in protecting the unprotected.[19]

SGN publicizes its consistent ethic vision through the publication of ads in national and local publications. These ads contain the Mission Statement, followed by the names of the people and groups that have committed themselves to the consistent ethic of life. SGN has placed ads in *Christianity Today*, the *New Oxford Review*, the *National Catholic Reporter*, and *The Nation*.

As of December 1993, 130 organizations and 210 individuals had joined the Seamless Garment Network. The organizations include Agnostics for Life, the Pro-Life Alliance of Gays and Lesbians, the Christian Center for Women (Nigeria), and various Catholic Worker communities. The individuals who have endorsed the SGN Mission Statement include three Nobel Peace Laureates: Mairead Corrigan Maguire, Adolfo Perez Esquivel, and the Dalai Lama.[20]

Carol Crossed, the executive director, explains, "the Seamless Garment Network is a federation of member organizations. The consistent ethic movement is just that, a movement, not an organization. The SGN is an umbrella; we try to serve, publicize and encourage the movement."[21]

DIOCESE OF ROCHESTER

A third example of a consistent ethic of life effort is the Consistent Life Ethic (CLE) Program of the Diocese of Rochester, New York. This program was the result of a communal discernment process from 1990-1993 by the Roman Catholics in this ten-county diocese of upstate New York. The synod, as this discernment and education process was known, led to a commitment by the diocese to the consistent ethic of life as one of four major priorities. The Consistent Life Ethic Program was established, given substantial funding ($140,000), and put under the able direction of full-time Consistent Life Ethic Coordinator, Dr. Suzanne Schnittman. Through a wide variety of initiatives the Diocese of Rochester is beginning to experience the vision of the consistent ethic of life, while at the same time the people of the diocese are shaping the future direction of this vibrant moral and spiritual tradition.

Two of the more visible efforts of Rochester's CLE program are the Consistent Life Ethic Awards, and grants. Each year the diocese names five people who symbolize the meaning of the Consistent Ethic of Life. These people, along with all those nominated, are lifted up for the church as witnesses to the Gospel call to protect life and reject violence. At a banquet and a reception all the nominees and awardees are recognized for their efforts at living out the consistent life ethic.

The CLE effort in Rochester also includes fund-raising to provide grants for CLE programs in the diocese. Creative initiatives are funded under the "venture grant" heading. The program also supports established programs under the heading "operational grants." This money, annually about $30,000, is dispersed to groups and programs such as women's shelters, homes for pregnant women, hospices, organizations addressing the death penalty, education on nonviolence, and experiential teen retreats on the CLE.

Through these initiatives the Diocese of Rochester is educating its members in the meaning of the consistent ethic of life. This ethic is articulated in its 1997 Strategic Plan, which reads,

> Roman Catholics will treat all people with dignity and respect, because, as a gift from God, all life is sacred. We will defend all people, especially powerless and marginalized people who are threatened by forces we oppose including: abortion, the death penalty, euthanasia, economic injustice, violence and war.
>
> Through strong parish leadership, we will nurture life in our own families and champion those threatened by personal, public and institutional neglect and by violence, prejudice or injustice. We will express our commitment to life in teaching and preaching and in individual and communal action. We will work to transform current social structures and behaviors in to a more creative and imaginative Christ-centered society which affirms nonviolence, justice and the sacredness of all life.[22]

The above sampling gives a sense of how the consistent ethic of life movement is visible in ecclesial and secular expressions. This movement is supported by diverse groups and individuals who do fit the traditional categories of "liberal" or "conservative." One such individual whose name is associated with the consistent ethic of life more than any other person is Cardinal Joseph Bernardin.

Part II. Cardinal Bernardin's Pastoral and Moral Vision

Cardinal Bernardin emerged as an effective leader among the American hierarchy, including his skillful handling of the drafting of bishops' pastoral letter *The Challenge of Peace*. His fellow bishops were not going to let him rest on his laurels. Only seven months after the promulgation of the pastoral letter (May 1983) he was assigned to be chairman of the National Conference of Catholic Bishops' Pro-Life Committee. He moved quickly from evaluating nuclear deterrence to analyzing abortion.

Bernardin immediately saw connections between the two issues, and committed himself to "shaping a position of *linkage* among the life issues."[23] The pastoral letter on war served as a starting point for the consistent ethic of life. "The central idea in the letter is the sacredness of human life and the responsibility we have, personally and socially, to protect and preserve the sanctity of life."[24]

Bernardin identified a dominant cultural reality present in both modern warfare and modern medicine that leads to a "sharper awareness of the fragility of human life," namely, "our technology." He believed that the challenge of technology with its troubling questions "along the spectrum of life from womb to tomb creates the need for a consistent ethic of life."

> For the spectrum of life cuts across the issues of genetics, abortion, capital punishment, modern warfare and the care of the terminally ill. These are all distinct problems, enormously complicated, and deserving individual treatment. No single answer and no simple responses will solve them. My purpose, however, is to highlight the way in which we face new technological challenges in each one of these areas; *this combination of challenges cries out for a consistent ethic of life.*[25]

Bernardin accurately realized that the selling of a consistent ethic of life in the church and in society begins with "the honest recognition that the shaping of a consensus among Catholics on the spectrum of life issues is far from finished."[26]

The first audience for consensus building is *within* the Catholic community. Bernardin said, "We need the kind of dialogue on these issues which the pastoral letter generated on the nuclear question. We need the same searching intellectual exchange, the same degree of involvement of clergy, religious, and laity, the same sustained attention in the Catholic press."

The secondary focus of consensus building is "sharing our vision with the wider society." In this regard, Bernardin offered two suggestions regarding substance and style:

1. The substance of a Catholic position on a consistent ethic of life is rooted in a religious vision. But the citizenry of the United States is radically pluralistic in moral and religious convictions. Therefore, to be effective in society Bernardin would state his case in non-religious terms that members of different faith convictions or citizens with no faith communities might find morally persuasive.

2. Recognizing that the issues of war, abortion, and capital punishment are emotional and often divisive questions, Bernardin urged a style governed by the following rule: "We should maintain and clearly articulate our religious convictions but also maintain our civil courtesy. We should be vigorous in stating a case and attentive in hearing another's case; we should test everyone's logic but *not question his or her motives.*"[27]

DISTINCT YET INTERRELATED ISSUES

Cardinal Bernardin identified the ways life was being threatened:

- nuclear war threatens life on a previously unimaginable scale;

- abortion takes life daily on a horrendous scale;

- public executions are fast becoming weekly events in the most advanced technological society in history;

- and euthanasia is now openly discussed and even advocated.

He recognized that "each of these assaults on life has its own meaning and morality; *they cannot be collapsed into one problem.*" Yet, Bernardin argued that "they must be confronted as *pieces of a larger pattern....* I am persuaded by the *interrelatedness of these diverse problems....*" This is a delicate tension to maintain—seeing their connectedness but also maintaining the distinctiveness of each issue.

The consistent ethic of life challenges both the anti-abortion activists and the anti-death penalty people to begin to see the common ground they share in defending life. Bernardin was criticized after his 1983 address at Fordham by respondents who maintained the separateness of abortion and capital punishment. They argued that the principle of protecting *innocent* life distinguished the unborn child from the convicted murderer. "Other letters stress that while nuclear war is a threat to life, abortion involves the actual taking of life, here and now." To these criticisms he responded, "I accept both of these distinctions, of course, but I also find compelling the need to *relate* the cases while keeping them in distinct categories."[28]

The creative edge of the consistent ethic of life is that it challenges Catholics and others to recognize *both* the distinctiveness of these issues and their relatedness:

> And it is very necessary for preserving a systemic vision that individuals and groups who seek to witness to life at one point of the spectrum of life not be seen as insensitive to or even opposed to other moral claims on the overall spectrum of life. Consistency does rule out contradictory moral positions about the unique value of human life. No one is called to do everything, but each of us can do something. And we can strive not to stand against each other when the protection and the promotion of life are at stake.[29]

CUTS TWO WAYS

In his 1983 address Cardinal Bernardin clearly linked pro-life advocacy and social justice:

> If one contends, as we do, that the right of every fetus to be born should be protected by civil law and supported by civil consensus, then our moral, political and economic responsibilities do not stop at the moment of birth. Those who defend the right to life of the weakest among us must be equally visible in support of the quality of life of the powerless among us: the old and the young, the hungry and the homeless, the undocumented immigrant and the unemployed worker. Such a quality of life posture translates into specific political and economic positions on tax policy, employment generation, welfare policy, nutrition and feeding programs, and health care. Consistency means we cannot have it both ways: We cannot urge a compassionate society and vigorous public policy to protect the rights of the unborn and then argue that compassion and sig-

nificant public programs on behalf of the needy undermine the moral fiber of the society or are beyond the proper scope of governmental responsibility.[30]

The cardinal was criticized on two counts. First by those who claimed he had confused two different moral issues and second, by those who claimed that he expected everyone to do everything. On the first count, he reiterated that "surely we can all agree that the taking of human life in abortion is not the same as failing to protect human dignity against hunger." Having said that, he goes on to say that "but... let us not fail to make the point that both are moral issues requiring a response of the Catholic community and of our society as a whole." He continued,

> The logic of a consistent ethic is to press the moral meaning of both issues. The consequences of a consistent ethic is to bring under review the *positions of every group in the Church which sees the moral meaning in one place* but not the other. *The ethic cuts two ways,* not one: It challenges pro-life groups, and it challenges justice and peace groups. The meaning of a consistent ethic is to say in the Catholic community that our moral tradition calls us beyond the split so evident in the wider society between moral witness to life before and after birth.[31]

On the second issue he responded that the consistent ethic does not expect "everyone to do everything." Rather it challenges single issue groups to explore how their issue is related to other life issues. Cardinal Bernardin was grounded in reality when he noted that

> There are limits of time, energy and competency. There is a shape to every individual vocation. People must specialize, groups must focus their energies. The consistent ethic does not deny this. But it does say something to the Church: It calls us to a wider witness to life than we sometimes manifest in our separate activities.[32]

MORAL VISION TO PUBLIC POLICY

The heart of the consistent ethic of life is that it is a *moral and pastoral vision* for the Catholic community, a vision not yet fully realized. It is a vision of where the church should be headed, as Father Bernard Häring would say, a *Zielgebot,* a "goal-command." The church has not completed the journey, but is on the way toward that vision of Gospel living.

While the consistent ethic of life is first to be lived within the church community, it is not a narrow, sectarian ethic, meant only for the "beloved community." Bernardin believed the consistent ethic of life sets the agenda for working with other religious groups and society as a whole. He had a nuanced sense of how the consistent ethic of life translated into public policy. In his address at the CEL Conference in Portland Oregon, on October 4, 1986, Bernardin discussed the transition from moral analysis to public policy.

Some in the church believe the church's moral teaching should be the norm for public policy. This is a type of automatic transference of morality to public policy. Cardinal Bernardin favored a second approach traced through Father John Courtney Murray back to Thomas Aquinas and Augustine. This second approach translates the moral teaching into policy decisions that are feasible and realistic.

In brief, Cardinal Bernardin recommended that we take into account the following five points as we move from moral vision and moral analysis to public policy choices:

1. that civil discourse in the United States is influenced and shaped by religious pluralism;

2. that there is a legitimate secularity of the political process;

3. that all participants in the political process must face the reality of complexity, i.e., these discussions are based on empirical evidence about which there is disagreement and complexity;

4. that there is a distinction between civil law and morality; and

5. that some issues are questions of public morality and others of private morality. A persuasive case has to be evident that an action violates the rights of another or that the consequences are so important that the civil law ought to be invoked to be deemed "public morality."

Bernardin recognized that it was a complex process to move from our religious convictions to public policy in a religiously pluralistic society. "But we have been able to do it—by a process of debate, decision-making, then review of our decisions."[33] Cardinal Bernardin pointed to the civil rights movement, which has gradually become part of our national consciousness as it moved from the activists' agenda through the churches and legislative bodies: "philosophers, activists, politicians, preachers, judges, and ordinary citizens had to state a case, shape a consensus, and then find a way to give the consensus public standing in the life of the nation."[34]

AN UPHILL JOURNEY

Advocates of the consistent ethic of life must be realistic about the challenge ahead of them. There is substantial support for abortion rights, for physician-assisted suicide, for the death penalty, not only in the Catholic community but also in American society as a whole. Bernardin began in his own backyard by rallying support among his fellow bishops. In 1985 the NCCB adopted the consistent ethic theme for its revised Plan for Pro-Life Activities.[35] This is a first step toward a broader endorsement of the consistent ethic of life in the Catholic community.

It is a daunting task to build a consensus in the church and in society around the vision of the consistent ethic of life, but Bernardin was optimistic. In one of his last addresses on the consistent ethic of life, presented at Georgetown University's Woodstock Theological Center, on March 20, 1990, Bernardin saw potential for support of the ethic in the sixty percent of Americans who do not identify themselves completely with either of the pro-life or the pro-choice camps. He was willing to work for incremental gains, such as setting limits on abortion. "To convince this 60 percent of the populace of the wisdom of at least limiting abortion would be a major advance for life." This is where the appeal of the consistent ethic of life may be helpful:

> I am convinced that moving the middle depends upon projecting a broad-based vision which seeks to support and sustain life. It will not be enough to be against abortion; we need to show convincingly that we are for life—life for women and children; for life, in support of the very old and the very young; for life which enhances the chance for the next generation to come to adulthood well-educated, well-nourished, and well-founded in a value structure which provides a defense against the allure of drugs, violence and despair.[36]

Bernardin also realized that there is and will be resistance, but such resistance should not lead to a defensive or sectarian response. Here, Bernardin was a master of presenting his principles, but presenting them in a way that was persuasive rather than preachy. He was open to other perspectives, because he believed, along with Vatican II that "we have much to learn from the world."

Let me conclude this section on Cardinal Bernardin's vision of the consistent ethic by quoting the ending of his 1990 address at Woodstock. It says a lot about the strength and openness of this approach.

> The substance of the consistent ethic yields a style of teaching it and witnessing to it. The style should be prophetic, but not sectarian. The word "prophetic" should be used sparingly and carefully, but a truly consistent ethic of word and deed, which protects life and promotes it, is truly a work of God, hence a prophetic word in our time. Such a vision and posture inevitably will meet resistance. But we should resist the sectarian tendency to retreat into a closed circle, convinced of our truth and the impossibility of sharing it with others. To be both prophetic and public, a countersign to much of the culture, but also a light and leaven for all of it, is the delicate balance to which we are called.
>
> The style should be persuasive, not preachy. We should use the model of the Second Vatican Council's *Pastoral Constitution on the Church in the Modern World*: We should be convinced that we have much to learn from the world and much to teach it. We should be confident but collegial with others who seek similar goals but may differ on means and methods. A confident church will speak its mind, seek as a community to live its convictions, but leave space for others to speak to us, help us to grow from their perspective, and to collaborate with them. May my words this evening contribute to this confidence.[37]

Part III. Pope John Paul II— "In defense of humanity"

On October 16, 1978 the cardinal of Warsaw, Karol Wojtyla, was elected pope. Those who were standing near him when he first heard the news said that "for a moment he went perfectly still, and his face turned as white as a dead man's." But after he had accepted the office, announced that he would take the name John Paul II, and donned the white cassock, he took on such an air of confidence and comfort in the office that "one would have thought he had always been Pope."[38] Wojtyla was the first non-Italian to become pope since the Dutchman Hadrian VI in 1523, and at the age of 58 he was the youngest pope since Pius IX in 1846.

His relative youth was evident in the vitality and energy with which he tackled the work of bishop of Rome. His charismatic and ruddy style broke through papal stereotypes. For example, pope watchers claimed that "popes don't sing"—well this one did and does. During his first trip abroad to attend the conference of Latin American bishops at Puebla, Mexico, he joined in singing the old Mexican favorite "Cielito Lindo" in a working class area of Guadalajara. The crowd was whooping it up when the pope stood to speak. Suddenly over the public address system there boomed a beautiful baritone joining in the "hi-yi-yi's." In Tokyo in 1981 the pope was being entertained by the rock quartet, the Dark Ducks. Before they realized it the Ducks had become a quintet; the pope had picked up a microphone and was singing with them.[39]

This pope reaches out to the poor with a human touch and a word of hope. In the *favela* of Vidigal, Brazil, where 20,000 people live in shacks of wood or mud along narrow streets that are quagmires of mud and fetid water, the pope stopped at least five times to kiss the children as he climbed the hill. At one point he turned abruptly to enter a three-room shack to embrace an aged woman who was shocked to have the pope in her home.[40]

On his third trip to Poland when Solidarity, the worker's union, was outlawed, he spoke the forbidden word in season and out of season. He rekindled the spirits of the workers whose hopes were half-stifled by the repressive tactics of the communist regime. He said everything that Lech Walesa, the workers' leader, was not allowed to say without punishment. General Jaruzelski complained that John Paul had treated the government with greater severity than usual. The pope responded with a smile: "No, I didn't. All I did was to quote your own Constitution." It was clear who really defended the rights of the proletariat.[41]

Andre Frossard, a French author and friend of the pope who has traveled with him and conversed with him on many topics, summarized his grand design as "the defense of humanity. It was a total defense...and it mobilized and went into action either successively or simultaneously on the political front, the social front, and the spiritual front." Frossard believes that "every one of John Paul II's encyclicals has to do with some aspect of human life or human activity, and in the same way, all his addresses...plead for social justice and sincere goodwill among men."[42]

Pope John Paul II truly advocates the consistent ethic of life:

- he has defended worker rights in his visits to Poland and in his very important encyclical *Laborem Exercens*, on the 90th anniversary of *Rerum Novarum*;

- he has continued the church's commitment to the poor and addressing issues of economic injustice in his social encyclicals, *Sollicitudo Rei Socialis* and *Centesimus Annus,* and in his visits to rich and poor nations alike;

- he has spoken out clearly that the death penalty is not the answer for our concerns about criminal justice. As a powerful witness that reconciliation, not vengeance, is the answer he visited with Mehmet Ali Agca, his attempted assassin, in prison;[43]

- he has spoken repeatedly against abortion, especially in the encyclical *Evangelium Vitae, The Gospel of Life;*

- his position on euthanasia is equally clear, starting with the well-written *Declaration on Euthanasia* in 1980 from the Congregation for the Doctrine of the Faith to the 1993 encyclical, *Evangelium Vitae;*

- he has also been limiting the circumstances in which resorting to war is morally acceptable; it was clear during the Persian Gulf war that he did not see it as a justifiable conflict.[44]

While it is not fair to reduce a prolific and complex papacy to one theme, it is also fair to see his use of the papacy as putting into action the reality of the consistent ethic of life.[45]

THE GOSPEL OF LIFE

Evangelium Vitae, The Gospel of Life, which was issued on March 25, 1995, defends life as sacred from the "very beginning until its end" not as an absolute value but as a "primary good respected to the highest degree. Upon the recognition of this right, every human community and the political community itself are founded." For followers of Christ, Pope John Paul II sees "the value of every human life and the right to have each life respected" as the church's "good news," an essential part of the Gospel. In other words, the incarnation reveals not only God's love for humanity but also the "incomparable value of every human person.... The Gospel of God's love for man, the Gospel of the dignity of this person and the Gospel of life are a single and indivisible Gospel" (par. 2).

This is a substantial linking of the Good News of salvation with the Good News of the value of every person, which means that the church cannot separate its religious message from its social message.

The pope's strongly worded defense of life is necessary, he says, because of "the extraordinary increase and gravity of threats to the life of individuals and peoples, especially where life is weak and defenseless. In addition to the ancient scourges of poverty, hunger, endemic diseases, violence, and war, new threats are emerging on an alarmingly vast scale" (par. 3). The goal of the encyclical is

> meant to be a precise and vigorous reaffirmation of the value of human life and its inviolability, and at the same time a pressing appeal in the name of God: Respect, protect, love and serve life, every human life! Only in this direction will you find justice, development, true freedom, peace and happiness! (par. 5)

He hopes that the church will offer "new signs of hope" to the world:

> to all the members of the church, the people of life and for life, I make this most urgent appeal, that together we may offer this world of ours new signs of hope and work to ensure that justice and solidarity will increase and that a new culture of human life will be affirmed for the building of an authentic civilization of truth and love. (par. 6)

Attacks Against Life:
A "Culture of Death"

In reflecting on the violence of Cain against his own brother Abel, the pope addressed God's question to Cain—"What have you done?"—to our contemporary society. John Paul identified the various sources of attacks against life, including:

- threats from nature that are made worse by the indifference and negligence of those who could help;

- situations of violence, hatred which leads to murder and war and genocide;

- violence against children due to poverty, malnutrition, and hunger;

- war and the arms trade;

- death caused by ecological destruction;

- criminal drug culture;

- attacks on the earliest stages of life and life in its final stages.

These diverse attacks on life are cause for deep analysis of western society's cultural roots. As the pope analyzed western culture he saw widespread moral uncertainty and skepticism and a structure of sin that denies solidarity. These forces can be described as a "culture of death" and a "conspiracy against life," which he sees as "a war of the powerful against the weak."

He believes that this "culture is actively fostered by powerful cultural, economic, and political currents which encourage an ideal of society excessively concerned with efficiency." In concrete terms the pope describes this culture of death in this way:

> A life which would require greater acceptance, love and care is con-sidered useless or held to be an intolerable burden, and is therefore rejected in one way or another. A person who, because of illness, handicap or, more simply, just by existing, compromises the well-being or lifestyle of those who are more favored tends to be looked upon as an enemy to be resisted or eliminated. In this way a kind of "conspiracy against life" is unleashed. This conspiracy involves not only individuals in their personal, family or group relationships, but goes far beyond, to the point of damaging and distorting at the international level relations between peoples and states. (par. 12)

While the encyclical engages in this broad cultural analysis, many paragraphs focus on the attack on life found in *abortion and euthanasia*. On these issues there are no surprises but rather a powerful and repeat-ed condemnation of abortion. In two places Pope John Paul II summons all the authority he has to articulate, in a noninfallible way, the church's teaching that a "direct abortion...always constitutes a grave moral disor-der" (par. 57 and 62). He also clearly confirms that "euthanasia is a grave violation of the law of God" (par. 65). The doctrinal "weight" of these passages is given different readings. I agree with the noted theologian Father Francis Sullivan that the letter is "an authoritative, but noninfalli-ble teaching of the ordinary papal magisterium."[46]

Death Penalty

Pope John Paul's treatment of the death penalty was the most publicized section of the encyclical. James Megivern writes in his excellent historical and theological survey of the death penalty that Pope John Paul II "had more to say about capital punishment than had any previous pope in a comparably authoritative document. His spirited repudiation of death as a punishment was all but total, to the consternation of many."[47] John Paul brings up the death penalty in three places.

1. In paragraph 9, John Paul concludes that "not even a murderer loses his personal dignity, and God himself pledges to guarantee this," as can be seen by God's protection of the murderer Cain.

2. In paragraph 27 John Paul points with pride to "a growing public opposition to the death penalty."

3. The fullest treatment of capital punishment is in paragraph 56. After quoting from the 1992 *Catechism of the Catholic Church*, Pope John Paul all but closes the door on capital punishment in stating that "punishment... ought not go to the extreme of executing the offender except in cases of absolute necessity...*such cases are very rare if not practically nonexistent.*"

In this section John Paul restricts the use of the death penalty further than previous teaching. Almost immediately after the publication of *Evangelium Vitae* Cardinal Ratzinger admitted that the *Catechism of the Catholic Church* would have to be revised in light of the papal teaching on the question. Two and a half years later when the Catechism was revised, the section on capital punishment was changed to include the very wording of *Evangelium Vitae*: "cases of absolute necessity of the execution of the offender 'are very rare, if not practically nonexistent.'"[48]

It is striking to see how quickly the church altered its official teaching.[49]

Cultural Transformation

To confront the "culture of death" Pope John Paul urges that "we must build a new culture of life." It is "new" because

- it will be called upon to solve "today's unprecedented problems affecting human life";

- it will be ecumenical as well as interfaith in its scope (par. 95).

The first step in this cultural transformation "consists in forming consciences with regard to the incomparable and inviolable worth of every human life." The cultural transformation will be expressed in "the courage to adopt *a new lifestyle* consisting in making practical choices—at the personal, family, social, and international level—on the basis of a correct scale of values: *the primacy of being over having, of the person over things"* (par. 98). This would be a radical cultural transformation for Western materialistic societies.

"Profoundly Consistent"

Evangelium Vitae offers a broad analysis of western societies in the ways in which contemporary culture threatens life and where there are "signs of hope" that are resisting the "culture of death." The letter did not intend to address all of the life issues, but focused primarily on *abortion and euthanasia.* The thrust of the letter is on the consistent ethic of life without using those exact words or without giving a balanced treatment to main issues of the ethic. The closest Pope John Paul comes to using the phrase "consistent ethic of life" is found in paragraph 87:

> Where life is involved, the service of charity must be profoundly consistent. It cannot tolerate bias and discrimination, for human life is sacred and inviolable at every stage and in every situation: it is an indivisible good. We need then to "show care" for all life and for the life of everyone.

In this encyclical, Cardinal Bernardin and others in the consistent life movement received a powerful and welcomed, though implied, endorsement of the consistent ethic of life.[50]

POSITIVE RECEPTION

How did *Evangelium Vitae* play in Peoria? Probably, pretty well—at least it received "good press" in Chicago. The *Chicago Tribune* praised the encyclical in an editorial:

> It is hard to brush off the pope's assertion that there is a growing "culture of death" in the world when the daily news in the world's richest country is of babies being discarded like trash, or children dropping other children from tall buildings; when the society seems in a headlong rush to put to death as many criminals as rapidly as possible; when in the name of reform, legislators ram through policies whose predictable results will be to increase the economic pressures on poor women to have abortions; when zealots preach that murder is justified to save unborn babies; when advocates of "choice" adopt locutions that permit them to avoid ever saying what it is that is chosen.[51]

Moral theologian Charles Curran believes there is wide support for the direction of *Evangelium Vitae:* "John Paul II's basic thesis about a failure to respect the sacredness and dignity of human life is shared by many people today," and "probably the majority of Catholics and of theologians are in fundamental agreement with the thrust of the teaching on abortion and euthanasia from the moral perspective...."[52]

AREAS IN NEED OF ONGOING EVALUATION

A number of questions are raised by *Evangelium Vitae* and the consistent ethic of life. This is not surprising: it is a moral vision that is still "a work in progress." I will briefly discuss five issues.

As we have seen from the discussion of capital punishment, *Evangelium Vitae* has already had an impact on the church's teaching on the morality of the death penalty. Pope John Paul II and the Congregation for the Doctrine of the Faith revealed how naturally the church can update and revise its official teaching on a very complex moral and social question. This *revising of church teaching* on the death penalty is instructive for other areas of the church's moral guidance. From this example it is clear that the church exercises its moral leadership by *interpreting, evaluating, and changing,* if necessary, its teaching in light of a new historical and social context. This approach is undertaken quite naturally and automatically on some of the life issues, such as war, the death penalty, and economic justice, but is not followed in other areas, such as abortion and euthanasia. The revision of the church's teaching on the death penalty raises the first question of the consistent ethic of life, namely, *how and when the Roman Catholic church revises its moral teachings.*

The second troubling question deals with *morality and public policy.* One of the more controversial sections of *Evangelium Vitae* deals with the relationship of morality to civil law. John Paul maintained that civil law must be in conformity with the moral law. He did admit that the law may tolerate an evil where its prohibition would cause even more serious harm, but civil law may not "legitimize as a right of individuals" an offense that violates the fundamental right to life. The encyclical expects those in public office will work for legislation to protect the unborn. The pope recognizes the reality of political compromise when a politician supports a less than fully protective law where the alternative is a more permissive law.

According to Father Richard McCormick, "What will make this section a matter of continuing controversy is its failure to wrestle realistically with one of the basic reasons for pluralism on abortion: the different evaluations of the fetus." The issue is that many people view the fetus with developing value and claims, as it grows and comes closer to term. McCormick notes that until there is more agreement about the value of the fetus, "public policy will remain sharply contentious and the task of legislators correspondingly complex. Indeed, a strong case can be made that the attempt to solve the evaluative problem by legislation bypasses our duty to persuade, to change minds and hearts."[53]

Fathers Charles Curran and Richard McCormick support the direction of *Evangelium Vitae*, but argue that the reality of carrying it out in a pluralistic society "is somewhat more complex than the encyclical recognizes."[54] On this point, the direction taken by Cardinal Bernardin, I believe, is better suited for the American context.

INCONSISTENCY OF METHOD

A third area of tension is the question of the mode of moral reasoning employed on the different life issues. This criticism has been raised by moral theologians such as Christine Gudorf, Richard Gula, and others. For example, in determining the morality of war, the death penalty, or capitalism, the magisterium applies moral principles to the specific situation in a way that involves *weighing all the factors involved including the context, circumstance, the consequences, and possible outcomes*. A "prudential judgment" is offered after all of these factors are weighed and evaluated. This is the approach taken by Pope John Paul as he evaluates the morality of the death penalty.

A *different methodology* is employed by the magisterium in the area of sexual and medical ethics. Father Richard Gula notes "... Catholic sexual ethics and medical ethics pertaining to reproduction have achieved a degree of certainty, precision, and consistency of moral judgment which we do not find in the documents on social ethics."[55] Gula continues:

> The church's epistemological claims in regard to natural law in social matters are more modest, *more cautious, and more nuanced* than those in sexual ethics and medical moral reproductive matters. In social ethics, the church readily accepts the inevitability of conflict on the philosophical level as well as in social life.

> ...From such a perspective, the church accepts conclusions of the applications of general principles which are *limited, tentative, and open to revision....*[56]

Christine Gudorf, a moral theologian at Xavier University in

Cincinnati, points out that "the Catholic church uses proportional con-sequentialism in public-realm issues, and a deontological natural law approach in private-realm issues." She continues:

> When we consider the methodological inconsistency between the church's treatment of war and abortion, it is small wonder that fem-inists charge the church with misogyny because of its apparent dis-trust of women as moral decision makers. Women with the medical option of abortion seem, in the bishops' eyes, to be a greater danger to life than men armed with tanks, missiles, and bombs.[57]

Professor Gudorf identifies a grave dilemma for the Catholic church.

> Though I do not believe that the source of the inconsistency is misogyny, I do feel that the continuation of methodological incon-sistency that discriminates against women as moral persons is pos-sible only in a climate of misogyny. In a society where many, and potentially all, women are not in control of their own bodies, but are raped, beaten, and molested by fathers, husbands, and strangers, as well as subjected to medical care which often treats care of women's bodies as if they were not women's to control—in such a society we move in entirely the wrong direction when we refuse to allow women final responsibility for their bodies' reproduction.[58]

There is a bit of work to be done here to reconcile this methodologi-cal *inconsistency* in the ethic of life, which seeks to be *consistent*.[59]

A fourth area in need of further reflection is the *scope* of the consistent ethic of life. There is no set canon of which issues are included in the ethic. The Diocese of Rochester includes six issues: abortion, war and vio-lence, the death penalty, economic injustice, and euthanasia. The Seamless Garment Network adds "racism" to the list and Feminists for Life include "sexism." The consistent ethic of life would be strengthened if it were extended to include all forms of violence against life. I recom-mend it include addressing the violence done to gay, lesbians, and trans-gender people. The dignity and rights of gay and lesbian people are vio-lated by the heterosexism of our society and church.[60]

If the consistent ethic of life is concerned about the violence done to all forms of life, the next step is to extend the moral vision and move-ment to include concern for *creation and the biosphere*. We now know that our pollution affects all people, especially the poor, but it also affects the unborn child in utero. Concern about the unborn would naturally include a concern that they be free of the damaging effects of alcohol, drugs, and pollution. In a Catholic perspective all of life is seen as sacred and as a reflection of God. We are to value creation not only because we depend on animal and vegetative life for our own existence, but also because it is part of God's holy creation. As we will discover in the last chapter of this book, pollution is also linked with racism and poverty— the poor and people of color often suffer disproportionally because of the placement of toxic waste sites, or the mining and manufacturing of hazardous ores and chemicals. The consistent ethic of life will be strengthened if it is extended to include all of life.

A fifth area of further reflection is voiced by the noted Protestant ethicist James Gustafson. Gustafson offers general support for the consistent ethic of life.

> I think, however, that the strong presumption in favor of the protection and promotion of human life the consistent ethic of life expounds finds no significant dissent among contemporary Protestant theologians, and that the deepening and enlarging of the implications of that presumption which Cardinal Bernardin espouses not only corrects earlier Roman Catholic teachings on particular matters but Protestant ones as well.[61]

Professor Gustafson goes on to point out a weakness that he sees as a Christian ethicist:

> It is my conviction, however, that while the consistent ethic of life justifies commendable moral attitudes and backs commendable moral and public choices, its articulation tends to avoid stating the ambiguities that are often consequent to its application…. I think we all need to be more forthright about the ambiguity that is part of life because the well-being of individuals and the well-being of others including "larger wholes" is not harmonious.[62]

In keeping with the instincts of Protestant ethical reflection, Gustafson is more attentive to the impact of sin in the world. According to Gustafson, our moral world is not "consistent" and "harmonious" but more often ambiguous and tragic. A harmony may be present in our vision of the next life or it may be in some "highly abstract ideal order, but it is not in many decisions about how human life is to be protected and promoted—not only life and death decisions but daily ones of no highly notable consequences." He concludes by noting that "whether we are directed by a consistent ethic of life or a significantly different one, *recognition of ambiguous and sometimes tragic choices affects our attitudes and our actions.*"[63]

Professor Gustafson's interjection helps to correct the tendency in Roman Catholic moral theology to underestimate the tragic and conflictual nature of the moral life. The moral vision of the consistent ethic of life would be enriched by addressing Gustafson's concern.

Conclusion: Confronting a Culture of Violence

The consistent life movement and the writing and witness of both Cardinal Bernardin and Pope John Paul II have focused attention on a central issue in Western societies: violence is used as a way of solving complex social and personal problems. Pope John Paul speaks of "a culture of death" to describe the deep cultural forces that shape our attitudes and choices. The U.S. bishops used the language of "Confronting a Culture of Violence" in their 1994 pastoral message with that title. In that well-written message the bishops confront American Catholics with the stark realities of American culture.

In the late 1960s in the midst of the Vietnam War; the race riots in Washington D.C., Newark, and Chicago; and the violent protest and police brutality of the Chicago Democratic Convention, the African-American activist H. Rap Brown succinctly quipped that violence "was as American as apple pie." The Kerner Commission's report on Civil Disorders picked up Mr. Brown's remark as a part of its wake-up call to the American people. The U.S. Catholic bishops also used Rap Brown's thesis as they noted, "Sadly, this provocative statement has proved prophetic. No nation on earth, except those in the midst of war, has as much violent behavior as we do—in our homes, on our televisions, and in our streets." The bishops list some of the gruesome realities of American life:

- we face far higher rates of murder, assault, rape, and other violent crimes than other societies;

- the most violent place in America is not in our streets, but in our homes—more than 50 percent of the women murdered in the U.S. are killed by their partner or ex-partner;

- 13 American children die every day from guns;

- our entertainment media too often exaggerate and even celebrate violence—children see 8,000 murders and 100,000 other acts of violence on television before they leave elementary school;

- the violence of abortion has destroyed more than 30 million unborn children since 1972.[64]

RESOURCES FOR RESPONDING

Unraveling the "spiral of violence" in the United States requires *cultural transformation* that goes much deeper than simply "getting tough" on criminals.[65] As the bishops put it, "fundamentally, our society needs a moral revolution to replace a culture of violence with a renewed ethic of justice, responsibility, and community.... We must confront this growing culture of violence with a commitment to life, a vision of hope, and a call to action." The bishops identify nine "assets" that the Catholic community brings to the challenge of confronting a culture of violence:

- the *example and teaching* of Jesus Christ;

- the *biblical values* of respect for life, peace, justice, and community;

- *our teaching* on human life and human dignity, on right and wrong, on family and work, on justice and peace, on rights and responsibilities;

- *our tradition* of prayer, sacraments, and contemplation which can lead to a disarmament of the heart;

- *a commitment to marriage and family life*, to support responsible parenthood and to help parents teach their children the values to live full lives;

- a *presence* in most neighborhoods—our parishes and schools, hospitals and social services are sources of life and hope in places of violence and fear;

- an *ethical framework* which calls us to practice and promote virtue, responsibility, forgiveness, generosity, concern for others, social justice, and economic fairness;

- a *capacity for advocacy* that cuts across the false choices in national debate—jails or jobs, personal or social responsibility, better values or better policies;

- a *consistent ethic of life* which remains the surest foundation for our life together.[66]

The bishops conclude their pastoral message with the compelling call to action from the grandmother of the five-year-old boy who was dropped to his death by two children in Chicago because he wouldn't steal candy: "We hope somebody, somewhere, somehow, will do something about the conditions which are causing our children to kill each other." The bishops respond, "we can be the 'somebody.' Now can be the time."[67]

Confronting a culture of violence is an enormous task for Christians and for society, but the first step is defining the problem,which both the bishops and Pope John Paul have done by looking at the systemic and cultural causes of violence. The antidote for a culture of violence is the consistent ethic of life—"the surest foundation for our life together."

A FINAL WORD

Eileen Egan, Pat Goltz, Carol Crossed, Humberto Medeiros, Joseph Bernardin, and Pope John Paul II have given us a good start on the consistent ethic of life in their activism and pastoral leadership. Much work needs to be done to explore the social, ethical, and theological dimensions of this movement. We have a good beginning, but a long way to go.

As the church develops the consistent ethic of life it must first apply the ethic *within the church* in order to be a credible spokesperson and witness in the world. Writer Daryl Domning asks: "Is it too much to ask that moral leaders donning the 'pro-life' mantle should cleanse their own institutions of spirit-killing sins such as sexism, racism, pharisaism, child abuse, exploitation of workers and persecution of loyal critics?"[68]

No, it is not too much to ask. The vision of a consistent ethic and spirituality of life invites us to nurture and not to crush life.

Discussion Questions

1. Archbishop Medieros believed the Catholic life ethic must be "comprehensive and consistent" to appeal to the American conscience. If this is true, why has the consistent ethic of life been such a "hard sell" to American Catholics?

2. Cardinal Bernardin elaborated important considerations in moving from the moral vision of the consistent ethic of life to public policy. How do you evaluate his suggestions in this regard?

3. Pope John Paul II has restricted capital punishment by saying that "such cases are very rare if not practically nonexistent." Subsequently the Catechism was also revised to reflect the revised papal position. What does this tell us about the development and process of changing the church's social teachings?

4. How do you evaluate the "culture of violence" in the United States described by the U.S. bishops? Is violence "as American as apple pie"?

5. As the consistent ethic of life links abortion, poverty, euthanasia, war and violence, and capital punishment, it argues that the taking of life is the wrong direction for our society. Where are the "cutting edges" in your own thinking about the consistent ethic of life? Which issue or issues trouble you as you assess your commitment to a nonviolent way of living?

9

Latin American Bishops' Conference— Liberation Theology

Our review of Catholic social teaching and movements has primarily focused on European and North American realities. We have examined the theology and spirituality of two minorities in the United States: Mexican American farm workers led by Cesar Chavez, and African Americans. Now it is time to review the vibrant theological and social justice agenda of Latin America. In fact, some would claim that "the really 'interesting' theology is now flowing from the South to be translated for eager readers in Europe and the United States..."[1]

In Part I we will survey the "official" social teachings of the Latin American church as articulated by *El Consejo Episcopal Latinoamericano*, CELAM (The Episcopal Conference of Latin America), the organization bringing together all the Latin American national bishops' conferences, and in Part II we will explore the "unofficial" ecclesial movement known as "liberation theology."

Part I. Latin American Bishops' Conference

THE CONTEXT: EXPLOITATION IN A LATIN CHORD

Just as the Europeans exploited the land and the people of the New World in North America, so the Europeans who came to Latin America exploited the people and the resources of the land. Already in 1511 Father Antonio de Montesinos told his wealthy congregation in Hispaniola (Dominican Republic): "You are in mortal sin...for the cruelty and tyranny you use in dealing with innocent people." "Tell me," he demanded of the estate owners, "by what right or justice do you keep these Indians in such cruel and horrible servitude.? ... Are these not men? ...Have they not rational souls, are you not bound to love them as you love yourselves?"[2]

The Spanish colonizers of Latin America came from a culture that had been shaped by centuries of a common cause of sword and cross: the Crusades and the Inquisition. The Argentinean historian and ethicist Enrique Dussel summarizes the historical context:

> By the sixteenth century the Christian people of Spain were inured to war. The ideals of Christendom and Crusade continued to live on in Spain long after they had faded from the consciousness of other peoples in Europe, because the struggle against the Muslims continued for many centuries. They gradually pushed back the frontiers of the encroaching Muslims, conquering Granada in the same year that Columbus discovered America.

> These frontier-fighters continued their struggle here in the new world, crusading against the native empires of this region.[3]

While a few brave preachers like Montesinos and Bartolomé de las Casas chastised the Spanish and Portuguese for their greed and cruelty the Catholic church had meanwhile entered into an alliance with Spain and Portugal to help spread Catholicism in the new lands.

> The fusion of cross and sword was officially sanctioned by Rome, almost from the first discoveries by Columbus, through a system called the "real patronato de Indias." Under this system the papacy conceded most of this power to the Spanish crown, including the exclusive right to license ecclesiastics to work in Latin America. Thus from the very beginning, the region's Church was a dependent partner of the state....

Journalist Penny Lernoux noted that this situation "has survived to modern times and is a root cause of the growing divisions between a Church of accommodation and a Church of liberation."[4]

A. FROM MEDELLÍN TO SANTO DOMINGO

CELAM, the Latin American Episcopal Conference, was established in 1955 as a means of linking the various national conferences of bishops of Central and South America. The Latin American Episcopal Conference is made up of representatives from every country in Latin America who gather for a two-week meeting approximately every ten years. The first meeting was held in Rio de Janeiro in 1955. A second meeting wasn't scheduled until after some of the dust had settled from the Second Vatican Council, which had ended in 1965. It was held in August of 1968 in Medellín, Colombia, to coincide with Pope Paul VI's visit to the International Eucharistic Congress, which was also being held in Colombia, in Bogota.

The purpose of the gathering in Medellín was to examine the situation in Latin America in light of the insights and directions of the Second Vatican Council. The poverty in Latin America had worsened in the 1960s. Even the bishops were shocked at the scope of the socioeconomic problems. According to Brazilian bishop Candido Padin, who helped to organize the meeting, "None of the bishops had ever imagined that the reality in Latin America had reached such inhumane proportions. We were all shocked after three opening papers that graphically described the continent in which we lived."[5]

After discussions, slide presentations, and hard data on the reality of poverty in their countries, the bishops began to have a global vision of the extent of the problems. Bishop Padin admitted that "for many of those attending...it was an eye-opening experience as well as cause for fright, because the situation was much worse than they had suspected. So the delegates were prepared to make a commitment."[6]

The document that the bishops approved at Medellín did commit the church to addressing the economic and social problems before them. For the first time the Latin American hierarchy recognized that the continent was living in a "situation of sin" and "institutionalized violence." They wrote:

> In many instances Latin America finds itself faced with a situation of injustice that can be called institutionalized violence, when, because of a structural deficiency of industry and agriculture, of

national and international economy, of cultural and political life, "whole towns lack necessities, live in such dependence as hinders all initiative and responsibility as well as every possibility for cultural promotion and participation in social and political life," thus violating fundamental rights. This situation demands all-embracing, courageous, urgent, and profoundly renovating transformations. We should not be surprised, therefore, that the "temptation to violence" is surfacing in Latin America.[7]

The poverty and oppression of the masses was especially scandalous in countries that claimed to be "Catholic." In many places, according to the Medellín documents, the upper classes and "foreign monopolies" representing an "international imperialism of money" were responsible for the "institutionalized violence" suffered by the poor.

The bishops encouraged the poor to take an active role in the construction of a new society:

The Latin American church encourages the formation of national communities that reflect a global organization where all of the peoples but more especially the lower classes have, by means of territorial and functional structures, an active and receptive, creative and decisive participation in the construction of a new society.[8]

A few paragraphs later the bishops urged the strengthening of peasants' and workers' unions: "Therefore, in the intermediary professional structure the peasants' and workers' unions, to which the workers have a right, should acquire sufficient strength and power." Regarding the rural poor and Indian populations, the bishops recognized that improving their situation

will not be viable without an authentic and urgent reform of agrarian structures and policies. This structural change and its political implications go beyond a simple distribution of land.... This will entail...the organization of the peasants into effective intermediate structures, principally in the form of cooperatives; and motivation toward the creation of urban centers in rural areas, which would afford the peasant population the benefits of culture, health, recreation, spiritual growth, participation in local decisions, and in those which have to do with the economy and national politics.[9]

These were far-reaching and radical changes in the exercise of "people power." What the bishops envisioned is an empowering of the poor:

> *It is necessary that small basic communities be developed* in order to establish a balance with minority groups, which are the groups in power.... The church—the people of God—will lend its support to the downtrodden of every social class so that they might come to know their rights and how to make use of them.[10]

The bishops were not naive about the risks involved in bringing power to the poor. In the section on peace, they bluntly admit that many of the wealthy would resist such efforts and try to sabotage the church's effort. They name

> a lamentable insensitivity of the privileged sectors to the misery of the marginalized sectors.... It is not unusual to find that these groups, with the exception of some enlightened minorities, characterize as subversive activities all attempts to change the social system which favors the permanence of their privileges. As a natural consequence of the above-mentioned attitudes, some members of the dominant sectors occasionally resort to the use of force to repress drastically any attempt at opposition. It is easy for them to find apparent ideological justifications (anticommunism) or practical ones (keeping "order") to give their action an honest appearance.[11]

The bishops recommended ecclesial structures be established to continue the work of human liberation.

> The Commission of Justice and Peace should be supported in all our countries.... The episcopal conferences will create commissions of social action or pastoral service to develop doctrine and to take initiative, presenting the church as a catalyst in the temporal realm in an authentic attitude. The same applies to the diocesan level. Furthermore, the episcopal conferences and Catholic organizations will encourage collaboration on the national and continental scene with non-Catholic Christian churches and institutions, dedicated to the task of restoring justice in human relations.[12]

Its Impact

The document's strong social criticism, cutting language, and prophetic commitment "sent shock waves through the continent and beyond, to Europe and North America." Lernoux captured something of the shock created by the Medellín document: "Rich or poor, radical or reactionary, the Latin Americans were dumbfounded: how could traditionally conservative bishops have written such a document!"[13]

The bishops proposed to help transform their societies through radical changes in liturgy and evangelization, including education of the poor and the promotion of popular organizations, especially the Christian grass-roots communities—the base communities.

Penny Lernoux, after interviewing some of the progressive Medellín bishops, argued that in espousing the cause of the poor, the bishops made three major breakthroughs:

1. "Of foremost importance was the church's rupture with existing social and political structures in order to promote a transfer of power to the impoverished masses."

2. Second, Medellín meant "the renunciation of centuries of state patronage and the transformation of the Church into a servant of the poor, with neither privileges nor riches."

3. And finally, "Medellín was a fundamental commitment to work for the construction of a community Church instead of the vertical Church we inherited with its pyramid of power."[14]

This sounds like a revolutionary change of direction in the Latin American hierarchy, and it was. But it must also be kept in perspective. The Medellín document contains sixteen sections. Only three sections, the ones dealing with justice, peace, and poverty, carried a new perspective and caused a reaction. Moreover, the other thirteen sections "offered little novelty or inspiration." The three sections that broke new ground did so in a very embryonic way. While the bishops named "institutionalized violence" *they did not go on to analyze the causes of this violence* or to offer an alternative. Despite all this, the words were radical, considering the source, and were seen as a "green light" by social activists and liberation theologians.

A minority of prophetic bishops led by Archbishop Dom Helder Camara of Recife, Brazil, and Bishop Padin had worked with consultants and the progressive leadership of CELAM to have these critical passages included. Even during the meeting, not all were in favor of the new approach. The conservative bishops from Colombia objected to the document. "Thanks to the liberating influence of Vatican II and the predominance of prophetic bishops in the CELAM hierarchy, the momentum for change carried the meeting."

As Bishop Padin later admitted "those who did not participate in the conference reacted with shock and fright. But even among the participants were bishops who would later claim they did not realize the significance of what they had signed, just as other prelates earlier had disclaimed Vatican II on the same grounds." Lernoux's conclusion: "Thus while the commitment made at Medellín was irreversible, only a minority of bishops would heed its call."[15]

Jesuit theologian Alfred T. Hennelly explains the impact of Medellín in these words:

> There can be little doubt that the Medellín conference marked a momentous watershed in the history of the church in Latin America, analogous but with significant differences to the effect of the Second Vatican Council on the universal church. The most significant difference was not that Medellín discovered the world of the poor.... Rather, in my opinion its importance was to institutionalize in its decrees the experience and practice of a significant number of Catholics in every stratum of the church from peasants to archbishops. It thus provided legitimation, inspiration, and pastoral plans for a continent wide preferential option for the poor, encouraging those who were already engaged in the struggle and exhorting the entire church, both rich and poor, to become involved.[16]

Medellín Misused and Attacked

As noted above, some bishops resisted the approach of Medellín, and others did not realize what they had approved. The document was used and misused by partisans on the right and the left.

On the left a group known as "Christians for Socialism" seized the Medellín document as an endorsement of their partisan political agenda. In Argentina, the Third World Movement of priests cited Medellín to rationalize their close identification with the left wing of the Peronist party.

Those on the right also misused and attacked the approach of the Medellín documents. Conservative theologians and bishops in Latin America and Europe attacked Medellín and liberation theology. From Rome, Cardinal Garrone, the prefect of the Congregation of Education, wrote a widely publicized letter chastising the CELAM leadership for placing too much stress on "liberating education," which, he warned, could lead to politicization.

Roger Vekemans, a Belgian priest working in Bogota, criticized liberation theologians and the direction of Medellín. In the process he found moral and financial support in the West German Catholic missionary groups *Adveniat* and *Miseror*, as well as financial support from conservative Catholic Harry John, of the DeRance Foundation in Milwaukee. With the support of Colombia's conservative Cardinal Anibal Munoz Duque, Vekemans founded the Research Center for Development and Integration of Latin America (CEDIAL) in Bogota and established the magazine *Tierra Nueva* in order to try to undermine Medellín and liberation theology.[17]

Eventually, over 100 German theologians challenged Adveniat's support of Vekemans' work. Karl Rahner, Herbert Vorgrimler, Johannes Metz, Ernst Kasemann, and others demanded an explanation of why the agency was financing an "attack...which endangers autonomous church evolution in Latin America...and is causing divisions between theologians and bishops in the national Churches."[18]

Three years after the CELAM Conference at Medellín the 1971 synod of bishops would commit the church universal to the same orientation when they said, "Action on behalf of justice and participation in the transformation of the world fully appears to us as a constitutive dimension of the preaching of the Gospel, or, in other words, of the Church's mission for the redemption of the human race and its liberation from every oppressive situation."[19] This synod document helped to galvanize those working for social justice in all areas and levels of the church. The commitment of Medellín echoed through the whole church and was amplified by the bishops' meeting in Rome.

New Leadership at CELAM

The four years following the bishops' conference at Medellín was a time of euphoria for those intent on carrying out its vision. It was a time of new possibilities for a just society and for a new church dedicated to the service of the poor. Some clergy, religious, and bishops moved into the poor *barrios* to live and work with the poor. There was a flurry of activism, conferences, workshops, and efforts at spreading the message of Medellín to all Latin America and beyond.

For others in the church, these years were a time of organizing resistance to the orientation of Medellín and liberation theology. The combination of euphoria and resistance in the Latin church surfaced the extraordinary paradox in Catholicism—"a curious dialectic between diffusion and resistance to the documents of Medellín."[20]

In November 1972, the dialectic swayed in favor of those who resisted the orientation of Medellín. At the CELAM meeting Bogota's new auxiliary bishop, Alfonso Lopez Trujillo, was elected the secretary general of CELAM, a position he held until 1979, when he was elected the president of CELAM, a position he held until 1983. Under the previous leadership CELAM had been on friendly terms with liberation theologians. Now, under Bishop Trujillo's leadership, CELAM moved in the opposite direction. When Trujillo retired as president in 1983 his followers were firmly in control of the conference, and they continued to implement his policies, which have consistently opposed the advances of Medellín and liberation theology. Father Hennelly calls Trujillo's election "one the most crucial events in this period.... I would emphasize that this is an astonishing spectacle: within the brief space of four years, an organization that was speeding along the road of implementation of Medellín was suddenly thrown into reverse gear, with a great shock to all involved."[21] The Vatican supported the direction Bishop Trujillo was taking. They also rewarded him with higher honors, naming him archbishop of Medellín in 1979, and cardinal in 1983.

CELAM at Puebla

The third general assembly of the Latin American Bishops' Conference was scheduled for the Fall of 1978 in Puebla, Mexico, ten years after the Medellín conference. The death of Pope Paul VI in August and the death of Pope John Paul I a month later postponed the conference until the end of January 1979, so that the new pope, John Paul II, could attend. Under Bishop Trujillo's leadership the conference was to be the venue for reversing the direction of Medellín. In preparation for the conference, the new CELAM staff with help from Father Vekemans, produced a preliminary consultative document entitled "Present and Future Evangelization in Latin America." The Preparatory Document (PD), as it came to be known, was a 214-page tome, triumphalist in tone, and authoritarian in its view of the church. It renounced Medellín's commitment to the poor and the oppressed in favor of doctrinal orthodoxy and political accommodation.

While the PD was an effort to steer the church away from the direction of liberation theology and Medellín, the result was just the opposite. Penny Lernoux recounts that, "Because it so patently denied Medellín and all that had happened in the Church since, the green book [the PD] set off a continent-wide debate unprecedented in scope and depth. In contrast to Medellín, when very few laypeople were involved in the preparations, thousands of Christian grass-roots communities discussed the Puebla consultative document with their priests and bishops."

This was exactly the hope of Medellín—that all levels of the church would come to a new social awareness. Hennelly points out the irony: "A document aimed at control of the conference actually opened it up to valuable contributions from every sector of the church, causing it to become a much more participatory and democratic event than the Medellín conference."[22] One community reported the insights of its reflection: "We have discovered the limits of this system.... We have experienced a new power which liberates us from the fear of dying."[23]

Many of the bishops rejected Trujillo's document; even his fellow Colombian conservative bishops did not support his approach. A new document was prepared by a small team of bishops that met under the leadership of Cardinal Aloisio Lorscheider, the president of CELAM. This new draft was shorter, more concise, and incorporated the language of Medellín, reemphasizing the church's commitment to the poor.

Joseph Comblin, a Belgian theologian who has taught in Latin America, evaluated the documents of Puebla in the following way: "the reader's first impression is finding here a confirmation of Medellín—a fact of profound consequences. Puebla is not an 'explanation' of Medellín.... Agreement results from the fact that Puebla took its stand on the same ground as Medellín.... Puebla testifies that Medellín's spirit has deeply permeated Latin American thinking."[24]

The focus of the conference was "evangelization" in Latin America. The delegates shaped the 21 sections of the document on how the church could evangelize effectively and with integrity in the Latin American setting. For example, Puebla renewed Medellín's commitment to a "preferential option for the poor" in light of the challenge of evangelization. Comblin explains:

> This option had become the ground for restructuring pastoral ministry; many activities that served rather the upper and middle class were abandoned so as to share the lot of the poor and to find the best way to help them in their strivings for integral human liberation. Puebla approves this movement and asks of the entire church a "conversion" to such liberating evangelization.[25]

While there was no repudiation of the direction of Medellín at Puebla, there were some new approaches and new themes.

1. Puebla addressed human dignity in terms of *human rights* in light of the outrages against human rights in Latin America. The struggle for human rights is a mandate of the "preferential option for the poor, because, as Comblin explains, the poor are "the first victims of repressive systems."

2. A number of sections of the document condemned the theory, ideology, and practice of *"National Security"* regimes.

3. While Medellín looked at the impact of internal colonialism, Puebla addressed *foreign colonialism* and asked the church to further a new economic order in the service of humanity.

4. Puebla gave serious consideration to the problems of the *indigenous and women*, stressing the contributions they can make to both Latin America and its church.[26]

Let me conclude this brief review of Puebla with the words of a liberation theologian from El Salvador, Jon Sobrino: "Medellín was a leap ahead, Puebla is a step ahead. True, Puebla is not Medellín's 'quantum leap,' but such advance does not come every ten years."[27]

CELAM at Santo Domingo

Thirteen and half years later the Latin American Bishops' Conference would meet in the fourth general assembly of CELAM on the 500th anniversary of Columbus' voyage to the new world, October 12-28, 1992. If we continue Jon Sobrino's metaphor, it would be fair to say that the Santo Domingo meeting was neither a quantum leap, nor an elegant step, but a *"shaky* step into the future."[28]

In 1983 Pope John Paul II, in a talk to the Latin America bishops during his visit to Haiti, announced the date, place, and topic for the next CELAM assembly: beginning October 12, 1992, in Santo Domingo, Dominican Republic, on the topic of "New Evangelization."[29]

In the nine years between the pope's announcement and the opening of the conference, the bishops and the church of Latin America were to prepare by studying the preparatory "Consultative Document." The first draft of this consultative document was released by the CELAM staff in 1991, but the Latin American bishops rejected it because it did not incorporate the work and ideas of the national bishops' conferences. "Ironically, therefore, it appears that the *consultative* document was rejected, because it had *not consulted* the bishops and also because it did not follow in the path of Medellín and Puebla."[30]

A much improved second draft was released in February 1992, entitled *Secunda Relatio*—Latin for "Second Report." This draft did exactly what a consultative document was supposed to do; it was an excellent synthesis of the ideas of all the national conferences. In the opinion of Alfred Hennelly, this was the "most important and substantive document of the conference, precisely because it represented the carefully considered theological and pastoral views of the bishops throughout the entire continent."[31]

The Second Report, however, was not acceptable to Vatican officials and to conservative Latin American bishops. The Vatican was not happy that the Second Report had been made public and had been given to a group of theologians who were to prepare a working document for the bishops to discuss and amend at the meeting.

The Vatican tried pressuring CELAM's general secretary, Brazilian Bishop Raymundo Damaseno Assis, into resigning. Bishop Assis, who had the support of many of the Latin American bishops and theologians, refused.

Because the Vatican was not able to remove Bishop Assis, they appointed an adjunct secretary to the CELAM meeting, the ultra-conservative Chilean Bishop Jorge Medina Estevez.[32] Bishop Medina was a lifelong friend and supporter of the former Chilean dictator General Augusto Pinochet. Medina had not been chosen by his fellow Chilean bishops to represent Chile at Santo Domingo. His fellow bishops strongly opposed his appointment to the conference and to such an influential position.

In a second move to control the meeting, Pope John Paul II appointed the Vatican Secretary of State, Cardinal Angelo Sodano, to chair the conference along with two other co-presidents: Cardinal Nicolas de Jesus Lopez Rodriguez, the archbishop of Santo Domingo, the host city, and Monsignor Cipriano Calderon Polo, the secretary of the Pontifical Commission on Latin America (responsible for ongoing liaison with CELAM). Rome was directly interfering in the Latin American bishops' process—a crass violation of the principle of subsidiarity.

The *Second Report* was reworked by Bishop Assis and his assistants and released as a new document called the *Documento de Trabajo*, the *Working Document*. This document was sent to Rome in April of 1992, only six months before the beginning of the conference. It took the Vatican several months to approve the document. This meant that there was little time for widespread distribution and discussion of the document by clergy, laity, and base communities and, therefore, less feedback from the church to the bishops attending the meeting.

On the very first day of the meeting in Santo Domingo, the adjunct secretary to the meeting, Bishop Medina, announced that the *Working Document* was to be discarded—after all those years of work and revisions! This threw the conference into chaos, according to Father Jorge Luis Aleman, a theologian consultant at the meeting: "But, for unknown reasons, the fundamental (working) document was simply nullified by the presidency with no explanation. You can imagine, then, what it means to have 300 people trying to write a new document without knowing what is its purpose."[33]

The bishops would not be discussing the *Working Document* as a framework for the meeting, but were subjected to a Vatican-approved process that included several days of long, primarily conservative, and useless lectures of material already familiar to the delegates. Then the bishops were allowed to break up into thirty smaller working committees. The work of these thirty groups was not discussed in plenary sessions but was submitted to the central drafting committee. "Obviously, this division into committees, while useful and perhaps necessary, divided the bishops and further impeded strong leadership among the Latin bishops."[34]

Because the *Working Document* had been set aside the bishops needed a new outline as a framework for the final document of the conference. Up until the last few days of the conference it wasn't even clear that there was going to be a final document. The lack of a working draft was resolved by adopting the framework and many of the ideas of Pope John Paul II's lengthy opening address to the conference. The pope's speech took a middle-of-the-road approach: it did not open any new paths, but also did not close any doors. His address covered three major themes: 1) a "new evangelization," 2) "human development," and 3) "Christian culture." These three themes were transformed into the framework for the three chapters of the final text.

Archbishop Luciano Mendes de Almeida of Brazil, the chair of the drafting committee, led the effort to write the final document. In the view of some senior prelates Archbishop Mendes "saved Santo Domingo."[35] Mendes' committee worked through long nights and a frantic final weekend to produce a document that took into account the work of the thirty subcommittees as well as interventions from individual bishops and bishops' conferences. The rushed process is evident in the text, which bears the weaknesses of material written in haste: poorly organized, with little prophetic energy.[36]

The final example of control by Rome was that the Vatican would review the final document before it could be published. Only the introductory "Message" from the bishops was left as written. The changes made by the Vatican after the meeting were mostly small, but they were not trivial changes, and "they represent a further watering-down of a text that already had been robbed of much of its power." Peter Hebblethwaite, a longtime Vatican observer, gives a sampling of the changes made by the Vatican's Commission on Latin America—the italicized words needed to be amended, according to the Vatican.

- The revisions start with the opening sentence: "Summoned by Pope John Paul II and impelled by the Holy Spirit of God our Father, *we bishops of the Church of Latin America and the Caribbean, assembled at Santo Domingo...* were in continuity with Medellín and Puebla." Becomes: "the Bishops taking part in the IVth General Conference of Latin America..." The bishops weren't even allowed to name themselves. Not being allowed to name oneself is one of the most subtle, yet powerful methods of oppression. Hebblethwaite adds "the Caribbean bishops, mostly black and French- or English-speaking, with their distinctive culture, were eliminated, and the authority of the text is reduced by attributing it only to those who were actually present."

- References to women's roles were scrutinized. The bishops had written, "New evangelization should involve the determined and active promotion of the dignity of women; that presupposes *also a rethinking of the role of women within the church and pastoral work.*" The Vatican editors reworked it to read: "that presupposes a deepening of the role of women in the church and in society." "Deepening" presumes an acceptance of the status quo; whereas, "rethinking" implies the possibility of change.

- The bishops approved, "In the reading of scripture, *we have to overcome anachronistic interpretations that fail to recognize women's dignity, proclaim with force what the gospel prefigures for women and favor a reading of the word of God which, beginning from women themselves, disclos-*

es the contribution of the feminine vocation to God's plan." The new version reads: "In the reading of scripture, we have to proclaim with force what the gospel means for women and develop a reading of the word of God which discloses the contribution of the feminine vocation to God's plan." The important words "beginning from women themselves" are deleted. The Vatican, as we shall see when we look at the U.S. bishops' pastoral on women, does not want to begin theological and pastoral reflection with women's experience. The revised text no longer warns against reading our sexist attitudes and practices back into Scripture, or asking questions of the New Testament, such as, "did Jesus ordain women as priests?" which are anachronistic. Jesus did not ordain anybody, in *our* understanding of ordination.

- In speaking about Amerindian culture the bishops wrote, "In the amalgam of elements that make up the indigenous community, the Earth is life, *a sacred place, the feminine face of God,* the integrating center of community life." The "feminine face of God" is struck out. Such a phobia, that even when describing American Indian, non-Christian religion, the linking of feminine with God is deleted!

- The bishops offered a word of repentance: "Unfortunately, with regard to slavery, racism and discrimination, there have been situations from which *men of the church* were not absent." The Pontifical Commission substituted "the baptized" for "men of the church." "They were not making a point about inclusive language either. It is rather an apologetic attempt to let churchmen off the hook."[37]

As we shall discuss below, the Vatican's persistent interference in the process and content of the Santo Domingo conference violates the principle of subsidiarity, which the church has taught since 1931.

Content

As a generalization, it is fair to say that the introductory profession of faith, chapter 1 on "new evangelization," and the doctrinal and ecclesiological sections—which makes up about half of the total document—are conservative in orientation. Chapter 2 on "human development" and chapter 3 on "Christian culture" are more progressive. One observer at the conference evaluated these progressive chapters with the following comment: "While the conservative, spiritualising theological straitjacket imposed on the bishops was frustrating, it could not in the end conceal the real life of the Church in Latin America."[38]

In this brief survey it is not possible to work through the Final Report chapter by chapter. I will comment on the central question of theological method and conclude with two examples.

A Shift in Methodology

Following the orientation begun at Vatican II, the Medellín documents approached the question of theological method by beginning with "reading signs of the times," that is, with an analysis of the current realities. Medellín used the social sciences to understand the current realities and then turned to theological and pastoral reflections. This method, initiated by Father Cardijn in the 1930s (see chapter three), came to be known as the "ver-juzgar-actuar" approach (see-judge-act). In theological terms it was known as the "hermeneutical circle" or the "pastoral circle." This method assumes that theological reflection begins with an analysis of the current reality and not with ahistorical theological principles. "There can be no theology without a prior historical reality, and God cannot be found in texts from the past without discerning *God's reality in the present.*"[39]

This experience-based method for doing theology was rejected by the Vatican-controlled presidency of CELAM IV. Father Jon Sobrino explains, "In Santo Domingo the presidency imposed the principle of judging-seeing-acting: theology comes first, followed by observation of the world, and then by application of theology to the world."[40] The Vatican-controlled presidency reversed the order from seeing, judging, acting to judging, seeing, acting. The "judging" would be done by those who were responsible for orthodoxy in the church. Then the doctrinal truths could be applied to the situation—the "seeing"—and acted upon. This reversal restored the classical method of "a priori," deductive theology, rather than the historical, inductive approach initiated by Vatican II.

As this is played out in the document we get a Christology "from above" rather than "from below." The Christology of Santo Domingo, which is considered the backbone of the whole document, is not based on

> Jesus of Nazareth but on an abstract Christ.... Jesus is *judged* as the Christ, without looking first at the reality of that Christ in Jesus. Thus the historical Jesus disappears, who was present in Medellín, in *Evangelii Nuntiandi,* and in Puebla,...who is certainly present in the most committed communities from which have come the most

martyrs; and who of course is present in the theology of liberation. In Santo Domingo, the choice was made to begin by proclaiming the Christ of faith rather than seeing the Jesus of Nazareth.[41]

The second example of not beginning with the Latin American reality, of not "seeing" reality, in the Final Document is the incredible silence on the martyrs of the Latin American church. Sobrino calls this "the most dreadful consequence of not beginning by 'seeing' reality." He continues, "No one understands, especially in countries like El Salvador and Guatemala, why the martyrs were not only not highly valued but not even mentioned." It is hard to estimate how many Christians have been martyred in Latin America since Medellín. In one small country, El Salvador, during a one-year period (January 5, 1980 to February 27, 1981) there were 300 attacks on the church, including 39 assassinations, 19 bombings, 43 shootings at church buildings, and 30 robberies.[42] Archbishop Oscar Romero was one of those killed while he celebrated Mass on March 24, 1980. Father Sobrino feels the loss personally: his six Jesuit colleagues were killed on November 16, 1989, along with their two housekeepers. Sobrino's name was on the list of those to be executed. His justified anger increases:

> In Latin America, martyrdom is not anecdotal or exceptional, but a massive and indistinguishable reality: it is the new thing, the grace, the credential and seal of the most genuine evangelization that has occurred between Medellín and Santo Domingo. This silence is therefore absolutely incomprehensible, highly suspicious, and above all, terribly impoverishing.

Sobrino explains the rich legacy and source of "new evangelization" that the martyrs are for the Latin church. His reflections are worthy of quoting at length.

> To ignore the martyrs really means ignoring the signs of the times, both because they describe what best characterizes the era...and because by their quality, they express God's presence in our midst. It also means denying ourselves an irreplaceable hermeneutic principle by which to understand Jesus, because today's martyrs—unlike most of those in past history—have died like Jesus, for the same reason that Jesus died, because structurally, they lived like Jesus. It also means ignoring the historical and theological origin of the church itself, born out of the martyrdom of Jesus; to pursue the life of Jesus in the hope of resurrection...

...The fact of martyrial love and the grateful recognition of it by Christians—is good news, it is evangelization for the poor of this world. Even though it may scandalize the powerful.

...The martyrs...it is they who in our days re-create the gospel that Paul preached: Jesus the martyr, crucified and resurrected. For that reason too, it is simply incredible that Santo Domingo did not mention the martyrs, the best that the Latin church had produced, the best that we have.[43]

The *Second Report* had a fine treatment of the martyrs but this did not find its way into the Final Document—a loss to the Latin American church and the church universal.[44]

THE VOICE OF LATIN AMERICA

As is evident from the tortured process leading up to and including the Santo Domingo conference, there was a great struggle for control among the various theologies of Latin America and Rome. At times, the voice of the Latin American bishops was almost lost as a Vatican-controlled process and leadership intervened. Commentators have suggested that we will find the clearest reflection of the Latin American voice if we consult the rejected *Second Report* and the discarded "Working Document."[45] The only piece of the final document that was written by Latin American bishops themselves and not by others at the conference is the seven-page "Message of the Fourth General Conference to the Peoples of Latin America and the Caribbean." This message "incontestably manifests the true theology of the Latin American church. Not only that, but it encapsulates the profound depths of the soul, heart, and mind of the peoples of Latin America and the Caribbean. It was written by the true inheritors of the noble legacy of Medellín and Puebla."[46]

In an effort not to lose the true Latin American voice, many bishops, religious, theologians, and laity throughout Latin America are promoting the Santo Domingo documents as a "package"—including the rejected "Second Report" and the "Working Document," along with the "Final Document." For instance, an educational pamphlet written by theologians Carlos Zarco and Pablo Richard, suggests that the Vatican-approved "Final Document" should be discussed using the two earlier documents as starting points.[47]

CONCLUSION: THE SPIRIT OF MEDELLÍN SURVIVES

What is so glaringly evident is the amount of Vatican involvement and interference in the workings of the CELAM assemblies at Puebla and Santo Domingo. This struggle and tension reveal the conflict between two visions of church: the one a centralized and obedient church under the leadership and control of Rome, and the second a local church that is culturally and historically diverse, semi-autonomous, in unity with the universal church. Jon Sobrino believes this control is exercised by Rome to check the Latin American church, which was "developing its own evangelical identity."[48] Does Rome fear too much distinctiveness in the local churches?

We can also view the tension, as theologian Monsignor William Shannon phrases it, between the Matthean model of church, which is focused on authority and order, and the Johannine model of an egalitarian, "community of disciples" church. Both of these models and visions of church are present in the Catholic experience of church.[49] The struggles at Puebla and Medellín are a playing out of the struggle between these two visions of church on an international stage. The drama of Santo Domingo is the story of the Vatican's hierarchical and authoritarian model completely dominating the egalitarian church. The balance between these two models was lost—to the detriment of the whole church and its evolving tradition. The church in Latin America, and in Rome, is weaker when this kind of control is exercised.

Yet despite these drastic measures of control, the egalitarian church was present in the bishops and showed through in places in the text. The church of the people, the church that was given birth at Vatican II and Medellín is still alive. "Medellín is not dead. That church no longer enjoys a favorable wind, but it is there. Administrative measures may be used to neutralize it, but that identity still supports the church's pastoral practice, theology, evangelization, and faith."[50]

The euphoria of the post-Vatican II church is gone. The optimism of the Medellín-era is tempered by many harsh realities in society and in the church. Bishop Luiz Demetrico Valentini, the president of the Brazilian episcopal conference's social pastoral commission, articulated the mood:

> The prophetic voices of the Brazilian conference of bishops were much stronger in the past. Today, the episcopal conference is more timid. People are tired. We are facing a very complicated situation of impoverishment—it is much more difficult to believe in concrete solutions than it was 25 years ago. People are disillusioned. The

utopias we dreamed of at the time of Medellín, that we were sure
were quick in coming, never materialized, and the problems and
suffering of the majority of our people are much worse.[51]

The spirit of Medellín's preferential option for the poor is still alive in
Latin America. Despite all the control efforts by the traditional church,
ministers and laity on the grass-roots level continue to enflesh the vision
of Medellín, the vision of the gospel. For example, Sister Maria Cecilia
Garcez took a leave from her congregation because her superiors did not
support her living in the street with abandoned children. "For my congregation, my leaving is probably seen as a division," said Sister Garcez,

> but for me, it is a radical deepening of my gospel commitment. I live
> on my small salary, and sometimes it's hard for me to meet my own
> needs. But religious life protected me too much. I never felt cold. I
> never felt hungry. Now, though, when I share in the suffering of the
> street children, when I begin to help them find alternatives, this is
> when I feel the true charism of communion with God.... No bishop
> or archbishop or pope, for that matter, is going to make us detour
> from our gospel commitment. They can create obstacles by not sup-
> porting us, but this treasure, this conscience in Christ we have
> obtained, no pope can take it away.[52]

The evangelical commitment to the poor is still a powerful vision in the
Latin American church despite the disillusionment of fighting persistent
and dehumanizing poverty. The commitment to the poor is also seen in the
vibrant theological and pastoral movement known as liberation theology.

Part II. A Pastoral and Theological Movement: Liberation Theology

In 1955 when Bishop Angelo Rossi was visiting a remote area of his diocese of Barra do Pirai, Brazil, an old lady told him, "On Christmas day,
the three Protestant churches were all lit up and jammed with people. We
could hear their hymns. But our Catholic church was shut, all its lights
out, because we had not found a priest to say Mass for us." The words of
the woman raised a fundamental question: if there are no priests, must
everything stop? Can't someone call the community together for prayer?
Bishop Rossi responded as many other bishops around the world have—

by launching a program to select and train peasant and worker catechists in regions where the priests seldom visited. Often this person was one of the local leaders, a school teacher or principal.

In the bishop's name, these local leaders gathered the people at least once a week to pray, to hear the Scriptures, and to keep alive the sense of being a faith community. One of the isolated communities wrote back to the bishop: "Dear Bishop, for the first time we celebrated Holy Week in our island. The one who celebrated it for us was our young school teacher."[53]

By September 1958 there were 475 of these community coordinators who called the people together for prayer—novenas, litanies, May devotions, morning and evening prayer—and religious instruction. The coordinators also baptized in emergencies and spiritually assisted those who were dying. With the community's help they built simple meeting halls, instead of costly chapels, which served as places for worship and religious instruction, and as elementary schools and places for sewing classes and other practical courses. The local community with support from the bishop was responding to its physical and spiritual needs as a faith community. This was the beginning of the *Comunidades Eclesiales de Base* (CEB), Basic Christian Communities—a key component in liberation theology's initial phase.

The process of the church creatively responding to the needs of the people, by training and empowering laypeople in their local communities, opened the door to radically new ways of thinking about the church and social justice. The development of the basic ecclesial communities movement was one of *three formative forces* that gave birth to liberation theology. The other two were the conscientization educational method of Paulo Freire, and a critique of economic development with a growing ideological awareness in the universities. All three of these had their beginnings in the mid to late 1950s. Two of these were "movements" that involved the poor.

BASIC ECCLESIAL COMMUNITIES

The basic ecclesial communities, as noted in the previous story about Bishop Rossi, are small groups of Catholics, often coordinated by lay leaders, who meet regularly for prayer, worship, and communal reflection on their religious and secular lives. They also stress responsibility, communication, mutual assistance, and friendship, and thus they create active and effective communities—in contrast to the often passive and anonymous experience of church prior to the CEBs.

When the bishops met in Medellín they blessed what had already developed in the field. Medellín did not invent the CEBs but its endorsement of them helped them spread across Latin America. The CEB mode of being church was revolutionary for the church and for society. It was revolutionary in three ways.

First, the leadership and organization are at the *grass-roots* level. The lay leaders are from the local community. In that way the CEBs are self-sufficient, having the leadership come from within rather than being dependent on an occasional visiting priest from outside the community. In this way the priest is not the center of the community; as St. Paul remarked, the minister is not the lord of the faith, but a fellow worker (2 Cor 1:24).

Second, the CEBs give the people an experience of a *working democracy*. The lay leaders are chosen by their peers and are not elevated or "removed" in any sense from the community. There is democratic participation and decision making at every step. In this way, the participation of all is encouraged.

Finally, the participation in the CEBs develops a sense of *self-worth and self-confidence* in the people who have been ignored in the past. For example, Maryknoll Sister Joan Petrik, who worked for seven years with peasants in the mountains of La Libertad, El Salvador, recalled that when she first arrived in Tamanique,

> "every time a child died the family would say 'It's the will of God.'
> But after the people became involved in the Christian communities
> that attitude began to change. And after a year or so I no longer
> heard people in the communities saying that. After a while they
> began to say, 'the system caused this.'" Sister Joan observed that after
> a time one could walk into a village where CEBs had been estab-
> lished and identify their members by the way they carried them-
> selves. CEB members, the nun recalled, "walk upright, their heads
> held high, with self-confidence." The other peasants shuffled along,
> their heads bowed.[54]

PAULO FREIRE

In the middle 1950s Paulo Freire, a Brazilian educator, devised a new and effective way to teach illiterate peasants how to read. His team would visit an area and listen to the discourse in the community. They would come up with a list of about 17 "generative words" from that community. These were words that were meaningful in the community. For instance, if the trans-Amazon road was being cut through the community, the word *camino*, road (or the Portuguese equivalent), would be a generative word. By breaking up the syllables of these 17 words ("ca-min-no") and discussing the impact of the road on their lives, Freire and his associates could teach adults to read the newspaper in about five weeks. They not only could read, but they were well on their way to *analyzing their situation*, their reality *(realidad)*, with a critical eye. For instance, they would ask questions like, who is going to benefit from this new road? who decided we need this road? how will it change our community and our culture? The peasants experienced what Freire called *concientizacao*, *"conscientization,"* which roughly translates into English as "consciousness-raising." They moved from being "objects" to "subjects" who no longer passively and fatalistically accepted life but now, as subjects, wanted to help shape life.

This awakening of the people's "conscience" had some powerful side-effects, both politically and in terms of the church. Father Hennelly summarizes the situation.

> In the process of teaching literacy to peasants, Freire intended also to liberate them from socio-cultural enslavement by becoming aware of their own dignity and rights, aware, too, of the real causes of their oppression, and of the urgent need to become active agents of their own destiny in seeking avenues of change. Obviously, this did not please governments that preferred peasants to accept passively their designation as brutes or animals, and Freire has been exiled from a number of Latin American countries, including his homeland, Brazil.[55]

SOCIAL ANALYSIS

A third formative component came from social analysts working in academic circles. One strain was the growing awareness in the universities that both the state and the church were using ideologies to legitimate injustice. Fear of communism and the ideology of national security were often used to label activists as "subversive" or "communist." These agents of change were labeled as enemies of the country (e.g., as in the case of Paulo Freire). In analyzing the situation in their countries, some found that *Marxist categories* helped to describe the reality. For instance, Marx pointed out that when the state is called upon to adjudicate the claims of the peasants against the wealthy land owners, the state will use the rhetoric of "justice" and "human rights" but in reality will side with the interests of the wealthy elites whose wealth and power determine social policy. For some in Latin America this analysis helped to explain the reality of political and economic power in their country.

Another strain of economic and social analysis was beginning to unmask the true beneficiaries of economic "development." Analyses of foreign aid from the United States revealed that 95 percent of the aid from the United States was tied to U.S. products and delivery systems.[56] Most of the money was coming right back into U.S. hands. Other analysts described the economic situation in terms of "dependency" of the Third World countries on the dominant economies of the First World nations. They envisioned "liberation" from the cycle of dependency that had kept the masses of poor people in a spiral of life-draining poverty.

These three threads: the base communities movement, the conscientization educational methods, and the critical analysis of ideologies provided a fertile bed for liberation theology to take root. A concrete example of this "germination" of the formative forces of liberation theology can be seen in the life of one of its architects: Gustavo Gutiérrez. The story of his theological journey illustrates how the pieces of liberation emerged out of the historical context of Latin America in the late 1960s.

THE THEOLOGICAL JOURNEY OF GUSTAVO GUTIÉRREZ

Gustavo Gutiérrez is the best known liberation theologian.[57] He was born in 1928 in Lima, Peru. Although he was born in "old Lima" he was not part of the aristocracy, for he did not live in the "desirable" part of town, and he was a mestizo, sometimes condescendingly referred to as a "half-breed," part Hispanic and part Quechuan Indian. From birth he was positioned among the oppressed of his nation. He also suffered physically when he was a child. Between the ages of twelve and eighteen he was at first bedridden and then confined to a wheelchair because of a severe case of osteomyelitis that left him with a permanent limp.[58] His own social class and suffering helped him to see the world from the bottom.

At first he studied medicine but changed directions in college and decided to study theology and philosophy in preparation for the priesthood. His studies took him to various cities, including one semester in Santiago, Chile, and four years in Belgium at the University of Louvain. At Louvain Gutiérrez studied philosophy and psychology from 1951-55. It was here that he became close friends with Camilo Torres who was studying social sciences. After finishing his studies in philosophy Gutiérrez moved to Lyon in southern France to study theology from

1955-59. After his ordination in 1959 he spent one semester at the Gregorian University in Rome before returning to Lima where he became a professor of theology at the Catholic University, and also served as the chaplain for the National Union of Catholic Students.

Father Gutiérrez's classical training in European theology would be challenged by the powerful political upheavals in Latin America. He identified three events that forced a remaking of his theological orientation.

First, in 1964, Msgr. Ivan Illich of New York City organized a meeting in Petropolis, Brazil, to discuss the pastoral activity of the church in Latin America. As part of this conference Gutiérrez developed the understanding of "theology as critical reflection on praxis."

A year later, in 1965, armed groups began to fight to liberate Latin America from its dependent status. The violent situation and the new political awareness in Latin America posed problems for the classical theology Gutiérrez had learned in Europe. He could not ignore the social upheavals, especially with his friend Father Camilo Torres joining a militant rebellion in Colombia. Torres was soon killed in the mountains. Gutiérrez shifted his focus to analyzing the underlying social and political causes of poverty and injustice.

The third formative event for Gutiérrez was a course on poverty that he taught in Montreal in July, 1967. In working on this course he began to view the poor from a new perspective: as a social class and as bearers of God's Word.

From these experiences Gutiérrez went on to sketch out a rough draft of liberation theology for a conference in Chimobote, Peru. He published this draft in 1969 under the heading of "Hacia una teologia de la liberacion." *Hacia* means "toward" a theology of liberation. In 1971 he published his book *Teologia de la liberacion: Perspectivas*, which was translated and published in English in 1973 as *A Theology of Liberation*.[59]

Henri Nouwen reflected on the importance of this book:

> There is a little man in Peru, a man without any power, who lives in a barrio with poor people and who wrote a book. In this book he simply reclaimed the basic Christian truth that God became human to bring good news to the poor, new light to the blind, and liberty to the captives.
>
> Ten years later this book and the movement it started is considered a danger by the greatest power on earth.

> When I look at this little man, Gustavo, and think about the tall
> Ronald Reagan, I see David standing before Goliath, again with no
> more weapon than a little stone, a stone called *A Theology of
> Liberation.*[60]

A Change of Method

In 1967 Professor Gutiérrez articulated the distinctive method of liberation theology in which he defined theology as "critical reflection on praxis." (*Praxis* is a Greek word that is translated as "practice," but it has a
richer meaning in this context. In this setting praxis is understood as
action that attempts to transform societal injustice.) With these few words
he signaled a radical shift in theological method from the classical
approach that puts the emphasis on orthodoxy, "correct doctrine," which
then is applied to the concrete situation. The liberational method
emphasizes beginning with the concrete situation and a commitment to
transforming praxis: orthopraxis. As he clarified in his book,

> first is the commitment of charity, of service. Theology comes after-
> wards, it is the second act.... The pastoral activity of the Church does
> not flow as a conclusion from theological premises. Theology does
> not produce pastoral activity; rather, it reflects upon it. Theology
> must be able to find in pastoral activity the presence of the Spirit
> inspiring the action of the Christian community.[61]

This approach to theological reflection puts the emphasis on transforming service, *praxis*, rather than on having correct doctrines. It is clear
why this approach ruffled the feathers of those concerned with correct
doctrine. Liberation theologians maintain that those who are engaged in
transforming activity have an epistemological privilege, that is, they see
and know the truth of the unjust situation better than those who are part
of the elite or aristocracy. Often those engaged in transforming activity
against injustice are the poor. Therefore the poor and those who work on
behalf of the poor share in the epistemological advantage of seeing and
knowing the truth of the unjust situation better than those defending the
status quo.

This method turns classical theology on its head: it is not the learned
in the isolation of their libraries who discover truth, but those "in the
trenches" of working with the poor, and the poor themselves. There is
still a role for the professional theologian in liberation theology, but the

theological method presumes a commitment to and engagement with *transforming activity* rather than isolated contemplation.

It is clear why such a method is threatening to those who are defending the status quo, both in the church and in society. The power of their position is undercut by a new way of thinking. That is why the Vatican leadership rejected the liberational approach and restored the classical method at Santo Domingo. They wanted to emphasize the importance of "correct doctrine," which is determined by those in authority, as the starting point. They replaced the see-judge-act method with the judge-see-act approach. The "judgment" refers to determining the correctness of one's theology—orthodoxy. This was the starting point in classical theology, and the traditionalists wanted to restore it to its place of primacy in the Latin American church.

OPTION FOR THE POOR

What is most distinctive about liberation theology is that it takes the experience of the poor seriously. Clodovis Boff tells of a bishop he met in the arid region of northeastern Brazil, a famine stricken area. The bishop

> was shaking. "Bishop, what's the matter?" I asked. He replied that he had just seen a terrible sight: in front of the cathedral was a woman with three small children and a baby clinging to her neck. He saw that they were fainting from hunger. The baby seemed to be dead. He said: "Give the baby some milk, woman!" "I can't, my lord," she answered. The bishop went on insisting that she should and she that she could not. Finally, because of his insistence, she opened her blouse. Her breast was bleeding; the baby sucked violently at it. And sucked blood. The mother who had given it life was feeding it, like the pelican, with her own blood, her own life. The bishop knelt down in front of the woman, placed his hand on the baby's head, and there and then vowed that as long as such hunger existed, he would feed at least one hungry child each day.[62]

Liberation takes the experience and scandal of such poverty as the starting point for its commitment to the poor. The Boffs write that "in the light of faith, Christians see in them the challenging face of the Suffering Servant, Jesus.... The Crucified in these crucified persons weeps and cries out: 'I was hungry... in prison... naked' (Matt. 25:31–46). Here what is needed is not so much contemplation as effective action."[63]

Liberation theology, as a movement, empowers the poor—gives them the space—to articulate the issues of their "faith seeking understanding":

> The right to engage in theological reflection is part of the right of an exploited Christian people to think.... Christians have the right to think through their faith in the Lord, to think out the experience of their own liberation. They have the right to reclaim their faith—a faith that is continually diverted away from their experience of being poor—in order to turn it into an ideological exposé of the situation of domination that makes and keeps them poor.

This kind of theological reflection by the poor is linked with their liberation. Gutiérrez reminds us that "we dare not forget that all reflection is a way of exercising power in history.... It makes a real contribution to the transformation of history—to the destruction of the system of oppression and the construction of a just and humane society."[64]

Liberation theology emerged as a way of theologizing that can be summarized as:

1. an interpretation of Christian faith from the suffering, struggle, and hope of the poor;

2. a theological critique of society and its ideological underpinnings;

3. a critique of the practice of the church and of Christians.[65]

These central points explain why liberation theology "rocks the boat" for the church and society as it challenges the current arrangements of ecclesial, economic, and political power.

THREE LEVELS OF LIBERATION THEOLOGY

Liberation theology is a name for a broad ecclesial movement that includes the people in the pews, the people in the base communities, the religious, the priests and bishops, and the professional theologians. Leonardo and Clodovis Boff describe the three levels of liberation theology. At the "base" or foundation of the church is the laity, especially those in CEBs and Bible study groups, who, like the theologians, are juxtaposing their faith and the situation of oppression. The reflection of the laity is "the basic constituent of liberation theology." This level, labeled "popular" by the Boffs, is primarily an oral reflection—a spoken theology. Popular liberation theology is often more than speech; it is expressed in gesture, symbol, and street theater. For example, one gospel study group presented the situation of prostitutes today with a placard: "Last in society, first in the kingdom."

The Boffs reported that during a course on the Apocalypse, another group

> prepared their morning prayer by devising a silhouette show of a dragon with seven heads confronting a wounded lamb. They invited those present to give names to the dragon's seven heads. Men and women came forward and wrote, as best they could: "multinational," "Law of National Security," "foreign debt," "military dictatorship," and names of various government officials held to be against the people. And below the lamb someone wrote: "Jesus Christ, Liberator." And a woman came forward and added: "The people of the poor."[66]

Sometimes the insights of this "popular" theology are gathered and shared with others. Father Ernesto Cardenal tape-recorded his base community's Sunday reflections in Nicaragua from 1975-1977 and published them in Spanish and English.[67] Frances O'Gorman gathered the stories and voices of 35 poor women in two hillside *favelas* in the South Zone of Rio de Janeiro. She notes that "the women tell their stories but reveal a history marked by a past of slavery and exploitation, a history involved in the present-day struggle to confront sociopolitical and economic oppression, a history reaching out for the fullness of life for all."[68] Students of liberation theology and ministers in Latin America have also gathered the insights of people in the communities where they are working. Jennifer Atlee, who has worked in Nicaragua since 1984 with her husband Tom Loudon, has collected and reflected on the popular theology of suffering from eight communities in the arid northwestern region of Nicaragua.[69]

The second level of liberation theology is called "pastoral theology" in the sense that it is the faith reflection of pastors and bishops and other ministers of the gospel. These ministers are trained in theology, but their primary ministry is the pastoral ministry of parishes, schools, and retreat centers. These ministers are nourished through pastoral study days, congresses, or workshops. They are often the bridge between the grass-roots and the theologians.

The third level of liberation theology is the reflection undertaken by the theologians. Some of the theologians publish articles and texts that help to disseminate their thinking. They dialogue with each other and clarify their thinking through theological forums. The liberation theologian does not try to articulate a theology apart from some form of praxis or engagement. "In the field of liberation, trying to know theology alone means condemning oneself to knowing not even one's own theology. So liberation theologians have to be at times pastors, analysts, interpreters, advocates, brothers or sisters in faith, and fellow pilgrims."[70]

A BIBLICAL AND SOCIAL SPIRITUALITY

Gustavo Gutiérrez remarked during a video interview that he has been preaching in parishes for decades and has not mentioned liberation theology in his homilies. He said he doesn't have to; he has the gospel.[71] The gospel is the liberating text for the church. Archbishop Helder Camara commented in 1976 that he has been accused of being a communist because of his work with the poor. He rejected that cold war label by bluntly stating, "I don't need communism, I have the gospel."[72] These comments signal how this movement is deeply rooted in the Bible.

The people in the base communities find their own experience reflected in the Bible. As the Brazilian Frei Betto puts it, the people in the base communities "look at the bible as in a mirror to see their own reality." They understand the Bible in terms of their own experience and reinterpret that experience in terms of biblical symbols and stories. In theological language we refer to this as the "hermeneutical circle"—as interpretation moves from experience to text and back to experience.[73]

Liberation theology views "spirituality" in very concrete and social terms. "Every true theology springs from a spirituality—that is, from a true meeting with God in history. Liberation theology was born when faith confronted the injustice done to the poor."[74] Jon Sobrino concurs:

> ...this theology wishes to take account of, and constitute a response to, concrete historical church reality, with its real cries and real hopes. The very fact that liberation theology is an account of something concrete, formulated for the purpose of turning that concrete reality into something really new, demonstrates that a particular spirit has been present in the very execution of its task. And it is because the theological task has been executed with spirit, we think, that this theology has made spirituality something central.[75]

For Sobrino liberation spirituality begins with the universal spirit in people as its confronts real life. "Spirituality is the spirit with which we confront the real. It is the spirit with which we confront the concrete history in which we live, with all its complexity." In confronting the real the following are necessary:

- *be honest with the real.* Intellectually, this means grasping the truth of concrete reality; practically, it means responding to the demand made by that reality.

- when confronting the injustice of the concrete reality, the spirit responds with *mercy and compassion.*

- the spirit requires our *fidelity,* despite our personal and social fear and masking of the real. *Love and hope* are part of the spirit's response: "Love and hope... are two sides of the same coin; the conviction, put in practice, that reality has possibilities. Love and hope mean helping to bring to light the better, the more humane, presently gestating in the womb of reality."

- the present reality is both challenge and grace—"reality is also Good News, not merely demand."

Sobrino summarizes these insights:

> Honesty with the real, fidelity to the real, and allowing ourselves to be carried forward by the real, are acts of spirit that, in one form or another, by action or omission, every human being performs. Thus we have called them, all three taken together, fundamental spirituality, because they concern every human being.

Christian spirituality, according to Father Sobrino, is "no more and no less than a living of the fundamental spirituality that we have described, precisely in the concrete manner of Jesus and according to the spirit of Jesus. This is the following of Jesus."[76]

As Sobrino "unpacks" the spirit of Jesus, he highlights two elements: the poverty of the incarnation and Jesus' mission of proclaiming the Reign of God. Both of these elements reflect an "option for the poor," which is a core commitment of the theology of liberation.

CHALLENGES FOR LIBERATION THEOLOGY

Since its emergence in the late 1960s liberation theology has come under scrutiny from theological, political, and ecclesiastical quarters. The Congregation for the Doctrine of the Faith (CDF) issued two

"Instructions" on liberation theology in 1984 and 1986. The first document raised questions about the use of Marxist thought in liberation theology, and it criticized "certain forms" of liberation theology that:

1. turn the political dimension in Scripture into "the principal or exclusive component" leading to "a reductionist reading of the Bible";

2. adopt Marxism uncritically and allow theology to become captive to Marxist ideology; and

3. attack authority in the church. CDF warned that certain forms of liberation theology create an opposition between the church of the poor and the hierarchical church, by promoting base communities whose members often lack the theological training and capacity to discern.[77]

The second document published two years later was less critical of liberation theology. In fact, it did not treat liberation theology directly but presented its own version of what a theology of liberation should look like. It stressed "freedom," which was described primarily as personal and spiritual and as more fundamental than any social, earthly liberation.[78]

When the first document was issued, the primary reaction of many who were familiar with liberation theology was to wonder which liberation theologians it was talking about. The uncritical use of Marxist categories is not evident in the works of any prominent liberation theologians. Commentators agreed that liberation theology does challenge church authority when it excludes lay involvement. Leonardo Boff would claim that the base communities "reinvent" the church; it is a revolutionary movement within a heavily hierarchical church.[79] I would argue that the base community movement is a necessary corrective that restores the egalitarian and personal dimensions that are part of the Catholic tradition and rooted in the Johannine community of "beloved disciples."

Regarding the second "Instruction," both Leonardo Boff and Gustavo Gutiérrez spoke favorably about its approach. While they may disagree with the subordination of the sociopolitical to the personal-spiritual, the letter did accept many of the commitments of liberation theology including:

• liberation as an important theme of Christian theology;

• leaving the application of this theme to local churches;

- recognition of the need to change unjust structures in society;

- affirmation of the base communities as a "source of great hope" and a "treasure for the whole church";

- asserting the poor were justified in taking action, through morally licit means—including armed struggle as a last resort—to secure structures that would protect their rights.[80]

In addition to the Congregation for the Doctrine of the Faith's concerns, another collection of critics is found among the hierarchy and the theological community. Members of the hierarchy include the previously discussed Archbishop Alfonso Lopez Trujillo of Colombia, and Archbishop Bonaventure Kloppenburg of Brazil. Theologians include: Roger Vekemans, Karl Lehmann, Heinz Schurmann, Olegario Gonzales de Cardedal, Hans Urs von Balthasar, Dennis McCann, and Richard Neuhaus. Other critics include the philosopher Michael Novak and political theorist Paul Sigmund.[81]

Challenges to liberation theology have also come from the women's movement, indigenous peoples movement, and ecological movement. These groups have challenged liberation theology to broaden its analysis beyond economic impoverishment to include racial, ethnic, cultural, and sexual oppression. Ecological thinkers have called for a reevaluation of the anthropocentric bias underlying liberation theology which implies a hierarchical ordering of creation.

Indigenous people claim that they do not want to be seen as one more facet of liberation theology. Rather, according to Diego Irarrazaval, the director of the Aymara Institute on the Peruvian Altiplano, "indigenous theology" has an "alternative character" rooted in its distinctive sources: "a worldview based on reciprocity, ritual coherence, and oral wisdom." The sages and elders of these indigenous peoples (Mayan, Quechua, and Aymara) have begun to identify the specific, intrinsic worth of Amerindian religious customs and beliefs. They are also discarding the approach that their traditional religions are simply stages leading to Christian evangelization. These reflections are helping liberation theology move toward religious pluralism and interfaith dialogue.[82]

Some ecological theologians have challenged the assumption of both classical and liberation theology that humans have primacy in the natural world. They also question the "option for the poor" if it does not include the rights and dignity of all creation. As we will see in a later chapter, some environmentalists are also recognizing the necessary link between concern for the environment and justice for exploited people. So far, at least one liberation theologian, Leonardo Boff, has consciously addressed the question of ecology—in his text *Ecology and Liberation: A New Paradigm*.[83]

Feminists and mujeristas have also raised questions about the sexism present in liberation theology, including its images of God.[84] Their hope is expressed in the words of the Brazilian theologian Ivone Gebara.

> This is my hope: The day will come when all people, lifting their eyes, will see the earth shining with brotherhood and sisterhood, mutual appreciation, true complementarity.... Men and women will dwell in their houses; men and women will drink the same wine, and dance together in the brightly lit square, celebrating the bonds uniting all humanity.[85]

In response, liberation theologians are beginning to address these important questions. More important, voices are being raised up from these communities to articulate their own realities and concerns. The method of liberation that begins with reality is accepted by these critics; they simply want more diverse people at the theological roundtable.

"A POINT OF NO RETURN"

Liberation theology has named a new way of doing theology: theology as critical reflection praxis. This can only be done in the local situation as Christians confront the injustice in their community and institutions. There is no "one" universal objective liberation theology; there are as many liberation theologies as there are communities engaged in this process. Liberation theology, although originating in Latin America, is not just a theological and pastoral movement for the developing nations. It can be used by faith communities throughout the world. I would argue that the synod process followed by the Diocese of Rochester, as described in chapter eight on the consistent ethic of life, is a liberation theology approach.[86] Father Michael Crosby has written a liberation theology for North Americans in his book, *Spirituality of the Beatitudes: Matthew's Challenge for First World Christians*.[87] Father Alfred Hennelly's recent book, *Liberation Theologies: The Global Pursuit of Justice*, surveys how liberation theology has taken root and is thriving among diverse groups: Africans, Asians, Latinos, African Americans, ecologists, and among world religions.[88]

The Uruguayan theologian Juan Luis Segundo points out that "count-less Christians have committed themselves to a fresh and radical inter-pretation of their faith." For them this process "represents a point of no return." He writes

> It is my opinion that the "theology of liberation," however well or poorly the name fits, represents a point of no return in Latin America. It is an irreversible thrust in the Christian process of creat-ing a new consciousness and maturity in our faith. Countless Christians have committed themselves to a fresh and radical inter-pretation of their faith, to a new re-experiencing of it in their real lives. And they have done this not only as isolated individuals but also as influential and sizable groups within the church.[89]

Segundo wrote that in 1975. Despite controversy and resistance the "movement" of liberation theology has continued to spread and perme-ate the church, even when it is not called liberation theology.

Conclusion

The Medellín conference in 1968 ushered in a new era in the Latin American church. It sanctioned the Catholic church's move toward iden-tifying with the poor and breaking its historic ties with the wealthy and powerful elites. This new direction was fueled by the emerging theology of liberation. Medellín, in turn, encouraged the spread of a liberational approach to ministry and theology.

Voices were raised, and interventions from Rome challenged the direc-tion of Medellín and liberation theology. The "winds have changed," and the optimism of the early 1970s has given way to a somber realism. While the exuberance is not evident, the slow work of liberation contin-ues, despite ecclesial and societal obstacles.

Liberation theology and Medellín have opened a way of doing theology and being church that has taken root in many other countries and among other groups who are marginalized. The church has also been blessed dur-ing this time by the witness of the martyrs of liberation. Their suffering has highlighted the violent tactics that are used against movements of libera-tion, but their witness also reveals the fidelity and grace of God's prophets.

Phillip Berryman situates liberation theology in Latin America against a broader backdrop.

> ...Latin American liberation theology—however important in itself—

is but one aspect of a much larger movement, the emergence of the excluded—women, non-whites, the poor—onto the stage of history. Its fate is inseparably bound up with that larger movement.[90]

The emergence of "the excluded" and a theology that supports their participation in the goods of society and the church is not going to disappear, despite the efforts of those who defend the unjust status quo and try to muffle their voices. We can expect continued conflict over liberation theology and the empowerment of the excluded until all "men and women will drink the same wine, and dance together in the brightly lit square, celebrating the bonds uniting all humanity."[91]

Discussion Questions

1. The Latin American bishops meeting at Medellín described the situation of poverty in their countries as a form of "institutionalized violence" and committed the church to working with small basic communities so that the downtrodden "might come to know their rights and how to make use of them." In what ways do you see the bishops breaking the traditional linkage of church and state in Latin America by the new directions of Medellín?

2. Why did the Vatican-controlled leadership at the Santo Domingo meeting reject the experience-based method of liberation theology and substitute a method that begins with the church's official social teachings?

3. Gustavo Gutiérrez holds that "theology is critical reflection on praxis." What are the implications of such an approach?

4. Sister Joan Petrik notes that members of small Christian communities walk upright, their heads held high, with self-confidence while other peasants shuffle along, their heads bowed. Why are the base communities seen as threatening to those who wish to maintain the current system with its imbalance of power and wealth between the rich elite and the poor?

5. Jon Sobrino maintains that spirituality "is the spirit with which we confront the concrete history in which we live, with all its complexity." What are the implications of a spirituality that begins with confronting real life in all its complexity?

10

The Challenge of Peace and the Catholic Peace Movement

The previous chapter discussed a variety of theological and pastoral issues related to liberation theology and the struggle this movement caused between the local churches of Latin America and Rome. When we turn our attention to the question of war we see an entirely different dynamic at work. In a number of ways the leadership in Rome has been on the cutting edge of challenging the contemporary validity of the just war ethic. Church leadership has been positive in its response to the peace movement. As we shall see, the peace movement had a positive impact on the deliberations of the Second Vatican Council, which set the tone for church teaching for the following thirty years.

This chapter chronicles the unfolding of Catholic thought about the morality of war in this last half of the twentieth century, the peace movement in the United States, the U.S. bishops' pastoral letter on war and peace, the case study of the Iraqi war, the future agenda for building a

275

theology of peace, and some concrete examples of how collective nonviolence has been effective. We begin by focusing on the role of the "local church" in articulating official church teaching. (Local church is a generic term that usually means diocese, but in this context I am using it to refer to the national church.) This will help us to appreciate the role of the U.S. bishops' conference in articulating the church's social teaching as it is presented in the pastoral letters we will be discussing here and in the following chapter.

THE NATIONAL CONFERENCE OF CATHOLIC BISHOPS:
ITS TEACHING ROLE

Like the Episcopal Conference of Latin America, the National Conference of Catholic Bishops in the United States was formed before the Second Vatican Council but has taken on a new significance and authority because of the ecclesiology of Vatican II with its emphasis on collegiality.[1] (Collegiality refers to the recovery by Vatican II of the early church's understanding of the "college of bishops" as the central authority of the church. The emphasis on collegiality is meant to balance the distorted view of authority which sees all authority residing in the pope.) In the arena of social teachings the national conferences of bishops were encouraged to take up their own initiative by Pope Paul VI's apostolic letter, *Octogesima Adveniens*. Pope Paul encouraged the "local church" to engage in theological reflection and pastoral action, rather than looking to Rome for "a solution which has universal validity."

> In the face of such widely varying situations it is difficult for us to utter a unified message and to put forward a solution which has universal validity. Such is not our ambition, nor is it our mission. *It is up to Christian communities to analyze with objectivity the situation which is proper to their own country,* to shed on it the light of the Gospel's unalterable words and to draw principles of reflection, norms of judgment and directives for action from the social teaching of the church. (par. 4)

Father J. Bryan Hehir, a noted Catholic moralist and longtime staff member for the U.S. bishops' conference, reasons that "this text was an invitation to the local churches to be sources of insight, the author of ideas which could move from the edge of the church to the center." Pope Paul, in keeping with the ecclesiology of Vatican II, was lifting up the importance and responsibility of the "local churches," that is, the diocese and national conferences. Father Hehir notes that the invitation did not go unheeded: "The Brazilian hierarchy's human rights ministry in the 1960s and 1970s, the emergence of the theology of liberation throughout Latin America in the same period, and the development of the pastoral letters of the 1980s all testified to *the potential of the local churches to be teachers in social ministry.*"[2]

Pope Paul VI realistically acknowledged in *Octogesima Adveniens* the limitations of his office and the Vatican curial offices by not trying to offer "a ready-made model" (par. 42) for the complex social issues in each country. The strength of the papal teaching, according to Hehir, "lies in its ability to project a vision, to protect principles and values of abiding moral significance and to call the community of the faithful to forms of service and witness in the social arena." The distinctive role of papal and Vatican teaching is to stress the catholicity of the church as it defines *values and principles* to be held by all Roman Catholics.

While Rome offers an essential service for the church, its general teaching has the disadvantage of being isolated from specific settings. This is where the *local church* must come into play by giving the general principles a specificity that is not possible on the universal level. *Specificity* for Hehir means "the ability to enter the concrete complexity of a problem, and to engage the public discussion by which social policies are shaped and influenced."[3] It should be clear that the local church and the universal church are interdependent, each serving a crucial role within the church community. Ideally, there should be a two-way street: the center teaching and learning from the local churches and vice-versa.[4]

AN OPEN PROCESS

Beginning in the early 1980s, the U.S. bishops have taken a new approach to the formulation of their pastoral letters in that they have tried to engage the entire U.S. Catholic church in the discussion of the issues they treat in the letters. In other words, they have not followed the "closed" methodology used by the pope and the Vatican. The Roman methodology uses an individual or a small group of advisers who generally work in secret with a limited consultation by other "experts." For example, many believe that the encyclicals of Pope John Paul II are primarily from his hand with only minimal consultation. The popes have not used an "open" process for drafting official teaching. The North

American and Latin American bishops, on the other hand, have used an open process in the drafting of recent pastoral letters.

As we saw in the previous chapter, the Latin American bishops circulated "working documents" prior to both the 1979 Puebla conference and the 1992 conference at Santo Domingo. These documents allowed local faith communities and theologians to give input and evaluation. Their counterparts in the North followed a similar procedure of making early drafts of their pastoral letters on peace, the economy, and women available for discussion prior to approval. For each of the three letters the bishops' conference named a committee of five bishops who represented the diversity of theological opinion within the bishops' conference as a whole. Consultants who have a special expertise were also named to serve the committee. The bishops' committees began their work with a "listening phase" which sought out the experience and wisdom of experts, specialists, various organizations within the church, and ordinary folk. These listening sessions were often done through two- or three-day "hearings," which were repeated in different parts of the country and focused on different disciplines and constituents.[5]

After the initial "hearing" phase the committee with its consultants wrote a first draft, which was released to the entire church and the general public. The initial drafts were intended to stimulate discussion of the issues involved, that is, to put them on the agenda of parishes, dioceses, and diverse groups both within the church and within society. Subsequent drafts were revised in light of the committee's assessment of the responses they had received to earlier drafts. The bishops' committees for both the peace pastoral and the pastoral on the U.S. economy circulated three public drafts. Each of the drafts was amended slightly before receiving overwhelming support by the bishops when the final vote was taken. The pastoral letter on women also went through three drafts, but the process was altered because of strong concerns from the Vatican, and, as we shall see in a later chapter, the final draft was not approved by the bishops.

Although this is a very lengthy process for drafting a pastoral letter, both Cardinal Bernardin and Archbishop Weakland, who chaired the respective committees, have commented on the importance of the process. While addressing his fellow bishops at the November 1982 meeting, Bernardin said, "The process of discussion, writing, and witness which already has been generated by the statements of bishops and particularly the pastoral may be the most important long-range consequence of our efforts. Today the issue of war and peace is identifiably a line in the Catholic Church." A few years later Archbishop Weakland would echo similar sentiments. "We remain convinced of the importance of this process, an importance that goes beyond the perfecting of a text. The text is ultimately only a catalyst for a larger process of 'forming church.' It is a vibrant and creative way of using modern communications and the possibilities inherent in them to reflect together on what discipleship means for the world today."[6]

In comparison with the secretive Vatican process of producing magisterial statements the U.S. bishops' methodology is as newsworthy as the controversial issues discussed in the letters.

CHURCH TEACHING ON WAR AND PEACE SINCE POPE PIUS XII

It is important to situate the U.S. bishops' pastoral letter, *The Challenge of Peace*, against the backdrop of papal teaching and the position of Vatican II.[7] Church teaching on war has changed dramatically since the time of Pope Pius XII (1939-1958).

The teaching of the church on the morality of war reflects the changes in warfare through the centuries. "With the development of the modern industrial state the church was once more confronted with a new context for war. Large conscript armies, modern weaponry, and the economic burdens of large-scale war all conspired to make warfare more destructive than previous ages imagined."[8] Because of the increasingly destructive scale of war the First Vatican Council expressed horror at the scope of modern warfare. Pope Benedict XV, who was elected shortly after the outbreak of the First World War in 1914, protested against the inhumane methods of warfare and made several strenuous efforts to bring about peace.

Pope Pius XII, who was elected at the outbreak of World War II in 1939, contributed to the church's teaching on the morality of warfare by enunciating two basic convictions: first, that all wars of aggression were to be prohibited and second, that defensive war to repel aggression was reluctantly necessary. He also redefined the meaning of the "just cause" in the church's just war theory. Prior to Pius XII the church had accepted *three* just causes: to vindicate violated rights, to repel an unjust attack, and to avenge an injury. Pius XII restricted the just cause to one, namely, to defend against aggression. This appeal to self-defense could not automatically justify a war. Pius believed that if the damage caused by the war outweighed the injustice done by the aggressor, the attacked nation would have to endure the injustice rather than resort to war. From his perspective the outbreak of war might be worse than tolerating the injustice.

While Pope Pius XII urged that nations seek the way of peace he also recognized the right of national self-defense. "There can be verified in a nation the situation wherein, every effort to avoid war being expended in vain, war—for effective defense and with the hope of a favorable outcome against unjust attack—could not be considered unlawful."[9] The Franciscan Kenneth Himes notes that "Pius' conviction regarding national self-defense was so firm that in the same message he declared a Roman Catholic could not in good conscience refuse to participate in a war declared by legitimate authority."[10]

Pius' teaching would be overturned by the Second Vatican Council. His position had been based primarily on his understanding of the role of the individual vis-à-vis legitimate authority. The work of John Courtney Murray and others helped the church to recognize the limits of authority and the primacy of individual conscience.

The papacy and writing of Pope John XXIII began a new era in Catholic reflection on the just war tradition. Pope John took a more international approach on the notion of the common good. He taught that just as individuals must support and contribute to the common good of their society, so too, the nation-states must regulate themselves to contribute to the global common good.

> John never explicitly denied the just-war theory in *Pacem in Terris,* but his silence about the right of national self-defense coupled with his opposition to nuclear war created a mood of questioning on the topic of warfare. With his death it was left for Vatican II to treat the question of war. The context for the episcopal discussion, however, *was a growing papal disenchantment with modern war.*[11]

The Pastoral Constitution on the Church in the Modern World, *Gaudium et Spes,* turned the papal disenchantment into a call for "an evaluation of war with *an entirely new attitude*" (par. 80). The bishops pointed to the "horror and perversity of war [which] are immensely magnified by the multiplication of scientific weapons. For acts of war involving these weapons can inflict massive and indiscriminate destruction far exceeding the bounds of legitimate defense." A few sentences later the bishops utter their only condemnation in all the Vatican II documents: "Any act of war aimed indiscriminately at the destruction of entire cities or of extensive areas along with their population is a crime against God and man himself. It merits unequivocal and unhesitating condemnation" (par. 80).

It was clear that the development of new weapons, especially nuclear weapons, pushed the church to reexamine its teaching on the morality of war. The Catholic church questioned whether modern warfare had ceased to be a politically rational enterprise. This "new attitude" was articulated in Vatican II. The second major change in the church teaching focused on the right of conscientious objection.

In sharp contrast to the teaching of Pope Pius XII in 1956, the bishops of the council in 1965 supported the right of conscientious objection. "Motivated by this same spirit," they declared in *Gaudium et Spes*, "we cannot fail to praise those who renounce the use of violence in the vindication of their rights..." (par. 78). A footnote clarified the issue by noting that "here, as in the following Article's reference to the treatment of conscientious objectors, the Constitution does not demand sacrifice of the principle or right of self-defense. Its language is strongly positive, however, in referring to those who espouse a policy of nonviolence." The next paragraph in the text urged the legal protection of conscientious objectors: "Moreover, it seems right that laws make humane provisions for the case of those who for reasons of conscience refuse to bear arms, provided however, that they accept some other form of service to the human community" (par. 79).

The change in official teaching on the question of conscientious objection was dramatic—in less than a decade Pius XII's rejection of the right of individual conscience was overturned. The groundwork for this change had been developed by the ethical and theological work of John Courtney Murray as well as by "the movements toward conscientious objection that took place in the 1960s and 1970s, movements often led and supported by the Catholic laity."[12] Again, we see the interplay of unofficial movements shaping the development of official teachings.

Pope Paul VI continued the momentum of Vatican II by reinterpreting the church's teaching on pacifism and the just war ethic. By writing on human and economic development, especially in *Populorum Progressio*, Pope Paul promoted serious reflection on the *conditions for peace* in the world. He is remembered for this adage: "*If you want peace, work for justice*." In 1965 he gave an impressive address at the United Nations headquarters in New York City where he reiterated, "War, never again." In 1968 he initiated the annual celebration of the World Day of Peace, which helped to keep the church focused on issues of war and peace.

When the bishops of the United States turned their attention to the American Roman Catholic church's response to war and deterrence, their reflections were shaped by the discussion at Vatican II and the leadership of Pope Paul VI.

Part I. "The Challenge of Peace"

THE PROCESS

Prior to the November 1980 meeting of the National Conference of Catholic Bishops, Bishop Francis Murphy, an auxiliary bishop of Baltimore and a member of Pax Christi, asked that the bishops prepare a *concise summary* of the church's teaching on war and peace and a strong educational effort on those issues within the church.

At the meeting itself Bishop Murphy posed the question, "Do we need to speak more specifically about the nature and numbers of nuclear armaments, about the morality of their development and use, and especially about the morality of diverting massive human and material resources to their creation?"[13] Other bishops spoke both for and against the idea, and finally the NCCB leadership took the recommendation under advisement and organized a five-member committee that included:

- Joseph Bernardin, archbishop of Cincinnati serving as the chairperson;

- Thomas Gumbleton, auxiliary of Detroit and president of Pax Christi;

- John O'Connor, auxiliary bishop of New York and the Military Ordinariate (overseeing all the military chaplains);

- Daniel Reilly, bishop of Norwich, Connecticut; and

- George Fulcher, auxiliary bishop of Columbus, Ohio.

The issues of nuclear weapons and peace had taken on a new urgency in November of 1980 as Ronald Reagan had just been elected to the presidency. Reagan had campaigned strongly against the SALT II arms limitation treaty negotiated by President Carter—which had been endorsed by the bishops. Reagan also called for a massive arms buildup and for a more militant stand against the U.S.S.R. James Castelli, a journalist who had access to the bishops' committee files, noted the catalyst provided by

Reagan's hawkish posture: "Reagan's election—with the rhetoric and policies he brought to office—was the single greatest factor influencing the bishops' discussion in November 1980 and all that followed."[14]

Consultants who advised the bishops' committee in an ongoing fashion included members of the NCCB/USCC staff, especially

- Edward Doherty and Father J. Bryan Hehir, chair of the USCC's Office of International Justice and Peace;

- Father Richard Warner representing the Conference of Major Superiors of Men;

- Sister Juliana Casey representing the Leadership Conference of Women Religious; and

- Dr. Bruce Martin Russett, professor of political science at Yale and editor of the *Journal of Conflict Resolution*, who was the principal consultant.

Sister Casey was the only woman in the process, and as such, had some telling insights. First of all she stopped taking notes during the hearings because a former government official mistook her for a secretary; she felt some truth to the notion that men talk about issues like war in terms of abstractions, while women see them in terms of people. She was also struck by the internal process of the committee. Meetings weren't preplanned, the way women religious plan things; Bernardin always set the agenda at the start. She noted, "We never stopped after some of the testimony to talk about how we felt about what we had heard, even when everyone was visibly moved. Women would have talked about how they had changed."[15] Later she reflected on the sexism endemic in the institutions and ethos of government.

> In all our meetings with departments of the government, the only other women I ever saw were receptionists, secretaries and cleaning women. I often felt lonely and alienated. I slowly began to realize that this was not simply because I was the "only woman," but rather because as the only woman, I was very much alone in a world view, a relationship to reality. Sexism is an evil. Nowhere is it more evil than in making of war.[16]

The worldview that she was referring to was "a strikingly different world view from that proposed in the 'real' male-dominated world."

It is a world where language is inclusive, imaginative and celebratory of the feminine. Logic is expanded beyond the limited (and dangerous) horizon of abstract, objective rationality to include creation, imagination and vision. Power is not domination, control, power-over, but rather energy which grows in relation, which enables and empowers others. Relationship is fundamental to development, enables caring, and dissipates the need for enemies.[17]

Before releasing their first draft the committee held fourteen hearings that included testimony from 36 witnesses, from Secretary of Defense Caspar Weinberger to peace activists. (Only three of the 36 were women, a scripture scholar and two peace activists.) The response to the first draft, which was published in the *National Catholic Reporter* in June 1982, was both voluminous and mixed. The strongest criticism came from Archbishop Philip Hannan, who had raised questions during the discussion of these issues at the Second Vatican Council. Hannan argued that the draft would hurt the U.S. negotiating position and was at odds with the pope's U.N. speech; he wanted to scrap the pastoral and simply distribute the U.N. address.[18]

The second draft was released in October 1982 in time for the November meeting of the NCCB. This draft drew more secular attention. *Time* magazine (November 29, 1982) had Bernardin's picture on the cover as the lead story, "God and the Bomb: Catholic Bishops Debate Nuclear Morality." Jim Castelli believed that "with the publication of the second draft, the American Catholic bishops as a body clearly emerged as the major moral critic of American—and, for that matter, Soviet—nuclear policy."[19]

After the second draft was released the committee met in Rome with Vatican officials and bishops from France, West Germany, Great Britain, Belgium, Italy, and the Netherlands. The meeting, held January 18-19, 1983, surfaced the differences between European and American pastoral letters. The European tradition was to focus on principles while the Americans dealt with principles *and specifics*. Concerns were raised about specific recommendations of the letter that would be seen as binding church principles that differed from those of the universal church. The question of the teaching authority of the NCCB was raised by the members of the curia, especially Msgr. Jan Schotte, the secretary of the Papal Commission *Iustitia et Pax*.[20]

Many changes were recommended by Bishop O'Connor including softening the language from "halt" to "curb" the testing, production, and deployment of strategic weapons.

A third draft was released in preparation for the May 2-3, 1983 meeting of the NCCB in Chicago. Recommendations and amendments continued to pour in. Archbishop Hannan raised many challenges to the text at the meeting but he did not win many votes.[21] After making a number of changes to the third draft, including returning to the stronger language of recommending a "halt" to nuclear weapons testing, production, and deployment, the letter was approved by a vote of 238 to 9.

CONTENT

The pastoral letter *The Challenge of Peace* is divided into four parts. Part I covers a biblical discussion of peace and the ethical tradition of the just war ethic, as well as the value of nonviolence. Part II addresses the morality of nuclear weapons and nuclear deterrence. This section establishes a sliding scale of moral judgments about the use of nuclear weapons:

- targeting population centers is judged to be absolutely immoral;

- first use of nuclear weapons is opposed on the basis of prudential judgment—meaning that there is room for disagreement on this as the conditions and facts may change; and finally,

- the letter acknowledges a narrow moral permissibility for second strike, counter-force (i.e. against military targets and not population centers) retaliation.[22]

Part II also conditionally accepts deterrence as a short-term necessity as nations take concrete steps to move away from reliance on nuclear weapons. The most controversial issues are dealt with in this section of the letter.

Part III offers suggestions for reducing the danger of war, arms control, conflict resolution, and the importance of social order based on justice as the foundation of true peace.

Part IV suggests a spirituality of peace as well as educational programs within the church to build a reverence for life.

Two Traditions: Pacifism and Just War

Following the lead of *Gaudium et Spes* the bishops' letter supports pacifism and conscientious objection to war as a legitimate Christian position. The U.S. bishops opt, in effect, for a stance of pluralism in regard to the moral evaluation of war: both the just war ethic and pacifism are accepted as justifiable moral positions. The biblical and theological foundation for this is found in the dual dimensions of the kingdom of God—"the already" and the "not yet." Father Ken Himes explains.

> Pacifism is a path to be taken by those who remind the world of the fullness of God's promise of peace, while just war proponents choose on the basis of their recognition of the unrealized nature of the kingdom of God. Since both dimensions of God's message are true, it is present reality and future promise, those who live in the "in-between times" must develop an ethical stance toward war that encompasses both aspects of God's message.[23]

The bishops discuss the traditional categories of the just war ethic and then give them a contemporary interpretation. Within the just war ethic there are two sets of principles, one for determining the "right to go to war," known as *jus ad bellum,* and a second set of principles governing the tactics used during the war, *jus in bello.* The U.S. bishops' restatement of these principles can be summarized as follows (par. 85-110):

A. *Jus ad bellum* (why and when recourse to war is permissible)

1. *Just cause*—to protect innocent life and secure basic human rights; not as retribution;

2. *competent authority*—war must be declared by legitimate authority, those responsible for public order;

3. *Comparative justice criteria*—challenges both sides to recognize the limits of their "just cause" and to ask if the rights and values that are in conflict justify the taking of human life;

4. *Right intention*—related to just cause and the pursuit of moral order as the basis of peace; it challenges unnecessarily destructive acts or imposing unreasonable conditions, such as unconditional surrender;

5. *Last resort*—all peaceful alternatives must have been exhausted;

6. *Probability of success*—questions the irrational resort to force or hopeless resistance, yet it also leaves room for "proportionate" witness to key values;

7. *Proportionality*—the damage to be inflicted and the costs incurred by war must be proportionate to the good expected by taking up arms.

B. Jus in Bello ("Even when the stringent conditions which justify resort to war are met, the conduct of war, i.e., strategy, tactics, and individual actions, remains subject to continuous scrutiny in light of two principles")

1. *Proportionality*—this criterion asks, "once we take into account not only the military advantages that will be achieved by using this means but also all the harms reasonably expected to follow from using it, can its use still be justified?" (par. 103)

2. *Discrimination*—this principle prohibits directly intended attacks on non-combatants and non-military targets (in nuclear weapons strategies these are called "counter-population" targets as distinguished from "counter-force" targets).

"These two principles, in all their complexity, must be applied to the range of weapons—conventional, nuclear, biological, and chemical—with which nations are armed today" (par. 110).

When the bishops discuss pacifism they are very clear that pacifism is a choice for *individual* believers. Echoing *Gaudium et Spes* (par. 79), the bishops endorse pacifism as an option for individuals; it cannot be required of nations or of individuals. Himes concludes: "Thus, those believers who maintain that pacifism is an essential aspect of Christian faith and therefore a duty rather than option do not find support in Catholic social teaching."[24]

Other Christian denominations known as the "peace churches," such as the Mennonite, Bruderhof, etc., rely primarily on the tradition of the New Testament and the early church, and argue that pacifism is the true ethic of the disciple of Jesus the nonviolent one. The closest that the post-Constantinian Roman Catholic church has come to calling pacifism a duty is to see it as a vocational duty that is required by one's state of life as a cleric or as a member of a religious order. The rejection of war was required by the higher morality of the evangelical counsels that were adhered to by those in religious life. This two-level spirituality and ethic have been officially eroded by the Vatican II's theology, which called *all* Catholics to a full evangelical spirituality and discipleship.

As the Catholic tradition continues to follow the advice of Vatican II—to have its moral reflection more clearly rooted in the Bible and be Christ-centered—I believe we will see a shift in the church's understanding of pacifism. The official teaching is finding it harder and harder to justify war in the modern era. This means that the tradition of nonviolence will be recovered and receive greater emphasis in the future. The Catholic tradition is still working on this question.

For the time being, the official Catholic position on pacifism can be summarized by the following three statements.

1. Pacifism is an option individuals may choose. Both conscientious objection and selective conscientious objection are supported by Catholic teaching. The latter is premised on just war theory, while the former is derived from the legitimacy of pacifism (par. 233).

2. Pacifism requires a clear commitment to resist injustice and a desire to promote human rights and the common good. Sectarian withdrawal is not an option for Roman Catholics.

3. The pacifism approved by Catholic social teaching is based on the freedom of the person and the right of individual conscience. It is not a duty for all but an option for those who discern a moral call to oppose war.[25]

The pastoral letter suggests that the two traditions "complement one another" in three ways: 1) "they share a common presumption against the use of force as a means of settling disputes" (par. 120; 2) "both find their roots in the Christian theological tradition"; and 3) they "often converge and agree in their opposition to methods of warfare" (par. 121).

By speaking about both the just war ethic and pacifism within the Christian ethical tradition the bishops restore to a place of prominence the pacifist tradition that, since the Crusades, has been relegated to fringe groups in the church. The bishops restore something of the "not yet," to the Catholic reflection on war: Christians are not to accommodate themselves to the norms of the culture that suggest that the violence of war is an acceptable way for nations to settle their disagreements.

There are some unresolved problems with proposing a pluralism on the level of moral theory. Fr. Ken Himes explains: "It is clear that individuals can opt for either pacifism or just war and find support in the documents. At the level of moral theory, however, it is more difficult to hold onto both pacifism and just war." Himes goes on to say that

> there seems to be a confusion in the pastoral whereby complementarity is equivalent to just war having something in common with paci-

fism. That is not sufficient, however, and obscures the real point, which is that pacifism and just war theory are in opposition to one another. They challenge each other, and they cannot both be right. Either war is sometimes permissible or it is not. There is no alternative.[26]

This question needs further discussion. It may be that the "either/or" logic presented by Father Himes does not do justice to the complexity of the question. It may be more fruitful to think in terms of the creative tension of a "both/and" approach because each tradition highlights important values that must be considered in conflictual and unjust situations.

The Question of Deterrence
On the question of the morality of deterrence the bishops take a moderate or centrist position. By so doing they were criticized by those on the right and those on the left. Among the Catholic pacifists the pastoral letter is seen as useful but neither profound nor prophetic. The pacifist Gordon Zahn and others argue that the logic of the Christian tradition and the nature of contemporary warfare will lead to a pacifist tradition for the Catholic church. (There is evidence of such a movement within influential Catholic circles, as we will discuss in a later section.)

Ethicists and commentators on the right are divided into two groups. One group, including George Weigel and Michael Novak, argues that the tradition of moderate realism within Catholicism, which they claim is the authentic tradition, was abandoned by the bishops because of the influence of progressive staff and theologians such as Father Bryan Hehir. Weigel argues that "the" Catholic position as developed by John Courtney Murray has been distorted and abandoned in the bishops' letter. Murray had said that "since limited nuclear war may be a necessity, it must be a possibility."[27] Hehir responded that, "those accused regard their work as development of the tradition, not its corruption."[28]

A second group of conservative thinkers criticize the bishops for tolerating the evil of deterrence that directly threatens to kill the innocent. This group of critics holds that the prohibition on killing the innocent is a moral absolute whether the context is abortion or civilian deaths in a nuclear war. Although conservative in their orientation John Finnis, Joseph Boyle, and Germain Grisez conclude that on this question *they share the perspective of the nuclear pacifists* that a deterrence based on killing the innocent is immoral. They accuse the bishops of caving in to "consequentialist" moral reasoning rather than maintaining the high moral ground of teaching the duty not to kill innocent life.[29] While the position of Finnis-Boyle-Grisez is a minority position, it is stronger today than it was when nuclear deterrence first confronted the Christian community. These critics from the right are aligned with critics from the left as both groups agree that a Christian must be a nuclear pacifist.

The bishops' position, a *conditional acceptance of deterrence*, argues that *the intention* to use nuclear weapons that will kill many noncombatants does not cover all the moral aspects of the complex question, as the Finnis group maintains. The morality of nuclear deterrence is not reduced to paying attention to *one* moral absolute. Hehir explains: "Without disputing the pedigree of the moral reasoning, and while recognizing the internal logic of the argument, one can still remain unpersuaded by the conclusion. It is not clear that intentionality captures the full range of moral judgment needed to assess the reality of deterrence."[30] Ethics of intention is balanced off by the ethics of consequence, in that the intention to cause harm may have actually prevented that harm from occurring, and is therefore a lesser evil.

According to the bishops' position, no single factor in the moral evaluation settles the question. There is a certain "untidiness" that "leaves both moralists and plain citizens less than satisfied with its conclusions."[31] The bishops have chosen to remain with the complexity and "untidiness" of the issue as they try to push the agenda toward safer and saner long-term goals, as discussed in Part III of the letter.

ITS IMPACT

Has this pastoral letter had any impact on the attitudes of Roman Catholics toward war and defense spending? The National Opinion Research Center, directed by Father Andrew Greeley, a sociologist, undertook a survey "to prove that pastoral letters have no impact." Greeley was surprised to find that his hypothesis was wrong. The 1983 peace pastoral brought about an "astonishing" shift against defense spending among Roman Catholics. According to Greeley the pastoral "appears to be the most successful intervention to change attitudes ever measured by social science." The pastoral letter seems to be the only factor that could account for a 22 percent shift in Catholic views on arms spending between 1983 and 1984. By comparison, Protestant views on arms spending remained unchanged during that same period.

In 1983, *before* the pastoral was issued, the Research Center found that

32 percent of both Catholics and Protestants thought that too much money was being spent on weapons. "A year later the percentage was still 32 percent for Protestants but 54 percent for Catholics; a change in attitude by perhaps 10,000,000 Catholics."

Greeley pointed to two reasons for this shift in thinking. The first was a matter of timing: the pastoral letter came at a time when many people who had not voted for President Reagan were becoming increasingly uneasy with his military spending policies. The pastoral letter coincided with their growing discontent with the President's military build-up—which had been one of the reasons motivating the bishops to write the letter in the first place. The second factor in the letter's success was that "it was an effective media event. The fact that non-churchgoers changed as much as the churchgoers shows that the knowledge causing the shift came through the media, not through reading the pastoral itself or hearing about it in church."[32]

FIVE AND TEN YEARS LATER

Five years after the writing of the *Challenge of Peace* an ad hoc committee of the bishops reviewed U.S. nuclear policy. Their report was called *Building Peace: a Pastoral Reflection on the Response to the Challenge of Peace,* and its companion document was entitled *A Report on the Challenge of Peace and Policy Developments 1983-1988.* These documents reaffirmed the conditional acceptance of deterrence and noted the breakthrough in arms control with the 1987 Intermediate Nuclear Forces (INF) Treaty. The committee also evaluated the Strategic Defense Initiative (SDI) and concluded that the risks seriously outweighed the benefits and that the deployment of SDI would not meet the moral criteria of the pastoral letter.[33]

In 1991, eight years after completing the pastoral letter, Cardinal Bernardin noted that *The Challenge of Peace* and the *Report* were both important texts for the 1980s but times have changed. "...It is not sufficient simply to amend the texts of the last decade. They spoke to the questions of the moment." These earlier documents focused on the question of "means." In fact, most of the debate about nuclear weapons focused on this question of means, the question of strategy, and the ethics of nuclear strategy. Because of the radical reshaping of the Soviet Union in the 1990s, Bernardin argued, the focus should shift to the question of *political ethics.* By this he means that the

...relations between the superpowers and their relations with others should be cast in terms of a framework of order, justice and change in world politics. It is the kind of framework found in *Pacem in Terris* and *Sollicitudo Rei Socialis*; the empirical political circumstances of the past made the moral vision seem unreachable. Today, this kind of conception of order is the precondition for addressing more specific issues of politics, strategy, and economics.[34]

Cardinal Bernardin and other bishops continued their reflection on the new international political order at the end of the Cold War. A subcommittee was established by the bishops' International Policy Committee to reflect on the implications of the liberation of Eastern Europe. The chairperson of this subcommittee, Bishop Daniel Reilly, commented that

this exciting, challenging, and often frustrating search for new directions invites the Church to take seriously two aspects of its role in the modern world. First, according to the Second Vatican Council, the Church has the responsibility to read "the signs of the times" and interpret them in light of the Gospel. Second, the method for doing this is respectful dialogue with the world.

Bishop Reilly realized that the discernment process was a two-way street for the church. "In short, the Church has something to learn and something to teach about the shape of the post-Cold War world."[35]

Bishop Reilly's subcommittee produced a statement on the tenth anniversary of the peace pastoral in 1993, entitled *The Harvest of Justice Is Sown in Peace*.[36] According to Reilly the statement

represents the most comprehensive reflection by the U.S. bishops to date of the moral and religious dimensions of peacemaking after the Cold War. It looks back to some of the unfinished business of the peace pastoral, namely, the validity of the just-war tradition and the issue of nuclear weapons. It also looks ahead at issues that were not among the primary concerns of a decade ago, such as the more central role of the United Nations and other multilateral institutions, the problem of religious and nationalist violence, and the moral dimensions of economic sanctions and humanitarian intervention.[37]

The principles of the just war theory would not sit on the shelf. They were used by both opponents and proponents of the 1991 Gulf War. This war serves as a test case for evaluating the morality of war at the end of the twentieth century.

A TEST CASE: THE PERSIAN GULF WAR

On August 2, 1990 the Iraqi army under the command of Saddam Hussein began a military annexation of Kuwait. On January 16, 1991 President George Bush decided to use military force against Iraq after Saddam Hussein refused to meet the January 15th deadline for withdrawal from Kuwait. Was this a justified war by the criteria of the just war theory?

The president defended his decision as a just war: "The war in the gulf is not a Christian war, a Jewish war, or a Muslim war—it is a just war."[38] Many others questioned its morality including Pope John Paul II,[39] the Society of Christian Ethics,[40] a statement by American Catholic theologians and professors of religious studies,[41] bishops, ethicists, and philosophers.[42] The president, too, had many supporters who accepted the "necessity" of this war.[43]

The Gulf War raised many troubling questions including

- what is the morality of sanctions?

- is a just war theologically unacceptable and incompatible with basic Christian values?

- does the just war criteria leave out of the analysis some vital piece of information, such as a longer view of the history of conflictual area or the consistency of the nations involved?

- does the just war theory contain so many indeterminate elements and potentially contradictory considerations that it is impossible to apply? For example, how do we make a decision if the cause is just but the means are disproportionate?[44]

- what about the long-term effects on the civilian population?[45]

The answers to these and other questions are clear for those who take a pacifist stance on war in general or this war in particular. For those who try to employ the just war thinking the moral terrain is filled with ambiguity and uncertainty as they try to determine if this war was "proportionate" and did not attack innocent civilians. My personal judgment is that the United States and its allies should have taken more time to pursue less violent means (e.g., sanctions). President Bush felt he had exhausted other means during the 166 days between the invasion of Kuwait and the beginning of the allied air strikes against Iraq. But in terms of the long history of tension in that region, I wonder if four and a half months was enough time.

The moral evaluation of that war has continued beyond its conclusion as we recognize its true costs—for Iraq and for our own servicemen and women. Theologian John Langan suggests the case is not closed on the Gulf War:

> The issues raised by the Gulf War are still to a large extent unresolved and will be reinterpreted in different ways depending on the fate of the various political regimes in the area and on the outcome of the negotiations between Israel and its Arab neighbors which began in Madrid in November 1991. Our judgments of proportionality in particular are likely to be altered as we understand more deeply the factors at work in the war and as we grasp in more detail the intentions of the various agents.[46]

JUST WAR—"UNATTAINABLE CRITERIA"?

The experience of the Gulf War caused many moral theologians and Christians to rethink and evaluate their attitude toward war. The editors of the influential Italian Jesuit theological journal, *La Civiltà Cattolica*, did their thinking out loud in a fourteen-page editorial in the July 6, 1991 issue of that journal. Msgr. William Shannon, a theologian and Thomas Merton scholar, reminds us that this editorial "carries special weight because *La Civiltà* is often used as a vehicle for 'official' church statements...."[47] (During Pope Paul VI's papacy the pope would personally review the journal prior to publication, which gave its editorials a semi-official status.) "The editorial filters [the] long Christian tradition through the recent events of the Gulf War in such a way that *a dramatic and radical rethinking* of that tradition emerges."[48]

The editors ask: "What can be said about this theory of the 'just war'?" They answer their own question:

> Before all else, we have to realize that it was not intended to "justify" war, but rather to limit its frequency and cruelty by assigning conditions and very precise and strict rules that must be fulfilled before a war can be defined as "just".... But *the theory has a serious flaw: Its conditions are unattainable; a war cannot really be conducted according to the criteria required for a just war.*

A few lines later they ask another question in light of the devastation caused by the 90,000 tons of bombs dropped on Iraq: "Or do we not rather have to say a 'just war' is impossible because, even when a just cause is present, the wrongs that wars produce by their very nature are so grave and dreadful that they can never be justified in the light of conscience?" The writers are suspicious of the "just cause" criteria:

> But what is an even more serious problem with the "just war" theory is that the "just cause" is used most of the time to give a moral and juridical guise to a war one intends to wage for purposes quite different from those that have been officially stated.

> *This shows that the theory of the "just war" is untenable and needs to be abandoned.* With the single exception of a war of pure defense against an aggression actually taking place, one can say that "just wars" do not exist and that there is no "right to (wage) war."[49]

Some have suggested that the unsigned editorial is "preparing the way for a repudiation of just-war theory by the magisterium."[50] William Shannon asks, "Is the Catholic church in the process of becoming a 'Christian Peace Church'?"[51] Whatever weight is given to this editorial it is clearly "symptomatic of a growing dissatisfaction with the just war theory."[52]

Dissatisfaction with justifying war has been part of the Christian community since the days of the first followers of Jesus.[53] It is certainly evident in the vibrant peace movement in the United States that preceded the writing of the bishops' letter on peace.

Part II. Catholic Peace Movement

The Catholic peace movement in the United States had a very slow beginning. For instance, during World War I, only four of the 3,989 conscientious objectors were Roman Catholic—that is, *one tenth of one percent.* Many factors explain the lack of resistance to war by American Catholics. They were immigrants trying to prove their patriotism. This combined with a heavy emphasis on obedience to lawful authority, and a concomitant weak sense of the value of individual freedom of conscience. During World War II the number of Roman Catholics claiming conscientious objection rose to 223 out of a total of 11,887. 135 of the 223 who claimed CO status were formally classified as COs. In addition to these 135 Catholic conscientious objectors, 61 Catholics refused induction and were imprisoned. Roman Catholics represented about *one percent* of COs during the Second World War.

Catholic resistance to war changed significantly during the Vietnam conflict. By 1969 2,494 Catholics had received CO status, or 7.3% of the 34,255 conscientious objectors.[54] While this raw data needs to be interpreted and examined in the specific context of each war, it does reveal a drastic increase over a fifty-year period, and it suggests the growing influence of a Roman Catholic peace movement.

The consistent and often lonely voice for the radical evangelical stance of pacifism in the early years was Dorothy Day and other members of the Catholic Worker. Founded in 1933 the Catholic Worker maintained its commitment to nonviolence throughout World War II, despite a great loss of support. By 1945 twenty of the thirty-two Worker Houses had closed and their newspaper had lost over 100,000 subscribers.[55] The Catholic Worker put the integrity of its mission above the expediency of institutional survival and growth.

In 1937 a pacifist offshoot of the Catholic Worker, known as PAX, was formed. A few years later this group changed its name to the Association of Catholic Conscientious Objectors (ACCO). ACCO helped to oversee the placement of the 135 Catholic draftees who had received a CO status. The COs were required to work in unpaid service in isolated work camps during the duration of the war plus six months. Camp Simon, the Catholic camp, was established in two locations (Stoddard, New Hampshire, and Warner, New Hampshire). The financial support for the camp came from the Catholic Worker and later other Protestant Peace Churches. The Catholic hierarchy did not support the CO camp during the war.[56]

During the Second World War advocates of the just war ethic used its categories to challenge the morality of some of the tactics used during the war. The most notable critic of the morality of Allied tactics was a professor at Fordham University, John C. Ford, S.J. In 1941 Ford defended the right of Catholics to be conscientious objectors, and then in 1944 he challenged the morality of obliteration bombing and the concept of "total war." His condemnation was based on the principles of proportionality of the means used and discrimination, that is, the immunity of innocent civilians. Ford went so far as to imply that in the modern era, with the availability of weapons of vast destruction, the very concept of a just war seemed naive and outdated. This theme would echo through the halls of the Second Vatican Council twenty years later and would be repeated with clarity by the editors of *La Civiltà Cattolica* in 1991.

VATICAN II ERA

In 1962, twenty-five years after PAX had been started by the Catholic Worker movement, Eileen Egan revived it as a lobbying and pressure group to attempt to change Catholics' attitudes about war and peace. Members of PAX and the Catholic Worker would be vocal advocates for change in attitudes during the Second Vatican Council.

A good number of progressive bishops wanted Vatican II to condemn nuclear weapons, but the American delegation was generally not in that camp. With the exception of Cardinal Ritter of St. Louis, who even sought the condemnation of the possession of nuclear weapons, the American bishops, along with the British bishops, did not feel that "banning the bomb" was realistic. A pacifist delegation including Dorothy Day, Eileen Egan, James Douglass (a Catholic theologian and critic of the just war tradition), Philip Scharper (a journalist), and Gordon Zahn (a CO from World War II) went to Rome to lobby their cause. They were supported by Thomas Merton, who sent an "open letter" to the council calling for a condemnation of nuclear war and support for conscientious objection. Eileen Egan, Dorothy Day, and others undertook a fast to dramatize the issue. Ronald Musto, a historian of the peace movement, records that "with the help of Bishop John Taylor the pacifists eventually got their opinions to the floor of the Council. They won the support of other American bishops like Fulton J. Sheen, who adopted Cardinal Ottaviani's position outlawing all modern war."[57]

The discussion of freedom of conscience at the council, which had preceded the discussion of war and nuclear weapons, prepared the bishops for the issues raised by the pacifists. As Himes noted,

> pacifists saw the necessity of rescuing individual conscience from the overreaching claims of the modern state in regard to military service. Their agenda for defending the right of conscientious objection fit in well with Vatican II's emphasis on the dignity of the person and the rights of conscience. Thus, despite its support for the just war tradition's claim of a right to use force in self-defense, the Council, in deference to the rights of conscience, also supported the option of pacifists to refuse to participate in the military.[58]

The council did go on to support conscientious objection as well as to condemn weapons of vast destruction. These were significant decisions that would have a reverberating effect in the U.S.: "The impact of Vatican II in the United States was decisive. Amid the conflict of Vietnam, Catholics

were suddenly awakened to the hard fact that their church had always recognized the call of peace and was now actively challenging Catholics to
awaken their consciences to the need for positive peacemaking."[59]

THE TRAUMA OF VIETNAM

In November 1964 Thomas Merton led a retreat at Gethsemani,
Kentucky, that brought together Daniel and Philip Berrigan, James
Forest, Tom Cornell, and John Heidbrink from the Fellowship of
Reconciliation (FOR), as well as leading Protestant peace activists,
including A. J. Muste, John Howard Yoder, and W. H. Ferry. As a result of
this retreat the Catholic Peace Fellowship (CPF) was started, with Cornell
and Forest as full-time staff and Daniel Berrigan and Thomas Merton as
directors. CPF, as an affiliate of the interfaith Fellowship of
Reconciliation, did not attract a large membership, perhaps due to its
requirement of pacifism as a condition for membership; but its members
were very visible in anti-war protests.

As the war in Vietnam intensified, CPF became the primary outlet for
individual Catholic radicalism. Tom Cornell had publicly burned his
draft card at an anti-Vietnam war rally in Union Square, New York City,
in November 1962. In May 1964 he burned his card again with another
Catholic Worker, Christopher Kearnes. In August 1965 others burned
their draft cards as protest against the war; among them were thirty-two
Catholic Workers. Because of these protests, Congress passed the Rivers
Act, which made draft card burning a federal offense. The burnings continued, but now the protesters were arrested and imprisoned. Soon more
than draft cards were being burned.

On November 9, 1965, Roger LaPorte, a former Trappist novice and a
Catholic Worker, burned himself to death in front of the United Nations
Building as a protest to the war. He had followed the example of the self-
immolation of Buddhist monks in Vietnam. "The Catholic Worker was
shaken to its roots, and Catholics all across the country were awakened
to the agony of Vietnam for the first time."[60]

In October 1967 Philip Berrigan led a protest in Baltimore in which
he and others poured blood on draft records in an effort to awaken the
Pentagon and the American people to the responsibility for the bloody
war. In May 1968 a group of nine Catholic activists entered the Selective
Service headquarters in Catonsville, Maryland, carried out draft files, and
burned them with napalm. The police waited until the nine had com-

pleted the Lord's Prayer and then handcuffed them and led them away. Similar protests took place in Milwaukee and Chicago.

In November 1971 the American Catholic bishops condemned the war in Vietnam as unjust, and eventually the war would come to a demoralizing end.

The protesting against the American war machine would continue, but now its focus was on nuclear weapons. The protesters took their inspiration from the words of the prophets Isaiah and Micah, "They shall beat their swords into plowshares, and their spears into pruning hooks" (Is 2:4; Mi 4:3). Their actions are referred to as "Plowshares":

- on September 9, 1980, eight people including Dan and Phil Berrigan entered the General Electric plant in King of Prussia, Pennsylvania, and symbolically "disarmed" Mark 12A warheads;

- ramming and "disarming" nuclear submarines in Groton, Connecticut;

- pouring blood in a GE nuclear warhead plant;

- disarming components of the Cruise, Pershing, and MX missiles at the AVCO plant in Wilmington, Delaware;

- hammering a B-52 bomber armed with Cruise missiles at Griffiss Air Force Base, Rome, New York, on Thanksgiving Day 1983;

- pouring blood on and hammering Pershing II components at the Martin Marietta plant in Orlando, Florida on Easter 1984.[61]

PAX CHRISTI

Another arm of the burgeoning Catholic peace movement, Pax Christi USA, was less dramatic and radical in its witness to peace. The U.S. chapter of Pax Christi was started in May 1975. Pax Christi is the only Catholic peace movement that seeks membership throughout the world. Membership in Pax Christi USA has grown steadily since 1975—by the time of its October 1981 conference in Richmond, Virginia, it had grown to 5,000 members, 46 of them bishops. One reason for its appeal is that it explicitly "embraces a pluralism of positions on peace issues among its members."[62] While there has been a strong and articulate pacifist voice in Pax Christi from the beginning, espousing pacifism is not and, according to the statutes of the movement, cannot be, a condition of membership.

The movement was founded by French laity who, after World War II, sought reconciliation with their German neighbors. The bishop of Lourdes, Pierre-Marie Theas, became its first enthusiastic leader. Pope Pius XII endorsed the movement in 1948, and it gradually became an international organization spreading throughout Europe and Australia. Today there are national sections also in Canada and the United States, with organizing efforts being made in a number of countries in Asia and the Pacific, as well as hopes of organizing in Africa.

Pax Christi works on the grass-roots level through programs of prayer, study, and action. The organization seeks to influence public opinion and opinion within the church on matters of peace, justice, and human rights. Its professed aim is "to work for peace for all people, as the fruit of justice, while always witnessing to the peace of Christ."[63]

The movement is a good example of collaborative ministry of hierarchy and laity. Pax Christi was founded by laypeople and has always elected a bishop as its international president, a practice followed by most national sections. In the U.S. chapter bishops Thomas Gumbleton of Detroit and Carroll Dozier of Memphis agreed to serve as "moderators" in its beginning. Laypeople continue to form the majority of the membership and are the majority on the international executive committee, which is democratically elected.

Pax Christi, respectful of the Catholic church's tradition, seeks to educate and conscienticize Catholics to the ways of peace, and it seeks to make the institutional church an instrument of peacemaking. In this regard Pax Christi draws upon the witness of the gospel and Catholic social teaching as the foundation of its work. In 1963 the movement adopted Pope John XXIII's encyclical *Pacem in Terris* as its charter. This encyclical provides a broad and consistent framework for peace as founded on the four pillars of truth, love, justice, and freedom.

Pax Christi focuses on the individual and the institutional route to peace. Individually it seeks to "convert" individual Catholics to the attitudes and work of peace. This entails a theology and a spirituality of peace. "Unlike many other single-issue peace movements, Pax Christi has the strength that comes from fostering the spiritual and theological development of its own members along with its work on social issues."[64] On the institutional level Pax Christi addresses the peace agenda within the church—for example, Bishop Gumbleton's work on the committee drafting the bishops' pastoral letter, and within the national and international arenas:

The movement has consultative status with the Economic and Social Council of the United Nations, and in 1983 was awarded the UNESCO Peace Education Prize for its work in stimulating the growth of an international peace climate. The organization regularly makes interventions in the UN Commission on Human Rights in Geneva, and also has organized fact-finding missions and visits of solidarity to Central America, Haiti and Brazil.[65]

Pax Christi is rooted in the Catholic tradition but is equally committed to working ecumenically with other Christian churches and on an interfaith basis with the major world religions. While there has been some "cooling off" of the ecumenical movement since Vatican II, Pax Christi is forging ahead on the national and international levels. For example, in the early 1980s five faith-based peace movements in the U.S. with national memberships joined together in the "New Abolitionist Covenant" to promote education and citizen action on the threat of nuclear weapons and related issues. The five national organizations are Sojourners, Fellowship of Reconciliation, World Peacemakers, The New Call to Peacemaking (a joint program of the historic peace churches), and Pax Christi. "Since that time the group has grown and meets annually for a retreat aimed at discerning the signs of the times and strengthening the bonds that unite these groups in their commitment to work for peace as the fruit of justice."[66]

FUTURE TASKS

From the witness of official statements of the Second Vatican Council, the popes, and the U.S. bishops, it is evident that the Roman Catholic church is moving to a very strict interpretation of the just war ethic. This means that a justifiable war is almost impossible in reality. Members of the peace movement would share that assessment. Yet the majority of American Catholics are uninformed regarding their church's present stance. The task of both the just war ethic advocates and the pacifists is to continue challenging the use of war as a means of conflict resolution so that people in the pews would share this overwhelming presumption against war and to promote peacemaking attitudes and strategies.

Sister Mary Evelyn Jegen suggests four tasks in promoting peace within the Catholic community.[67] First, the Catholic social ethic tradition must *continue the recovery and development of biblical theology on the question of nonviolence.* "We cannot bring the riches of our faith tradition to this search [for nonviolent social structures and mechanisms] unless we root it in a continuing and disciplined scripture scholarship. Simply repeating what has already been achieved, or translating it into more effective educational materials, will not do."

Second, the church should *support a history of peace* to overcome the attitude toward history as our past "periodized by wars."

Third, "positive peace is above all a cultural enterprise." This means *building cultural attitudes* that see peace as "the state in which all spontaneously desire one another's welfare." In this cultural agenda the women's movement has an indispensable role to play. "The intersection of the women's and peace movements can bring into focus ways of communication, of organization of power, of ways of dealing with conflict, of structures of mutuality that offer needed alternatives to structures of domination and subordination." The cultural emphasis means giving more attention to the affective dimension of human life in the social construction of peace. "Stoicism, the stiff upper lip, is appropriate for making war; it is not appropriate for making peace. On the contrary, it is compassion that is the necessary and primary response that will characterize the peacemaker." Two other cultural arenas are, first, to pay much more attention to the victims of violence—both war and the violence of structural poverty and, second, to realize the limitation of legal remedies for violence. Jegen believes that the research and production of biological, chemical, and bacteriological weaponry continues because there is no strong cultural abhorrence of these weapons.

> The fact that chemical weapons have had a comeback after a recess in their use after World War I demonstrates the power of culture to decide the limits of law.... Practices like child abuse, incest, and torture are prevented more by cultural taboos, by a collective sense of moral abhorrence, than by any amount of legislation.

Finally, Sister Jegen asks us to evaluate our work in terms of its effect on creating that state in which all spontaneously desire one another's welfare, relationships with those not in our group or nation, and the care of the earth. This vision is also articulated in the consistent ethic of life, which challenges the Catholic community to shape a cultural attitude that rejects the violence of abortion, poverty, capital punishment, euthanasia, and war.

MORE THAN A DREAM—NONVIOLENCE THAT WORKS

Sister Jegen's words may strike us as the "wish list" of a pacifist—disconnected from reality. The truth is that the experience of nonviolent attitudes and strategies is not only found in the imagination of a pacifist. There are historic situations and movements that put flesh and bone on this agenda for the future.

In a previous chapter we discussed the nonviolent strategy of the United Farm Workers Union led by Cesar Chavez. The most convincing evidence of the effectiveness of Christian nonviolence is to look briefly at three other amazing stories of communal nonviolence that worked.

Part III. Effective Nonviolence

1. POLAND'S SOLIDARITY MOVEMENT

Poland has known external oppression for many decades. In this century alone Polish citizens faced domination under Nazism and then under Soviet Stalinism. It is a miracle that a nonviolent revolution and a nonviolent spirituality blossomed in a country that has experienced so much violence and domination. The struggle for human rights and freedom in Poland in the 1980s was the catalyst for other Eastern European countries as well.

We will connect with the story of Polish oppression in 1952, when eight Polish bishops and over 900 priests were imprisoned. In the following year Cardinal Stefan Wyszynski, the Archbishop of Warsaw, was declared an enemy of the state and imprisoned. In 1961 the communist government suppressed all religious education. Despite these efforts the Marxist-Leninist regime in Poland was not able to silence the church. Michael Duffey, a moral theologian at Marquette University, comments:

> Beneath the bleakness of Polish life, a ferment of spiritual renewal and an alternative social reconstruction was underway. The Church promoted a radically different social vision. Against the state dogma of the necessity of class conflict and of hatred toward all who impeded the rise of the socialist state, it preached the necessity of love and forgiveness.... *The Church proclaimed the power of nonviolent Christian love in a repressive environment.* It helped to educate the people in alternative form of political participation (avoiding confrontation with security forces, riot police, and the Soviet troops waiting across the border).[68]

Workers picked up the spirit of resistance expressed in the words of Cardinal Wyszynski, "If a citizen does not demand his rights, he is no longer a citizen but a slave."[69] They began to protest food shortages and to demand a voice in the reform of the Polish economy. In December 1970 the shipyard workers in Gdansk staged a strike and demanded the establishment of trade unions that would not be controlled by the state. Polish authorities retaliated by declaring a state of emergency and cutting off all communications. Several hours later hundreds of workers attempted to report to work, unaware that the state authorities had ordered the shipyard closed. Polish troops opened fire on the workers as they emerged from the railroad station on their way to the shipyard. Many were killed and hastily buried. The official death toll was set at 26 although it was clear that many more had died.

A decade later, in August of 1980, another strike broke out at the Gdansk shipyard. Lech Walesa, who had been a leader in the 1970 strike, wanted to avoid a repetition of the bloodshed. They vowed to stand their ground but in a nonviolent way:

> We will not abandon the shipyards and we will not give the militia any reason for intervening. Should they try to break up the strike before it winds up, we will not do anything against them. We don't struggle, we won't get into fights; we will merely sit down and drag the peace. They can come in and carry us away, all 16,000 of us, one by one.[70]

The workers were successful in their nonviolent tactics. The community responded to the strikers' needs, lifting food over the shipyard fences and celebrating Mass among the striking workers. The workers were so committed to avoiding violent behavior that they banned alcohol during the strike. Their nonviolent resistance was contagious—it spread throughout the region and eventually included 400 factories throughout the country.

After two weeks, the government agreed to the workers' demands: "Solidarity" was born and a nonviolent social revolution spread like a grass-fire across Poland and Eastern Europe. Things did not change overnight, however, and tension remained high in the fall of 1980 when the Soviet leader, Leonid Brezhnev, threatened to send in Soviet troops. The leaders of Solidarity looked for ways to work with the Polish leaders; they did not call for the overthrow of the Marxist regime; nor did they directly attack socialism. The church set a conciliatory tone. Cardinal Jozef Glemp advised, "Let us look at ourselves truthfully. We shall see our own sins... and this will allow us to see the good done by the other side."[71] A joint church-government commission was established that set national unity as a priority "regardless of the differences in world outlook or political views."[72]

In December 1981 the old guard struck back. Prime Minister General Wojciech Jaruzelski declared a "state of war" against Solidarity, which was now 10,000,000 members strong. Solidarity was banned, the leaders were imprisoned, and martial law was imposed. The situation was bleak, yet the church continued to speak out. The Polish bishops' conference called on the regime to lift martial law, to release all political prisoners, and to renew dialogue with Solidarity. On the practical, grass-roots level the church assisted workers who had been fired and imprisoned and provided aid to their families.

This time the international timing was right. The Soviet leaders had their own problems in the Soviet Union and told General Jaruzelski to handle his domestic problems; there would be no Soviet reinforcements. Solidarity outlasted General Jaruzelski and his Communist Party. In 1983 the Solidarity leaders were released from prison, and Walesa was awarded the Nobel Peace Prize. In accepting the award Walesa confirmed his beliefs that "we can effectively oppose violence only if we do not resort to it... We will defend our rights but will not allow ourselves to be overcome by hatred...."[73]

2. EAST GERMANY IN THE 1980S

A strategy and spirituality of nonviolence was also strong in the churches of East Germany. As a Lutheran pastor in Leipzig put it, the churches were "the shield against Communist attack, the shelter of action groups, the champion of the reforms and the voice of nonviolence."[74] For 45 years the Communist regime, the German Democratic Republic (GDR), had marginalized the Protestant churches and those who tried to practice their faith.[75] But the Lutheran and Catholic churches resisted in a variety of ways:

- Already in 1960 the Lutheran church had established a "Peace Decade" (Friedensdekade), ten days every November devoted to prayer and repentance.

- In the early 1970s the Lutheran churches initiated an "Education for Peace" program that provided young people with a different worldview from the Party's emphasis on the necessity of class conflict. Week-long workshops on peace were organized.

- In the city of Halle an annual ecumenical "Bridge Worship" for justice and peace was started in 1980.

- In 1981 Nicholas Church (Nikolaikirche) in Leipzig became the center of a weekly prayer session for peace.

- In 1987 the churches in several cities began to discuss social issues and the churches' role in dealing with them. These meetings often concluded with public candle-lit processions through the streets.

- In the mid-1980s the environmental groups who found a home in the churches also raised questions and challenged the GDR.

It was clear that the churches in East Germany were becoming meeting places for believers and nonbelievers to study and raise questions of resistance and reform.

In the fall of 1989 everything came to a boil:

> More and more people began to participate in the peace prayers at the Nikolaikirche in Leipzig. Soon the church was no longer able to hold all of the people. Many thousands of them stood in the street around the church.... The government had to act. Would it again use guns and tanks?... The situation was at a breaking point.[76]

As the Communist regime lost popular support the church arranged talks between reformist groups and the government. These talks were often held in church facilities and chaired by church officials. The Lutheran bishop of Leipzig, Johannes Hempel, pleaded for calm on both sides of the stand-off. The Berlin Wall was cracking. After four decades of repression and fear, *"God had blessed them with unyielding patience and unconquerable nonviolence.* They had overcome their fear and found their voice and self-respect again."[77]

These nonviolent popular movements were also effective in Hungary, Bulgaria, and Czechoslovakia. In Moscow itself people around the world witnessed the power of nonviolent protest as large crowds shielded Boris Yeltsin and other elected officials in the Parliament from the threatening military forces outside. The Russian Orthodox church distributed 4,000 Bibles to the soldiers and demonstrators. Patriarch Alexis of the Russian Orthodox church threatened that any soldiers firing on the people would be excommunicated. 1989 stands as an historic year in the transformation of Europe.

3. THE PHILIPPINES' NONVIOLENT REVOLUTION OF 1986

In 1986 the Philippines was ripe for revolution. For twenty-one years the country had been ruled by Ferdinand Marcos. During those years he had consolidated his power through control of the military and the economy. He used the fear of communism to crush political opposition. In 1972 Marcos declared marital law and arrested thousands of his opponents including Benigno Aquino, the opposition leader. Mr. Aquino was imprisoned for eight years until his release to travel to the U.S. for heart surgery. In August of 1983 Aquino returned to the Philippines but was assassinated as he walked from the plane.[78] Aquino's widow, Corazon Aquino, picked up the baton of opposition.

Would the Philippines explode from the decades of oppression and institutionalized violence? Would the army split into two camps and start a civil war? The answers to these historic questions were played out on television for the world to see. In February of 1986 people around the world

> watched nonviolence at work in the Philippines: on television we saw masses of unarmed people blocking tanks, soldiers accepting flowers from nuns, military and church leaders urging soldiers to refuse orders to shoot their fellow citizens. And soon we saw that nonviolence had indeed worked. With almost no bloodshed, and none caused by the opposition, a dictator was forced from power and the popularly elected choice became president. In one particular instance, *we actually saw nonviolence succeed.*[79]

This miracle of a nonviolent revolution had not dropped ready-made out of the heavens. Many laity and clergy had been working for years and decades to prepare for this nonviolent transfer of power. Already in the 1970s Francisco Claver, the bishop of Bukidnon, was working to convert his fellow bishops and their people to active nonviolence as the only legitimate Christian response to both the violence of the Marcos regime and the communist New People's Army (NPA). Bishop Claver gradually gathered about thirty like-minded bishops who reflected on their people's situation in light of the gospel. These bishops encouraged acts of nonviolent resistance when faced with government harassment and killings. This initial group of bishops influenced the other seventy bishops of the country to stand up to the Marcos oppression. Prior to this the official church had not challenged the denial of human rights by the Marcos government, directly responsible for the growth of the counterviolence of the New People's Army.[80]

The bishops supported a nonviolent movement that was already growing in the Philippines. A married couple from Austria, Jean and Hildegard Goss-Mayr, and an American Methodist, Richard Deats, helped to provide *training in nonviolence* to the Catholic and Protestant communities respectively. As leaders in the Fellowship of Reconciliation the three led seminars for peasants, bishops, labor leaders, nuns, and priests. In their work they focused on analysis of the structures of oppression and on personal spiritual conversion. The Goss-Mayrs insisted that the violence in society and the violence in our hearts cannot be separated.[81] From these seminars a nonviolent movement in the Philippines, known as AKKAPKA, was formed under the energetic leadership of Father Blanco. AKKAPKA with a staff of nine set to work building base communities and giving in-depth seminars on active nonviolence. Forty seminars on nonviolence were held in thirty provinces throughout the Philippines during 1984-85.

At the end of 1985 AKKAPKA changed its tactics in response to Marcos, calling for a "snap" election for February 1986. Now they concentrated on encouraging people to vote their consciences, helping to train people in nonviolent defense of the ballot boxes, and setting up "Tent Cities." The tent cities were for prayer, fasting, and nonviolent training; they were set up in ten highly populated areas. Half a million people were trained in nonviolence and how to defend the voting boxes without weapons. The trainees were successful when Marcos' forces tried to steal the people's votes.

These tent cities were instrumental in the eventual success of the nonviolent campaign. Hildegard Goss-Mayr described what went on in one tent city:

> One tent was set up right in the banking center in Manila, where the financial power of the regime was concentrated. There in a little park, this big prayer tent was set up. And around this prayer tent, people who promised to fast and pray would, day and night, have a presence and carry within the fast and with the prayer the whole revolutionary process. And I think we cannot emphasize this enough: that in this whole process, there was always this unity—of outward nonviolent action against the unjust regime and of that deep spirituality that gave the people the strength later on to stand up against the tanks and to confront the tanks—this force of fasting and prayer. And in the celebrations of the Eucharist, they would point out that we are not fighting only against flesh and blood, we are fighting against the demons of richness and exploitation and hatred that we have to cast out from our people—from ourselves, from the military, from Marcos and his followers. And that we must use this arm together with the organized nonviolent resistance.[82]

The nonviolent movement also used the Catholic radio station, Radio Veritas, to communicate the message of active nonviolence. Peggy Rosenthal, author and educator, reported that "not only did Radio Veritas coordinate the whole resistance, broadcasting continual reports of what was happening, but around the clock it also read passages of Martin Luther King, Jr., the Sermon on the Mount, and Gandhi, urging people to follow these examples."[83]

Cardinal Jaime Sin, the archbishop of Manila, played a pivotal role in birthing the nonviolent transfer of power. He was instrumental in the creation of the National Citizens' Movement for Free Elections (NAM-FREL), which was "a watchdog group that had marshaled half a million people in a vain attempt to ensure honest elections."[84] The February 7, 1986 election was, by all accounts, the most fraudulent in Filipino history. Marcos claimed a victory. The Philippine bishops condemned it in a pastoral letter. Cardinal Sin celebrated a Victory Mass for Mrs. Aquino, and he, with the other bishops, urged the people to engage in nonviolent action and civil disobedience as the gospel way of overcoming the unjust system. The people responded with a massive display of "people power."

In those historic and dramatic days the hierarchy, rooted in the Catholic social tradition, had combined with the courage and leadership of the people to forge a nonviolent way out of an intolerable situation. The tradition and the popular movements had converged in a nonviolent show of strength and unity—a combination that could not be intimidated or stopped by the amassed wealth and power of a dictator.

Conclusion and Ongoing Questions

Not all movements of nonviolence are immediately effective. The brutality of the Chinese in crushing the nonviolent resisters in Tiananmen Square shows that nonviolence is not always successful. Of course, success can be measured in different ways and by different timetables. Nonviolent resistance "wins" when it is faithful to its own principles, which include:

- defeating evil, not defeating people;

- not humiliating their adversaries but winning them over;

- acknowledging the truth as they see it and the truth their adversary has to contribute;

- holding their position firmly, but not as if it were infallible;

- giving time to their adversaries so that they may see the evil in their ways and turn away from it;

- refusing to kill their adversary for that destroys their own quest for truth.[85]

As the history of the church's teaching on the morality of war has evolved and shifted in response to changing nature of warfare itself, it is natural to expect that this living tradition will continue developing. The following five areas will need further discussion.

First, *the relationship between the just war tradition and pacifism* needs further examination. The pastoral letter described the two "distinct moral responses...having a complementary relationship" (par. 74). What does this mean?

What common ground do the pacifists and just war thinkers share, and how do we describe the ethical and theological points of divergence?[86] James Turner Johnson, a Protestant social ethicist, has argued that just-war thinking and pacifism "have something profoundly in common: a searching distrust of violence."[87] This common ground, as well as the dissimilarities of the two traditions, needs further examination.

A second problem area is how are the just war theory and pacifism played out in *revolutionary situations*. Kenneth Himes reminds us that, "it is not always easy...to determine in a revolutionary situation how the criteria of competent authority, last resort, or probability of success are to be assessed." He sees a restrictive use of revolutionary violence: "At the present time, it appears that Catholic social teaching generally opposes recourse to violence on behalf of societal change but does not rule out revolutionary violence in principle."[88] I would remind us that Pope Paul VI's treatment of the question in *Populorum Progressio* left the door open for justified use of revolutionary violence in situations "where there is manifest, long-standing tyranny which would do great damage to fundamental personal rights and dangerous harm to the common good of the country" (par. 31).

Liberation theologians have been wrestling with this question for many years. One of the clearest treatments of the question is from a Methodist theologian from Argentina, Jose Miguez Bonino.[89] An important difference between the just war thinkers and the liberation theologians is who is being addressed as agents and actors. While the just war thinkers aim their remarks primarily at persons in power, theologians of liberation speak first to those persons who have been marginalized by the dominant economic and political power structures. Liberation theologians focus more on the structures of injustice that prevent the possibility of peace and undermine the hope for fulfilling the basic needs of the poor. Liberationists from the Third World are more interested in the relationships between the First World nations and Third World nations than in the relationships among nations of the First World. For the Third World nations are often in a dependent situation wherein their economies and political realities are unduly controlled by powerful nations of the First World. This dependent situation cannot be the basis of lasting peace.[90]

Further reflection is needed in a third area: how do we evaluate *"humanitarian intervention"* or "peacekeeping missions"? Pope John Paul II helped to define the starting point for reflection in his 1992 address to the International Nutrition Conference. He maintained that "humanitarian intervention [is] obligatory where the survival of populations and entire ethnic groups is seriously compromised. This is a duty for nations and the international community."[91] Some of these interventions involve the use of military force.

A fourth area of ongoing reflection is *how to construct effective theologies and ethics of peace.* Theologian Stephen Lammers puts it this way: "The issue here is how little reflection there has been on how the Catholic community might display its beliefs about peace, whatever these beliefs might be."[92] Our theology of peace begins in our homes, neighborhoods, and schools as we teach each other less violent ways of resolving our conflicts so that when we come to international conflicts we have been trained to think of nonviolent solutions.

The final focus for reflection and action is how to *link our concern about war and militarism with other life issues in the consistent ethic of life.* As we have seen in this chapter there are specific moral and social questions about armed conflict that call for resolution and a nonviolent spirituality. But there are many dimensions in this arena that connect with the other life issues. The common substratum is to recognize the "culture of violence" that shapes our attitude and behavior in all areas of life. If as a church we can constructively name and heal our violent cultural underpinnings we will be on the way to addressing many of the social issues raised in this book.

Discussion Questions

1. The U.S. bishops' pastoral letter gave a conditional acceptance of nuclear deterrence as a short term necessity. Do you agree with the moral reasoning of their position?

2. How do we evaluate the criteria of the just war? Are they "unattainable criteria" in today's world? How do you evaluate the Gulf War in terms of the just war criteria?

3. The just war theory is also applied in revolutionary situations. Do you believe there can be a morally justifiable revolution that includes the use of force and armed conflict?

4. Do you see any common threads and preconditions for success in the nonviolent movements discussed in this chapter, i.e., Poland, East Germany, and the Philippines?

5. How do you understand the relationship between the two Christian positions on war: the pacifist and just war ethic?

11

Economic Justice for All and "From Charity to Advocacy"

Part I. Economic Justice for All

This chapter will examine the U.S. bishops' moral analysis of the U.S. economy, as articulated in their 1986 letter, *Economic Justice for All*, and the reevaluation of those issues ten years later. We will also explore how the church has committed itself to working for social change and social justice through two important movements and organizations: Catholic Charities and the Campaign for Human Development. These two movements reveal the activist side of the institutional church as it moves from works of charity to the social ministry of advocacy and empowerment. It is clear that both the bishops' moral reflections and these two "movements" are shaping the face of Catholic social tradition.

The two-year debate during the drafting of *The Challenge of Peace* had propelled the bishops into the forefront of the national debate on the morality of nuclear weapons and the nuclear freeze movement. Some

313

commentators claimed that because of the "success" and publicity surrounding the "peace pastoral" the bishops had now turned their attention to the economic arena to build on their newfound "activism."[1]

The truth of the matter is that even though the pastoral letter on the economy was approved three years after the peace pastoral, both letters had their origins in the November 1980 meeting of the bishops. After that meeting the leadership of the National Conference of Catholic Bishops established two committees to begin the drafting process. Because of the pressing debate on SALT II and limiting nuclear weapons the committee on the economy decided to hold back and let the committee on nuclear weapons go through the drafting process first.

There is a certain irony in that the stimulus at the November meeting for a moral appraisal of the U.S. *capitalist* economy came in response to a letter the bishops were discussing on Marxist *communism*. Bishop Peter Rosazza, auxiliary bishop of Hartford, made a motion that the Bishops' Committee on Social Development and World Peace study both the positive values and the injustices of capitalism. "If we publish a document on Marxism," Rosazza pointed out, "we'll be criticized elsewhere for not seeing the faults in our own system if we make no reference to capitalism." Bishop Rosazza said it was two French priests, two of this classmates, who started him thinking. The French priests wondered why the bishops had gone through the trouble of writing a pastoral letter on Marxism—"hardly a burning pastoral issue in the United States. Why not a letter on capitalism?"[2]

Another bishop, William Weigand of Salt Lake City, who had worked in Latin America for ten years, agreed that it would be good to have *a paragraph* on the evils of capitalism. A year later, in November of 1981 when the committee was established with Archbishop Rembert Weakland as chairperson, it was no surprise that Bishops Rosazza and Weigand were also on the committee, along with Archbishop Donnellan of Atlanta and Bishop Speltz of St. Cloud, Minnesota.

I'm sure Bishop Weigand had no idea that his suggestion for "a paragraph" on capitalism would turn out to be a 208-page pastoral letter, and that it would take six years, dozens of meetings, many long hearings, and poring through thousands of pages of responses to produce. Such are the ways of bureaucracy, even in the church.

This letter, like its predecessor on nuclear weapons, was in the news from the first draft released in November of 1984 until the fourth draft was overwhelmingly approved, 225 to 9, at the November 1986 meeting.

THE PROCESS: BISHOPS AS LEARNERS AND TEACHERS

Experts from various fields as well as the poor themselves were involved in the process of drafting this letter along with the bishops and staff. I attended one of these three-day hearings at Notre Dame University in December 1983. As I mentioned in a previous chapter, the visual image of the five bishops on the committee sitting in the front row of the audience, *listening and taking notes* as various economists, business and governmental leaders addressed the issues of the economy struck me at the time and stays with me. The bishops were in their *listening and learning mode,* which is an important part of leadership and exercising a teaching authority. The bishops sat and listened to hours of testimony and discussion from GM officials, economists, government officials, and people who work with the poor. The first draft lists 16 hearings prior to the drafting of the letter.[3] After the first draft was released in November 1984 the bishops invited people across the country to respond, and they received a mountain of responses, criticisms, and suggestions.

Archbishop Weakland commented on the process: "More than anything else, we hope the second draft will be a valid confirmation of the process used. The insights and criticisms of many people have affected this second draft—just as the first draft was based on the shared reflections of the many hearings that preceded it."[4]

I served as the chairperson of the Diocese of Rochester's Consultative Panel on the Economics Pastoral Letter. Our committee, which reviewed the four drafts, felt that many of our recommendations were heeded. It was a rewarding experience to have a sense that our feedback, along with that of many other groups around the country, was being taken seriously. I recall the comment of one of our panel members, Judy Schley, who was the assistant director of research at Kodak Park. She said she felt as if the bishops had been listening to her, as if she had spoken to them directly.

Archbishop Weakland said that, "as a committee, we realize that our ideas and concepts have grown and have been improved by these contributions. For this reason we are grateful and give thanks to God." He concluded his remarks by taking the spotlight off the text:

> We remain convinced of the importance of this process, an importance that goes beyond the perfecting of a text. The text is ultimately only a catalyst for a larger process of "forming church." It is a vibrant and creative way of using modern communications and the possibilities inherent in them to reflect together on what discipleship

means for the world today. It has afforded us bishops an opportunity for performing our role as moral teachers in a unique way.

Moral theologian Richard McCormick underscored that the content and process reflected a new collegial vision of church that is "broadly consultative, questioning, critical, open, appropriately tentative."[5]

Why the Bishops Were Writing
The bishops had a twofold purpose in mind. First, "to provide guidance for members of our own Church as they seek to form their consciences about economic matters." Second, "to add our voice to the public debate about the directions in which the U.S. economy should be moving" (no. 27).

BIBLICAL AND MORAL VISION
After setting the context for their effort in chapter one, the bishops sketch out in chapter two the moral vision that guides their discussion of economic life. The centerpiece of this Judeo-Christian worldview is the sacredness of humanity: "The dignity of the human person, realized in community with others, is the criterion against which all aspects of economic life must be measured" (no. 28). The bishops see this teaching as "the fundamental conviction of our faith" namely, that "human life is fulfilled in the knowledge and love of the living God in communion with others" (no. 30).

The Bible reveals this basic truth in all its narratives, laws, poetry, and letters. The bishops summarize the biblical themes of creation, covenant, justice, community, and discipleship, all of which shape the way Christians view economic life. Even though the Bible tells of communities in a pre-industrial society, these themes and values continue to be relevant for shaping our attitudes, policies, and personal decisions at the beginning of the third millennium.

The bishops summarize the rich tradition of Catholic social teachings. Central to this tradition is the understanding of justice that has evolved through the centuries. After reviewing the traditional categories of commutative, distributive, and social justice the bishops explore a new dimension of justice, *justice as participation:*

- Basic justice demands the establishment of minimum levels of participation in the life of the human community for all persons. (no. 77)

- Recent Catholic social thought regards the task of overcoming these patterns of exclusion and powerlessness as a most basic demand of justice. Stated positively, justice demands that social institutions be ordered in a way that *guarantees all persons the ability to participate actively* in the economic, political, and cultural life of society. (no. 78)

This is an important development in the church's understanding of justice; it sets up a clear yardstick of how to evaluate the justice of a community, namely, if the community is effective in enabling people to participate in the economic, social, and political life of their community. It is a violation of justice when a person is marginalized or not allowed to participate. This yardstick of justice applies to society and to the church community as well. As we will see, the bishops note that the church itself must "practice what it preaches" to be a credible witness to its social principles.

After establishing the right of all to participate in the economic, political, and social life of the community, the bishops develop the biblical heritage to require special attention to the needs of the poor:

- *The obligation to provide justice for all means that the poor have the single most urgent claim on the conscience of the nation.* (no. 86)

- As individuals and as a nation, therefore, we are called to make a fundamental "option for the poor." (no. 87)

The bishops explain this commitment as "the obligation to evaluate social and economic activity from the viewpoint of the poor and the powerless." This obligation "arises from the radical command to love one's neighbor as one's self.... The prime purpose of this special commitment to the poor is to enable them to become active participants in the life of society. It is to enable *all* persons to share in and contribute to the common good" (no. 88).

The implications of this "option for the poor" are radical and comprehensive for society and for the church. We have a long way to go in transforming the rhetoric into reality. There are small, but significant signs of the church's commitment to this option for the poor. As we shall see, the Campaign for Human Development is an example of the church using some of its resources for empowering the poor.

Chapter two concludes by reviewing the rights and duties of workers, managers, and owners, as well as the proper role of government. It highlights the importance of "subsidiarity"—keeping programs close to the local level.

The moral reference points and principles discussed in this chapter are neatly summarized in a framework of six principles presented in the executive summary at the beginning of the letter, under the heading of "A

Pastoral Message" (12-18). Ten years later the bishops expanded the six principles to ten. Later in this chapter we will present these ten principles for reflection, judgment, and action.

SPECIFIC POLICY ISSUES: "PRUDENTIAL JUDGMENTS"

Chapter three of *Economic Justice for All* uses the principles and biblical themes to evaluate four specific areas of economic life: *unemployment, poverty, agriculture,* and *developing nations.* Here the bishops attempt to translate the general principles into specific policy recommendations, also known as "prudential judgments."

By using the language of "prudential judgments" the bishops are signaling that not everything in this letter be given the same moral weight. While they expect their policy recommendations to be taken seriously, these prudential judgments do not carry the same moral certainty as the basic moral principles. Hence, the bishops presume agreement on the general principles and *they expect disagreement* on the specific recommendations. Their expectations did not go unfulfilled.

Approaching moral teaching with two levels of moral certainty is not new. This methodology is used in their previous pastoral letter *The Challenge of Peace*, in 1983, and also in their 1919 statement, *Program on Social Reconstruction.* In the "Foreword" of the latter document we find:

> Its practical applications are of course subject to discussion but all its essential declarations are based upon the principles of charity and justice that have always been held and taught by the Catholic Church, while its practical proposals are merely an adaptation of those principles and that traditional teaching to the social and industrial conditions and needs of our own time.

By comparison we do not see this kind of moral reasoning at work in other church documents on moral issues, such as birth control, sterilization, and homosexuality. In the area of sexual ethics the church claims more certitude for its practical applications, and some hierarchical leaders will not tolerate disagreement with church teaching in the public arena.[6]

While the bishops *assumed* general acceptance of their moral principles, that assumption is unwarranted. As Archbishop Weakland would discover, many Catholics who wrote to him about the pastoral letter were deeply committed to an individualistic ethic that is contrary to the communitarian moral vision of the Bible and the church's social tradition.

Economists and other critics also challenged the moral assumption that community and common good are central moral categories. Milton Friedman noted "the collectivist moral strain that pervades the document," which he found "repellent."[7] On both levels of the teaching—principles and policy recommendations—there are significant disagreements and diverse opinions. The bishops would do well to recognize that situation as they exercise their teaching office.

The letter offers dozens of policy recommendations. Because of the limitations of space I will only pick out a few examples from the four issues.

Employment

- We recommend that the fiscal and monetary policies of the nation—such as federal spending, tax, and interest rate policies—should be coordinated so as to achieve the goal of full employment. (no. 156)

- We recommend expansion of job-training and apprenticeship programs in the private sector administered and supported jointly by business, labor unions, and government. (no. 159)

Poverty

- The tax system should be continually evaluated in terms of its impact on the poor. (no. 202)

- Welfare programs should provide recipients with adequate levels of support. This support should cover basic needs in food, clothing, shelter, health care, and other essentials. (no. 212)

Food and Agriculture

- Moderate-sized farms operated by families on a full-time basis should be preserved and their economic viability protected. (no. 233)

- Effective stewardship of our natural resources should be a central consideration in any measures regarding U.S. agriculture. (no. 238)

Developing Nations

- The United States should do all it can to ensure that the trading system treats the poorest segments of developing societies fairly and does not lead to human rights violations. (no. 269)

- Rather than promoting U.S. arms sales, especially to countries that cannot afford them, we should be campaigning for an international agreement to reduce this lethal trade. (no. 289)

PARTNERSHIP

In chapter four the bishops ask for "a new American Experiment: Partnership for the Public Good." In this chapter they offer visionary, longer-range perspectives on the U.S. economy. Their basic assumption is that there is "unfinished business" in the "American experiment."

> The nation's founders took daring steps to create structures of participation, mutual accountability, and widely distributed power to ensure the political rights and freedoms of all. We believe that similar steps are needed today to expand economic participation, broaden the sharing of economic power, and make economic decisions more accountable to the common good. (no. 297)

They recommend, in general, "a greater spirit of partnership and teamwork...competition alone will not do the job" (no. 296). They envision "new institutional mechanisms for accountability," for employees, managers, and shareholders, including such ideas as giving workers a greater voice in determining work conditions, cooperative ownership, discussion of plant closing with workers, and developing community-wide cooperative strategies in which churches play a role.

Because of the debate about the role of government in economic planning the bishops suggest that it is time "to move beyond abstract disputes about whether more or less government intervention is needed, to consideration of creative ways of enabling government and private groups to work together effectively" (no. 314). They suggest three criteria for planning (318-320):

1. First, "all parts of society, including government, must cooperate in forming national economic policies." This will require greater cooperation among all citizens and a sharpened concern for the common good.

2. Second, the primary criterion for judging national economic policies should be their impact on the poor and the vulnerable, "those who fall through the cracks of our economy."

3. Third, "the serious distortion of national economic priorities

produced by massive national spending on defense must be remedied." Devoting so much of the national budget to military purposes has been disastrous to the poor and vulnerable in the United States and elsewhere.[8]

CHURCH'S EXAMPLE

In the final chapter, the bishops draw on the liturgical and spiritual resources of the faith community to help bring about the attitudinal, practical, and political changes needed. They also reflect on the church as an economic actor.

> Together in the community of worship, we are encouraged to use the goods of this earth for the benefit of all. In worship and in deeds for justice, the Church becomes a "sacrament," a visible sign of that unity in justice and peace that God wills for the whole of humanity. (no. 331)

The bishops call for a "worldly spirituality":

> For the laity holiness is achieved in the midst of the world, in family, in community, in friendships , in work, in leisure, in citizenship. Through their competency and by their activity, lay men and women have the vocation to bring the light of the Gospel to economic affairs.... (no. 332)

It is important for laity to realize that they too have a "vocation." When the church prays for vocations, it should be praying that all the baptized will respond generously to their vocation to bring the Gospel to their families, communities, and workplaces. In the opening "Pastoral Message" the bishops spoke very clearly of this call to holiness in the marketplace. "Like family life, economic life is one of the chief areas where we live out our faith, love our neighbor, confront temptation, fulfill God's creative design, and achieve our holiness" (no. 6).

The bishops bring the letter home in the second part of chapter five, where they examine "Challenges to the Church." Here they discuss the importance of the church's educational mission to the poor and the need to educate all its members on the biblical and social justice tradition of the church. The church also sees that one of its important challenges is how to serve the family as the basic building block of any society.

Finally, the bishops address themselves and the whole church as an economic actor. All that has been said about acting with economic justice applies, first and foremost to the church itself. *"All the moral principles that govern the just operation of any economic endeavor apply to the Church and its agencies and institutions; indeed the Church should be exemplary."* They echo the words of the 1971 synod of bishops' statement *Justice in the World*:

> While the Church is bound to give witness to justice, she recognizes that anyone who ventures to speak to people about justice must first be just in their eyes. Hence, we must undertake an examination of the modes of acting and of the possessions and lifestyle found within the Church herself. (no. 40)

The bishops admit that "we would be insincere were we to deny a need for renewal in the economic life of the Church itself..." (no. 349). The bishops selected five areas for reflection: wages, rights of employees, investments and property, works of charity, and working for economic justice. In this section the bishops committed themselves to providing sufficient livelihood and social benefits for church employees. At the same time they call on every Catholic to take seriously the implications of this letter in all areas of their personal and public life. They stated that "true charity leads to advocacy" (356) and drew upon their experience with the Campaign for Human Development, which "confirms our judgment about the validity of self-help and empowerment of the poor." They offered some words of support and encouragement for all members of the church who are already living out the goals of this letter:

> We bishops know of the many faithful in all walks of life who use their skills and their compassion to seek innovative ways to carry out the goals we are proposing in this letter. As they do this, they are the Church acting for economic justice. At the same time, we hope they will join together with us and their priests to influence our society so that even more steps can be taken to alleviate injustices. Grassroots efforts by the poor themselves, helped by community support, are indispensable. The entire Christian community can learn much from the way our deprived brothers and sisters assist each other in their struggles. (no. 357)

The letter is a call to all in the church to take its vision seriously, from the workers and owners in the pews to the bishops and clergy who oversee the administration of the church's resources.

ORGANIZED OPPOSITION

Even before the first draft of the pastoral letter on the U.S. economy was released, a great deal of debate and controversy surrounded the anticipated document. In the United States at least five groups were organized or mobilized to affect or discredit the bishops' letter. These included

1) "The American Catholic Committee" headed by Philip Lawler, who urged Catholics to join him in fighting the "few influential Church bureaucrats [who] are pushing the American Church into partisan political controversies. This year, they will be urging the Bishops to make a radical statement on the economy."[9]

2) "The Institute on Religion and Democracy," which had led an attack on the National Council of Churches aired on "60 Minutes," now turned its attention to a major new focus on economic issues and the bishops' letter. They started a "Church Economic Programs Information Service" that, for $2,000 per year, will provide corporations and other organizations with a bulletin ten times a year, five hours of research, and access to seminars. A headline from their March 1984 bulletin read, "Business Told to Lobby Bishops."

3) "The Ethics and Public Policy Center" headed by Ernest Lefeber (who withdrew his nomination for Assistant Secretary of State for Human Rights in the face of Senate opposition), turned its attention to the bishops' letter, including holding a meeting on "how business should respond to the letter." They too were urged to lobby their bishops. They held a number of symposia to bring together business leaders, analysts, philosophers, and theologians to discuss the issues raised by the letter on the economy.

4) "The Catholic Study Council" had worked on nuclear and Central American issues and turned its attention to producing literature and developing strategies to influence the process of the economics pastoral.

5) The most notable group was "The Lay Commission on Catholic Social Teaching and the U.S. Economy," which was headed by former Treasury Secretary William Simon with Michael Novak serving as vice-chairman. The Lay Commission included 30 business and government leaders such as J. Peter Grace, who chaired

President Reagan's Commission on proposed cuts in the federal government; and Alexander Haig, former Secretary of State under President Reagan. The group held its own set of hearings parallel to the bishops' process and produced their own "pastoral," which they distributed before the bishops released their letter. The 106-page booklet was mailed to every Catholic parish in the country—that is, over 19,000 free copies were sent out. The "lay letter" was written by Michael Novak with consultation from J. Brian Benestead, Robert Spaeth, Ernest Fortin, and Ralph McInerny.[10]

Two years later the "lay commission" issued a statement on the third and final draft of the bishops' letter. Novak and Simon begin by commending the bishops for the "improvements introduced since their first draft." They were "gratified to see how many points we raised—particularly concerning the family—found their way into the bishops' final draft." The authors praise the bishops for their intention to lift the poor out of poverty, although they do not agree with their strategies for doing this. Novak and Simon were also happy to see statements in the letter in favor of a capitalist economy and that the bishops' letter opened up dialogue.

After pointing out these "improvements" in the third draft the lay committee went on to list a few "defects," including:

- a failure to grasp what makes poor nations into developed nations;

- deficient understandings of *political economy* (the relative roles of government and the free economy);

- excessive trust in the state and its officials;

- an inadequate grasp of crucial concepts such as enterprise, markets, and profits;

- significant confusions about economic rights;

- fateful confusions between defense spending and spending on weapons;

- a preference for "solidarity" over pluralism; and,

- an inadequate exposition of "liberty."[11]

It is clear from the Novak and Simon critique that they are committed to a different priority of values from that of the U.S. bishops. As we step back from the debate it is evident that the drafting process achieved its purpose of getting business and moral leaders to *engage in a dialogue* about the morality of American capitalism. This doesn't mean that all in the dialogue will agree with one another, but something happens when people are honestly open to hearing each other. Each side is transformed by an attentive hearing of the other party's experience and point of view. To a certain extent the lay committee felt that they were heard by the bishops—not to the extent they would like, but heard, nonetheless. The question remains: to what extent did the lay committee "hear" what the bishops were saying?

Such a dialogue also reveals that the participants do not agree on all issues. Although some "convergence" may emerge many areas of "divergence" will remain. Some of these disagreements relate to basic assumptions, the way of prioritizing the values and needs, the participants' experience and one's class, race, and gender. For instance, the Novak and Simon approach would have the bishops focus on personal virtues and promoting "family values" and not get involved in economic analysis. They argue that "more important" than any flaws in the current economic system is the "larger breakdown in the moral/cultural traditions upon which our political and economic systems ultimately rest." The virtues that they believe are the church's proper domain include the following:

> Such critical moral habits as personal responsibility, trust, high aspiration and hard work, marital commitment and strong family life, postponed gratification, and the sustained pursuit of education are at the opposite pole from lax sexual standards, teen-age pregnancy, abortion, single-parent households, and dropping out from school. The moral traditions of the United States, both individual and social, need invigoration. *It is in this area, more than in matters of economic expertise, that the bishops have a special role.*[12]

The bishops obviously disagree with Simon and Novak about the range of episcopal competency and responsibility. The bishops, in keeping with the Catholic social teachings tradition, refuse to be limited to personal, sexual, and family values. The Catholic tradition is not only concerned about values in the home, but about values in the marketplace and how these values affect people, policies, and institutions in the workplace.

THIRD WORLD CRITICISM

Clodovis and Leonardo Boff, liberation theologians from Brazil, also critiqued the pastoral letter in a number of important areas:

- The U.S. bishops did not undertake a broad *systemic analysis*, but only seem intent on reforming the current system of capitalism. "Without doubt the American bishops strike vigorously at the apparatus; yet, they do so only to repair it and not to replace it."

- The Boffs noted that the U.S. bishops do not accept the thesis that the poverty of the Third World is the result of exploitation by the capitalists of the First World. Among liberation theologians this thesis is referred to as the *theory of economic dependency.* (Archbishop Weakland responded that these theories were examined by the bishops' committee but were not accepted as proven.)

- The bishops' letter does not have a clear and enunciated social theory to accompany their economic analysis. The Boff brothers criticize the letter as being a *functional analysis* of capitalism and not a systemic one. A systemic analysis would explore the relationship between economics and political power. This is a serious absence, according to the Boffs and others, for the letter only takes an ethical approach to economic issues but does not reveal the underlying linkages to the political arena and the question of who has the power to make decisions.[13]

THREE PERSPECTIVES

We have sampled some of the criticisms of the bishops' letter on the economy: one from the "right" and one from the "left." It is evident from both the lay letter and the liberation theologians that we are dealing with drastically different economic and political worldviews or mindsets. Most authors identify three worldviews: the neo-conservative or free market, the liberal, and the radical or liberationist.[14] We will review these three worldviews to assist us in understanding the conflicting analyses of the letter. A fourth worldview will be added to the list.

1. The free market or neo-conservative mindset, as its title suggests, "regards the free market as the essential principle of society, assuring economic growth, personal freedom, and the relative justice of equal opportunity."[15] The neo-conservative would remove the interference of government in the economic sectors, reduce or eliminate the welfare system, weaken labor organizations, and trust in the "trickle down" theory to help the poor—or simply tolerate existing levels of poverty and unemployment. The groups discussed above that were organized to lobby the bishops can be situated in this mindset.

2. The liberal tradition "favors a government-sponsored industrial policy to guide privately owned corporations and promote the industrial growth that will create employment.... Liberals rely on Keynesian economics, that is a national economy in which government subsidizes the industries and intervenes in the market to overcome the periodic slumps and depressions associated with capitalism."[16] Liberals want to see the welfare system strengthened and reformed in a more humane fashion; they call for respect for organized labor, oppose discrimination, and foster equality of opportunity. (This is where many of the conservative critiques of the pastoral letter situate the bishops' thinking. Yet, while there is some truth in that judgment, the pastoral letter, as we shall see, does not neatly fit here.)

3. The radical mindset views poverty, unemployment, marginalization, and indifference to the poor not as unfortunate accidents in an otherwise acceptable system or as the unintended result of increasing cultural individualism. Rather the radical or liberationist sees these realities as the consequences of a politico-economic order created by the rich and powerful to enhance and protect their own privileges.[17]

Each perspective describes the problem of poverty and unemployment in different terms and suggests drastically different solutions as the following chart suggests.

Worldview	Poverty viewed as	Solution
Conservative	Attributed to laziness, ignorance, or wickedness	Pity and all forms of aid
Liberal	Economic and social backwardness	Reform of existing system
Liberationist	Oppression caused by exploitative systems	Revolution: creating an alternative system

Of these three perspectives where does the bishops' letter on the economy land? Many commentators would place the letter in the "liberal" camp and showing "leanings" toward the liberationist perspective.[18]

While this argument is defensible, I would suggest that Catholic social teaching in general and the U.S. bishops' pastoral letter on the economy in particular, do not fit neatly into any of these three perspectives. A fourth worldview is called for that could be called *communitarian*.

4. The communitarian worldview eschews the individualism implicit in both the neo-conservative and liberal perspective as well as the conflictual and dualistic assumptions of the liberationist. The communitarian perspective is rooted in the communal ethics of the Bible and Aristotelian and Thomistic social philosophies. In its modern expression the communitarian sees poverty and unemployment as a form of exclusion from participation in the economic life of the community. Poverty is wrong because it excludes a person from active participation in the economic project of the community. This exclusion is a form of injustice and treats one as a nonmember of the community. The pastoral states this very effectively.

> These fundamental duties can be summarized this way: Basic justice demands the establishment of minimum levels of participation in the life of the human community for all persons. The ultimate injustice is for a person or group to be treated actively or abandoned passively as if they were nonmembers of the human race. (no. 77)

If we were to add the communitarian to our chart, it would read:

Worldview	Poverty viewed as	Solution
Communitarian	Exclusion and injustice	Inclusion through structural reform

The communitarian approach is central to the biblical story and to Christian social ethics prior to the Enlightenment. As we discussed in the first part of this book, Catholic social teaching did not accept the premises of the Enlightenment with its emphasis on individual rights. The Catholic tradition continued to emphasize the common good and the duties and responsibilities of all to build up the community. This commitment to community has survived through the centuries and has been given various "faces," such as the "corporatively organized society" of the 1880s, the "solidarism" of Heinrich Pesch, or the "body of Christ" image of Virgil Michel.

More recently, Cardinal Ratzinger drew upon these communitarian roots to evaluate capitalism when he addressed a group of German industrialists gathered in Rome in November 1985. The cardinal revealed "a deep distrust of the capitalist system, especially as manifested in the United States."[19] His traditional roots showed through; we hear an "echo" of Archbishop von Ketteler's words in the cardinal's communitarian assumption: "It is becoming an increasingly obvious fact of economic history that the development of economic systems which concentrate on the common good depends on a determined ethical system, which in turn can be born and sustained only by strong religious convictions." As Archbishop Weakland commented on Cardinal Ratzinger's talk he noted how little coverage this talk received among the neo-conservative audience:

> Ratzinger does not openly condemn capitalism as intrinsically evil, but he does come close to it in the many questions he raises. Perhaps this is why his lecture, given to a conservative group of capitalist industrialists, has not been much quoted by the neo-conservative economists or political writers. He makes the point quite clearly that the former discussions on this point are not finished.[20]

Father David Hollenbach believes the pastoral letter achieved a "synthesis" between liberalism and communitarianism by assigning them to different domains of public life. The liberal theory of justice and rights connects with the *political* order, while the communitarian vision of the common good connects all the other areas of social activity. The synthesis emerges as the bishops push the liberal view of justice to include the economic realm. The bishops teach that justice means participation (in the economy), which is a fuller notion of justice than liberals would normally accept. The letter "argues that all persons have rights not only to the conditions necessary for political cooperation or participation, but to the basic conditions to be participants in the economic and social sphere as well."[21]

These four "worldviews" are able to serve as models or perspectives to evaluate not only the pastoral letter but also the criticisms and reactions to the letter.[22]

TEN YEARS LATER

When Archbishop Weakland, the chairperson of the bishops' committee, evaluated the letter after ten years, the first thing he pointed out was the value of the process used in drafting the letter. He believes the process of numerous hearings that preceded the first drafts of both the peace pastoral and the economics pastoral, which brought many actors into play, was "unique." The benefit of this time-intensive approach is that it "gave breadth and scope to the letter that it could not have otherwise obtained.... For an issue so complex the consultative process was most helpful. One of its finest features was also its ecumenical and interfaith dimension."

Archbishop Weakland recognized that not everyone was supportive of this unique procedure: "Some opposition came to that procedure from certain church quarters; namely, the fear was expressed that it could give the impression that the bishops were deficient in their knowledge of social justice and thus that their teaching authority would be diminished." Weakland, however, does not accept this criticism. "There is no reason to believe that the consultations gave that negative impression. On the contrary, most applauded the bishops for such openness and for listening to so many divergent views."

The sad fact is that such an open method might not be employed again. "If the letter were to be rewritten today, I am not sure that such a procedure would be engaged in." He points to a possible lack of energy, enthusiasm, and support by the bishops. His evaluation of the value of the procedure employed has not changed in the decade since working on the letter, "yet the procedure itself used for both the peace pastoral and the economic pastoral letter remains one of the major contributions of the two letters to the process of church teaching."

The second set of comments by Archbishop Weakland focus on the question of the length of the letter—it was just too long, and the bishops tried to accomplish too much. If the letter were to be rewritten, said Weakland, it should be divided up into three or four shorter letters: a first to discuss the principles of social justice from the biblical and natural law traditions, a second letter that would apply the principles to several distinct areas, and a third to discuss the demands of the gospel and social justice on our Christian life-style as individuals and as a church.[23]

In preparation for the tenth anniversary of the pastoral letter the bishops approved a 17-page "Pastoral Message" because "the nation needs to hear its message once again and to respond to its continuing challenges."[24] A year later on November 12, 1996 the bishops approved in a unanimous voice vote a ten-point framework to serve as "principles for reflection, criteria for judgment and directions for action."[25] Brevity has caught on. The ten principles are:

1. The economy exists for the person, not the person for the economy.

2. All economic life should be shaped by moral principles. Economic choices and institutions must be judged by how they protect or undermine the life and dignity of the human person, support the family, and serve the common good.

3. A fundamental moral measure of any economy is how the poor and vulnerable are faring.

4. All people have a right to life and to secure the basic necessities of life (e.g., food, clothing, shelter, education, health care, safe environment, economic security).

5. All people have the right to economic initiative, to productive work, to just wages and benefits, to decent working conditions, as well as to organize and join unions or other associations.

6. All people, to the extent they are able, have a corresponding duty to work, a responsibility to provide for the needs of their families, and an obligation to contribute to the broader society.

7. In economic life, free markets have both clear advantages and limits; government has essential responsibilities and limitations; voluntary groups have irreplaceable roles, but cannot substitute for the proper working of the market and the just policies of the state.

8. Society has a moral obligation, including governmental action where necessary, to assure opportunity, meet basic human needs, and pursue justice in economic life.

9. Workers, owners, managers, stockholders, and consumers are moral agents in economic life. By our choices, initiative, creativity, and investment, we enhance or diminish economic opportunity, community life, and social justice.

10. The global economy has moral dimensions and human consequences. Decisions on investment, trade, aid, and development should protect human life and promote human rights, especially for those most in need wherever they might live on this globe.[26]

CHANGING ATTITUDES

The moral principles are offered to guide reflection and to lead to a conversion of attitude in the Catholic community and broader society. Two attitudes in particular that need special attention because of their impact in the economic arena and on the role of the church are American individualism and attitudes about charity and advocacy.

Archbishop Rembert Weakland came face to face with American individualism during the six-year process of writing the economics pastoral letter. He commented that he had received "stacks of letters from Catholics around the country saying things like: 'I have worked hard for what I got and I am going to keep it. God has been good to me. The lazy slob next door has no rights for what I have earned.'"[27] These responses revealed to Weakland how committed his fellow Catholics are to an extreme version of individualism. He described these Catholics as "hyper-individualists." Since receiving those letters Weakland is more intentional about how he preaches. He wants to make sure that his "preaching is not giving support to that hyper-individualism." "For a while, I have to admit," he says, "I preached an enormous amount about personal virtue and never talked about community much." But his approach had changed. "Now I find I have to always emphasize what that Gospel means not just for me as an individual but for me as a member of a community. You and I have a burden in this American culture to make sure we preach that style and not reinforce what would really be a bad kind of biblical message."

A few years later he reflected on this question and named it "perhaps the most difficult pastoral task that is yet to be accomplished," namely, "to make people aware of the communal nature of their vocation both as a human person and as a baptized member of the church." Without a transformation of American individualism the goals of a just economy will be impossible. The church has its work cut out for it.

> So many sociologists point out the nature of our society and the Lockean individualism that permeates it. These fundamental influences, which go back to the founding of this nation, have been recently reinforced by psychological concerns about the self that can reach the point of a kind of collective narcissism. Combating such extreme individualism but coupling it with a wholesome respect for self and one's identity and worth will not be easy. The best way to help the economy, however, is to alter some of the selfish attitudes that pervade the society.[28]

A second pastoral task, according to Weakland, is to move from charity to advocacy.

> Charity is a necessary Christian virtue, but it is not an economic solution to any problem. It is easy to preach charity and thus to alleviate the signs of a problem at once. But the ultimate solution must be to help people to participate in the life of society by being able to make their contribution and not become wards of society.

The archbishop believes advocacy is the better route to pursue as we work to open doors so all can participate in the economy.[29]

Others agree with Archbishop Weakland's assessment of the importance of moving from charity to advocacy. According to philosopher William Murnion, the bishops' commitment to the preferential option for the poor will remain empty rhetoric unless the bishops help to organize the poor. In fact, without organizing the poor, the letter is "likely to foster only resignation in the poor, legitimizing rather than unmasking the injustice of the American economic policy."[30] As we shall see in the next section, the bishops' solid commitment to the empowerment of the poor through the Campaign for Human Development in the last 25 years "puts their money where their mouth is." The option for the poor is given concrete support in the bishops' commitment to advocacy and empowerment efforts at social change.

Part II. From Charity to Advocacy

CATHOLIC CHARITIES USA

The Roman Catholic community has a long tradition of not only analyzing social problems and teaching moral principles, but also of responding concretely in works of charity, service, and advocacy. In this section I will focus on two of the many Catholic agencies confronting social issues in the United States: Catholic Charities USA, and the Campaign for Human Development. Both of these anti-poverty programs give witness to the task of "moving from charity to advocacy."

Catholic Charities USA is a national network of 630 agencies and institutions serving 11 million individuals and families regardless of creed, race, sex, or age through community-based social programs.[31] As such it is the largest nongovernmental provider of diverse social services in the United States.

Catholic Charities was established in 1910 as a clearing house for mutual aid and discussion among the more than 800 Catholic institutions that were assisting children, the elderly, the sick, and the poor. Its remote beginnings can be traced to 1727 when the Ursuline Sisters came to New Orleans and started the first Catholic orphanage, the first home for "women of the street," and the first health care facility.[32]

From the very beginning Catholic Charities was not satisfied to provide only "charity" to the needy; rather they sought to understand the "causes of dependency" and to be an advocate for the poor to "secure to them their rights." The original statement of the purpose of the National Conference of Catholic Charities reads:

> The National Conference has been created to meet a definite situation. It aims to preserve the organic spiritual character of Catholic Charity. It aims to seek out and understand causes of dependency. It aims to take advantage of the ripest wisdom in relief and preventive work to which persons have anywhere attained, and to serve as a bond of union for the unnumbered organizations in the United States which are doing the work of Charity. It aims to become, finally, the attorney for the Poor in Modern Society, to present their point of view and defend them unto the days when social justice may secure to them their rights.[33]

The first president of Catholic Charities, Bishop Thomas J. Shahan, focused on the heart of the Christian obligation to care for the needy when he wrote that "the Magna Carta of Catholic charity was written on Mount Olivet, when Jesus Christ said to his disciples: 'For I was hungry, and you gave me to eat; I was thirsty, and you gave me to drink.'" Bishop Shahan also stressed the "overriding importance of preventive charity, that is, social change to avert the causes of human distress."[34]

The focus on "preventive charity" as well as immediate charity has been a hallmark of Catholic Charities throughout its history. Catholic Charities was an advocate for the poor when it played an initiating and assisting role in preparing the Social Security Act of 1935, public works programs for the unemployed, the National Public Housing Conference, national housing legislation, health insurance for wage earners, federal funding of specialized care for disabled children, and the first White House Conference on Families.

The advantages of preventive charity, according to Catholic Charities, are twofold: first, for the individual, who attains a better life and, second, for society, which gains a more productive participant. This approach pervades Catholic Charities USA's advocacy on public issues.[35]

In 1967 Catholic Charities initiated a renewal process within the movement. The process began with a board resolution and ended five years later with the publication of a report entitled *Toward a Renewed Catholic Charities Movement.* The document was the product of a working group, or "cadre" of people, which acted as a microcosm of the entire Charities movement. As Thomas Harvey reported, "their involvement with the renewal document became so intimate that it came to be known simply as the Cadre Report."

The Cadre Report, released in 1972, urged the members of Catholic Charities "to embrace organizational change and personal conversion" along with the direct services they were providing. It set the priorities of Catholic Charities in terms of three programs: social services, advocacy, and convening people to work on social issues. Three additional associate directors were hired by the national office to give attention to these organizational priorities.[36] These three priorities were reaffirmed and complemented a long-range planning committee in 1985. Under the title of *Countdown to the 21st Century* the planners identified three major goals:

- fostering quality social services based on identified need and developing responsive public policy through research and advocacy in order to enhance human dignity;

- promoting Catholic social teaching within the membership as well as with the general public; and

- developing leadership in order to further the church's commitment to social welfare and social justice in the church and society.[37]

More recently Catholic Charities completed a three-year evaluation process called *Vision 2000,* which gives direction to the future. One of four strategic directions makes empowerment one of the central services it offers. The president of Catholic Charities USA, Father Fred Kammer, explains that "empowerment means assisting people to come to understand and use their own abilities to deal with their problems." He connects empowerment to welfare reform:

> It shows up in our present services like job training. A number of agencies across the country have begun welfare-to-work programs. Because of welfare reform, we'll see more pressure on those programs, in terms of education and training, even by simply helping

people to realize that they can work. Many of them didn't finish
high school, never had jobs, and will therefore need a lot of support
to get into the work place and stay there.

"But," he asks, "what's going to happen in communities where there
just aren't enough jobs to go around? We need to do new thinking about
job generation, creating the jobs that people need as a way of empowering them. This is one of the big challenges our agencies are going to face
as we look toward the next century."[38]

The other strategic directions for Catholic Charities include involving
individuals, communities, and organizations in the effort to change the
sinful structures of our society that undermine family life and create
poverty. Catholic Charities will also seek to strengthen its relationship
with the rest of the Catholic Church and promote its social mission
throughout the world.[39]

Catholic Charities is present in each of the nation's 170 dioceses working to protect human dignity through services that include:

- adolescent pregnancy and substance-abuse counseling;

- refugee resettlement;

- child care;

- adoption;

- marriage counseling;

- day care;

- respite care;

- health, nutrition and shelter;

- care for frail elderly people; and

- care for children at risk.[40]

The most recent area of expanded services is in AIDS ministry. Father
Kammer reports that "we now provide social, hospice, and other services
to almost 20,000 people." He notes that there are over 500 separate programs offered under Catholic sponsorship, which shows "the wide and
deep response of the Catholic community to the AIDS pandemic."[41]

In the advocacy and public policy arenas Catholic Charities is active in meeting with state and county legislators, and with senators and congresspeople on the national level. Its educational efforts include printed materials, videos, forums, and workshops.

The local agencies work with parish communities and secular groups on a variety of social issues, addressing both the preventive and the restorative needs of justice and charity. Approximately 150,000 volunteers are involved each year in the work of Catholic Charities. This is truly a powerful witness to the church's commitment to the poor, which goes beyond rhetoric and is translated into meaningful direct service and advocacy.

The second Catholic program that is helping to shift the attitude of church members from charity to advocacy is the bishops' anti-poverty program, the Campaign for Human Development.

CAMPAIGN FOR HUMAN DEVELOPMENT

Two powerful events served as the backdrop for the establishment of the Campaign for Human Development: the impact of Vatican II and the social turmoil in the United States during the 1960s. The Campaign was an "offspring of a post-Vatican II church newly dedicated to responding to human needs, and a response to the social turbulence in American society at that time."[42] In 1967 and 1968 cities like Watts, Detroit, and Newark were literally on fire as despair turned to rage among poor black Americans. As people were trying to make sense of it all, black and white communities were further traumatized by the assassination of Martin Luther King, Jr., in April 1968, and two months later by the assassination of Senator Robert Kennedy.

Cardinal Dearden in Detroit provided strong leadership in word and deed to help rebuild the burned community. He defended the controversial phrase "black power": "there is much in the black power movement that we must recognize as valid and good...." He also announced that he would use one million dollars from the Detroit Archdiocesan Development Fund to make grants to groups of poor people. In setting up these grants he wanted to avoid patronizing and paternalistic programs: "We want to know what they need.... They will tell us what they need."[43]

As the bishops met in April 1968 they responded to the racism and social unrest by arguing, like Cardinal Dearden, that three areas needed attention:

- the need for self-determination for the poor;

- the need to change attitudes; and

- the need to change unjust social structures.

They set up an Urban Task Force "to coordinate all Catholic activities and to relate them to those of others working for the common goal of one society, based on truth, justice and love."[44] The following summer a 45-member Urban Task Force was established to tackle the twin crises of race and poverty. Members of the Task Force included USCC staff members John McCarthy and Monsignor George Higgins as well as priests from the newly formed Catholic Committee on Urban Ministry (CCUM), including Geno Baroni of Washington, D.C., Eugene Boyle of San Francisco, John Egan of Chicago, P. David Finks of Rochester, and James Sheehan of Detroit.

In August several members of the Task Force met for a retreat at Madonna House near Toronto. Baroni, Finks, and McCarthy were joined by Michael Groden of Boston, and Patrick Flood and Dismas Becker, both from Milwaukee. During the retreat the members of the Task Force came up with the idea of replacing the annual collection for Indian and Negro Missions with a major appeal to respond to domestic poverty. The proposal called for raising $50 million over a number of years.

Bishop Francis Mugavero of Brooklyn, New York, worked with other bishops to gather support for the proposal of the Task Force, which was discussed and approved a year later at the November 1969 meeting of the National Conference of Catholic Bishops. The bishops called for "a national Catholic crusade against poverty." In April 1970, the National Conference of Catholic Bishops voted unanimously to "raise funds to fight domestic poverty through a special collection to be launched in the Thanksgiving season." The bishops directed that the campaign be undertaken by the United States Catholic Conference, which is the bishops' civil organization (the NCCB is the ecclesial structure). To carry out the mandate of the bishops the USCC established the Campaign for Human Development, CHD, on July 28, 1970.

The Poor Have a Voice
What has been a distinctive feature of the Campaign for Human Development is that it *takes poor people seriously as agents of change* and not merely as recipients of the "charity" of others. From the very beginning CHD has stressed an empowerment approach. In officially launching CHD at a press conference in Chicago in October 1970, Bishop

Dempsey, its first national director, said the Campaign would allow the poor to tell the church what they need and get resources to allow them to follow up: "The vision and hearing of all this nation's people can no longer be clouded or dimmed with propositions based on suppositions of what we think would be good for the poor. It is the poor who must be masters of their destinies."[45]

The criteria for CHD funding are very clear in giving a voice to the poor:

1. The project must benefit a poverty group. *At least fifty percent (50%) of those benefiting from the project must be from the low-income community.*

2. *Members of the poverty group must have the dominant voice in the project.* At least fifty percent (50%) of those who plan, implement, and make policy (e.g., the board of directors, etc.) of a project, should be persons who are involuntarily poor. (Clergy, VISTA volunteers, students, etc., are considered by CHD to be "poor.")[46]

Institutional Change

The bishops called for new approaches to get at the root causes of poverty and racism.

> The magnitude and complexity of these problems in a time of rapid social change challenge us to a constant rededication of our efforts and, at the same time, calls for the creation of a new source of financial capital that can be allocated for specific projects aimed at eliminating the very causes of poverty.
>
> ... [T]here is an evident need for funds designated to be used for *organized groups of white and minority poor to develop economic strength and political power in their own communities.*[47]

CHD does not fund direct service projects such as day care centers, recreation programs, community centers, scholarships, counseling programs, direct clinical services, emergency shelters and food pantries, and so forth. These programs could apply to other groups for assistance. CHD looks for groups that empower the poor to begin tackling structural and systemic causes of poverty and racism. The "Guidelines" explain the type of institutional change CHD will support:

> Projects which are innovative and demonstrate a change from tradi-

tional approaches to poverty by attacking the basic causes of poverty and by effecting institutional change.

The "Guidelines" then explain what CHD defines as institutional change, namely:

a. Modification of existing laws and/or policies;

b. Establishment of alternative structures and/or redistribution of decision-making powers.[48]

Fund-Raising Program

In November of 1970 CHD undertook its first national collection, which totaled $8.4 million dollars, making it the largest single collection in the Catholic church in the United States to that time.[49] Twenty-five percent of the moneys collected was kept in the local dioceses to be used to fund smaller diocesan projects that fulfilled the CHD criteria. The remaining seventy-five percent of the 8.4 million dollars was sent off to Washington, D.C., to be awarded in national grants.

In a few cities, such as Los Angeles, Santa Fe, Philadelphia, and Denver, controversy arose concerning the work of some of the groups that were funded. Cardinal Krol in Philadelphia reported that

two complaints about Campaign projects in Philadelphia were absolutely ridiculous. I investigated them only for the record, since criticism had been public. Charges were shown to be utterly without foundation, and I may add, the exemplary Catholics who were defamed in each case would have had every right to pursue the matters in the courts.[50]

A number of factors led to a decline in the CHD collection in the following year, including the backlash by some Catholics, an economic recession, and inadequate promotional efforts. The total dropped to under $7.5 million in 1971 and $7.1 million in 1972. 1973 was the lowest amount at $7 million. After 1973 the collection has been steadily increasing and went over $13 million in 1993.[51]

Educational Effort

The second leg of the CHD effort was a national education and information program that was intended to "lead the People of God to a new knowledge of today's problems, a deeper understanding of the intricate forces that lead to group conflict, and a perception of some new and promising approaches that we might take in promoting a greater spirit of solidarity...."[52] The CHD staff developed educational modules on poverty and social justice that are used in schools in several dioceses. In October of 1972 CHD published the forty-page book *Poverty Profile*, which criticized public attitudes toward the poor. In 1974 CHD published a 208-page book, *Poverty in American Democracy: A Study of Social Power*, which criticized the gross maldistribution of wealth and income in the United States. Author Fred Perella argued that poverty and powerlessness threatened America's democratic institutions. CHD, in collaboration with the Communication Department of the USCC, produced film, radio, television, and printed media dispelling myths about poverty and the poor.

Controversial Empowerment

From the very beginning of CHD there has been criticism of this anti-poverty effort from both the right and the left. Some liberals, namely the National Association of Laymen (NAL), now defunct, challenged the bishops for not going far enough. It also urged full disclosure of church finances.

A lead editorial in *Triumph*, a conservative Catholic magazine of the time, recommended that the bishops drop the Campaign, lest they become "laughing stocks," and urged that "it is a patent duty of Catholics to protect their bishops by abstaining from the collection on November 22, [1970]."

The NAL criticism broke on November 15, 1970, just a week before the collection, and received national coverage on "The CBS News with Walter Cronkite." Mr. Cronkite did not air a response from Bishop Dempsey. Later, though, in a surprise move, the NAL endorsed the collection, urging the church to match contributions from parishioners. Just days before the collection, a second news report by Cronkite presented the Campaign in a more favorable light. This national TV coverage certainly helped to inform Catholics of this upcoming appeal and helped CHD to its successful outcome in 1970.[53]

After fifteen years of experience the bishops' conference decided to evaluate CHD to determine if it should be phased out in keeping with its "ad hoc status" or be incorporated into the NCCB on a permanent basis. The Oversight Committee turned to Father William Byron, the president of Catholic University of America, who organized a professional evaluation team. The comprehensive work of this team was completed by mid-1988. The Oversight Committee reviewed the team's work and made its recommendation at the November 1988 meeting of the National Conference of

Catholic Bishops: The bishops overwhelmingly voted to strengthen and expand CHD and to give it permanent status as a standing committee. CHD had passed through a rigorous scrutiny with "flying colors."

While the bishops were reviewing CHD another group was making its own evaluation of the church's anti-poverty program. In 1988 the Capital Research Center (CRC), based in Washington, D.C., published a 126-page booklet, *The Campaign for Human Development: Christian Charity or Political Activism?* The CRC, a spin-off of the conservative Heritage Foundation, includes among its sources of funding the John M. Olin foundation, whose director is William Simon—the same William Simon who led the charge against the bishops' pastoral letter on the economy. The perspective of the authors is very clear: they are comfortable with "works of charity" as the only appropriate Catholic response to poverty:

> Catholics might expect that money "dispensed by an organization clothed in the aura of the Church" and intended to address "the basic causes of poverty" would go to support the work of, say, Mother Teresa or Father Bruce Ritter's Covenant House, or possibly to "efforts to protect the unborn and provide the emotional and financial support that can encourage pregnant women to carry their babies to term." But Catholics who believe that are due to be disappointed, CHD has in mind no such recipients.[54]

The CRC authors are also disturbed that CHD does not adequately defend and encourage private property.

CHD's response identified CRC's distorted reporting:

> Under the guise of providing research, the authors' selectivity in citing names of persons who publicly supported the Campaign disclosed either their bias or their faulty research. From among the hierarchy they list Cardinal Joseph Bernardin and Archbishops John Roach and Rembert Weakland, all presumably from the "liberal-left wing" of the Church. Others on the public record who have endorsed CHD, but who are not cited by Poole-Pauken, include Cardinals John O'Connor and Roger Mahony. Most notably absent among those who have publicly endorsed CHD is Pope John Paul II.[55]

These criticisms revealed that not all Catholics were comfortable with the move from "charity to advocacy." William E. Simon's cover letter, which was included with the CRC booklet, articulated his acceptance of "traditional types of Catholic charities"; everything else he lumped together as "political activism" for the "radical left." "The book documents how this program of the U.S. Catholic Conference is a funding mechanism for radical left political activism in the United States, rather than for traditional types of Catholic charities."[56]

This debate about works of charity and works of justice and advocacy has been going on in the church since the time of the "Social Catholics" in Europe. It is no surprise then that when the church engages in programs of social political change conflict and controversy will follow.

Impact of CHD

It is hard to measure the impact of the Campaign for Human Development or how well it has achieved its goals. In anecdotal fashion we can say that:

- In Philadelphia, where health care was once denied to indigent people, pregnant women, the physically handicapped, and seniors on fixed incomes, it is now available.

- In rural North Carolina, where unemployment loomed as the only prospect, CHD's economic development program has enabled workers to own and manage their own businesses.

- In San Diego, where fear pervaded neighborhoods, police now patrol the streets, drugs have been driven out, harassment has ceased;

- In Texas, where the educational system failed, children now learn in a healthy and creative environment.

- In Columbus, where low-income residents were politically isolated and without power, they now have an effective voice in city halls and state legislatures through the successful efforts of church-based community organizations.[57]

These are just a few of the concrete changes people have seen in their lives because of the projects supported by CHD. While the amount of money invested has not been monumental, the $8 million annually in Campaign grants have had an eightfold leverage factor, meaning an additional $64 million a year for empowerment efforts. CHD staff members John D. McCarthy and Jim Castelli studied more than 300 groups that received Campaign grants from 1991-1993. Their study reveals that the groups funded by CHD serve about one half of the poor population in the United States.

Cardinal William Keeler of Baltimore cited the Campaign's impact in his 1994 address to his fellow bishops.

> CHD does more to help poor people help themselves than any other agency in the United States. CHD-funded groups have helped generate literally billions of dollars in private and public funds to assist low-income people, creating and saving jobs, for building and rehabilitating family homes, and for providing hope and a future for farm workers and immigrants.

The bishops signaled their support of CHD by giving it a standing ovation after Cardinal Keeler's address.[58]

CHD and Community Organizing

The consistent emphasis on "empowerment" sets the Campaign apart from other church charities. One of the most effective ways empowerment has been supported is through "community organization." A network of community organizations and training centers was taking root at the same time that CHD was being established. In many ways the story of community organizing since 1970 cannot be told without mentioning the crucial role CHD has played in many communities. By the late 1970s the leaders in printed media (*Time, Newsweek, The New York Times, The Washington Post*, etc.) described the rise of community action groups as a new source of strength for American society. "Virtually all the groups mentioned received CHD grants for their early organizing efforts. It is more than a coincidence that the growth of this movement paralleled the launching of CHD." The CHD Committee explained the rationale for this support: "There is no CHD priority for community organizing as such. Rather, community organizing is the way large numbers of poor people are choosing to effect institutional change."[59]

Community organizing is now being rooted in congregations. In 1994 there were 81 grants made to congregation-based organizing projects. An estimated 1,800 congregations nationwide participate in congregation-based community organizations (CBCO) with 1.5 million members from Catholic, Protestant, Jewish, and Muslim congregations. The CBCOs emphasize the building of relationships among people across ethnic, racial, and religious lines. While the groups focus on the immediate needs of the community, such as housing, police protection, gangs, and schools, the long term priority is to build alliances. "The goal is to create a power base of committed neighborhood residents that, over the long run, can strengthen families and the community."[60]

Conclusion

The basic assumption of this book is that the story of Roman Catholic social teaching in this country cannot be told only from the perspective of pastoral letters and encyclicals—as important as those documents are. The grass-roots social justice movements, Catholic service, and advocacy organizations are an essential part of the total story. Catholic Charities and the Campaign for Human Development validate the church's social teachings in the lives of millions of Americans—whether they realize it or not. These movements and programs take the words off the page and make them come alive as a source of hope for the community. Many times the social action and the movements articulate the theology of the community and the prompting of the Spirit *before* it has become part of the church's official teaching.

Peter Henriot, S.J., has pointed out the importance of the Campaign for Human Development in the shaping of the bishops' letter on the economy.

> Without the experiences of this creative program the pastoral letter would be only a one-sided response by the Catholic church to the serious problems facing this country. The Campaign also offers many important lessons of making changes in social structures. These lessons are drawn not from social theory, but from social practice.[61]

The pastoral letter *Economic Justice for All* endorsed the commitment to empowerment that is the heart of the CHD. The bishops stated, "We believe that an effective way to attack poverty is through programs that are small in scale, locally based, and oriented toward empowering the poor to become self-sufficient" (no. 200). The letter argues that "the most appropriate and fundamental solutions to poverty will be those that enable people to take control of their lives" (no. 188). Accordingly, the bishops endorsed programs and policies "oriented toward empowering the poor... empowered to take charge of their own futures...."[62]

The principles and practices of the Campaign are implicitly endorsed throughout the pastoral letter. The three themes of participation, empowerment, and education, which are central to CHD's mission, are also the backbone of the pastoral letter.

The U.S. Roman Catholic bishops have clearly contributed to the development of Catholic social teaching and tradition by the drafting and dissemination of their pastoral letter *Economic Justice for All*, and by their visionary and consistent support of the Campaign for Human Development since its inception in 1970. Through the Campaign the bishops and the church have helped people to find their voice and make a difference in their community. This same spirit is found in the vast network of Catholic Charities' agencies. In both of these anti-poverty programs the church is giving concrete expression to its social and moral vision. At the same time the institutional church is learning from these grass-roots experiences as it continues to reshape its life-giving tradition of justice, peace, and hope.

Discussion Questions

1. The pastoral letter declares that "basic justice demands the establishment of minimum levels of participation in the life of the human community for all persons." In what ways does this understanding of justice as participation serve as a criticism of church and society?

2. As is clear in this chapter, not all members of the church agree with the prudential judgments and competency of the bishops on economic matters. How do the bishops defend their positions?

3. Evaluate the ten principles that were issued on the tenth anniversary of *Economic Justice for All*.

4. The Campaign for Human Development was established to fund organized groups of the poor to develop economic strength and political power in their own communities. Is this the role of the church's social ministry? Explain.

5. If the church moves beyond traditional types of charity and direct service it is criticized for "political activism." How do you evaluate such a complaint?

12

Sexism:
Women's Voices—
Silent No Longer

After analyzing 100 years of Catholic social teachings in 368 pages, Donal Dorr points out nine areas where the tradition is weak or insufficiently developed. He notes that "perhaps the biggest lacuna in the social teaching of the Catholic Church is its failure to provide an adequate treatment of the issue of justice for women."[1] That "lacuna" is finally being addressed by church leaders, theologians, and the feminist movement. This chapter brings together a variety of approaches to this "missing piece" in Catholic social thought including:

- the role of women in official Catholic social teaching;

- the story of the attempted pastoral letter on women in the church and society by the U.S. bishops;

- the theological agenda of feminist theology; and

- how women of color view the challenge of overcoming sexism and cultural bias.

As we shall see, women's voices are silent no longer. Their words and actions have created a "stir" in the church. As Anne Carr, a noted Catholic feminist theologian, writes:

> The recent emergence—or perhaps explosion—of women's voices in the public realm of the church, in ministry, theology, and new forms of active leadership, has meant some *troubling questions and significant reorientations* of mind and heart for many women (and men) with regard to Christianity, especially Roman Catholic Christianity.[2]

Some of those "troubling questions and significant reorientations" will be examined in this chapter with the hope of bringing about a fuller understanding of the richness of the human experience—male and female.

Part I. Women in Catholic Social Teachings

A review of the first 70 years of modern Catholic social thought (1890-1960) reveals that women are seldom mentioned in papal documents. Women are usually included *implicitly* in the terms "man" and "family."

In Leo XIII's *Rerum Novarum* two themes are used to speak of women: 1) *women, like children, are dependent and in need of protection,* and 2) *women are "by nature" bound to the home.* According to Sister Maria Riley, O.P., of the Center of Concern in Washington D.C., and resource person on women in church and society, "these themes remain more or less constant throughout the body of Catholic social teaching."[3] Leo's worldview was paternalistic, authoritarian, and hierarchical with clearly defined roles for everyone in society and church. In this worldview a woman's place and role were divinely ordained according to her nature. Leo assumed women's role was in the family and did not elaborate upon her role in society. He focused on workers—which he presumed were men—and the family. If women or children worked outside the home, Leo considered this to be an aberration from the "natural law." Justice for workers meant that the rights of their families would be protected and that the men, as heads of families, would receive just wages. The assumption was that women as wives and mothers would be economically dependent on the just wage of the working male head of household.

In reality, women did not conform to Leo's "idealistic" worldview. They did work outside the home and so did their children. They were engaged in labor unions and political protest. But overall they were subject to the ethos of paternalism in church and society.

Pope Pius XI continued the same line of thinking in his 1931 encyclical *Quadragesimo Anno*. Women and children are again mentioned in the same sentence as we read in paragraph 71:

> But to abuse the years of childhood and the limited strength of women is grossly wrong. Mothers, concentrating on household duties, should work primarily in the home or in its immediate vicinity. It is an intolerable abuse, and to be abolished at all cost, for mothers on account of the father's low wage to be forced to engage in gainful occupations outside the home to the neglect of their proper cares and duties, especially the training of children.

Maria Riley argues that "women are not seen as autonomous adults. This habit of identifying women with children and other dependent persons has been the accepted norm in most Catholic writing, particularly in canon law."[4]

While it is clear that the institutional church was committed to a paternalistic worldview rooted in European culture and history, the popes were also reacting to socialists and communists who promoted the equality of women and men. As Pope Leo had overstated the role of private property, now he and his successors denied the equality of the sexes in the face of the revolutionary thinking of the socialists.

A shift in Catholic social teaching on gender equality begins with Pope Pius XII. Pius XII argued that men and women are equal in dignity and worth in the eyes of God. "But they are not equal in every respect. Certain natural gifts, inclinations and dispositions, are proper only to the man, or only to the woman, according to the distinct fields of activity assigned them by nature."[5] One area where Pius XII insisted on the same treatment of men and women was on the question of equal pay for equal work. (This principle had already been taught by the American bishops in their 1919 letter on social reconstruction.) Like his predecessors Pius XII disapproved of women working outside the home except when necessary and taught that men and women should not be doing the same work, because of the differences in their natures.[6]

Pope John XXIII continued the line of thinking of his predecessor in that "women's natural dignity, involvement in social life, and subordination to men's authority all fit together nicely in a complementary pattern."[7] John did acknowledge that women were becoming less passive in both domestic and public life, more conscious of their God-given dignity.

> It is obvious to everyone that women are now taking a part in public life. This is happening more rapidly perhaps in nations with a Christian tradition, and more slowly, but broadly, among peoples who have inherited other traditions and cultures. Since women are becoming ever more conscious of their dignity, they will not tolerate being treated as inanimate objects or mere instruments, but claim, both in domestic and public life, the rights and duties that befit a human person.[8]

Pope John explained that every person is endowed with intelligence and free will and has universal and inviolable rights and duties—political, economic, social, cultural, and moral rights. By including women explicitly in this document he is teaching that women have the same rights and duties as men. In paragraph 15 we read, "Human beings have, in addition, the right to choose freely the state of life which they prefer. They therefore have the right to set up a family, with equal rights and duties for man and woman, and also the right to follow a vocation to the priesthood or the religious life." (But this equality of rights does not pertain to access to ordination.) Maria Riley calls this the "double vision" with which churchmen view women.

Women are perceived by Pope John primarily as "mothers and wives":

> Indissolubly linked with those rights is the right to working conditions in which physical health is not endangered, morals are safeguarded, and young people's normal development is not impaired. Women have the right to working conditions in accordance with their requirements and their duties as wives and mothers. (par. 19)

Vatican II did not signal any dramatic breakthroughs for women, but there were significant events that began to change how women were perceived and eventually allowed gestures of participation. The major contribution of Vatican II was the new, official openness of the Catholic church to the changes created in modern Western societies by liberal democratic principles, including changes in women's status and role. As Rosemary Radford Ruether points out this new openness "was an important turning point. The Second Vatican Council created an atmosphere where a discussion among Catholics of women's rights in society and in the Church seemed possible."[9]

As the bishops and consultants gathered in Rome in 1962, women were conspicuous by their absence. Even the reception of communion by a woman became an issue, as Ruether recalled:

> The clerical male culture of woman-shunning was shockingly demonstrated early in the Council when a woman news reporter was denied Communion. The uproar over this incident brought some soul searching. On 4 December 1962, Cardinal Leon-Joseph Suenens made a famous intervention in which he called for an additional document that would consider the role of the Church in the modern world. During this intervention he noted the absence of women by declaring that "half of the Church" was excluded from the conciliar deliberations.[10]

By the beginning of the second session of the Council a few women auditors were appointed; by the end of the Council their number had grown to twenty-two—twelve lay women and ten women religious. One of the women consultants, Sister Luke Tobin, the Superior of the Sisters of Loreto in the United States and the head of the Leadership Conference of Women Religious, recalled that she and two others were appointed to the commission drafting the documents on the Church in the Modern World and the Apostolate on the Laity. The women were allowed to speak during the meetings of the commissions but did not have a vote. No woman's voice was heard in any of the plenary sessions of the Council; when the noted British economist Lady Jackson prepared a paper for the third general session it had to be delivered by a man.[11]

Sister Tobin recalled another incident that symbolized Catholic theology's attitude toward women. During a meeting of the commission on the Church in the Modern World the French theologian Yves Congar made a long and flowery speech on women's virtues. He then looked at one of the women auditors, a woman from Australia, Rosemary Goldie, head of the Vatican Commission on the Laity, and asked her opinion of his words. She replied that he could dispense with the flowery rhetoric; what concerned women was that they be treated as the fully human persons that they are.[12]

Ruether believes Ms. Goldie's forthright approach was effective for it is "echoed" in three statements in *Gaudium et Spes*:

- in the introduction, par. 9, which reads, "Where they have not won it, women claim for themselves an equity with men before the law and in fact";

- in the section on the family, par. 52, which maintains that the role of woman as mother should not be used to underrate "the legitimate social progress of women"; and,

- in the section on the right of every person to culture, par. 60, we read that "women are now employed in almost every area of life. It is appropriate that they should be able to assume their full proper role in accordance with their own nature. Everyone should acknowledge and favor the proper and necessary participation of women in cultural life."

In all the church documents there is a giving and a taking, an ambiguity about the rights of women. Women's "proper role" is determined by "nature"—read mother and wife. Yet, the very next sentence pushes forward with a positive statement on the "necessary participation of women." In commenting on the ambiguity of the text, Anne Patrick writes, "Thus, although the document does represent some progress on the question of justice for women, its tone and contents... betray a decidedly androcentric bias, indeed a blindness to the sexism in its understanding of human rights and dignity."

A few pages later she is more enthusiastic about *Gaudium et Spes*:

> ...There is no question that this document conveyed Good News to the faithful, and particularly to women. Its insistence on the full humanity of woman—fully equal to man and created with him in the divine image—represents a decisive break with a long tradition of misogynist Christian anthropology.... The import of this new understanding of woman's full humanity cannot be overstated, and its articulation by Vatican II in 1965 is to be celebrated.[13]

The most powerful section of *Gaudium et Spes* is found in paragraph 29 when it states that "with regard to the fundamental rights of the person, every type of discrimination, whether social or cultural, whether based on sex, race, color, social condition, language, or religion, is to be overcome and eradicated as contrary to God's intent." In these simple, straightforward words the church has given itself and society a radical goal.

Pope Paul VI continued the line of thinking of *Gaudium et Spes*. In his 1971 document *Octogesima Adveniens*, he defended women's equal right to participate in cultural, economic, social, and political life, but he also emphasized women's and men's difference: "We do not have in mind that false equality which would deny the distinctions laid down by the Creator himself and which would be no contradiction with woman's proper role, which is of such capital importance, at the heart of the family as well as within society" (par. 13). Maria Riley wonders, "Can a person having a proper role and vocation, predetermined by her nature and needing special protection, still be independent and have equal rights with a person who has no such qualifying and limiting definitions predetermined by his nature?"[14]

The 1971 synod document, *Justice in the World*, introduced the question of justice within the church regarding women. We read:

> Within the church rights must be preserved. No one should be deprived of his ordinary rights because he is associated with the church in one way or another. Those who serve the Church by their labor, including priests and religious, should receive a sufficient livelihood and enjoy that social security which is customary in their region. (par. 41)

I read the above section as including women, but the following sentence in the text could put a different spin on the previous quote. "We also urge that women should have their own share of responsibility and participation in the community life of society and likewise of the church" (par. 42). As a man, I read these sections to imply that paragraph 41 covered all people, even though the male pronouns are used, and the following paragraph gives specificity to the general principle by applying it in a focus way to women. Maria Riley, as a woman, is more suspicious about whether paragraph 41 is intended to cover men and women. She suggests that "The words, 'their own share' raise the questions, is women's share different from men's? If so, why?"[15]

In Pope Paul's other writings we find a continuing duality, as moral theologian Christine Gudorf notes. While the pope argues for "the civil rights of women as full equals of men" and for "laws that will make it possible for women to fulfill the same professional, social, and political roles as men," he also argues that "prudent realism" be used as women take on positions of making policy decisions. "Prudent realism" would take into account women's complementary "qualities of intuition, creativity, and a profound capacity for understanding and love." These "feminine" qualities are seen to complement the qualities that Pope Paul's predecessors saw in men—discernment, realism, prudence, and responsible decision making. Gudorf suggests that "the obvious reason for 'prudent realism' is Paul's concern for women's role in the family."[16] The pope wants to emphasize the equality of women and men, and yet he continues to present women in a stereotypical way.

On balance, Riley sees *Justice in the World* as a step forward for women's efforts at liberation.

> This document brings together several powerful themes that support women's struggle for justice in the church and in the world. In calling for justice in the church, especially for women, and in affirming social movements whereby people assume responsibility for their own lives to change oppressive structures, *Justice in the World* affirms women's struggle for liberation.[17]

It comes as no surprise that Pope John Paul II continued the line of thinking of Paul VI, with a slight reinforcing of traditional roles. In *Laborem Exercens*, written in 1981, John Paul recognized that women do work outside the home, yet he continued the tradition of emphasizing that the primary role of women is to be responsible for the family, and that the primary role of men is to be responsible for economic support of the family. Riley believes that John Paul is "reasserting the patriarchal model of family."[18] He is concerned that women are "having to abandon" their tasks as mothers, which is wrong for the family and for society. He therefore called for a "social re-evaluation of the mother's role," calling for the society to support a woman's role. He explains that "true advancement of women requires that labor should be structured in such a way that women do not have to pay for their advancement by abandoning what is specific to them and at the expense of the family, in which women as mothers have an irreplaceable role" (par. 19).

While this is an important challenge the pope is making, why doesn't he also call for a "social re-evaluation of fatherhood"? Doesn't fatherhood have an "irreplaceable role" as well?

A few months later Pope John Paul issued the encyclical *Familiaris Consortio*, his response to the synod discussion on the family. Here he condemned discrimination against women, repeated his emphasis on motherhood, and called for providing incomes for mothers at home because of children's need for the full-time presence of mothers.[19] This proposal caused quite a reaction, both "pro" and "con." Feminists saw it as a mixed blessing in that it gave value to work women do in the home, which is not valued monetarily in modern societies, but it also limited women to a narrow view of "women's work," namely, taking care of babies at home.

POPE JOHN PAUL II'S "ABSENT FATHER"

The most troubling contribution of Pope John Paul to the discussion of the role of women is the way he romanticizes conception, childbirth, and motherhood. It is reminiscent of Father Yves Congar waxing rhetorically on the virtues of women at the Second Vatican Council.

John Paul presents procreation as one of, if not the primary purposes of marriage, and he suggests that the primary bond within marriage is between mother and child:

> What is happening in the stable, in the cave hewn from rock, is something very intimate, something that goes on "between" mother and child. No one from outside has access to it. Even Joseph, the carpenter from Nazareth, is but a silent witness.[20]

In another address he says, "We should devote special care to mothers and to the great event that is peculiarly theirs: the conception and birth of a human being. This event is the foundation on which the education of a human being builds. Education depends upon trust in her who has given life."[21]

The role of Joseph as an "outsider" in a virgin birth is problematic for describing the relationship between husband and wife. It also distances the father from his parental role in conception, pregnancy, birthing, and educating the child. John Paul reflects a cultural attitude that excludes or limits the father's role in the birthing process.

There is no need to continue such limited and sexist thinking about the role of the father. As a father who participated in both of our children's births, I disagree with his unbalanced focusing on the mother and child—leaving men outside. That has been the problem with too many pregnancies and births. The father has not taken up his responsibility and as a result, impoverishes himself, the child, and the mother.

Christine Gudorf notes the dual discrimination in the pope's line of thinking:

> The writings of John Paul and his predecessors are open to feminist charges of sexism against women as well as *reverse discrimination*

against men. For while the restricting of mothers to the home and exclusive care of children may be regarded as discrimination against women the portrait of men that emerges from the writings of 20th-century popes, despite its depiction of men as rational and competent, is one devoid of capacity for nurture, intuition, compassion, and bonding (except with their mothers). The public world of men, as opposed to the domestic sphere of women, is characterized by harshness, toil, suffering and inhumanity.[22]

CELAM AND NCCB

The documents of the Latin American and North American bishops' conferences *do* introduce gender into their analyses of current social problems. The 1979 Puebla Document of CELAM identified marginalization of women from political, economic, and social life as the result of "cultural atavisms—male predominance, unequal wages, deficient education."[23] The Latin American bishops name various expressions of women's marginalization, including prostitution as a result of stifling economic situations, exploitation of women in the workplace, the overburdening of women in the family, and *the church's undervaluing of women*. That is an amazing acknowledgment by the Latin American bishops.

The 1979 Puebla document also emphasizes the church's traditional understanding of the role of women: "the fundamental role of the woman as mother, the defender of life and the home educator." But it goes on to call the church to "consider" the equality and dignity of women and to recognize the mission of women in the church and in the world. The document recognizes women's aspirations for liberation as an "authentic sign of the times." The bishops speak of being encouraged by women's initiatives and growing consciousness.[24] Maria Riley points out that "this document marks a significant advance in Catholic social teaching's recognition of the complex reality that shapes women's lives."[25]

Seven years later the North American bishops treated the complexity of the economic issues faced by women in some depth in *Economic Justice for All*. This letter was a breakthrough in its treatment of women and economic issues. "For the first time in a church document the language is clearly gender specific in order to illumine the different economic issues faced by women and men."[26] By treating women's economic issues throughout the document, rather than in one specific section, the letter avoids the impression that these are only "women's issues" rather than problems of the entire economic system that affect men and women. The letter examines and condemns the "feminization of poverty," calls for greater economic justice for women in the workplace, and recognizes the changing patterns in family with mutual responsibilities for both fathers and mothers.

The Latin American and U.S. bishops' documents reveal a willingness to see women in a more inclusive way, while the papal documents continue to see women primarily in terms of motherhood and in accord with their "proper nature." This tension emerged within the U.S. bishops' conference as they drafted their letter on women.

Part II. The Attempted Pastoral Letter on Women

In 1972 the National Conference of Catholic Bishops formed an Ad Hoc Committee on the Role of Women in Society and the Church with the charge "to address the concerns of women and to recommend action." This newly formed committee met with representatives of various women's organizations, researched a variety of issues, and in 1977 conducted a survey on the roles that women were and were not taking in the church. After dialogue with many women and after considering all the input, the committee recommended at the November 1982 bishops' meeting that the bishops address these concerns. In 1983 the bishops unanimously approved a proposal to develop a "pastoral document" that would consider the concerns of women. In March 1984 a drafting committee of six bishops was formed, including:

- Joseph L. Imesch, chairman, bishop of Joliet;

- Thomas J. Grady, bishop of Orlando;

- William J. Levada, archbishop of Portland, Oregon;

- Matthew H. Clark, bishop of Rochester, New York;

- Alfred C. Hughes, auxiliary bishop of Boston; and

- Amedee W. Proulx, auxiliary bishop of Portland, Maine.

Seven women consultants were invited to assist the bishops. These women represented different academic areas and different life-styles—married, single, in religious life, and as mothers:

- Dr. Mary M. Brabeck, associate professor of educational psychology, Boston College;

- Sister Sara Butler, MSBT, Ph.D., general councilor, Missionary Servants of the Most Blessed Trinity, Philadelphia;

- Dr. Ronda Chervin, associate professor of philosophy, St. John's Seminary, Camarillo, California;

- Dr. Toinette M. Eugene, provost and associate professor of education, society, and black church studies, Colgate Rochester Divinity School/ Bexley Hall/Crozer Theological Seminary, Rochester, New York;

- Dr. Pheme Perkins, professor of scripture, Boston College;

- Dr. Susan A. Muto, professor and director at the Institute of Formative Spirituality, Duquesne University, who served as the writer; and

- Sister Marielle Frye, MHSH, Ph.D., the staff member of the Committee on Women in Society and the Church of the NCCB.

The full committee met for the first time in November 1984 to plan the process for consultation that would prepare them to write the first draft. The committee proposed a dual listening process: one of Catholic women's *organizations* and a second *grass-roots* listening process in each diocese. Twenty-four national groups participated in the hearings, which began in March 1985. The grass-roots listening process was to be initiated by each bishop in his diocese and to involve as many women as possible.

The committee received "grass-roots" responses from 100 dioceses, involving approximately 75,000 women. The committee also heard from 60 college campuses and 45 military bases. As could be expected, the responses covered a variety of perspectives:

> ...ranging from disbelief and antagonism to enthusiasm and relief. We were asked repeatedly not to write this pastoral as if women were the problem, but to focus solely on the sources of discrimination against women in church and society. The best we bishops might do, others said, was to express contrition. Still others told us to write in support of Catholic tradition and the willingness of women to pass its values on to the next generation. They urged us strongly not to suggest changes that might reflect contemporary pressures rather than perennial teachings. (par. 8)

After four years of work the committee released its first draft in March 1988, a 99-page document entitled *Partners in the Mystery of Redemption: A Pastoral Response to Women's Concerns for Church and Society*. This draft was the product of five writings and revisions. The bishops were very conscious of reflecting what they heard from women during the consultation process. The very structure of the letter reflected the bishops taking their listening responsibility seriously:

> On the basis of reports received from the national hearings and from the diocesan listening sessions, we have chosen to discuss the concerns raised by Catholic women under four headings...women as persons, women in relationships, women in society, and women in the church. (par. 20)

Those four areas begin the four chapters of the letter. Each of these four chapters was divided into three sections: first a *report* on what the bishops had heard, second a *reflection* on the Catholic theological heritage, and third, a *response* "intended to show that we have listened to women's voices and taken them seriously, that we seek to remedy the injustices women denounce and to promote the positive values they advocate" (par. 20).

In June 1988 the bishops' conference held its first formal discussion of the proposed pastoral at their meeting in Collegeville, Minnesota. Comments from individual bishops included asking for a more detailed analysis of sexism, a fuller treatment of church teachings in some areas, and a revision of the text in light of the expected papal statement on women.

As the U.S. dioceses began their evaluation of the first draft, Pope John Paul II issued his 119-page document on women, *Mulieris Dignitatem (On the Dignity and Vocation of Women)* on August 15, 1988. The papal encyclical had a strong influence on subsequent drafts of the pastoral letter. To facilitate discussion of the draft with women's groups, the bishops' committee sponsored two meetings with diocesan women's commissions, one in Elkins Park, Pennsylvania, and a second on the West Coast in January and February of 1989.[27]

To the credit of the drafting committee the first draft truly reflected the diverse voices heard during the listening sessions. The text of the letter included actual quotes from women, including those who questioned the hierarchy's teaching on birth control and women's ordination. Thomas Reese, a well-informed observer of the bishops' conference, points out that "while the first draft was well received by most women, Vatican officials and many bishops insisted that the bishops must not just listen, but also teach." He continued, "as a result, the second draft dropped the quotations from women and adopted the style of a traditional pastoral letter."[28]

Two years after the first draft, on April 3, 1990, a second draft was released. The text was to be discussed at the November 1990 meeting of bishops, but in September, the administrative committee of the National Conference of Catholic Bishops changed directions. At the request of the Vatican the leadership of the NCCB postponed its discussion of the second draft until the U.S. bishops consulted with representatives of other bishops' conferences from around the world. Roman officials and many U.S. bishops found the first draft unacceptable. These critics insisted on an expansion of the sections on the ordination of women, birth control, sexual ethics, and respect for the authority of the magisterium. Father Reese notes that "as each draft became more acceptable to Rome, it became less acceptable to many U.S. Catholic women."[29]

The Vatican-initiated consultation took place in Rome on May 28-29, 1991. At these meetings the U.S. committee was asked to consider:

- changing the document from a pastoral letter to one of lesser authority,

- expanding the human anthropology section,

- removing a request for a quick resolution of a Vatican study on ordaining women to the diaconate, and

- developing more fully the Marian dimension of the church.[30]

Ten months after the Vatican consultation on April 3, 1992, a third draft of the letter was released and slated for discussion at the bishops' meeting to be held at Notre Dame University in June 1992. The plan was to vote on the pastoral five months later at the November 1992 meeting. The bishops had not discussed the second draft, which was tabled and revised because of the Vatican intervention. They were now asked to discuss the third draft.

Bishops Imesch and Clark both admitted that the changes made to the document in the third draft reflected the concerns expressed at the Vatican consultation. The consultation included Vatican officials and bishops of 13 other countries. The changes included:

- amending the second draft's urging that a Vatican study on admitting women to the permanent diaconate "be undertaken and brought to completion soon" was changed to a call for "continued dialogue and reflection" on various ministries such as the diaconate;

- expanding the role of Mary as the mother of the church and as someone whose "continuing fidelity" is an example for all Christians; and

- redoing the second draft's section on "human anthropology," which discusses the differences between men and women.

In commenting on the third draft, Bishop Clark said that the consultation "had its most significant impact on the first chapter" where there is an "expansion of the topic of human nature and what it means to be man and woman."[31] Clark noted that the section on "human nature" incorporates elements of Pope John Paul II's reflections on the subject from *Mulieris Dignitatem.* Commenting on the committee's decision to delete the call for a prompt study of the diaconate, Bishop Clark explained, "We were told by Vatican authorities that this simply was not going to happen for some time. We felt, 'Why create expectations or [raise] issues that are simply not going to [be acted on] now?'"

Bishop Clark went on to explain why the third draft dropped the discussion of the reasons traditionally given for not ordaining women to the priesthood. "This change comes in spite of evidence from the listening sessions conducted at the start of the pastoral-writing process that this issue is a deeply felt one.... 'We felt it would be beating a dead horse to merely repeat all the (reasons why) women are not being ordained. There is no way the document is going to solve the issue.'"[32]

The bishops' committee went along with three of the four recommendations from the international consultation. They did not accept the recommendation to downgrade the document from a pastoral letter to a statement with less authority.

At the June 1992 meeting there was considerable discussion and debate among the bishops on the third draft. As they began their meeting, "there were predictions that criticisms of both 'right' and 'left' would combine to end the effort to produce a pastoral on women's concerns."[33]

Bishops were upset about both the *process* of writing the letter, and its *content.* Bishop Austin Vaughan, a New York auxiliary, criticized what he called a lack of communication from the committee—"never a revelation of problems, no revelation of a minority report, no revelation of why...women left the committee." In view of the process used by the committee, Vaughan said, "If we were voting on the Hail Mary, I would vote it down."[34]

Other conservative voices argued that the letter lacked a sustained critique of "radical feminism" and a reasoned defense against the ordination of women. Progressive bishops also argued against the letter. Bishop Charles Buswell of Pueblo, Colorado, noted that "the document seems a response to our and the Vatican's concerns, not women's." Archbishop Rembert Weakland said that the letter was not "a healing" document. In view of the "many hurts among women on both sides," he thought this was a shame. In places the letter is "brusque and harsh."[35]

After the debate the bishops took a "straw vote" to move ahead toward a possible vote at their next meeting, November 1992. Journalist Jim Bowman noted that the vote "resulted in a virtual draw, suggesting the draft could not garner the two-thirds vote required for approval of a pastoral letter."[36]

In preparation for the November meeting the committee prepared a fourth draft for discussion. The committee responded to criticisms voiced at the June meeting. The majority of those bishops who spoke up wanted the letter to take a more conservative tack. Accordingly, committee members Archbishop William Levada and Bishop Alfred Hughes wrote the fourth draft.[37] (Hughes had issued a minority report to the third draft, objecting that it had not adequately upheld official church teaching on women. Levada had worked in the Congregation for the Doctrine of the Faith prior to his selection as the Archbishop of Portland.) The bishops' conference released the letter on September 2, 1992. The latest draft revealed the impact of the June discussion as well as some "undisclosed Vatican criticisms made in early August."[38] Some of the notable changes from the previous draft include:

- a major shift from a focus on sexism to a broader look at evils harming women;

- a move from a short affirmation of the teaching of the church on women's ordination to an extended defense of the official teaching and a rebuttal of counter-arguments;

- a shift from the approach of dialogue and shared examination that marked earlier drafts to an approach that emphasized the bishops' responsibility to teach "fundamental truths about the human person and...application of these truths";

- the addition of extensive teaching on sexual morality; and,

- the dropping of nearly all criticisms of alleged clerical insensitivity to women.[39]

The fourth draft was written to appease Roman officials and traditional bishops. In the process it alienated many women and progressive bishops. Thomas Reese reports that "opposition to the fourth draft was especially high among the women most involved in the church, including religious women, women theologians, religious educators and employees and volunteers in chanceries and parishes. Bishops reported receiving hundreds of letters against the pastoral, along with petitions from parishes."[40]

At the November 1992 meeting the bishops debated the fourth draft. When it came time for voting the letter failed to receive a two-thirds vote of the eligible voting bishops. After ten years of work 137 voted in favor and 110 voted against. The supporters lacked 53 votes, as 190 votes were necessary for passage.

The opposition to the letter had been growing since 1990. Moderates and progressives believed the letter in its later versions would do more harm than good. Archbishop Weakland spoke against passage, warning that it could create a reaction within the church as vast as that caused by *Humanae Vitae*. Passage, he believed, "would lose another generation, especially another generation of very wonderful women."[41]

The question of women's ordination emerged as the linchpin of the pastoral letter. Cardinal Bernardin acknowledged that "in all honesty, we must admit that the central question which has emerged and is driving our discussion regarding the pastoral is that of the ordination of women."[42]

Journalist Dorothy Vidulich commented that "as the debate unfolded, rightly or wrongly, progressive bishops were seen as arguing against the pastoral, as a sign of hope to women to keep the ordination discussion going; conservatives, meanwhile, were seen as arguing for the passage of the pastoral, as a means of upholding the ban on women priests."[43] With all the many issues women face in the church and society, and after so many years of work by the committee and the staff, it is tragic that the future of the pastoral letter came down to one ecclesial issue—women's ordination. This has become the litmus test.

Because the pastoral letter was not approved, the fourth draft was released as a "report" of the Ad Hoc Committee for a Pastoral Response to Women's Concerns "to encourage further dialogue."[44] In effect, the fourth recommendation of the Vatican consultation was fulfilled: the pastoral letter was downsized in authority.

EVALUATION

In this brief evaluation of the pastoral on women's concerns I will explore both questions of "process" and "content."

Process: Listening to Women—at First

The bishops' committee followed a process that had proved successful in their two previous pastoral letters, namely, they held a number of hearings and consultations on the topic in preparation for writing the first draft. The bishops listened to women—some 75,000 women in 100 diocesan consultations. In commenting on the role of women on the committee, chairperson Bishop Joseph Imesch noted in October 1989 that "we tried to include women as consultants. Women are full members of the committee. Nothing is decided by the bishops without the presence or agreement of the consultants." That is an amazing statement about the attitude of the committee *in its early days*. He continued, "in addition, *we went to women—over 75,000 of them—and asked them what their concerns were. We, the bishops, did not define women's concerns; women did.*"[45]

What I find most compelling and surprising is that women were allowed to speak for themselves in the text. The bishops used direct quotes from women in the first draft. By using women's own words, the bishops were giving great importance to the experience of women. They brought forward the good and the bad news; the way women felt affirmed and alienated by their church.[46] As the bishops' committee wrote in the first draft:

> Our first responsibility throughout these years of research and writing has been to listen to as many women as possible, to hear them speaking from the reality of their own experience. ...All women...agree that they want to be heard, taken seriously, and respected as persons baptized and called to Christ to the service of church and society. (par. 17)

The bishops took women seriously in this first draft. They heard women, and they let the women speak for themselves. This way of writing a pastoral letter was innovative and revolutionary, and because of that it was challenged by some women, some bishops, and some Vatican officials. Two women's groups, "Women for Faith and Family," a predominantly lay group of Catholic women based in St. Louis, and

"Consortium Perfectae Caritatis," an organization of women religious with its headquarters in Middleburg, Virginia, complained in a joint letter to the bishops that the process was flawed from the start because the bishops, instead of "exercising their teaching function," responded to a limited set of women's concerns. These two groups felt that the "listening session" that the bishops held during the development of the pastoral letter tended to attract discontented women. The questions posed during the hearings elicited mainly "predictable critical responses." They argued that the data collected during the listening sessions was given "far too much weight" in formulating the pastoral letter.[47]

Vatican officials also raised the question of the consultative process. Bishop P. Francis Murphy, an auxiliary bishop in Baltimore and, from 1978-89 a member of the NCCB Committee on Women, reported that "the most serious concern raised by Vatican officials was the consultation process used by the Imesch Committee. They asserted that bishops are teachers, not learners; truth cannot emerge through consultation." Bishop Murphy called the Vatican intervention "harmful pressure being exerted by Rome on the *legitimate process of discernment* underway in the Catholic Church in the United States."[48]

The committee's open and egalitarian process conflicted with the traditional hierarchical and closed process that the Vatican and the more conservative bishops preferred. These are two very different ways in which the bishops exercise their role as teachers.

The hierarchical model relies on the "classicist" worldview in which truth is already "given"; the teaching office communicates and applies the truth. The teacher's role is to articulate the clear and unchanging tradition.

The egalitarian model recognizes that all people and perspectives can contribute to a fuller understanding of truth. Truth is both something that we possess and something we are continually discovering and searching for in our historical journey. The egalitarian model stresses the whole people of God, the *sensus fidelium*—the "sense" or understanding of the all faithful, lay and ordained.

The Catholic tradition has both of these approaches in its history and current practice and it is not easy to hold the two together. The bishops' committee began with an egalitarian model but was forced to shift back to a hierarchical model of teacher.

The Vatican's complaint was not really about consultation, because the Vatican itself uses consultation in developing its teaching documents.

The question is really about *who* is qualified to offer consultation—is it only theologians who are *in agreement* with the official church teaching as it is understood at this time, or is it theologians and housewives who may disagree with the church's official, noninfallible teachings? The U.S. bishops violated Vatican tradition by including the voices of nontheologians who were critical of church practice and teaching in their document. According to the hierarchical worldview this egalitarian approach could not be tolerated.

Two secondary "process" issues were also identified: first, that the U.S. bishops themselves did not spend enough time discussing the various drafts and, second, that scholarly papers were not part of the process. In the ten-year process the bishops discussed the drafts only twice, at the June and November 1992 meetings. The discussion of the second draft that was to take place in November 1990 was postponed because of the Vatican request for a consultation. It was *four years* after the first draft was released that the bishops as a whole were finally able to discuss the document. These late discussions did not allow the bishops enough time to hear each other during the process.

The final process critique comes from Bishop Francis Murphy:

> Perhaps the greatest methodological problem of the process was the failure to set in motion an initiative parallel to the committee's listening process that would have engaged the scholarly community in preparing papers on the central issues of the debate for study by the bishops. In writing the pastorals both on peace and on the economy, the bishops were immensely enriched and their debate focused by the spoken and written contribution of experts in the fields. No such effort was made for the women's pastoral.[49]

While the open consultative process did receive criticism and was discarded by Vatican intervention it did bear fruit. Again, Bishop Murphy articulates its value:

> The real strength of the process is that the bishops' committee listened to a diversity of women who are members of the church's body. It consulted the experience of many whose talents and aspirations are unjustly overlooked, especially in the church. It brought this listening process into the public domain and opened a dialogue that cannot be dismissed or ignored. This raised awareness of women's concerns with the church, not only in the United States, but in a number of countries around the world. In the process, some

fundamental issues that go beyond women's concerns have been raised, issues such as ecclesiology, the role of Rome, the nature of our being church together.[50]

Content

It is difficult to comment on the content of the pastoral letter because the content changed significantly through the four drafts. Discussing the content is like trying to hit a moving target. I will highlight two of the issues that were at the center of the debate, namely the question of "complementarity" and sexism.

1. Complementarity or Equality

One of the central issues of debate was on the question of human nature and how to explain what it means to be female or male. The committee wrestled with this underlying issue and had two schools of thought on the question. Bishop Imesch describes the two approaches:

> What it boils down to is this: One group argues that complementarity implies the superiority of one sex over the other. And thus they want to downplay the differences between the sexes (over and above the differences involved in reproduction) and emphasize the common personhood shared by the sexes.
>
> A second group argues that to affirm the differences between the sexes is not to deny equality of full mutuality between the sexes. In other words, equality does not require identity. In his recent papal letter *On the Dignity and Vocation of Women*, the Pope assumes this second viewpoint.[51]

The texts of the earlier drafts reveal *both* approaches, which leaves them confusing and often contradictory. Regarding the second draft, critics from the Washington-based Center of Concern point out that "the fundamental contradiction shaping the document is that while equality is proclaimed foundational, differences are used to justify inequality in sensitive areas."[52] Women are denied access to ordination and full decision-making power in the church. This restriction undermines the church's teaching on the equality of women in the public arena.

On the one hand, the second draft affirms the equality of women and men and rejects the assignment of certain personality traits to either sex. It also rejects the assumption that one sex is incomplete without the complementary gifts of the other. On the other hand, the rest of the second draft fails to live up to these affirmations when it assigns stereotypical roles, and resorts to the language of complementarity. As the executive committee of the Leadership Conference of Women Religious pointed out in its August 9, 1992 statement, "Language about complementarity continues to cloud the issue and introduce a basis for distinction that is unacceptable in the context."[53]

The early drafts tried to appease both approaches, while the final draft was clearly in keeping with the papal school of thought maintaining that equality of the sexes is not undermined by the exclusion of women from holy orders. This debate continues even though the Congregation for the Doctrine of the Faith has said it is a closed issue.

2. Sexism and Patriarchy

While the various drafts of the letter condemn sexism—"understood as an erroneous conviction that one sex, male or female, is superior to the other in the very order of creation and by the very nature of things," the drafts accept the basic assumption of patriarchy defined by Catherine Spretnak—"that males should legitimately act as the controlling cultural fathers, while females should appropriately act as dependent minors."[54] Sexism was called a sin in Draft III, yet this draft had no adequate treatment of sexism. Again, Bishop Murphy explains:

> there was no treatment of the causes of sexism in our society and church, no discussion as to how sexism permeates the history of the church and its attitude and actions concerning women, no explanation about how sexism and patriarchy support and reinforce one another, no attempt to see how women's present experience of sexism could help shape the fundamental changes needed. The call for conversion in Draft III was presented in terms of personal relationships. It was not extended to conversion of church structures.[55]

The final draft did not improve on these deficiencies but watered down the condemnation of sexism by dropping the more powerful language of "sin" in favor of calling it "a moral and social evil."

The bishops condemn sexism but seem to accept the patriarchal structure of the church and its official theology, which are ecclesial expressions of sexism. I agree with Bishop Murphy's assessment that "the patriarchal family continues to serve as model and legitimating structure in our church." He adds:

Rule by man over woman, the pope states, is not part of God's plan. In fact, however, dominance pervades our church, a dominance that excludes the presence, insights, and experience of women from the "table" where the formulation of the church's doctrine takes place and the exercise of its power is discerned. It likewise excludes women from presiding at the table where the community of faith is fed. This *patriarchy continues to permeate the church* and supports a climate that not only robs women of their full personhood, but also encourages men to be domineering, aggressive, and selfish.[56]

CONCLUSION

The process of writing the four drafts of the pastoral letter on women's concerns brought to the surface many issues that church leaders, theologians, and laity will have to continue addressing. The troubled path of this attempted pastoral letter reveals how much work the Catholic community still has to do to address the dehumanizing sexism that permeates both society and the church. The failure of the pastoral letter confronts the church with the reality that this dialogue about the role of women and men will not be easy or settled in a few years. I recall the advice of an Orthodox priest to his Lutheran counterpart: "You Lutherans want to decide about sexuality? Talk about it for a century or so and then see where you're at."[57]

Two years after the vote on Draft IV the Committee on Women in Society and in the Church wrote a brief pastoral reflection called *Strengthening the Bonds of Peace* in which the bishops pledged anew, "through our committee structure, to continue the dialogue in a spirit of partnership and mutual trust and to implement the recommendations [of Draft IV] where possible." From their own experience they admitted that "to be committed to honest dialogue is no easy task." They hearken back to the wisdom of Pope Paul VI on the benefits of dialogue—benefits often lost in the polarization of the contemporary church.

> In the dialogue one discovers how different are the ways which lead to the light of faith, and how it is possible to make them converge on the same goal. Even if these ways are divergent, they can become complementary for forcing our reasoning process out of the worn paths and by obliging it to deepen its research, to find fresh expressions.... The dialogue will make us wise; it will make us teachers.

The bishops' committee concluded, "Once again, we urge the Church at all levels to establish structures to hear and respond to the concerns of women."[58]

The first two sections of this chapter have examined official church teaching on women in the church and in society. We now turn to a brief discussion of the diverse movement within society, church, and within theology, known as feminism.

Part III. Feminist Movements and Social Theology

In the previous section we noted how the U.S. bishops' committee was initially willing to let women's voices be heard in the first draft of their pastoral letter on women. As Anne Carr points out, the emergence of women's voices "has meant some troubling questions and significant reorientations of mind and heart for many women (and men) with regard to Christianity, especially Roman Catholic Christianity." The bishops too, have had to face "troubling questions and reorientations of mind and heart." But as the story unfolded we saw that women's voices were deleted from the letter and replaced with only men's voices. Some critics saw the final document as "a stark embodiment of the sin of sexism itself."[59]

These troubling questions are still part of the church at all levels even if some members of the church try to close down all discussion.On the positive side, women's voices are being heard in the church and in society as they speak out of their experience. Women's voices have always echoed through the church, even if from outside the hierarchical power structures. But these voices were not always "heard" by their contemporaries, nor do we have a full account of their contribution. What is new in these last 30 years is not that women are speaking out, but that they are presenting a systemic critique of the sexism in culture and religion. This systemic critique of the church, society, and culture is called *feminism*. Feminism is a diverse movement that empowers women to be seen, heard, and to participate, in all areas of society. It is an invitation to personally and structurally transform sexist and patriarchal attitudes, practices, and policies. It is a "systemic challenge to patriarchal or sexist economic, political and cultural structures, that is, to systems in which women are subordinated and excluded from full participation in the life of the society."[60] The feminist movement in the church intends to overcome the exclusion of women from church structures, policies, and the development and articulation of doctrine. An agenda that seeks to overcome exclusion is perceived as threatening to those who hold a traditional view of the church and its theology.

While the feminist movement is a recent development its roots connect with "all that women have done to survive and to resist oppression throughout the centuries."[61] "'Feminism' has served as a name for the growing body of theory and social practice based on experiences in the women's movement worldwide, a phenomenon that can be interpreted broadly to include all that women have done to survive and to resist oppression throughout the centuries."[62]

Feminism has both a theoretical and a practical orientation. The theoretical focus covers all academic disciplines, including theology and ethics as well as political studies, economics, sociology, psychology, and cultural studies. The practical emphasis includes bringing about change in attitudes, policies, and structures in order to address the root causes of sexism. The common starting point for theory and the social practice is women's experience. "Beginning with women's experiences, feminism seeks greater well-being, mutuality in relationship, equality and participation for women, raising questions about structures for organizing all of life."[63]

Both women and men who are committed to these goals are considered feminists; it is not only the work of women.

Within the feminist movement there is great diversity; all feminists are not cut from the same cloth. Rosemary Radford Ruether describes the three major approaches within feminism in these words:

> Feminism is also a complex movement with many layers. It can be defined as a movement within *liberal democratic* societies for full inclusion of women in political rights and access to equal employment. It can be defined more radically in socialist and *liberationist* feminism as a transformation of the patriarchal socioeconomic system in which male domination of women is the foundation of all social hierarchies. Feminism can also be studied *in terms of culture* and consciousness, charting the symbolic, psychological, and cultural connection between the definition of women as inferior mentally, morally, and physically, and male monopolization of knowledge and power.[64]

The three broad groupings described by Ruether are rooted in different philosophical and political systems of thought and practice.[65]

1. The *liberal democratic* form of feminism is rooted in the liberal tradition of the Enlightenment, which forms the basis for political rights, democracy, and the capitalist system as practiced in the West. It emphasizes the equality and common human nature of all persons, and it seeks to extend to women, as individuals, political and legal rights within the current system.

2. The *socialist and liberationist* forms of feminism draw on the theories of Karl Marx, which stress the need for transformation of economic structures in order to effect positive change for women of all classes.

3. "Radical" or *cultural* feminism considers gender discrimination the root cause of all forms of oppression. It sees women's control of their own persons, especially their own bodies, as the core issue and it advocates separating from patriarchal institutions in favor of cultivating a women's culture through women-centered alternatives. Some radical feminists suggest the natural and moral superiority of women.

Another "layer" of diversity among feminism is found in identifying *women of color and diverse socioeconomic classes and cultures and religions*. These women "have challenged white, middle-class, North American feminists to broaden and deepen their analysis in light of the situations of all women, especially the poorest."[66] These groups of women have taken on different terms for their feminist thinking and action, including *"womanist"* and *"mujerista."* (These expressions of feminism will be discussed toward the end of this section.)

In the theological realm feminist theology has taken on a threefold agenda: 1) to point out the androcentric and misogynist bias of Christian theology and ministry, 2) to recover the lost history of women in the Christian tradition, which challenges the androcentric bias, and 3) to envision and reconstruct a Christian theology and ministry that is free of the bias against women and takes seriously the equality and experience of women.[67]

To carry out this threefold agenda women will have to have a public presence in the theological academy and in ministry. This is happening slowly, and not without obstacles, as women have only recently had access to theological education in seminaries and ordained ministry in many Christian traditions. Much solid work has been done in these areas already.

1. NAMING THE ANDROCENTRISM AND MISOGYNISM OF THE JUDEO-CHRISTIAN TRADITION

Feminist theology begins with the simple historical recognition that the dominant orientation of Christian theology has been written by men. Women have been historically excluded from shaping the public tradition of theology. As Ruether notes, "This means that males, and indeed males of the dominant class and race, have unconsciously been assumed to be the normative human persons." She continues:

> ...women have been defined as possessing an inferior and non-normative humanity, to be more responsible for the origins of evil than males, to be more prone to sin than males, to be in a state of subjugation, both as an expression of their lesser nature and as punishment for their role in original sin, to lack the image of God and to be unable to represent Christ and to be unordainable.[68]

Some of the first work in feminist theology took the form of a critique of the male bias of classical theology. In 1968 Mary Daly, a Roman Catholic trained in the theological faculty of Fribourg, Switzerland, wrote her first book, *The Church and the Second Sex*, on the sexual bias of the whole Christian tradition. In the same year a Norwegian Catholic feminist, Kari Borresen, wrote a comprehensive study of the role of gender in the anthropology of St. Augustine and St. Thomas Aquinas. Other studies have also explored the sexist distortion of classical theology and particular authors throughout Christian tradition.[69]

The Bible both denigrates and upholds women, yet the patriarchal motif predominates:

> Passages in the Hebrew Bible that associate the female with matter, chaos, and evil (especially the figure of the temptress Eve who led Adam to sin) and New Testament injunctions to women about silence in the Christian assembly and subordination to male "headship" underscore ancient patriarchal attitudes that legitimate notions of the inferiority and subordination of women.[70]

The church "fathers" were generally more distrustful of women. Tertullian described women as "the devil's gateway," the "first deserter" of the divine law. Clement of Alexandria observed that a woman should be covered with shame when she thinks "of what nature she is"; and Augustine held that "in her the good Christian likes what is human, loathes what is feminine." In the twelfth century Thomas Aquinas continued the misogynist tradition, maintaining that a "woman is defective and misbegotten," and "is in the [natural] state of subjection."[71]

These anti-woman teachings have been used to exclude women from theological study and teaching and from public ministry and ordination in the church.

2. RETRIEVAL OF WOMEN'S HISTORY
AND THEOLOGICAL REFLECTION

While the term "feminist theology" is relatively recent the voices and witness of women have shaped and influenced the church and society throughout history. Feminists are recovering those muted voices by rereading history. The liturgical and leadership roles of women are being examined as extending as far back as Miriam's dance after the Israelites crossed the Red Sea. Archaeologists are examining evidence that women, as well as men, presided over the liturgy in the early church. Giorgio Otranto, the director of the Institute of Classical and Christian Studies in Bari, Italy has published his findings from literary and epigraphical sources (sarcophagi, graffiti, etc.,) that testify to women priests in the early church.[72]

A major movement of "feminist" criticisms of the misogynist use of biblical texts and an affirmation of women's right to leadership in the church and society was flourishing in seventeenth-century England. For example, the Society of Friends developed a systematic hermeneutic of Scripture that affirmed women's equality in Christ and their inclusion in preaching.[73] In the United States there were women preachers in many of the religious sects of the Civil War era.

The work of recovery of women's history and theological reflection in the Christian tradition flows from the desire to find new "foremothers for a feminist theology." This historical recovery often means revisiting traditional areas of doctrinal conflict.

> Reexamination of marginalized early christian groups, such as gnostics and Montanists, or new study of popular christian texts, such as the apocryphal gospels, may expand the reading of christian tradition to include traditions more affirmative of women's participation.[74]

The retrieval work also revisits women who were accepted and recognized in their own day, such as Mary, Teresa of Avila, and Catherine of Siena, as well as bringing to light the writings of neglected women, such as the twelfth-century mystic Hildegard of Bingen. This research gives us a fuller understanding of the ways women have shaped the tradition and opened the door for a more inclusive theology and ministry.

3. FEMINIST THEOLOGICAL CONSTRUCTION TODAY

In the construction of feminist theology women's experience is seen as the contemporary category by which sexist theology can be evaluated. Ruether explains that "women's experience" is not limited to gender-specific biological experiences such as pregnancy, childbirth, and breast-feeding children. Rather "women's experience" means primarily "women's critical experience of the devaluation of her person under patriarchal domination and her own journey of liberation." She continues, "these stories of women's experience can serve as critical paradigms for critique of sexist ideologies and also for new symbols affirmative of women's full humanity. Storytelling thus becomes an important source for feminist theology."[75] Stories keep alive the liberating experience of women who struggle against sexist attitudes and behavior. The construction of an inclusive theology and ministry will begin with and take seriously the experience of women.

Experience as the Essential Starting Point

Susan Secker of Seattle University explains that "the reason we women are insisting upon the truth of our experience is because of a fundamental 'contrast experience' we encounter as we do our theology." She elaborates that the "contrast experience" recognizes the absence of women's perspectives and voices in the Christian theological tradition. From this experience feminists have developed the (hermeneutical) principle that

> whatever denies, diminishes, or distorts the full humanity of women must be presumed not to reflect the divine or an authentic relation to the divine, or to reflect the authentic nature of things, or to be the message or work of an authentic redeemer of community of redemption.[76]

Secker focuses her discussion of the importance of these "contrast experiences." "The import of these contrast experiences is especially significant with the Catholic tradition which holds that through human experience we come to know and respond to God." If this is so, then insights from over 50 percent of the human race, women, must be incorporated into our notion of what "the human" is. Insights from women's experience are needed to qualify and correct our Christian anthropology, which has been written almost exclusively by men.

Besides this corrective to our theological anthropology, women's experience brings another dimension to our way of doing theology and moral reflection. Women's experience as a source for theology "starts from a groundedness in the concrete. Theology starts with reflection on everyday living."[77] Sally Purvis, from Candler School of Theology, Emory University, claims that feminist ethics blurs the boundaries between "the secular" and "the sacred." She continues,

> Women's stories contain many accounts of their encounters with God in the most ordinary tasks: bathing children, gardening, making a salad, watching a sunset comprise important parts of my spiritual autobiography. The vast new literature in feminist Christian liturgies often reflects a reclaiming of, or a new emphasis on, the ordinary as sacramental—an insight that has been part of Christian theological claims from the beginning.[78]

In the sacramental-liturgical realm rich insights about God's presence are also being articulated by feminist theologians and liturgists. In the ethical-moral realms the reflected experiences of women of every class and color are being offered to the theological community as well. The disciplines of biblical studies and systematic theology have seen very creative feminist theological discourse. One of the most central theological questions is how we name God and what metaphors for God we accept as normative. Can we add to the sacred trinity of names, Father, Son and Spirit, the feminist names of Lover, Friend, and Mother?[79] Can we image the world as God's body?[80] Can we include images from nature, as the Bible does, to describe God? Can we speak of God as the gentle wind, the eagle, the bear, or the powerful lightning?[81]

Is It Being Taught?

The church and theological disciplines are enriched by feminist contributions to theology. But these insights will not be heard in the church unless they are accepted and taught in seminaries, universities, and theological centers around the world. Feminist theology, says Rosemary Ruether, will not help to reshape the Catholic tradition

> until those who control what is taught as christian history and thought are willing to incorporate this material into the curriculum and reshape the teaching of theology to reflect feminist critique. Needless to say, this can only happen when feminist theology becomes not merely a marginal and occasional item in the theolog-

ical curriculum, but is regarded as a major perspective through which to teach the foundational tradition.[82]

The insights of feminist theology will help the church become inclusive only if it is taught in our schools and preached in our places of worship. Feminist theological and ministerial reflection and practice are further enriched by women of color who are claiming their own voice as "womanist" and "mujerista" feminists.

WOMANIST THEOLOGY

Feminist theology among African American women is distinguished from white feminist theology. Delores Williams, a womanist theologian at Union Theological Seminary, calls it "a vision in its infancy." The term "womanist" comes from the novelist Alice Walker, who traced it to the black folk expression "You are acting womanish," meaning "wanting to know more and in greater depth than is good for one...outrageous, audacious, courageous and willful behavior." Walker insists that a womanist is also "committed to survival and wholeness of entire people, male and female."[83] A womanist is a black feminist or feminist of color.

> Walker situates her understanding of a womanist in the context of nonbourgeois black folk culture. The literature of this culture has traditionally reflected more egalitarian relations between men and women, much less rigidity in male-female roles, more respect for female intelligence and ingenuity than is found in bourgeois culture.

> The black folk are poor. Less individualistic than those who are better off, they have, for generations, practiced various forms of economic sharing.[84]

Walker and Williams point to black heroines like Harriet Tubman, whose liberation activity earned her the name "Moses" of her people. Williams notes that,

> this allusion to Tubman directs womanist memory to a liberation tradition in black history in which women took the lead, acting as catalysts for the community's revolutionary action and for social change. Retrieving this often hidden or diminished female tradition of catalytic action is an important task for womanist theologians and ethicists. Their research may well reveal that female models of authority have been absolutely essential for every struggle in the black community and for building and maintaining the community's institutions.

Womanist theologians bring to light the crucial role of black women in the black community's struggle for liberation. "By uncovering as much as possible about such female liberation, the womanist begins to understand the relation of black history to the contemporary folk expression: 'If Rosa Parks had not sat down, Martin King would not have stood up.'"[85]

Womanist theology is beginning to define the categories and methods consistent with its broad theological and ecclesial agenda. Williams identifies four elements:

1. A *multidialogical orientation* that encourages womanist theologians to advocate and participate in dialogue and action with many diverse social, political, and religious communities concerned about human survival and liberation. In this dialogue and action the womanist will keep her speech open to oppressions of other cultures and groups, but will focus on "the slow genocide of poor black women, children, and men by exploitative systems denying them productive jobs, education, health care, and living space." Notes of discord may be heard in the dialogue, similar to a jazz symphony that breaks the norms of harmony.

2. A *liturgical intent* that will consciously and critically impact upon the foundations of liturgy, "challenging the church to use justice principles to select the sources that will shape the content of liturgy."

3. A *didactic intent* that highlights the teaching function of womanist theology, especially in terms of new insights about the moral life based on "justice for women, survival, and a productive quality of life for poor women, children, and men." Tensions about obedience, love, and humility are present in black literature sources. Womanist theology must teach the church the different ways God reveals prophetic word and action for Christian living.

4. The fourth element is a commitment both to reason and to the validity of *female imagery and metaphorical language* in the construction of theological statements. The language of womanist theology will be rich in female imagery, metaphor, and story. For the black church, this kind of theological language may be quite useful, since the language of the black religious experience abounds in images and metaphors.[86]

Delores Williams, Kate Cannon, and other black female preachers and ethicists focus on the biblical story of Hagar as the most illustrative and relevant to African American women's experience of bondage and survival. Williams explores the story of Hagar more fully in her text, *Sisters in the Wilderness: The Challenge of Womanist God-Talk*.[87]

Hagar was the mother of Ishmael, who was cast into the desert by Abraham and Sarah, but protected by God. Because of the discrimination and exploitation she experienced, Hagar is seen as the prototype of the struggle of African American women. As an African slave, homeless and in exile, a surrogate mother, Hagar is an image of survival and defiance for black women today. Hagar's "forced motherhood," "single motherhood," and "surrogate motherhood" has also been part of black women's experience. Hagar's religious resilience and encounters with God, and her surrogacy and wilderness experience are all themes that connect with the cultural and literary traditions of African American women, as well as their contemporary struggles.

Professor Williams dialogues with black theology as well as white feminist theology. She and other womanist theologians demonstrate how approaching theology consciously informed by an awareness of the realities of black women results in a rich and vibrant contribution of theological discourse.

A number of Roman Catholic women have contributed to the womanist theological conversation. They include the late Sister Thea Bowman, Toinette Eugene, who served for a number of years on the committee drafting the women's pastoral letter, Dominican sisters Jamie Phelps and M. Shawn Copeland of the Catholic Theological Union in Chicago and Marquette University, respectively, and Diana Hayes, who teaches at Georgetown University. Diana Hayes notes one area, among others, in which Catholic womanists can make a significant contribution—a reinterpretation of the role and presence of Mary.

> Too often seen as a docile, submissive woman, Black Catholic womanists, instead see a young woman sure of her God and her role in God's salvific plan.... We relate to her by sharing in her experiences as women who are also oppressed but who continue to bear the burden of faith and to pass on that faith to generations to come.... She is a role model, not for passivity, but for strong, righteous, "womanish" women who spend their lives giving birth to the future.[88]

Catholic, Protestant, and Jewish womanist theologians are gradually weaving a chain of flowers like the girls in the black community do. Bess

B. Johnson reminds her readers that girls weren't allowed to play tug-o-war with the boys,

> so we figured out how to make our own rope—out of...little dandelions. You just keep adding them, one to another, and you can go on and on.... Anybody, even the boys, could join us.... The whole purpose of our game was to create this dandelion chain—that was it. And we'd keep going, creating till our mamas called us home.

Delores Williams comments that "like Johnson's dandelion chain, womanist theological vision will grow as black women come together and connect piece with piece. Between the process of creating and the sense of calling, womanist theology will one day present itself in full array, reflecting the divine spirit that connects us all."[89]

MUJERISTA THEOLOGY

Women of Hispanic background are also doing theology out of their concrete cultural and historic experience. One of the first issues to sort out is how to name one's reality and one's self. Jeanette Rodriguez-Holguin, a theologian from Seattle University, explained at the 1992 Catholic Theological Society of America meeting that this is not an easy task. Even the word "experience" is not the word a Hispanic person would use. *La realidad*, one's reality, is a better term for describing one's experience in Spanish. Rodriguez also pointed out that the word "Hispanic" is a Eurocentric term developed by bureaucrats for political expediency and is not a self-defining word. She prefers "Latina" because it speaks of ethnicity. "Deep in my heart, I believe that being a Latina has nothing to do with what country one lives in. Rather, it is a state of soul, not one of mind, not one of citizenship." Rodriguez also uses "Chicana" to refer to her political consciousness of a people aware that they were born and raised in the United States. But in naming herself she prefers "Latina."

Rodriguez maintains that "latinas share the belief that we have the right to maintain our cultural heritage, a heritage that we maintain despite 500 years of 'influence.'" They recognize what a struggle it has been, and is, to maintain their Latina culture. As Virgilio Elizondo writes in *The Future is Mestizo*,

> we had learned about the greatness of the American experience and we hold it in great reverence. What we had not studied was the cruel injustices involved in the process of nation-building (Christianizing,

civilizing): the massacres of the natives, the slave trade, the systematic impoverishment of the Mexican inhabitants of the Southwest.[90]

In light of their history of struggle for equal dignity, Latinas, according to Rodriguez, describe their reality with words like "conquest and resistance, borderlands, ...integrity, anger, pain, economically and politically marginalized and multiple identities." She goes on to explain, "Other women may have multiple identities in terms of their roles, but I am talking about something much more profound: A woman from a dominant culture does not have to learn my point of view to survive, but Mexican American women have to know the ways of the dominant culture."

Rodriguez quotes from Gloria Anzaldua's book *Borderlands: The New Mestiza* to give us a sense of this clash and blending of cultures:

> ...*la mestiza* is a product of the transfer of the cultural and spiritual values of one group to another... the *mestiza* faces the dilemma of the mixed breed: which collectivity does the daughter of a dark-skinned mother listen to?... Cradled in one culture, sandwiched between two cultures, straddling all three cultures and their value systems, *la mestiza* undergoes a struggle of flesh, a struggle of borders, and inner war.... The coming together of two self-consistent but habitually incompatible frames of reference causes *un choque*, a cultural collision...a swamping of her psychological borders. She has discovered that she can't hold concepts or ideas in rigid boundaries.... Rigidity means death.... The new *mestiza* copes by developing a tolerance for contradictions, a tolerance for ambiguity. She learns to be an Indian in Mexican culture, to be Mexican from an Anglo point of view. She learns to juggle cultures. She has a plural personality, she operates in a pluralistic mode....

Rodriguez then turns to a very earthy metaphor to explain her point. "Indigenous like corn, like corn, the *mestiza* is a product of crossbreeding, designed for preservation under a variety of conditions. Like an ear of corn—a female seed-bearing organ—the *mestiza* is tenacious, tightly wrapped in the husks of her culture. Like kernels she clings to the cob; with thick stalks and strong brace roots, she holds tight to the earth—she will survive the crossroads."[91]

Rodriguez notes that with these two cultures come conflict and questions of identity. Another woman had confided in her that "sometimes the Latina in me doesn't understand or is in contradiction to the Anglo educated side of me. Sometimes I feel like one cancels out the other. And

I feel like nothing." Mujerista theology recognizes that experience of nothingness and calls women to be something and someone: a *Latina*, a *mestiza*, a *Chicana*, a person who survives at the crossroads of her cultures.

Mujerista theology names that experience of "nothingness" as "anthropological poverty," which "includes and goes beyond material poverty." The Cuban American theologian Ada María Isasi-Díaz explains that "this anthropological poverty threatens to despoil us of our very being." Latina women struggle on many levels for their very existence, their survival, and the survival of their community.[92]

In the face of material and anthropological poverty mujeristas point out the two ways Hispanic women assert their "being" and their value. First, *they act*. That is, they do what is necessary to survive. Latinas know they "have to act, that whatever is going to happen is going to happen because they see to it that it happens.... All of them insist in their own way that only if they depend on themselves can they depend on God." Professor Isasi-Díaz has interviewed nine women and uses their own words in the text as part of her mujerista method and content. (It is a method similar to what the bishops' committee did in its first draft of the pastoral letter on women.)

The second "generative theme" that Isasi-Díaz hears in women is a "strong awareness, almost a passion, for *claiming and asserting their value* and their self-worth." For example,

> Even Marta, who claims to have low self-esteem, struggles valiantly to separate that negative image from her belief, her knowing, that she is good, very good. Julieta's husband tries to control her by insisting that God might not have forgiven her working as a prostitute, and at times he seems to succeed in planting in her a seed of uncertainty. But then, almost out of nowhere, comes Julieta's assertion that she knows she is of value to God, that she is a good mother, that her children love her.[93]

As Professor Isasi-Díaz worked with these women she became more convinced that "these women want their voices heard, that they believe they have a contribution to make to the doing of *mujerista* theology."[94]

Dialogue with Anglo feminists

Mujerista theologians such as Ada María Isasi-Díaz seek to carry on a dialogue with Anglo feminists. Isasi-Díaz begins this dialogue by pointing out two defining characteristics of her theology: it is *liberationist* and *cultural*. She concludes by noting the common cause of all feminist efforts—

confronting sexism.[95] Mujerista theology sets itself off from liberal feminism in that it does not seek participation in the current economic and political structures as do some feminists in First World countries. "We do not seek to participate in oppressive structures but to change those structures; our goal is not equality but liberation." Mujerista theology is *radical and liberationist* in its approach.

Mujerista theology is also a *cultural theology*, which distinguishes it from liberal feminism because mujerista theology focuses more clearly on cultural oppression. "'As residents in an alien land'... our religious understandings are intrinsic to our struggle against assimilation. We struggle to maintain the values of our culture as an intrinsic element of our self-identity and our struggle." Latin women in the North American context have a cultural struggle that most Anglo feminists do not have to confront.

Mujeristas do share with other feminists a common commitment to confront sexism. "It is *feminist theology* because we know that the oppression of women by men is an intrinsic element of all oppression. The struggle against sexism and its incarnational mode, patriarchy, is a significant element of our doing theology."

As the three perspectives suggest, *mujeristas* share common ground with other feminists but also have different approaches and additional struggles when compared with Anglo feminists. At times, they are even marginalized by other feminists: "*Feministas hispanas* have been consistently marginalized within the Anglo feminist community because of our critique of its ethnic/racial prejudice and its lack of class analysis."[96]

Susan Secker and Jeanette Rodriguez-Holguin, colleagues at the University of Seattle, are good examples of the dialogue between white and Latina feminists. They have wrestled with the starting point of "women's experience" from their diverse perspectives.[97] Ellen Leonard says the value of this dialogue is that it helps to

> clarify how experience can be used as a resource for feminist thought by pointing to the danger of overlooking difference in the search for commonality. It insisted that women must name their own experience with their own voices rather than have it named by others. This has implications for theological method. If women are to give content to the wisdom which diverse racial and cultural groups provide about the meaning of their experience as women, doing theology cannot be the work of isolated scholars. It requires a collaborative and dialectical model.[98]

Conclusion

Professor Leonard's words provide a fitting theme to draw this diverse chapter to a close. Much of the chapter has chronicled the difficulty the teaching office of the Roman Catholic church has faced as it struggles to hear the voices of women, and to let the messages it hears help transform the church, while it also listens with a critical ear to the voices of tradition. The dynamic process of the church creatively shaping the tradition as it hands it on is happening in our day. With it comes frustrations, power struggles, and, it is to be hoped, the conversion of all involved.

I would like to let a woman have the last word in this chapter. Ada María Isasi-Díaz's thoughts are a fitting conclusion:

> Mujerista theologians believe that the preferential option for the poor has to be more than a conceptual claim and that in order to do so it has to yield specific praxis. A key praxis it must produce is the recognition that all Latinas engaged in the struggle to survive— the struggle for liberation—are capable of speaking our own word, naming our own reality, reflecting upon and making explicit our own religious understandings and practices.[99]

Discussion Questions

1. Bishop Francis Murphy notes that while sexism is condemned by the church the dominance of men over women "pervades our church." Do you agree with his assessment? If so, how can we deal with this dichotomy?

2. The process of writing the pastoral on the role of women included the "voices" of women in the first draft. Why is the removal of those voices from the text so controversial?

3. What are the common elements in feminist thinking and where do you see distinctive features of the various schools of feminist thinking?

4. Why is attention to inclusive language so significant in combating sexism?

5. One of the debated questions among the bishops and their critics was whether to employ the notion that male and female are "complementary." How do you understand the attempt to hold together the two assumptions that men and women are both *equal* and *complementary*?

13

An Emerging
Earth Ethic

This final chapter focuses on Catholic social teaching on the environment, an area that has been largely ignored in the official documents. After reviewing and evaluating the recent documents, I engage in a theological review of the obstacles and resources that must be examined if a vibrant "earth ethic" is to take root in the Catholic community and tradition of social teaching. As we will see, leadership on environmental issues is often found in secular arenas as well as in non-Christian religions. These are some of the movements and religions Roman Catholics will need to listen to and dialogue with in the future.

Part I. Catholic Teaching on the Environment

In the spring of 1962 the American marine biologist Rachel Carson published her ground-breaking book *Silent Spring*, on the devastating effects

385

of environmental pollution. She feared that because of the toxic effects of pesticides we were headed for a "silent spring" when life would flourish no more on the earth.[1] A few months later, in the Fall of 1962, the Second Vatican Council began. But the question of the environment was *not* on the list of issues to be discussed during the four years of the council meetings.[2] The tone of the Vatican II documents, especially *Gaudium et Spes,* was to praise the accomplishments of modern technology. The council fathers, like many of their contemporaries, were dazzled by the marvels and promise of modern science and technology in "mastering" nature. "Through his labors and his native endowments man has ceaselessly striven to better his life. Today, however, especially with the help of science and technology, he has extended his mastery over nearly the whole of nature and continues to do it."[3]

The Vatican II documents did not raise any critical concerns about the harmful side of modern technology, science, and industrialization. In 1967, two years after the close of the council, Pope Paul VI issued his encyclical on economic and human development, *Populorum Progressio.* But this document was also silent on the negative impact of industrialization on the biosphere.

In 1971, after the first Earth Day in 1970 and while the Club of Rome—a group of European industrialists—was beginning to analyze the impact of industrial growth and population increase on the environment, the official teachings of the Catholic church *began* to name environmental degradation. In *Octogesima Adveniens,* Pope Paul briefly noted that "man is suddenly becoming aware that by an ill-considered exploitation of nature he risks destroying it and become in turn the victim of this degradation."[4] In this brief statement the pope remains somewhat abstract; he does not make any specific reference to what is happening to the water, the air, the forests. "The destruction of species or ecosystems is not seen as in itself a moral and religious problem."[5]

"The first significant environmentalist declaration in a magisterial document," according to Thomas Landy, associate project director of the Leadership Education Project at the John F. Kennedy School of Government, Harvard University, "occurs in the 1971 synod document, *Justice in the World,* which essentially characterized environmental degradation as a violence carried out by wealthy consumers against the poor."[6] Here we see the influence of the Third World bishops who emphasize the impact of the consumption of the First and Second World economies:

> Furthermore, such is the demand for resources and energy by *the richer nations*, whether capitalist or socialist, and such are the effects of dumping by them in the atmosphere and the sea that irreparable damage would be done to the essential elements of life on earth, such as air and water, if their rates of consumption and pollution, which are constantly on the increase, were extended to the whole of mankind. (par. 11)[7]

Sean McDonagh, an Irish missionary working in the Philippines, comments that "this is one of the few texts in which the growth mania of the modern industrial consumer society is mentioned. However, the data are not clearly arranged and the analysis is not rigorous enough to challenge one of the most strongly held tenets of our modern society: that we must continue to have economic growth, otherwise we will stagnate and our way of life will collapse."[8]

As we saw in a previous chapter, the 1971 synod did have a powerful effect in calling for the creation of peace and justice centers. Many dioceses and bishops' conferences took this charge seriously and formed social concerns committees and centers. Some of these centers began to address environmental issues. The pope's own justice and peace center, the Pontifical Commission *Iustitia et Pax* (Justice and Peace) addressed the environmental question in one of its publications issued in 1973, *A New Creation? Reflections on the Environmental Issue*. This reflection paper, written by the well-known British economist Barbara Ward (Lady Jackson), was part of series of brochures published after the 1971 synod to continue the discussion initiated by the synod's focus on "Justice in the World." Barbara Ward's fine paper did not carry any formal authority, but it did encourage Catholics to reconsider their attitude toward creation, just as Rachel Carson's work had done a few years earlier.

Ecological concerns were soon on the front pages of newspapers as forums appeared in all sectors. With the variety of events, including the 1972 United Nations Conference on the Human Environment held in Stockholm, "people wondered openly whether they were witnessing a turning point in history, the end of an era, the beginning of a new age."[9]

Iustitia et Pax continued to work on issues of social justice, including the environment, as these topics emerged on the political landscape. For instance, during the 1977 U.N. Conference on the Law of the Sea, the Pontifical Commission issued a position paper that emphasized the church's teaching on "the universal purpose of created things" as it related to the use of the resources of the sea.[10] But the environment did not receive any sustained and systematic attention.

POPE JOHN PAUL II

It is in the later writings of Pope John Paul II that the Catholic church begins to more *formally* address issues of the environment in its magisterial teaching. In 1979, in *Redemptor Hominis*, John Paul outlined the primary directions of his teaching, namely, a theological anthropology that holds that "the human person is the primary and fundamental way for the church, the way traced out by Christ himself."[11] This sentence summarizes John Paul II's humanism, which serves as the foundation of his concern about justice, development, and the environment.

In this encyclical he began to break with the optimism of Vatican II and his predecessors Paul VI and John XXIII. He expressed a fear that humanity may not be "developing and progressing," but "regressing and being degraded." The indications of this are seen not only in the social and political order's inability to care for the needs of so many but also in the economic order's "depleting the earth's resources of raw materials and energy at an ever-increasing rate and putting intolerable pressures on the geophysical environment" (par. 15-16).

The pope responded to the misinterpretation of Genesis 1:28 that distorts the words of the Bible to justify domination and exploitation of creation. The text reads "God blessed them and God said to them, 'Be fruitful and multiply, and fill the earth and subdue it, and *have dominion* over the birds of the air and *over every living thing* that moves upon the earth.'"[12] The pope affirmed that creation is ordered to meet human needs but he warned against needless exploitation. "It was the Creator's will that man should communicate with nature as an intelligent and noble 'master' and 'guardian,' and not as a needless 'exploiter' and 'destroyer'" (par. 15). He explains that "the essential meaning of this 'kingship' and 'dominion' of man over the visible world, which the Creator himself gave man for his task, consists in the priority of ethics over technology, in the primacy of the person over things, and in the superiority of spirit over matter" (par. 16). While this is a beginning of a correction of the ruthless domination over nature, it still maintains a dualism of spirit over matter and keeps humanity at the center of the universe.

This dominant anthropocentrism of Roman Catholic teaching concerns many environmentalists who see this dualism and anthropocentrism as at the heart of our disregard for creation. Father Sean McDonagh argues that "while this is a marked improvement on the domination ethic, this is still fundamentally anthropocentric. It encourages environmental preservation because it is ultimately in the interest of humans. It does not begin with an understanding of the totality of God's creation and then seek to decipher the role of humans within the total biosphere."[13]

In 1981 on the 90th anniversary of *Rerum Novarum* Pope John Paul II issued *Laborem Exercens,* an encyclical on human labor.[14] While the letter updates the church's teaching on the "condition of the working class" it barely addresses the impact of human labor on the environment. This was a missed opportunity to connect concern for the dignity of the worker with concern for the dignity of creation and the call for human labor that respects and enhances our natural environment.

Another missed opportunity took place in 1984 when the synod of bishops discussed the theme of reconciliation. Only one speech at the synod, by Bishop Stephen Fumio Hamao of Japan, called for reconciliation between humanity and the natural world. Bishop Hamao urged that "work for peace will be effective if all men become aware of their deep connection with nature, especially with all living beings. Man must not only dominate nature, but also seek harmony with it and admire in it the beauty, wisdom, and love of the Creator. Thus men will be freed of their frenzy for possessions and domination and will become artisans for peace."[15]

Bishop Hamao's message, with its clear Buddhist overtones, was not picked up by Pope John Paul when he presented his teaching on reconciliation in response to the synod, in the apostolic exhortation *Reconciliatio et Poenitentia* (*Reconciliation and Penance*). In the exhortation the pope emphasized the divisions and conditions that lead to the breakdown of peace, but peace and harmony *with nature* were not included in his analysis. In the discussion of sin, no mention was made of the abuse of nature as a sin against God and creation. In discussing the rituals of reconciliation no mention was made of rituals to heal the scars and exploitation of mother earth.

At the very end of 1987 Pope John Paul II issued the encyclical *Sollicitudo Rei Socialis* (*On Social Concern*), which addressed ecology in a fairly substantial way. John Paul expanded the notion of true development initiated by Pope Paul VI in *Populorum Progressio*. To Pope Paul's teaching that development integrates human rights, spiritual values, and opportunity for growth without being subordinated to economic indicators alone, Pope John Paul II adds a new respect for the natural world and for environmental sustainability. We read:

> Nor can the moral character of development exclude respect for the beings which constitute the natural world...called the "cosmos."...A true concept of development cannot ignore the use of the elements of nature, the renewability of resources and the consequences of haphazard industrialization—three considerations which alert our conscience to the moral dimension of development. (par. 34)

Sean McDonagh offers an assessment of *Sollicitudo*, noting its strengths and weaknesses from a Third World perspective:

> The encyclical rightly challenges and often condemns development theories and strategies which give precedence to economic over social or moral considerations and in the process aggravate the plight of most people living in the Third World. The Pope recognizes that development for a fraction of humanity—the middle class in First World countries and the Third World elite—has been achieved through exploiting cheap labour and primary commodities from Third World countries. He overlooks the fact that it has also been achieved at the cost of precious topsoil, the elimination of forests with their unique flora and fauna and the poisoning of their rivers, springs, lakes and air.[16]

Finally, in 1990 we have a document from a pope devoted *exclusively* to environmental concerns—Pope John Paul II's World Day of Peace Message, *Peace with God the Creator, Peace with All Creation*.[17] This text is a *breakthrough* in Roman Catholic official teaching on the environment; the style is lively, the coverage is comprehensive, the analysis is incisive and communicates a note of urgency. The text addresses specific problems and does not remain on an abstract philosophical level. It looks at the "greenhouse" effect, acid rain, soil erosion, destruction of marine resources, tropical deforestation, and the waste of resources consumed by spending on armaments. In moving to a deeper analysis of the root causes of our ecological crisis the pope offers a *critique of technology* that is a significant shift from previous magisterial teaching. He also warns that *consumerism and instant self-gratification* are root causes of our environmental predicament.

> Modern society will find no solution to the ecological problem unless it takes a serious look at its life-style. In many parts of the world, society is given to instant gratification and consumerism

while remaining indifferent to the damage which they cause....
Simplicity, moderation, and discipline, as well as a spirit of sacrifice,
must become part of everyday life, lest all suffer the negative consequences of the careless habits of a few. (par. 1)

At the end of the statement Pope John Paul II broadens the "pro-life"
agenda of the church: "Respect for life and for the dignity of the human
person extends also to the rest of creation, which is called to join man in
praising God (cf. Ps 148:96)" (par. 16). This document opens a new
chapter in the church's teaching on the moral and religious nature of
respect for creation.

Father McDonagh was enthusiastic about the 1990 message, calling it
"a landmark in the greening of the Church. One hopes and prays that the
pope's voice will be heard and acted upon in parishes, Church schools,
and dioceses around the world."[18] McDonagh did have two critical comments on the statement: one on the lack of attention to the impact of
ecological destruction on poor women, and the second on the refusal to
look at the pressure that rapid population growth places on the limited
resources of the biosphere. I would add the criticism that our environmental vision must not only include the impact on women but also how
racism and environmental pollution are often linked. (We will pick up
these criticisms in the next section after we have finished giving the
chronology of the official teaching.)

Centesimus Annus *and* Evangelium Vitae
—*Ecologically Disappointing*

A year after the 1990 Day of Peace message the pope seemed to return to
his previous approach to environmental issues—that of benign neglect.
In *Centesimus Annus* (1991) John Paul continued to focus on consumerism as the reason for environmental devastation. In this letter the
pope is supportive of market structures while he also urges people to
avoid consumerism. The market system is dependent on consumerism,
so, it is hard to have it both ways. Tom Landy comments that "what John
Paul gives in consideration to the environment with one hand, he takes
back with the other." The pope turned his attention from ecological devastation to focus on the "more serious" destruction of the *human* environment. "Only the year before, in his 1990 World Day of Peace address,
he had offered a more articulated vision of the relationship of ecological

degradation to poverty, and of the need for eradication of poverty if environmental protection is to have meaning and take root. Unfortunately, the nuance of that message is somewhat lost in *Centesimus Annus*."[19]

On March 25, 1995, Pope John Paul II issued his 11th encyclical, *Evangelium Vitae* (*The Gospel of Life*).[20] The cardinals of the church who met in Rome in April 1991 had asked him to reaffirm the value of human life in the light of present circumstances and attacks threatening it today.

Pope John Paul II did defend the value of human life especially in terms of dual threats of abortion and euthanasia. Minimal attention is given to how the "Gospel of Life" extends to the rest of creation—two out of 194 pages. In these sections the pope clearly establishes the "lordship which God bestows on man. It is a matter first of all of dominion over the earth and over every living creature" (par. 42). Later in the document he quotes, approvingly, Gregory of Nyssa: "Man is a king. Created to exercise dominion over the world." John Paul tempers this kingship and dominion:

> Man's lordship however is not absolute, but ministerial: It is a real reflection of the unique and infinite lordship of God. Hence man must exercise it with wisdom and love, sharing in the boundless wisdom and love of God.... Through obedience to God's holy law...he is the "minister of God's plan." (par. 52)

There is little or no sense that humanity is part of creation as fellow creatures with other species, each deserving respect. In fact, John Paul seems to go out of his way to establish the gap between humanity and the rest of creation: "The life which God gives man is quite different from the life of all other living creatures inasmuch as man, although formed from the dust of the earth, is a manifestation of God in the world, a sign of his presence, a trace of his glory.... In man there shines forth a reflection of God himself" (par. 34). What does this say about the rest of creation? Doesn't creation also reflect the presence and the glory of God?

Evaluation of Papal Teaching on the Environment

We may wonder why Pope John II hasn't continued the fine directions laid out in his 1990 statement. As outsiders to Vatican realities we really do not know. My suspicion is that the two recent encyclicals truly reflect the mind of the pope on ecology, for they are consistent with the minimal attention given to this topic in previous statements. The 1990 statement could be seen as a positive "blip" on the screen, but it did not signal a major redirection on the question. The pope also is surrounded by a variety of advisors with different approaches to ecology. The very influential Cardinal Joseph Ratzinger, the prefect of the Congregation for the Doctrine of the Faith, has criticized environmentalists. According to Sean McDonagh, "He threw cold water on the ecumenical meeting in Assisi in 1986 organized by the World Wide Foundation." The "Greens," are "a blend of ill-defined romanticism with elements of Marxism and even stronger strains of liberalism—none of which he has much time for." Ratzinger is very critical of the environmentalists' position. Cardinal Ratzinger claims that some environmentalists have a

> somewhat antitechnical, somewhat antirational concept that has an antihumanist element. It presents man as having, by his thinking and action, destroyed the beauty and equilibrium that once existed. That would mean that man had moved backward in regard to himself. That seems to me the position of one who no longer recognizes himself in himself, who even has a kind of hate of himself and his history. [21]

If Pope John Paul II shares the perspective of Cardinal Ratzinger it is clear why the *Evangelium Vitae* has a defensive tone of reestablishing or clarifying human dominion over creation. To be fair, John Paul does not defend the domination of creation; rather, he reinforces a vision of creation and ecological ethics that is clearly anthropocentric. He teaches that humanity is different from the rest of creation and we are to be ministers of God's plan. The use of patristic and medieval images of "lord" and "king" can inadvertently support notions of humanity's attempts to "master" nature and exploit the rest of creation for our needs and desires. The language he used and the passages from the Bible that he selects tend to create or maintain a dualism between humanity and the rest of creation, just as the pope maintains a dualism of the spiritual over the material.

The 1990 statement may represent other voices in the Vatican, perhaps the Pontifical Commission *Iustitia et Pax*, scientists at the Pontifical Academy of Sciences, or the voices of other bishops and national conferences that had issued pastoral letters on environmental issues prior to 1990, including the bishops of the Philippines, the Dominican Republic, Guatemala, and northern Italy.[22]

In defense of the encyclical *Evangelium Vitae,* it is clear that abortion and euthanasia are serious moral issues in all First World nations. They are complex questions that deserve sustained moral, biblical, and theological reflection, as found in the letter. My criticism is that Pope John Paul II missed an opportunity to develop a holistic vision that addresses *all the threats to life*—life in all its diverse and rich expressions. The "Gospel of Life" should cover all areas of life, human and non-human. That vision has taken root in some parts of the church and many groups and religions outside of the church. One example of Catholic teaching on the environment that takes a different approach is the 1988 pastoral letter of the bishops of the Philippines.

FILIPINO BISHOPS: "WHAT IS HAPPENING TO OUR BEAUTIFUL LAND?"

The bishops of the Philippines take an entirely different approach. They were not afraid to write a pastoral letter that listens to the wisdom of tribal peoples and simple Filipinos, as well as to scientists and environmentalists. The Filipino bishops have produced a document that is "distinctly Filipino in its references and attitudes. Its emphasis is not an appeal to the encyclical tradition... .Though balanced and orthodox, it does not appear to be looking over its shoulder toward Rome."[23] The Filipino bishops view ecology as the ultimate "pro-life issue."

The theology of the letter is simple and straightforward. It is based on the creation themes of Genesis, the covenant with Moses before the people of Israel entered the promised land, and the simple exhortation to choose life over death, "that you and your descendants will live" (Deut 30:19–20). The letter successfully links concern for the poor with concern for the environment. It first describes the pervasive destruction of the forests and coral reefs and the resulting loss of topsoil and fishing grounds. In rupturing the relationship with the land and the sea the people also suffer. For the poor, the outcome is less nutritious food, poorer health, and an uncertain future. So the bishops of the Philippines call for an end to a "plunder economy of consumption, greed, and disregard for others." Such an exploitative mentality, they argue, erodes both the human and natural ecologies.

Tom Landy notes:

> The Filipino document is an interesting contrast to much of the first world discourse on the environment. First of all, it lacks any individualist reference or appeal to rights. It only speaks of relationships, community, shared faith, our ability to learn from and nurture each other.... The document only speaks of "we" and exhorts Filipinos as a community to solve the problems that only Filipinos

as a community can solve. While perhaps not noticeable, the presumption of community may be the most important contribution the document makes to larger discourse.[24]

The universal church could and will learn something from this non-clerical letter and the way the bishops were willing to listen to their people as they put forward a positive and inclusive vision.

Part II. Obstacles and Debated Questions

The previous sections have sketched out the emerging teaching on the environment from official Roman Catholic sources. The teaching seems to be unfolding in fits and starts rather than in a consistently developing body of thought. In some ways the papacy may find itself in a defensive and reactionary role amid the ecological movements and debates of contemporary society. The church's teaching on birth control, its anthropocentrism, its attitude toward women have all been identified as obstacles to a more vibrant ecological theology. We will summarize that debate in order to gain a better understanding of both the obstacles and opportunities that are part of the Roman Catholic emerging ethic of the environment.

JUDEO-CHRISTIAN ANTHROPOCENTRISM

In March 1967 the historian Lynn White, Jr., touched off a long-term debate on the role of Christianity in the ecological crisis with his article "The Historical Roots of Our Ecological Crisis," which appeared in *Science* magazine. White's thesis was that the Judeo-Christian tradition preached the message that it is *wrong to exploit people* but it is *right and proper to exploit nature*. He argued that an irreverent or dismissive attitude toward nature is grounded in Christian teaching and is widely accepted in the Western Hemisphere among both Christians and non-Christians.

In White's view, Christianity, by vigorously embracing Genesis' mandate to hold "dominion" over the earth and to "fill and subdue it," broke the hold of animistic belief in the intrinsic sacredness of nature. In this way Christianity set the preconditions for the emergence of modern science and technology in the West and thus bears a heavy burden of responsibility for our ecological degradation today. As White put it:

> Both our present science and our present technology are so tinctured with orthodox arrogance toward nature that no solution for

our ecological crisis can be expected from them alone. Since the roots of our trouble are so largely religious, the remedy must also be essentially religious, whether we call it that or not. We must rethink and refeel our nature and our destiny.[25]

Professor White concluded that Christianity was the most anthropocentric religion that the world had seen and that the environment had suffered incalculably as a result of rationalizations derived from anthropocentrism. Other analysts have also laid the blame for ecological destruction at the feet of Judeo-Christian theology.[26] Many theologians interested in ecology adopted the White thesis uncritically. Other theologians evaluated White's thesis and, while admitting it had some truth, found it unconvincing.[27] One of them, Sister Anne M. Clifford, wonders whether White "may be overly influenced by what 'dominion' implies to the mind of a twentieth-century English speaker."[28] At the same time his writing and the works of other environmentalists have caused a reexamination of our interpretation of the notion of "dominion" as described in the book of Genesis.[29]

While White's thesis can be debated, the important question underlying the debate is, how do Roman Catholic theological and moral teachings shape a Catholic's attitude toward nature and creation? There are themes and threads in the Judeo-Christian tradition that tend to support a disregard for nature. There are also significant aspects of the Christian tradition that provide a positive rationale for respecting and healing the earth. The various church documents we have been discussing have been trying to articulate the theological vision of a pro-environment ethic. It is important to be attentive to the underlying theological themes and assumptions that may undercut a constructive eco-theology. These, *potentially negative, assumptions* include a fear of pantheism, a disregard for this life in favor the next life, dualism, asceticism, hierarchical worldview, and the church's attitude toward women and sexuality, population control, and environmental racism.

When the Hebrew people accepted radical monotheism, they rejected belief in many gods. God was seen as transcendent, standing apart from nature. Jews and Christians, in their *radical monotheism*, refused to identify God with nature and believed in God's power over nature. By separating God from 'nature, the earth may have become less holy to monotheists than it had been or is to pantheists. The church feared the tendencies to see God in creation as a reversion to pantheism. Church leaders and theologians often overreacted to this fear of pantheism.

Another obstacle to appreciating nature is found in Christianity's teaching about heaven and the next life. In the Christian vision, our union with God in heaven is the ultimate value; everything else is of secondary value. This has led to giving less importance to the things of this life. Augustine, for instance, taught that we should use the things of this life, but not enjoy them—they may distract us from our true destiny and home. The image he suggested was that we should use creation like a shipwrecked person would cling to a plank to reach home.

DUALIST THINKING

The assumption that reality consists in dual realms: earth and heaven, time and eternity, matter and spirit, good and evil, the natural and the supernatural, has been a constant temptation and heresy for Christians. In dualist thinking the spiritual, non-material reality is more highly valued. The Manichaean version of dualism that infected the church of the fourth, fifth, and sixth centuries held that the created world was a product of the devil and that procreation itself was a great evil. Christian theology, even though it rejected the Manichaean heresy, is permeated with dualist thinking. Beginning with the Greek Fathers and Augustine the church has implicitly accepted the neo-Platonic thinking that gave greater importance to the spiritual and rational realms. The soul was viewed as "imprisoned" in the body. Yes, the creed taught the sacredness of the body ("resurrection of the body") but the lived spirituality of many generations of Christians exhibited a fear and distrust of nature and their own bodies. Christian spirituality included a strong emphasis on *asceticism*, which requires self-denial and discipline of the body so as to enable one to reject the temptations and sin of this life, clarify and focus one's desires, and thereby draw closer to the transcendent God.[30]

The Christian church in its spirituality and its theology adopted a *hierarchical worldview* in which everything and every class of people are assigned a place. The higher levels control and direct the lower levels. Anthropocentrism, patriarchy, and domination often follow. In the patriarchal system male metaphors for God, such as Father, King, Ruler, and Lord are commonly used. As was noted above, Pope John Paul uses these metaphors for God and human dominion over creation. As theologian and educator Eileen Flynn states:

> Anthropocentrism is the logical corollary of the patriarchal-hierar-

chical religious systems. The superior status of the male human is taken for granted along with the assumption that the goods of nature, ranked far below humans in the grading system, exist solely for the use of humans.[31]

SEXUALITY AND BIRTH CONTROL

Sexuality and women were (and are) both revered and feared in the Christian tradition. Christian tradition has been shaped by a patriarchal worldview that implies that women are inferior. When patriarchy is combined with hierarchical and dualist thinking the end product is not conducive to constructing a positive ecological theology and ethic. Roman Catholic theology and morality have been shaped by these anti-nature assumptions even though, ironically, the church's moral theology has been articulated under the rubric of "natural law."

The Catholic church's teaching on sexuality and birth control has been seen by many as an obstacle to developing a realistic and comprehensive ecological tradition. The official teaching of the church recognizes the importance of responsible parenthood and the need to limit the number of births. Bishop James Malone summarizes official teaching on this point:

> In the eyes of many people, the Catholic Church is saddled with much of the blame for what are generally perceived to be unsustainable population growth rates.
>
> But despite the misconceptions that some may hold, Catholic teaching does not favor the largest possible families. On the contrary, Pope Paul VI in 1967 asserted the need for responsible parenthood, which, he explained, was limiting family size to the number of children that parents could reasonably care for. But he opposed the use of certain methods of limiting family size that, he taught, ran counter to human dignity.
>
> This teaching has been affirmed by Pope John Paul II, and it has been affirmed and asserted by Catholic bishops.[32]

The conflict is not around the "what" but the "how." The official teaching accepts only those methods of birth control that respect the "natural rhythms" of the woman's ovulation cycle. Yet these methods are not the ones preferred by the majority of Catholic women.[33] Arguments from the Third World are found on either side of the debate, just as in the First World.[34] The church's teaching on contraception will continue to be debated.

The church's birth control teaching is also a reminder that population control can often be a First World response to social problems, as if to say: "We could solve these social problems if *the poor* did not have so many children." This implies that the middle classes and the rich do not want to change their consumption levels or redistribute the resources of the earth in a more equitable fashion. The church's position points out that the environmental problems we face cannot be resolved by only addressing the question of population control, but also by addressing questions of economic justice.

While admitting the value of these concerns about a contraceptive mentality and the question of economic justice, it also seems that the church's position inhibits a free and full discussion of the population issues as part of an ecological ethic. Can the Catholic church claim to be "pro-life" in the broadest sense of that term? Father McDonagh argues that:

> ...the pro-life argument needs to be seen within the widest context of the fragility of the living planet. Is it really pro-life to ignore the warnings of demographers and ecologists who predict that unbridled population growth will lead to severe hardship and an increase in the infant mortality rate for succeeding generations? Is it pro-life to allow the extinction of hundreds of thousands of living species which will ultimately affect the well-being of all future generations on the planet? ...Is it pro-life to ignore the increase in population levels to such an extent that the living systems in particular regions are becoming so impoverished that they will never recover?... In setting out to defend human life in a narrow anthropocentric context, we might be creating the conditions that will, in fact, endanger all life on earth.[35]

Later in his book *The Greening of the Church*, McDonagh argues that the official church is not taking leadership on the environment because it is not squarely facing the population problem.

> ...one reason why the leadership of the Catholic Church has given the ecological movement a wide berth is because of its position on population. Any comprehensive discussion of ecological problems inevitably includes a discussion of the rate of population growth. ...The Catholic Church is not facing up to the magnitude of this problem.[36]

RACISM AND ENVIRONMENTAL ABUSE

All citizens are affected by the health hazards associated with environmental pollution, such as poor air and water quality, but there is mounting evidence that ethnic and racial minorities suffer disproportionately. For example,

- The nation's largest hazardous waste landfill, receiving waste from 45 states, is located in predominantly black and poor Sumter County, Alabama;

- The predominantly black and Hispanic Southside of Chicago has perhaps the greatest concentration of hazardous waste sites in the nation;

- In Houston, Texas, six of the eight municipal landfills are located in predominantly black neighborhoods;

- The Navajo community in Shiprock, New Mexico, where over 100 million tons of uranium mill tailings flooded the Rio Puerco, is one of numerous Native American communities near uranium mills and nuclear facilities;[37] and

- A 1983 report issued by the U.S. General Accounting Office documented that 75 percent of hazardous-waste landfills were located in poor African American and Latino communities.[38]

The United Church of Christ Commission for Racial Justice has been studying this issue since 1982. After five years of study the Commission released a report that was the first comprehensive national study to document the disproportionate location of waste sites in racial and ethnic communities. Some of its findings are:

- Race consistently proved to be the most significant among factors tested in association with the location of commercial hazardous waste facilities;

- More than 15 million blacks and 8 million Hispanics lived in communities with one or more uncontrolled toxic waste sites; and

- Forty percent of the nation's total commercial hazardous waste landfill capacity was located in three predominantly black and Hispanic communities.[39]

The communities of racial minorities and the poor are often chosen intentionally because they have less political and economic power. For example, on December 12, 1991, the chief economist of the World Bank, Lawrence Summers, argued that toxic pollution *should be located in poor countries*. He boldly stated "I think the economic logic behind dumping a load of toxic waste in the lowest-wage country is impeccable and we should face up to that."[40]

The thread of racism is implicit in this "purely economic" line of reasoning because poor countries are overwhelmingly nonwhite. Recent studies found that race and under-representation on governing boards were significant factors, *independent of poverty and low incomes*.[41]

The Roman Catholic theologian Rosemary Radford Ruether addresses this linkage between the poor and the environment:

> The environmental movement needs to be about more than saving seals and defending public parks from lumber companies, although these are worthy causes. It needs to speak of environmental racism and classism, about the poisoning of the environments where poor black, Latino, and indigenous people live in inner cities and rural areas. An environmental movement that does not make these connections across class and racial lines is an escapism for hikers, and not a serious call for change in the industrial system's disregard of its ecological base.[42]

If the churches are to defend the dignity of every person, they will have to confront the reality of environmental racism that attacks the poor and people of color disproportionately.

At the same time people of color and the poor are not waiting for the official church to condemn the sin of environmental racism. They are creating culturally diverse grass-roots movements for environmental justice. "Formerly divided by race and class, and separated by geography, dozens of grass-roots groups over the last twenty years have begun to forge new alliances to combat corporations poisoning their communities, workplaces, and children."[43] Sometimes the grass-roots people lead, and church leadership follows.

This section has pointed out a few issues and assumptions that have been obstacles for Roman Catholic theology as it begins to construct a ecological theology. These underlying assumptions need critical reflection and purification before the church can move ahead. At the same time, the Catholic tradition has powerful theological and spiritual resources that can serve as the garden for a healthy earth ethic.

Part III. Roman Catholic Ecological Potential

While the official church teachings on the environment have been meager, Catholic moral and spiritual traditions have many resources that can be "recovered" and developed as the basis for vibrant ecological theology. Some of the more obvious resources are: the church's social teachings, sacramental theology and practice, spirituality, the "realism" of Thomistic thought, and the "catholic" orientation to be "inclusive" and "universal."

SOCIAL TEACHINGS

The official social teachings of the church offer a moral vision that can help shape a distinctive Catholic environmental ethic. In their 1991 statement *Renewing the Earth,* the U.S. bishops stated that the following "themes drawn from this tradition are integral dimensions of ecological responsibility":

- a *God-centered and sacramental view of the universe,* which ground human accountability for the fate of the earth;

- a consistent *respect for human life,* which extends to respect for all creation;

- a worldview affirming the ethical significance of *global interdependence and the common good;*

- an *ethics of solidarity* promoting cooperation and a just structure of sharing in the world community;

- an understanding of the *universal purpose of created things,* which requires equitable use of the earth's resources;

- an *option for the poor,* which gives passion to the quest for an equitable and sustainable world;

- a conception of *authentic development,* which offers a direction for progress that respects human dignity and the limits of material growth.[44]

These principles of the Catholic social tradition can be used to create a moral vision that is attentive to environmental issues.

SACRAMENTALITY

A second resource is Catholic sacramental theology, practice, and vision. According to Kenneth and Michael Himes,

> A sacrament is not a stand-in for something else, a visible sign for some other invisible reality. The essence of a sacrament is the capacity to reveal grace, the agapic self-gift of God, by being what it is. By being thoroughly itself, a sacrament bodies forth the absolute self-donative love of God that undergirds both it and the entirety of creation. The Catholic community has recognized seven particular events as being revelatory of grace. *But every creature, human and non-human, animate and inanimate, can be a sacrament....* The discovery that every creature, including oneself, is a sacrament of the love of God that causes all things to be provides the deepest foundation for reverencing creation. By its nature a sacrament requires that it be appreciated for what it is and not as a tool to an end, in Buber's terms, a sacrament is always "thou."[45]

The Catholic sacramental system uses the elements of creation: water, ashes, oil, fire, wine, and bread in sacred worship.[46] According to Bishop Anthony Pilla of Cleveland, "Catholic sacramental practice embraces the gifts of creation and uses them for praise and thanksgiving. Fundamental to that practice is the conviction that creation is itself holy and is appropriately used for worship."[47] We view all of creation as a sacrament of God.[48] We have rich biblical and theological and mystical traditions that tell us of the holiness of creation. These insights have not yet been fully expressed in our liturgy, in our ethical teaching, and in our behavior. The poetry of Thomas Merton, a socially engaged Trappist monk, captures this appreciation of the sacramentality of creation:

> The forms and individual characters of living and growing things, of inanimate beings, of animal and flowers and all nature, constitute their holiness in the sight of God.

> Their inscape is their sanctity. It is the imprint of His Wisdom and His reality in them.

> The special clumsy beauty of this particular colt on this April day in this field under these clouds is a holiness consecrated to God by His own creative wisdom and it declares the glory of God.

> The pale flowers of the dogwood outside this window are saints.

The little yellow flowers that nobody notices on the edge of that road are saints looking up into the face of God.

This leaf has its own texture and its own pattern of veins and its own holy shape, the bass and the trout hiding in the deep pools of the river are canonized by their beauty and their strength.

The lakes hidden among the hills are saints, and the sea too is a saint who praises God without interruption in her majestic dance.

The great, gashed, half-naked mountain is another of God's saints. There is no other like him. He is alone in his own character; nothing else in the world ever did or ever will imitate God in quite the same way. That is his sanctity.[49]

REREADING ST. THOMAS

While I do not want to err by reading "eco-theology" into Thomistic thought, I believe we are on solid ground if we reread Aquinas to discover his attitude toward nature. We shall reclaim insights from Aquinas that are helpful today, just as we recognize that not everything he wrote is of lasting value. I would highlight two central theological assumptions of St. Thomas that can be used as the foundation of an eco-theology: a) the sacredness of everything that exists, and b) that the diversity of creation more adequately reveals God than any *one* species—even humanity.

In the doctrine on creation in the *Summa Theologica* Thomas writes, "Because God by virtue of his essence is existence itself, therefore the existence of what He has created is necessarily a producing peculiar to His essence.... Therefore *God must be in all things, and in the most intimate manner.*"[50] Thomas teaches that every existing thing—whether alive or not, material or spiritual, perfected or wretched—everything that has existence, confronts us in the most direct way with the primal reality of God. This means that because the being of the world participates in the divine being that pervades it to its innermost core, the world is not only a good world, it is in a very precise sense *holy* and deserving of respect.

In another place in the *Summa Theologica* Thomas talks about the necessary diversity in creation:

> For God brought things into being in order that God's goodness might be communicated to creatures, and be represented by them; and because God's goodness could not be adequately represented by

one creature alone, God produced many and diverse creatures, that what was wanting to one in the representation of the divine goodness might be supplied by another. For goodness, which in God is simple and uniform, in creatures is manifold and divided; and hence the whole universe together participates [in] the divine goodness more perfectly, and represents it better than any single creature whatever.[51]

This thinking was revolutionary in its day, which accepted the Platonic categories that clearly separated God from the created order. It is still revolutionary today. If we appreciated these theological insights we would more easily translate that sense of the sacredness of creation into our contemporary theology and worship.

Other students of St. Thomas have been rereading his corpus to establish a linkage between his work and the contemporary development of a theocentric environmental ethic. Two recent doctoral dissertations have studied this question.[52] Pamela A. Smith suggests twelve themes of "ecothomism":

1. a faith-filled sense of the "unity of the world";

2. a reverence for all creatures;

3. an appreciation for the simultaneous "intrinsic value" and "instrumental value" of nonhuman creatures;

4. an active support of creaturely diversity;

5. the extension of moral consideration to all living things;

6. an exercise of providence on behalf of the universal common good;

7. a healthy hierarchicalism;

8. a general stance of nonaggression;

9. personal moderation and the search for sustainable living;

10. a commitment to Earth-healing and restoration;

11. the pursuit of integrally virtuous living; and

12. the study and reinterpretation of viable traditions.[53]

Continued discussion and analysis are necessary to clarify how to use

Thomistic theology and ethics as a resource for contemporary Catholic eco-theology.

CATHOLIC SPIRITUAL TRADITIONS

Politicians, activists, and analysts are saying that the ecological crisis is not just an economic or scientific problem, but a spiritual problem. For example, Vice President Al Gore's best-selling book, *Earth in the Balance: Ecology and the Human Spirit*, includes a specific call for a religious ethic of stewardship.[54] Tom Hayden, author and California state senator, explains his spirituality as an ecologist and politician:

> We need a spiritual base to sustain ourselves as human beings. I have come to the conclusion that being spiritual is not a choice on a menu of selections, but a matter of understanding that we are spiritual. It is part of being human to be connected to eternity and its cycles, to a living creation, something larger than ourselves.[55]

The Catholic tradition has many *spiritual traditions* that reflect a profound respect for God's creation. To be honest, the Catholic church also has spiritualities that are negative toward creation and the human body. It would be a shame if the richness of the spiritual tradition of a St. Francis of Assisi, a St. Benedict, or a Hildegard of Bingen were not constructive partners in the framing of a contemporary earth spirituality.

A few creative thinkers like Leonardo Boff, Matthew Fox, and Thomas Berry have been breaking new ground in this regard. An important linkage in a spirituality of creation is connecting our concern for the earth with our concern for the poor. Leonardo Boff, a Franciscan, has pointed out that the school where St. Francis gained his love for creation was actually his experience of ministering to lepers.[56] What allowed Francis to see the fraternity of all creation was the asceticism of poverty. Boff explained Francis' poverty as "a way of being by which the individual lets things be what they are; one refuses to dominate them, to subjugate them, and make them objects of the will to power." Francis, like the rest of creation, was a creature and therefore refused to dominate creation or other people.[57]

Concern for the poor and concern for all of life are cut of the same "seamless garment." The spiritual legacy of St. Francis pushes the church to link its concern for the poor with an equal regard for all of creation.

AN INCLUSIVE, WORLDWIDE PERSPECTIVE

This characteristic, like the previous ones, is a potential that needs to be developed. The very word "catholic" means universal, open to all. Both in membership and in methodology, the best of the Catholic tradition remains open, not closed in on itself, not parochial or sectarian. In practice, of course, the Roman Catholic church has not always lived up to this broad and inclusive perspective.

Openness to other religious voices is expressed in a number of ways: a) institutional collaboration, b) examining our pre-Christian roots, and c) a basic interest in and respect for the non-Christian perspectives.

1. An example of *institutional collaboration* (openness) is the establishment of the National Religious Partnership for the Environment in 1993. This partnership brought together the U.S. Catholic Conference, the National Council of Churches of Christ, the Coalition on the Environment and Jewish Life, and the Evangelical Environmental Network. While the member groups develop their own public policy initiative, the partnership has coordinated some joint lobbying and advocacy actions, such as the 1996 campaign opposing the revision of the Endangered Species Act.

The partnership sees its role as facilitating the religious connection on the environment as it emerges "spontaneously, independently, and diversely." In its first three years this broad-based interfaith and interdenominational alliance has distributed environmental education and action kits to nearly 10,000 congregations and has held leadership training for 2,000 key clergy and laypeople.

In February 1997 the National Partnership launched a three-year, $4 million campaign to make environmental protection part of the churches' response to the bipartisan abandonment of the poor, welfare reform, and other social justice issues. Citing the

> disproportionate rate of pollution-related disease in low-income neighborhoods—such as asthma, which is now the number one reason urban children are admitted to hospitals—the campaign is calling on the Clinton administration, Congress, and environmental groups to prioritize the needs of the poor in their programs to protect air, land and water.[58]

This partnership is a good start, but further outreach to other non-western religious traditions could be explored and developed, including Native American, Muslim, and Buddhist traditions.[59]

2. A second area of openness and "catholicity" is to reexamine our cultural and ethnic background to recover an appreciation of nature. Part of being Catholic is to be in touch with one's traditional roots and to be open to the voice of God in all people. Every ethnic community has the right and the challenge of understanding its *cultural and ethnic "roots."* The African American community has made significant efforts in this regard. The diverse Native American cultures are also struggling to protect their traditional cultural values. Asian Americans and European Americans should also be able to claim and celebrate their distinctive cultural heritage. Part of the challenge in all cultures is to discover the values that provide a respect and appreciation of creation. This may mean discovering and claiming the *pre-Christian cultural elements* that may have been forgotten or suppressed.

An example of this kind of cultural recovery is Tom Hayden's recent work *The Lost Gospel.* As a Roman Catholic, Irish-American, Tom has begun retracing his "Celtic spirituality as the lost gospel."

> My Irish ancestors could be called the Indians of Europe, a people who lived in clans and tribes, were warriors with a heroic view of life, and who communicated with spirits in the land and sea.... The early Irish created a culture that was energized and organized according to nature's sacred cycles.... Even after the Irish were converted to Christianity, their ties to nature spirituality remained so deep that theirs became the "greenest" church in Europe.

As the story unfolds Hayden notes that "thus the eternal aftermath to life increasingly became a consolation to a people who previously had rooted their spirituality in the seasons of the earth." He muses on the loss of these rich cultural roots: "I wonder today if the experience of expulsion from our own ethnic gardens doesn't reverberate as an unhealed pain in our memory and healing of loss."[60]

I suspect a similar story could be traced for all of our ancestors, whether they be the Germanic tribes who worshiped the sacred oak (which St. Boniface is "credited" with chopping down), or the Britons, or Scots or Vandals or Visigoths. It may be hard for us to connect with those distant cultures, but I believe we would benefit in many ways from knowing our deep, tribal heritage. We would find linkages with the tribal peoples of today, and we might find ways of correcting the dualism of our Christianity, which would provide a broader foundation for our ecotheology.

3. Openness to non-Christian spiritualities is another way to express and experience our catholicity. A Catholic approach to spirituality and theology maintains that God is free to speak to us in many ways and through many voices. The Catholic approach teaches that God spoke in a preeminent way in Jesus Christ, the Word of God, but God speaks in other ways as well—through nature, through the web of our relationships, even through *other religions*. Thomas Merton's life is an example of this. The last chapter of his life was a journey to the East to dialogue with Buddhist monks in Bangkok, Thailand. He wanted to hear of their understanding of God and learn from their spiritual journey.

The same openness to the East is happening in the environmental movement and in spirituality. For example, "in recent years both the Dalai Lama and Thich Nhat Hanh have spread a powerful environmental message to the West, deepening the green roots of Buddhism in America. The Dalai Lama proposes a visionary liberation of his people: '... my dream [is] that the entire Tibetan plateau should become a free refuge where humanity and nature can live in peace and harmonious balance.'" Thich Nhat Hanh is an exiled Vietnamese Buddhist living in France whose many works emphasize nature, reminiscent of St. Francis.[61]

Interfaith discourse is not just a dream. It has already begun. In 1986 representatives of five world religions, Christianity, Judaism, Hinduism, Islam, and Buddhism met in Assisi. Representatives of these faiths gathered in "a beautiful and historic act of celebration—of prayer" in the historic Basilica of St. Francis, the church where the saint is buried. This gathering was not called by a religious leader but by Prince Philip, the Duke of Edinburgh, in his capacity as president of the World Wide Fund for Nature.

Each of the faiths celebrated some aspect of their worship and ritual, such as choir music, dance, and the blowing of the ram's horn. Five thoughtful statements were delivered.[62] These statements explained each tradition's theological basis, "grounded in its own unique tradition and history, for supporting the conservation of nature." Conservationist William K. Reilly notes:

> Those statements are very powerful appeals to the faithful, to believers, to recognize the implications of their beliefs for their conduct regarding the environment. They have had a great influence on subsequent thinking within in each of those religions. Later the Bahais and the Sikhs joined in preparing statements of their own. A great deal of activity, of reflection, of research, has flowed from that event.

> All this occurred because Prince Philip believed that the cause of conservation was in very serious need of spiritual definition and reinforcement.[63]

Roman Catholic leadership did not take the initiative in these interfaith meetings. At times "the world" (a secular prince) will lead and the church will follow, but the Catholic church has the *possibility* of being a leader and not only a reluctant follower in recognizing the diverse ways God communicates with humanity.

Some of the most overlooked voices and witness of respectful living for the North American church are the voices and lives of America's *indigenous peoples*. The wisdom of the "first Americans" was noted by Bishop John McRaith of Owensboro, Kentucky:

> Until recently, concern for God's gifts of nature—the land, water, air and living things—was seen as an extremist approach and a threat to the established way of doing things. Now there is a growing realization that through our lack of respect for God's creation we are destroying our very life-support system, the Earth. The first Americans have always known this; in fact they understand that "the earth is precious to (God) and to harm the earth is to heap contempt on its Creator" (Letter of Chief Seattle to president Franklin Pierce, 1854).[64]

Any dialogue between Christianity and Native American worldviews must recognize that there are many voices and experiences to attend to. Native spokespeople say that there are over 500 distinct cultural traditions that still maintain sacred traditions and relations with creation throughout the North American continent.[65]

Despite the great variety of cultures and terrain the native peoples may occupy, there are common elements in their worldview and spirituality that would be beneficial for the larger community to appreciate and perhaps make their own. Let me share only a tiny sampling of this spiritual wisdom.

From the Six Nations Iroquois Confederacy, known as the Haudenosaunee ("Haudenosaunee" means "people who build," and is the proper name of the people of the Longhouse) we hear the following in their document entitled *Basic Call to Consciousness*:

> We believe that all living things are spiritual beings. Spirits can be expressed as energy form manifested in matter—grass matter. ...
>
> The original instructions direct that we who walk about on the Earth

are to express a great respect, an affection, and a gratitude toward all the spirits which create and support Life. We give a greeting and thanksgiving to the many supporters of our lives—the corn, beans, squash, the winds, the sun. When people cease to respect and express gratitude for these many things, then all life will be destroyed, and human life on this planet will come to an end....

The people who are living on this planet need to break with the narrow concept of human liberation, and begin to see liberation as something which needs to be extended to the whole of the Natural World. What is needed is the liberation of all the things that support Life—the air, the waters, the trees—all the things which support the sacred web of Life....

The renewable quality—the sacredness of every living thing, that which connects human beings to the place which they inhabit—the quality is the single most liberating aspect of our environment. Life is renewable and all the things which support life are renewable, and they are renewed by a force greater than any government's, greater than any living or historical thing. A consciousness of the web that holds all things together, the spiritual element that connects us to reality and the manifestation of an eagle or a mountain snowfall—that consciousness was the first thing which was destroyed by the colonizers.[66]

It is a shame to touch so briefly on a document so rich with spiritual, relational and ecological wisdom. Let me conclude with a few lines on "reciprocity—a foundation for balance:"

The general American Indian notion of reciprocity is fundamental to the human participation in world-balancing and harmony. Reciprocity involves first of all a spiritual understanding of the cosmos and the place of humans in the processes of the cosmic whole. It begins with an understanding that anything and everything that humans do has an effect on the rest of the world around us. Even when we cannot clearly know what that effect is in any particular act, we know that there is an effect.... Knowing that every action has its unique effect has always meant that there had to be some sort of built-in compensation for human actions, some act of reciprocity....

We are so much a part of the whole of creation and its balance that anything we do to perpetuate an act of violence [e.g., hunting], even when it is necessary for our own survival, must be accompanied by an act of spiritual reciprocation intended to restore the balance of existence....

Animals, birds, crops, and medicines are all living relatives and must be treated with respect if they are to be genuinely efficacious for the people.[67]

The Roman Catholic church is just beginning to open its doors to the spiritual wisdom of the Native American peoples. In 1992 the U.S. bishops recognized that "the coming of religious faith in this land began not 500 years ago, but centuries before in the prayers, chants, dance, and other sacred celebrations of native people."[68] Earlier when Pope John Paul II met with Native Americans he said, "I encourage you, as native people... to preserve and keep alive your cultures, your language, the values and customs which have served you well in the past and which provide a solid foundation for the future."[69]

The future is hopeful if the church is willing to listen to the wisdom and spiritual truth of Native American peoples to build a spiritual and moral vision that cares for "brother sun and sister moon" as well as all the creatures of the cosmos.

Conclusion

As we look back over official Catholic social teaching we see a tradition that has potential to offer a solid base for ecological theology. But that potential has not been well used in the church's teachings. Some Catholic theologians and activists have begun to explore these themes. There are only a few "green shoots" of creative articulation and vision. As of this date the official teachings have not shifted to include a consistent and wholehearted commitment to developing an ecological ethic and theology.

There is a fair amount of work to do on the Catholic church's "emerging earth ethic." The U.S. bishops realized in 1991 that the work is far from finished:

Although Catholic social teaching does not offer a complete environmental ethic, we are confident that this developing tradition can serve as the basis for Catholic engagement and dialogue with science, the environmental movement, and other communities of faith and good will.[70]

The best of the Catholic tradition will contribute to "this developing tradition" by a constructive and critical "engagement and dialogue" with the sciences, the environmental movement, and the spiritual and moral wisdom of other faith traditions as well. The very future of humanity and all life on earth depends on this joint effort.

Discussion Questions

1. Pope John Paul II has an uneven track record on environmental statements. What are some reasons for this?

2. Professor White blames Christianity for a domineering attitude toward nature. In what ways are his remarks true and in what ways do they distort Christian theology and practice?

3. The issue of population control is a complex question. What different perspectives are evident from a Third World perspective?

4. What are some linkages between racism and environmental injustice?

5. Which of the Roman Catholic "potentials" for developing a deeper theology of ecology do you find most compelling and promising?

6. How can the Catholic church be open to the "voices" of non-Christian spiritualities and understandings of creation without losing its own distinctive voice?

Conclusion

This book tells us something of the richness, diversity, limitations, and hope of the Catholic social tradition as it is expressed in the lives of men and women and in the documents it has inspired. Our treatment has not been exhaustive, but rather illustrative of what it means to live out the Christian faith in a complex society. There are other movements that could have been studied and other documents that could have been analyzed, but I hope that you have picked up on the richness of these lives and this moral vision.

It has been invigorating to write about the courageous Christians who are part of our tradition of social justice. My hope is that we will be faithful witnesses of this rich and developing tradition. Father John Coleman captures what I am trying to say:

> Ultimately, the future of this tradition will depend less on our ability to parrot its significant terms such as subsidiarity, a just wage, etc., and more on our ability to read the signs of the times in fidelity to the Gospel of human dignity as Leo, Pius XI and XII, John—with all their historical limitations, biases and failures—tried to do in their times. History will surely unveil all too well our shortcomings. May it also—as it does for this legacy of the popes—show our prophetic vision and courageous action.[1]

Source Notes

INTRODUCTION

1. Peter Henriot, Edward DeBerri and Michael Schultheis, *Catholic Social Teaching: Our Best Kept Secret* (Maryknoll, NY: Orbis Books, 1988).

2. Mary Elsbernd, "What Ever Happened to *Octogesima Adveniens?*" *Theological Studies* 56 (1995): 60.

3. Walter Abbott, ed., *Gaudium et Spes,* par. 11, *The Documents of Vatican II* (New York: Association Press, 1966), p. 209.

4. Edward Schillebeeckx, *Ministry: Leadership in the Community of Jesus Christ* (New York: Crossroad, 1981) and *The Church with a Human Face: A New and Expanded Theology of Ministry* (New York: Crossroad, 1985).

CHAPTER 1

1. Paul Misner, *Social Catholicism in Europe: From the Onset of Industrialization to the First World War* (New York: Crossroad, 1991), p. 79. For a history of this movement see; H. Daniel-Rops, "The Triumphant March of Social Catholicism," in *A Fight for God 1870-1939* (New York: Image Books, 1967), p. 128-165; J. B. Duroselle, *Les debuts du Catholicisme social en France: 1822-1870* (Paris: Presses Universitaires de France, 1951); Robert Talmy, *Aux Sources de Catholicisme Social: l'Ecole de La Tour du Pin* (Tournai: Desclee & Cie, 1963).

2. Misner, pp. 90-91.

3. Ibid., p. 91.

4. *Mainz Sermons,* quoted in George Metlake, *Ketteler's Christian Social Reform,* (Philadelphia: The Dolphin Press, 1912), pp. 34-35.

5. William E. Hogan, *The Development of Bishop Wilhelm Emmanuel Von Ketteler's Interpretation of the Social Problem* (Washington, D.C., 1946), p 165.

6. Misner, p. 505. While recognizing the importance of his leadership role in shaping social consciousness in Germany and in Europe, we can from our contemporary perspective note two rigid characteristics. First, Von Ketteler did not accept capitalism and offered instead a "corporatist" theory of the economy. To many Catholics this did not seem realistic, as capitalism was here to stay. Second, he placed an exaggerated emphasis on the role of the

Roman Catholic church. In his 1848 address to the first Catholic Congress Von Ketteler said, "It must now become evident which Church bears within it the power of divine truth. The world will see that to the Catholic Church is reserved the definite solution of the social question; for the State, with all its legislative machinery, has not the power to solve it." Edward Cahill, "The Catholic Social Movement: Historical Aspects," in Charles Curran and Richard McCormick, eds., *Readings in Moral Theology No. 5: Official Catholic Social Teaching* (New York: Paulist Press, 1986), p. 5. Today we would take a modest tone in articulating the role of the church.

7. Normand Paulhus, "Social Catholicism and the Fribourg Union," *Society of Christian Ethics: Selected Papers, 1980,* Joseph Allen, ed. (Waterloo, Ontario: Council on the Study of Religion, 1980), p. 65.

8. Cahill, p 12.

9. Ibid., p. 13.

10. Paulhus, p. 66.

11. Ibid., p. 69.

12. Normand Paulhus, "Fribourg Union," in Judith Dwyer, ed., *The New Dictionary of Catholic Social Thought* (Minneapolis, MN: Liturgical Press/Michael Glazier, 1994), p. 404; hereafter NDCST.

13. Cyrille Massard, *L'oeuvre sociale du Cardinal Mermillod: l'Union de Fribourg* (Louvain: Presses Universitaires, 1914), as quoted in Paulhus (1980), p. 64. A fuller study of the Fribourg Union is found in Paulhus' Ph.D. dissertation *The Theological and Political Ideals of the Fribourg Union* (Ann Arbor, MI: University Microfilms, 1983).

14. George Jarlot, "Les Avant-Projets de *Rerum Novarum,*" *Nouvelle Revue Theologique,* 81 (1959): 70-71, as quoted in Richard Camp, *The Papal Ideology of Social Reform: A Study in Historical Development* (Leiden: E.J. Brill, 1969), p. 79.

15. Camp, p. 73.

16. "1890 Minutes of the Fribourg Union, unedited documents," p. 21, cited in Paulhus (1980), p.74.

17. Ibid., pp. 78-79.

18. Ibid., p. 80.

19. "Rapport sur le regime corporatif—2e partie." Unedited manuscript, 1885, p.8, quoted in Paulhus (1980), p. 85.

20. Paulhus, "Fribourg Union," NDCST, p. 405.

21. Ibid., p. 405.

22. "L'Eglise dans le mond moderne" (Paris, 1975), p. 156; as cited in Marie-Dominique Chenu, *La Dottrina sociale della Chiesa: origine e sviluppo, 1891-1971* (Brescia: Queriniana, 1977), p. 12.

23. Michel Schooyans, perhaps too dramatically, states that "the actual publication of *Rerum Novarum* was profoundly surprising and unexpected... [it] stood out like a flash of lightning." "Catholic Social Thought to 1966; An Historical Outline," *Church Alert,* No. 17 November-December, 1977): 2.

24. Robert Bellah, et al., *Habits of the Heart: Individualism and Commitment in American Life* (Berkeley, CA: University of California Press, 1985).

25. Gerald Fogarty, "Leo XIII," NDCST, p. 546.

26. Ibid., pp. 546-547.

27. Aaron Abell, *American Catholicism and Social Action: A Search for Social Justice 1865-1950* (Garden City, NY: Doubleday, 1960), p. 73.

28. Fogarty, p. 546.

29. Stephen Pope, *"Rerum Novarum,"* NDCST, p. 829.

30. Henry Browne, *The Catholic Church and the Knights of Labor* (Washington, DC: Catholic University of America Press, 1949), p. 347; as cited by Francis Broderick, *Right Reverend New Dealer* (New York: Macmillan, 1963), p. 43.

31. Fogarty, p. 547.

32. David O'Brien and Thomas Shannon, eds., *Renewing the Earth: Catholic Documents on Peace, Justice and Liberation* (Garden City, NY: Image, 1977), p. 36; hereafter *Renewing the Earth.*

33. *"Rerum Novarum—A General Appraisal," Social Justice Review* (May/June, 1991): 72-73.

34. *"Rerum Novarum"* in David O'Brien and Thomas Shannon, eds., *Catholic Social Thought: the Documentary Heritage* (Maryknoll, NY: Orbis, 1992), pars. 51 and 62; hereafter RN.

35. RN par. 53.

36. Nell-Breuning, p.76.

37."Propriete, 'de Droit Naturel' These Neoscholastique et Tradition Scholastique," *Nouvelle Revue Theologique* 72 (1950): 582-86; as reported in Camp, 54-55.

38. *Social Justice Review,* p. 3.

39. Joseph Husslein, ed., *Social Wellsprings: Fourteen Epochal Documents by Pope Leo XIII,* (Milwaukee: Bruce, 1940), p. 234.

40. With the 100th anniversary of *Rerum Novarum* in 1991 a number of texts were produced to commemorate that event and to carry the discussion of Catholic social thought into the future.

The most obvious anniversary text was the encyclical of Pope John Paul II, *Centesimus Annus* (Washington D.C.: USCC, 1991). Other helpful texts include: John Coleman, ed., *One Hundred Years of Catholic Social Thought: Celebration and Challenge* (Maryknoll, NY: Orbis, 1991); Ronald Duska, ed., *Rerum Novarum: A Symposium Celebrating 100 Years of Catholic Social Thought* (Lewiston, NY: Edwin Mellen Press, 1991); George Weigel and Robert Royal, eds., *A Century of Catholic Social Thought: Essays on 'Rerum Novarum' and Nine other Key Documents* (Washington, D.C.: Ethics and Public Policy Center, 1991).

41. Anticlericalism should be understood in the broad sense of not only being anti-clergy, but anti-church as an influence in society.

42. Camp, pp. 5-6.

43. Ibid., p. 9.

44. Ibid., p. 8.

45. *Syllabus* 80, cited by S. Pope, NDCST, p. 829

46. Not all Catholics were opposed to socialism even though their pope and bishops were firmly opposed to this revolutionary movement. A few clergy joined the ranks of the social-ists. Father Thomas McGrady of Bellevue, Kentucky, as a utopian socialist, rejected *Rerum Novarum* for its acceptance of the profit motive, and he taunted Catholic leaders for their accommodation to the capitalist system. It is no surprise that he did not get along with his bishop, Camillus Maes, who eventually suspended him. McGrady left active ministry and retired in California. A second priest, Thomas Hagerty from Las Vegas, joined the socialist cause after experiencing the violent atmosphere of the Rocky Mountain mining camps. He became a very popular lecturer and was considered by one contemporary as "without a

doubt the brainiest and certainly one of the most eloquent speakers in the Labor and Socialist movement...." Jay Dolan, *The American Catholic Experience* (Garden City, NY: Image Books, 1985), p. 337.

Hagerty's radicalism caused his suspension; he worked with an anarchist group, the Industrial Workers of the World (the Wobblies) for some time, then ended up teaching Spanish under the alias "Ricardo Moreno" and by 1920 was on Chicago's skid row. James Hennesey, *American Catholics* (New York: Oxford University Press, 1981), 135.

More telling of Catholic grass-roots support for socialism than a few radical priests is the number of Catholics who supported socialist political candidates. Milwaukee was the best example of this. For a number of years in the early part of the twentieth century, the Socialist party ran the city of Milwaukee which was approximately 40% Catholic. Milwaukeeans elected a socialist mayor and over 1,000 socialist candidates to local office. David O'Brien, *Public Catholicism*, Second Edition (Maryknoll, NY: Orbis Books, 1996), p.135. The Socialist party was able to do this because German, Irish, and Polish Catholics voted for Socialists despite the anti-socialist stance of the pope, bishops, and clergy. See Dolan, p. 336.

47. John Coleman, "Development of Church Social Teaching," *Origins* 11 (June 4, 1981): 38.

48. Pope, p. 843.

49. Ibid., p. 843, emphasis added. A number of these points of lasting impact follow Stephen Pope's helpful summary, pp. 842-843.

50. Donal Dorr, *Option for the Poor: A Hundred Years of Catholic Social Teaching*, Revised Edition (Maryknoll, NY: Orbis Books, 1992), p. 16.

CHAPTER 2

1. Quoted in Zwierlein, *The Life and Letters of Bishop McQuaid, III*, p. 234, and found in Jay Dolan, *The American Catholic Experience: A History from Colonial Times to the Present* (Garden City, NY: Doubleday, 1985), pp. 313-314.

2. Dolan, pp. 311-312.

3. Ibid., p. 325.

4. Ibid.

5. Jeffrey Burns, "Knights of Labor," NDCST, pp. 513-514.

6. Dale Fetherling, *Mother Jones the Miners' Angel: A Portrait* (Carbondale: University of Illinois, 1974), p. 107.

7. Ibid., p. 193.

8. Mary (Harris) Jones, *Autobiography of Mother Jones* (Chicago: Charles H. Kerr and Co., 1925 [reprint edition New York: Arno Press, 1969]), p. 12.

9. Ibid., 12-13.

10. Fetherling, p.6.

11. Jones, p. 15.

12. Fetherling, pp. 6-7.

13. Dumas Malone, ed., *Dictionary of American Biography*, Vol. X (New York: Charles Scribner's Sons, 1933), p.195.

14. Fetherling, p.8.

15. Ibid., pp. 41-42.

16. Ibid., pp. 48-57.

17. Ibid., p. 8.

18. Ibid., p. 121; 107-108.

19. Ibid., p. 7.

20. Ibid., pp. 208-209.

21. Ibid., 203-204.

22. Jones, p. 242.

23. Fetherling, p. 211.

24. Ibid., p. 8.

25. Dolan, pp. 330 and 339.

26. In 1886 alone there were 1,572 labor strikes, some of them violent like the clash between labor and police on May 1 in Chicago's Haymarket Square in which twelve policemen were killed, as well as causing casualties among the workers.

27. Burns, p. 514.

28. Abell, pp. 68-71.

29. Burns, p. 514.

30. Dolan, p. 332.

31. Abell, pp. 68-71.

32. Burns, p. 515.

33. Dolan, p. 337.

34. Ibid., p. 338.

35. Ibid., p. 342.

36. Ibid., pp. 339-40.

37. This analysis is true today in areas of Brazil where large sections of the rain forest are cleared and held as unproductive cattle ranches to be sold when land value increases because of increasing population and migration.

38. Walter Rauschenbusch, *Christianizing the Social Order* (New York, 1912), pp. 91-92.

39. McQuaid to Corrigan, 28 December 1892, in Zwierlein transcripts, Archives, Saint Bernard's Institute, Rochester, NY, quoted in David O'Brien, *Public Catholicism* (New York: Macmillan Publishing Co., 1989), p. 85.

40. Ibid., p. 87.

41. *Breaking Bread: The Catholic Worker and the Origin of Catholic Radicalism* (Philadelphia: Temple University, 1982), p. 34.

42. Abell, p. 189.

43. Dolan, p. 345.

44. Joseph McShane, "Bishops' Program of Social Reconstruction of 1919," NDCST, p. 88.

45. Jeffrey Burns, "John Augustine Ryan," NDCST, p. 852. A summary of his thought with a critique is found in Charles Curran, *American Catholic Social Ethics: Twentieth-Century Approaches* (Notre Dame, IN: University of Notre Dame Press, 1982), pp. 26-91. Also see: Francis Broderick, *Right Reverend New Dealer: John A. Ryan* (New York: Macmillan, 1963); P. Gearty, *The Economic Thought of Monsignor John A. Ryan* (Washington: CUA Press, 1953); Joseph McShane, *"Sufficiently Radical": Catholicism, Progressivism, and the Bishops' Program of 1919* (Washington: CUA Press, 1986) and David O'Brien, *American Catholics and Social Reform: The New Deal Years* (New York: Oxford, 1968).

46. Broderick, *Right Reverend New Dealer*, p. 9.

47. Ibid., p. 8.

48. Ibid., p. 7.

49. Burns, p. 852.

50. *Northwestern Chronicle*, March 2, 1894, as cited by Broderick, pp. 20-21.

51. Broderick, p. 43.

52. John Coleman, "Vision and Praxis in American Theology: Orestes Brownson, John A. Ryan, and John Courtney Murray," *Theological Studies* 37 (1976): 23.

53. Ibid.

54. John Ryan, *Social Doctrine in Action: A Personal History* (New York: Harper, 1941), p. 136.

55. McShane, p. 89.

56. Curran, p. 29.

57. Curran, p. 91.

58. Ibid., pp. 90-91.

59. Coleman, p. 33.

60. O'Brien, *American Catholics and Social Reform* , p. 147; cited by Coleman, p. 21.

61. Abell, pp. 193-194.

62. Ibid., 192.

63. Ibid., 192.

64. Ibid., p. 192.

65. Administrative Committee of the National Catholic War Council, "Program of Social Reconstruction," in David Byers, ed., *Justice in the Marketplace: Collected Statements of the Vatican and the United States Catholic Bishops on Economic Policy, 1891-1984* (Washington, D.C.: United States Catholic Conference, 1985), par. 1, p. 367. Hereafter noted as "Program."

66. Ibid., par. 13, p. 372.

67. McShane, p. 89.

68. "Program," par. 16, pp. 373-374.

69. McShane, p. 90.

70. Ibid., p. 90.

71. Ibid.

72. Abell, pp. 208-209.

73. For example, the proposal that suggested a national employment service is not found in Leo's writing. In fact, Ryan had to use a "considerable mental sleight of hand" to square it off with Leo's thought. Ryan argued that "the right to a living wage was obviously dependent on a worker's ability to land a job in the first place," therefore, "he declared that the ideal of a national employment service was implied in the idea of a living wage." McShane, p. 90.

74. Ibid., pp. 90-91.

75. Ryan, *Social Doctrine in Action*, p.19.

76. Dolan, pp. 345-346.

77. Ibid., p. 259; also see George Higgins, "Toward a New Society," in Charles Curran and Richard McCormick, eds., *Readings in Moral Theology No. 5: Official Catholic Social Teaching*, (New York: Paulist Press, 1986), p. 53.

CHAPTER 3

1. Jay Dolan, *The American Catholic Experience*, pp. 345-346.

2. James Hennesey, "Pius XI," in NDCST, p. 740.

3. Virgil Michel's original thinking made a unique contribution not only to American Catholic social thinking but to the European approach to social issues. The German H. A. Reinhold noted: "We had no Virgil Michel in Germany. The close inter-connection of the liturgical revival with social reform... was never expressed in that forceful way in which you see it in the writings of the late Dom Virgil and *Orate Fratres.* ...America is in an enviable position.... While in Germany the leaders of the liturgical and social revival, both strong and powerful movements, never really met and sometimes antagonized and criticized each other—here you have a close cooperation of the two, a unity of both, right from the start." Paul Marx, *Virgil Michel and Liturgical Movement* (Collegeville, MN: Liturgical Press, 1957), p.185.

4. Ibid., p. 258.

5. Ibid., p. 263.

6. Joseph Chinnici, O.F.M., *Living Stones: The History and Structure of Catholic Spiritual Life in the United States* (New York: Macmillan, 1989), p.185.

7. Michael Baxter, "Reintroducing Virgil Michel: Towards a Counter-Tradition of Catholic Social Ethics in the United States," *Communio* 24 (Fall 1997): 503-504.

8. Virgil Michel, "Liturgy and Catholic Life," 234 (unpublished manuscript) quoted in Marx, p. 60.

9. Baxter, p. 527.

10. Dolan, pp. 408-409.

11. Debra Campbell, "Reformers and Activists," in *American Catholic Women: A Historical Exploration,* Karen Kennelly, C.S.J., ed. (New York: Macmillan, 1989), p. 175-76.

12. Dorothy Day, *The Long Loneliness: The Autobiography of Dorothy Day* (New York: Harper, 1952).

13. For a systematic development of the radical Catholic approach which is personified in Dorothy Day see the works of Paul Hanly Furfey. Charles Curran offers an excellent overview and analysis in *American Catholic Social Ethics: Twentieth-Century Approaches* (Notre Dame, IN: University of Notre Dame Press, 1982), pp. 130-71: hereafter "Social Ethics."

14. Dorothy Day, *House of Hospitality* (New York, 1939), p. 49.

15. Mark and Louise Zwick, "Dorothy Day and the Catholic Worker Movement," *Communio* 24 (Fall 1997): 424.

16. Ibid., p. 459.

17. Jansenism is the erroneous, but popular, belief among Roman Catholics that we prove ourselves acceptable to God by our rigorous ascetical practices.

Chapter V of *Lumen Gentium* is entitled, "The Call of the Whole Church to Holiness." Paragraph 40 reads, "Thus it is evident to everyone that all the faithful of Christ of whatever rank or status are called to the fullness of Christian life and to the perfection of charity."

18. Zwick, p. 444.

19. Ibid., p. 444.

20. "Street Saint," *Time* (December 15, 1980), p. 74.

21. Patrick Jordan, "An Appetite for God: Dorothy Day at 100," *Commonweal* 124 (October 24, 1997): 12.

22. Dolan, p. 411.

23. Jordan, p. 12.

24. *Loneliness*, pp. 148-9.

25. "Introduction," Dorothy Day, *The Long Loneliness: The Autobiography of Dorothy Day* (San Francisco: Harper and Row, 1952, 1981), p. xxiii.

26. Robert Ellsberg, ed., *Dorothy Day: Selected Writings* (Maryknoll, NY: Orbis Books, 1993), p. xv.

27. Zwick, p. 456.

28. *The Catholic Worker*, July-August 1965, p. 7.

29. Jordan, p. 17.

30. Ibid., p. 17.

31. Campbell, pp. 176-177.

32. Catherine de Hueck, "Friendship House and Its Staff Workers," *The Catholic World* 152 (February, 1941): 605-606.

33. During the same period Father John LaFarge was addressing the question of racism in southern Maryland through a multi-leveled approach including setting up schools, writing texts, and especially in setting up Catholic Interracial Councils. He established the first Interracial Councils in New York in 1934. These Councils were an outgrowth of a previous organization of African-American professionals, the Catholic Laymen's Union, which LaFarge had founded in 1927. Their goal was to cooperate with other local groups in combating racial discrimination and to eliminate racism from the policies and practices in the Catholic Church. By 1958, approximately forty such councils had been established in the United States. Michael Graham, "John LaFarge," NDCST, pp. 538-9.

34. Dolan, p. 405.

35. Alden V. Brown, "The Grail Movement to 1962: Laywomen and a New Christendom," *US Catholic Historian* 3 (Fall/Winter 1983): 150, as quoted Campbell, p. 177.

36. Janet Kalven, et al., "The Grail in America, 1940-1982" (unpublished manuscript) p. 4, as quoted by Dolan, p. 414.

37. *Mens Nostra*, No. 8 as found in Joseph Husslein, ed., *Social Wellsprings, Vol. 2* (Milwaukee: Bruce Co., 1942), p. 76.

38. Closer to the Vatican model of Catholic Action for women would be the formation in 1920 of the National Council of Catholic Women (NCCW) which was part of the recently formed bishops' National Catholic Welfare Council. The NCCW focused most of its energies on education, study clubs, dialogue on social topics, and administering immigrant aid. According to one historian, "its institutional ties [to the bishops' conference] appear to have inhibited its independent Christian witness." Campbell, pp. 174-175.

39. Dolan, p. 415.

40. Ibid., p. 416.

41. Campbell, p. 178.

42. James Hennesey, "Pius XI" NDCST, p. 739.

43. Abell, p. 173.

44. Hennesey, p. 740.

45. Marie Giblin, "Corporatism," NDCST, p. 244.

46. Richard L. Camp, *The Papal Ideology of Social Reform: A Study in Historical Development, 1878-1967* (Leiden: E.J. Brill, 1969), p. 37.

47. Ibid., p. 65.

48. The shorter text is available in English, *Ethics and the National Economy,* trans. Rupert Ederer (Manila: Divine Word Publications, 1988). The five-volume work which was originally published in Freiburg in Breisgau (Herder, 1905-1923) is now translated and ready to be published according to Ederer, see, "Heinrich Pesch, S.J.—A Reminder" *Social Justice Review* (July/August 1990): 146.

49. Curran, *Social Ethics,* p. 99.

50. Pesch's thought was very influential for members of the German American organization, Central Verein. The Central Verein, or Central Union, was a national federation of German American organizations that was concerned about social reform in the first part of the twentieth century. Frederick Kenkel led the Central Verein and used its publication, the *Central-Blatt and Social Justice* (later called the *Social Justice Review),* to popularize the solidaristic theory of Pesch among the German American community of the Midwest. In a more academic setting, William Engelen, S.J., who taught in Toledo and St. Louis, carried on the solidaristic tradition in the U.S. Engelen held that "functional and hierarchical structures such as characterized the medieval guilds should exist. Individualism, competition, and self-seeking are to be held in check. Order and harmony rather than competition and class struggle should reign. Labor and capital should not be opposed, but all those involved in the same type of work of vocation should be united in vocational groups. These vocational groups, however, must also recognize that they are part of the whole of society and work for the prosperity of all and for civic solidarity. These vocational and occupational groups would set just prices, pay just wages, determine the amount of production, and have some say in management." Charles Curran, "The Central-Verein and William J. Engelen'" in *Social Ethics,* pp. 113-14.

51. Marie Giblin, "Quadragesimo Anno," NDCST, p. 803. Gustav Gundlach was to become the writer of many of Pius XII's social allocutions.

52. Ibid., p. 804.

53. Oswald von Nell-Breuning, "The Drafting of *Quadragesimo Anno,"* in Charles Curran and Richard McCormick, eds., *Readings in Moral Theology No. 5: Official Catholic Social Teaching* (New York: Paulist, 1986), pp. 67-8 [emphasis mine].

54. Ibid., p. 66.

55. *Quadragesimo Anno,* in O'Brien and Shannon, *Catholic Social Thought:,* par. 88; hereafter QA.

56. John Cronin, *Catholic Social Principles: The Social Teaching of the Catholic Church Applied to American Economic Life* (Milwaukee: Bruce Pub., 1955), pp. 124-25.

57. *Divini Redemptoris,* 1937, no. 92.

58. In the writings of Thomas Aquinas we find three types of justice discussed: general or legal, commutative, and distributive. The three are not to be seen as three subdivisions of justice as was later thought in some of the manuals of moral theology, rather general justice is the basis of the other two types of justice. In other words *general justice is the foundational concept,* and commutative and distributive flow from this general notion of justice. Aquinas described the broad category of general justice as follows. "Now it is evident that all who are included in a community, stand in relation to that community as parts to a whole; while a part, as such, belongs to a whole, so that whatever is the good of a part can be directed to the good of the whole. It follows therefore the good of any virtue, whether such virtue direct man in relation to himself, or in relation to certain other individual persons, is referable to the common good. It is in this sense that *justice is called a general virtue."*

Then using the term legal justice, he adds, "since it belongs to the law to direct to the common good, as stated above, it follows that the justice which is in this way styled general, is called legal justice, because thereby man is in harmony with the law which directs the acts of all the virtues to the common good." Thomas Aquinas, *Summa Theologica* 2a2ae 58.5 (New York: Benziger Brothers, 1920).

Thomas' use of the term "legal" justice is quite different from our understanding of legal justice. We would think of courtroom justice and the legal system. By contrast, Thomas has a much broader understanding of legal justice. The notion of legal justice was also problematic for the ethicists of the 1840s. The notion of law had changed significantly from the way Thomas used it six centuries earlier. Aquinas understood law as an "ordinance of reason promulgated by the ruler for the common good." In his understanding the notion of law is linked with reason discerning the nature of things and the lawmaker promulgating or making explicit the implicit laws of human nature, the natural law. Law in Thomas conforms to the order of things perceived by reason and promulgated by the legitimate authority. In promulgating law the ruler is defending and promoting the common good. Law finds its authenticity in the promotion and defense of the common good, which is not in tension with the good of the individual. For the common good is never at odds with the good of the individual. In his understanding then, *law promotes the common good* as does the general virtue of justice, so he had no trouble linking the two terms together—legal justice.

By the mid-1800s, when the rediscovery of Thomistic thought was underway, it no longer seemed appropriate to keep the term legal justice, because the notion of law had changed dramatically. By the time of Father Taparelli in the 1840s law was associated with the positive laws of the modern state. In this sense law was not inherently linked to the order of reason and the natural law as for Aquinas, but now it referred to the authority of the lawgiver to make law regardless of the order of reason. "Under the influence of voluntarism, law was no longer seen as an expression of right reason but rather as an arbitrary decree of the powerful wielder of authority." See Normand Paulhus, "Uses and Misuses of the Term 'Social Justice' in Roman Catholic Tradition," *Journal of Religious Ethics* 15 (1987), p. 270.

The law's basis was the authority of the lawgiver, not its inherent conformity to the natural law and the common good. In this setting, legal justice is reduced to the obedience of the citizen to the laws of the State—a far cry from what it meant for Aquinas. To talk about the full meaning of justice Taparelli d'Azeglio and others felt they had to avoid the term legal justice because it would be misconstrued by their contemporaries so they chose the popular term "social" to express the Thomistic idea of full justice in the social order. But this term had its own "baggage" in the nineteenth century which also shaped the understanding of justice.

First of all, for someone familiar with the Thomistic notion of justice it is tautological to say social justice, for justice at its very root is social. The goal of justice in the Thomistic framework is the common good, which is an individual and social reality. Second, social, as it was used in the last century, had a connotation of distinction from or opposition to the political realm. The political realities pertained to the state and governmental dimensions and the word social pertained to societal dimensions, of which the political is one arena. Instead of stressing relationships as the unifying force of the whole, the term "social" now suggested potential antagonisms that may arise in those relationships, especially between the State and individuals (Paulhus, p. 269).

The classical view had emphasized the primacy of the common good with the demand it made on individual citizens. The new view put the focus on individuals and groups who were making their demands on the common good and the state. The *classical* (or *Thomistic*) view was kept alive in the solidarism of Pesch and others as they stressed the duties and obligations of individuals to the common good. The *modern view* stressed the rights of individuals and social groups, rather than duties to the common good. The modern view of legal justice has completely overshadowed the classical view.

What this discussion reveals is the extent to which Catholic social ethicists were influenced by the political philosophy of their time. Taparelli incorporated contemporary attitudes toward justice, law, and common good as he tried to express the Thomistic tradition. In so doing he shifted the tradition, some would say distorted it, without even realizing it.

For instance, the relationship of the individual to the common good took on a modern connotation in Taparelli's writing. He pictured the common good as something external to the members of society which must be redistributed to them by an exercise of distributive justice. For Aquinas the common good was not something external to the individual members of society, rather it already included their good, as they are parts of the whole. What emerged was a subtle antagonism between an individual's good and the common good, which was not part of the Thomistic perspective. The claims of individual good (rights) against the society's good (common good) were foreign to the classical understanding of the relationship of the individual to society. The common good now became the sum total of the individual's good and was seen as an alien good, an abstract good separated from the good of the individual.

59. J. Tonneau, O.P. as cited by Jean Yves Calvez, "Social Justice," *New Catholic Encyclopedia* (New York: McGraw-Hill, 1967), vol. 13, p. 319.

60. Daniel Maguire, *A New American Justice* (Minneapolis: Winston Press, 1980).

61. Michael Novak's works include: *Freedom with Justice: Catholic Social Thought and Liberal Institutions* (San Francisco: Harper & Row, 1984); *The Catholic Ethic and the Spirit of Democratic Capitalism* (New York: Free Press, 1993); *Catholic Social Thought and Liberal Institutions: Freedom with Justice* (New Brunswick, NJ: Transaction, 1989).

62. David Hollenbach, *Claims in Conflict: Retrieving and Renewing the Catholic Human Rights Tradition* (New York: Paulist, 1979) and *Justice, Peace and Human Rights* (New York: Crossroad, 1988).

63. The recovery plan of the New Deal in the United States echoed something of the vocational group system suggested by the encyclical. The National Industrial Recovery Act (NIRA) of 1935 established 731 codes to "induce and maintain united action of labor and management under adequate governmental sanction and supervision." By relaxing the anti-trust laws, the code authorities, controlled by business leaders, were empowered to check overproduction and extremely low prices, the result, it was held, of excessive and unfair competition, low wages, long hours, and child labor. The codes, therefore, provided for a minimum wage of $12-15.00 a week, reduced the work week to 40 hours, and abolished child labor. These changes were designed to stimulate re-employment, increase purchasing power and improve working conditions.

Despite these advantages, the NIRA, as it was implemented through the code authorities, did not include the voice of labor on the code committees. Labor had no direct voice in the new industry monitoring agency, nor was it represented at the policy shaping levels. The New Deal reforms in the United States, I believe, showed the difficulty of implementing the ideal vision suggested by the pope when the hard realities of political and economic power are not taken into account.

64. Cronin, *Readings*, p. 71; also see his treatment "Industry Councils in American Life," in idem, *Catholic Social Principles: the Social Teaching of the Catholic Church Applied to American Economic Life* (Milwaukee: Bruce Pub., 1950), pp. 227-253.

65. Abell, p. 267.

66. Ibid., pp. 267-8.

67. Andrew Greeley, "*Quadragesimo Anno* After Fifty Years," *America* 145 (August 8, 1981): 47.

68. Ibid., p. 47.

69. Herman Daly and John Cobb, *For the Common Good* (Boston: Beacon Press, 1989), pp. 16 and 18.

70. Giblin, p. 812.

71. James Hennesey, *American Catholics: A History of the Roman Catholic Community in the United States* (Oxford: Oxford University Press, 1981), p. 263

72. George Flynn, *American Catholics and the Roosevelt Presidency 1932-1936* (Lexington, 1968), p. 17 as quoted by Hennesey, ibid., p. 260.

73. Giblin, p. 812.

74. Hennesey, p. 259.

CHAPTER 4

1. David O'Brien, *Public Catholicism* (New York: Macmillan Publishing Co., 1989), p. 219.

2. Andrew Greeley chronicles this era in the Archdiocese of Chicago in *The Catholic Experience: An Interpretation of the History of American Catholicism* (Garden City, NY: Doubleday, 1967), pp. 247-274.

3. Hennesey, p. 203.

4. John Pawlikowski uses this phrase in reference to Murray. I believe it is appropriate to apply it Pope John as well. "Walking with, and Beyond, Murray: Catholic Participation in Public Life," *New Theology Review* 9 (August 1996): 29.

5. Walter Abbott and Joseph Gallagher, eds., *The Documents of Vatican II* (New York: America Press, 1966), pp. 712-713.

6. Donal Dorr, *Option for the Poor: A Hundred Years of Vatican Social Teaching*, Revised Edition (Maryknoll, NY: Orbis Books, 1992), p. 115 [emphasis mine].

7. Hans Langendorfer, "John XXIII," NDCST, p. 490.

8. *Commonweal* noted that Pavan "actively assisted Pope John in writing of *Mater et Magistra*," Pietro Pavan, "Pope John's Vision," 81 (November 13, 1964): 213. Pavan's other works include *Social Order* (1955), *Economic Order* (1957), *Democracy and Its Reasons* (1958), *The Catholic Laity in the Temporal Order* (1959) and *Laicism Today* (1962); more recently he has written two books on ecology *Voce della Natura: la Gran Madre* [The Voice of Nature: the Grand Mother] (Rome: Citta Nuova Editrice, 1976) and *L'Uomo nell' Universo* [Man/Humanity in the Universe] Rome: Edizione Centena, 1978.

9. Michael Campbell-Johnston, "The Social Teaching of the Church," *Thought* 39 (February 1964): 383.

10. "The World Wide Response" in Joseph Moody and Justus Lawler, eds., *The Challenge of Mater et Magistra* (New York: Herder and Herder, 1963): 156; first published as "*Mater et Magistra* and Its Commentators," in *Theological Studies* 24 (March 1963): 1-52. Campion's survey covered commentaries until the end of 1962; other important works came out after that date including Jean Yves Calvez, *The Social Thought of John XXIII: Mater et Magistra* (Chicago: H. Regenery Co., 1965); J. R. Kirwan *The Social Thought of John XXIII* (Oxford: Catholic Social Guild, 1964); John Cronin, *The Social Teaching of Pope John XXIII*

(Milwaukee: Bruce, 1963); idem, *Christianity and Social Progress: A Commentary on Mater et Magistra* (Baltimore: Helicon, 1965); and Paul-Emile Bolte, *Mater et Magistra, commentaire, IV Vols.* (Montreal: University of Montreal, 1964-1968).

11. Marcel Laloire, "L'encyclique 'Mater et Magistra,'" *Revue nouvelle* 34 (September 1961): 203; as quoted by Campion, p. 157.

12. Ibid., p.158.

13. "'Mater et Magistra'" *Stimmen der Zeit* 87 (November 1961): 116; as quoted by Campion, p. 158.

14. Jean-Yves Calvez,"La Socialisation dans la pensée de l'Eglise," *Revue de l'Action Populaire* (May 1962): 517-528; Jean Villain, "L'Encyclique *Mater et Magistra*: son apport doctrinal," ibid. (September- October 1961): 897-915; as cited by Campbell-Johnston, p. 382; J. R. Kirwan, "'Mater et Magistra': A commentary on Pope John XXIII's Encyclical," *Wiseman Review,* No. 489 (Autumn 1961), p. 196-230; cited by Campion, p.162. For many others it was a source of confusion. The term "socialization" does not appear in the official Latin text yet it does appear in the official French, Italian, English, and Spanish translations issued by the Vatican Polyglot Press.

15. Radio broadcast to the Congress of Austrian Catholics at Vienna, September 14, 1952: AAS 44 (1952): 792; quoted in Campbell-Johnston, p. 383.

16. Campbell-Johnston, p. 387.

17. "A propos d'une grande encyclique sociale," *Signes du temps* 3 (August-September), p. 21; as quoted in Campion, p. 164. For further bibliographical references see Bartolomeo Sorge, S.J., "Socializzaione e Socialismo," *Civiltà Cattolica* 114 (February 1963): 326-337; esp. 336-7.

18. "'Mater et Magistra': Rich and Poor Nations," *London Catholic Times* (July 21, 1961): 9.

19. Joseph Joblin, "The Papal Encyclical 'Mater et Magistra'" *International Labour Review* 84 (September 1961), reprint p. 16.

20. Philip Land, "Pope John XXIII: Teacher," *America* 106 (November 4, 1961): p. 149.

21. "*Mater et Magistra*: Liberal or Conservative?" *Social Justice Review* 54 (December 1961): 271.

22. "The Week," *National Review* 11 (July 29, 1961): 38 and "For the Record," *National Review* 11 (August 12, 1961): 77.

23. Land, p. 149.

24. *Gaudium et Spes,* in Abbott, *The Documents of Vatican II,* par. 43.

25. See Martin Hengel, *Property and Riches in the Early Church.* Translated by John Bowden, London: SCM Press, 1974; and William J. Walsh and John Langan, "Patristic Social Consciousness—the Church and the Poor," in John Haughey, ed., *The Faith That Does Justice* (New York: Paulist, 1977), pp. 113-152.

26. National Conference of Catholic Bishops, *Economic Justice for All* (Washington, D.C.: USCC, 1986), p. 68, par. 135. Also see the "Foreword" of the *Program of Social Reconstruction* in David Byers, ed., *Justice in the Marketplace: Collected Statements of the Vatican and the United States Catholic Bishops on Economic Policy, 1891-1984* (Washington, D.C.: USCC, 1985), p. 367.

27. *Lumen Gentium,* par. 37, in Abbott, *The Documents of Vatican II,* p. 64.

28. Pietro Pavan, "The Place of *Mater et Magistra* in Papal Social Teaching," *Christus Rex* 16 (December 1962): 242.

29. John Courtney Murray calls it a résumé of the three previous social encyclicals, *Rerum Novarum, Quadragesimo Anno,* and *Mater et Magistra.*

30. Herbert Vorgrimler, ed., *Commentary on the Documents of Vatican II*, Vol. V (New York: Herder and Herder, 1969), p. 329.

31. April 21, 1963, quoted by Thurston Davis, "Pope John's Letter," *America* 108 (May 18, 1963): 710.

32. John Murray, "The Peace that Comes of Order: Reflections upon the Encyclical 'Pacem in Terris,'" *Studies* 52 (Autumn 1963): 294.

33. "Praising the Pope," *Christianity Today* 7 (May 10, 1963): 42 [806].

34. "*Pacem in Terris*: Two Views," *Christianity and Crisis* 23 (May 13, 1963): 82.

35. Davis, p. 709.

36. Murray, *Studies* (1963): 295.

37. Ibid., 294 and 300. "*Vade-mecum*" is a Latin phrase for handbook or more literally "it-goes-with- me."

38. Murray, "Things Old and New in 'Pacem in Terris'," *America* 108 (April 27, 1963): 613. This is a summation of the pope's thought on these central concepts.

39. Ibid.

40. *Pacem in Terris* in O'Brien and Shannon, *Catholic Social Thought*, par. 112; hereafter PT.

41. David Hollenbach, *Claims in Conflict: Retrieving and Renewing the Catholic Human Rights Tradition* (New York: Paulist, 1979), p, 67.

42. Murray, "Things Old," p. 614.

43. William V. O'Brien, "Balancing the Risks," *Worldview* (June 1963): 11; as quoted in George Weigel, *Tranquillitas Ordinis: The Present and Future Promise of American Catholic Thought on War and Peace* (New York: Oxford, 1987), p. 88.

44. Reinhold Niebuhr, "*Pacem In Terris*: Two Views," *Christianity and Crisis* 23 (May 13, 1963): 83.

45. See Larry L. Rasmussen's Presidential Address at the 1991 Meeting of the Society of Christian Ethics, "Power Analysis: A Neglected Agenda in Christian Ethics," *The Annual of the Society of Christian Ethics* (1991): 3-17.

46. Darryl Trimiew, "The Economic Rights Debate," *The Annual of the Society of Christian Ethics* (1991): 95.

47. Ibid., p. 91.

48. Ibid., p. 95.

49. Ibid.

50. Michael Novak, "The Future of 'Economic Rights,'" in James Finn, ed., *Private Virtue and Public Policy: Catholic Thought and National Life* (New Brunswick, NJ and London: Transaction Publishers, 1990), pp. 76 and 80.

51. Trimiew, pp. 88 and 90.

52. Ibid., p. 89, references Warren Holleman, "Reinhold Niebuhr on the United Nations and Human Rights," *Soundings* 70 (Fall-Winter, 1987): 350 n. 2.

53. "Political Responsibility: Revitalizing American Democracy," *Crux* (October 28, 1991).

54. At the 1991 Convention of the Catholic Theological Society of America two papers were synopsized in a workshop entitled "American Catholic Social Ethics in the Murray Tradition: Possible Directions of Development." J. Leon Hooper's paper, "A Survey of John Courtney Murray's Influence Twenty-five Years after His Death," surveyed 112 texts from 1965 to 1990 that make explicit appeal or challenge to Murray's work. The second paper was Todd David Whitmore's "From Religious Freedom to Conditions for Witness:

Developing the Heritage of John Courtney Murray." A brief report of this workshop is found in *Proceedings of the Forty-Sixth Annual Convention of the CTSA*, Atlanta, June 12-15, 1991, Vol. 46, Paul Crowley, ed., pp. 136-137.

55. Charles Curran offers an excellent introduction and evaluation of the work of John Courtney Murray, in *American Catholic Social Ethics* (Notre Dame, IN: University of Notre Dame, 1982), pp. 172-232; at 232.

56. Richard McBrien, *Caesar's Coin: Religion and Politics in America* (New York: Macmillan, 1987), p. 117.

57. Ibid.

58. Ibid., p. 118.

59. Donald E. Pelotte, *John Courtney Murray: Theologian In Conflict* (New York: Paulist, 1975), p. 53.

60. Hennesey, p. 303.

61. Pelotte, p. 82.

62. Ibid., p. 82.

63. Hennesey, p. 303.

64. John Courtney Murray, "Freedom in the Age of Renewal," *American Benedictine Review* 18 (September, 1967): 323; see Pelotte, pp. 101-102.

65. Pelotte, p. 105.

66. Curran, p. 200 ff.

67. Ibid., pp. 177 and 207.

68. The illiteracy rates in the Catholic countries of Europe at the time of Leo were extremely high: Italy 62%, Spain 72%, Portugal 79%, 31% in Belgium, 28% in France. Cited by Curran, p. 210.

69. "The Problem of State Religion," *Theological Studies* 12 (1951): 158, 159, n. 6; as quoted in Curran p. 197.

70. Curran, p. 223.

71. Weigel, p. 177ff.

72. David Hollenbach, "Notes on Moral Theology: War and Peace in American Catholic Thought: A Heritage Abandoned?" *Theological Studies* 48 (1987): 717.

73. J. Leon Hooper, *The Ethics of Discourse: The Social Philosophy of John Courtney Murray* (Washington, D.C.: Georgetown University Press, 1986), p. 8.

74. John Pawlikowski, "Walking with, and Beyond, Murray: Catholic Participation in Public Life," *New Theology Review* 9 (August 1996): 24.

75. Ibid., p. 25.

76. John Coleman, "A Possible Role for Biblical Religion in Public Life," *Theological Studies* 40 (December 1979): 705.

77. *Woodstock Report* (March 1993): 3. An abridged and edited report of a public forum held at Woodstock Theological Center in January 1993 to commemorate the 25th anniversary of his death. J. Bryan Hehir who has worked for many years in the United States Catholic Conference, no doubt writing many of the bishops' statements on public policy and international issues, argues that faith language may not be the appropriate language for the public arena. He maintains that religious language and symbols are appropriate within the church community, whereas in the public arena, he says "I cannot agree that it [public theology] should be the dominant mode of policy discourse for the Church." Hehir prefers the

language of public *philosophy* over public *theology* when arguing public policy questions. J. Bryan Hehir, "The Perennial Need for Philosophical Discourse," *Theological Studies* 40 (December 1979): 710-13, at 711.

78. Pawlikowski, p. 25.

79. Pawlikowski, p. 29.

80. "Freedom in the Age of Renewal," *American Benedictine Review* 18 (September, 1967): 320; quoted by Pelotte, p. 106.

CHAPTER 5

1. Brown first coined this phrase, which was picked up the Kerner Commission on racial unrest in 1968 and repeated by the U.S. bishops in *Confronting A Culture of Violence: A Catholic Framework for Action* (Washington, D.C.: USCC, 1994), p. 4.

2. M. Shawn Copeland, "African American Catholics and Black Theology: An Interpretation," in James Cone and Gayraud Wilmore, eds., *Black Theology: A Documentary History, Volume II* (Maryknoll, NY: Orbis, 1993), p. 101.

3. Charles Moeller, "Pastoral Constitution on the Church in the Modern World: History of the Constitution," in Vorgrimler, *Commentary on the Documents of Vatican II, Vol V*, pp. 10-11.

4. Ibid., p. 15.

5. Ibid., p. 68.

6. Xavier Rynne, *The Fourth Session: The Debates and Decress of Vatican Council II September 14 to December 1965* (London: Faber and Faber, 1966), p. 212.

7. Bernard Häring, "Fostering the Nobility of Marriage and the Family," in Vorgrimler, p. 228.

8. At least in late 1965 the issue of birth control was an open question for Paul VI. Rynne reports that when the American moral theologian Father Ford "presented the Pope with the arguments of the intransigents [on November 29, 1964], the Pope was said to have replied: 'You, as a moral theologian, tell me there is only one way to look at this matter. On the other hand, Bishop Reuss is also a moral theologian and he tells me just the opposite. Go to him and argue the matter out. When you two moralists reach an agreement, come back to me with an answer." Three and a half years later, Pope Paul was to side with the conservative position against the advice of the Majority Report of the Papal Commission on Birth Control as he issued the encyclical *Humanae Vitae* on July 25, 1968.

9. Vorgrimler, p. 345.

10. Ibid., p. 345.

11. Joseph Gremillion, ed., *The Gospel of Peace and Justice: Catholic Social Teaching Since Pope John* (Maryknoll, NY: Orbis Books, 1976), p. 383.

12. Vorgrimler, p. 69.

13. Lois Lorentzen, "*Gaudium et Spes*," NDCST, p. 407.

14. Abbott, *The Documents of Vatican II*, pp. 268-270.

15. Lorentzen, p. 408; *Schema constitutionis pastoralis de ecclesia in mundo huis temporis: Expensio modorum partis secundae* (Vatican: Vatican Press, 1965), pp. 37-38.

16. Louis Janssens, "Artificial Insemination: Ethical Reflections," *Louvain Studies* 8 (1980): 3-29. Richard McCormick provides a helpful summary of this focus on the person in *The*

Critical Calling: Reflections on Moral Dilemmas Since Vatican II (Washington, D.C., Georgetown University Press, 1989), pp. 14-16.

17. Lorentzen, p. 410.

18. Manuel Velasquez, "'Gaudium et Spes' and the Development of Catholic Social-Ecomonic Teaching," in Judith A. Dwyer, ed., *Questions of Special Urgency: The Church in the Modern World Two Decades after Vatican II* (Washington, D.C.: Georgetown University Press, 1986), p. 187; hereafter *Questions*.

19. Anne Patrick, "Toward Renewing 'The Life and Culture of Fallen Men': 'Gaudium et Spes' as Catalyst for Catholic Feminist Theology," Dwyer, *Questions*, p. 59.

20. Copeland, p. 101.

21. Lorentzen, p. 415.

22. Robert McAfee Brown, "A Response," in Abbott, *The Documents of Vatican II*, p. 315.

23. Lorentzen, p. 414.

24. Antonio Moser and Bernardino Leers, *Moral Theology: Dead Ends and Alternatives*, translated by Paul Burns (Maryknoll, NY: Orbis Books, 1990), pp. 47-48.

25. Enda McDonagh, "The Church in the Modern World," in Adrian Hastings, ed., *Modern Catholicism: Vatican II and After* (New York: Oxford University Press, 1991), p. 110.

26. Gregory Baum, *Theology and Society* (Maryknoll, NY: Orbis Books, 1984), p. 14.

27. The Council on the Laity and the Commission *Iustitia et Pax* was established on January 6, 1967. *Iustitia et Pax* is a study commission to help catechize the church on social issues through working papers, and conferences. It also was an agency for ecumenical collaboration as well as serving as a resource for the hierarchy. An American, Msgr. Joseph Gremillion, was appointed the first secretary of the commission. See Stefan Swiezawski, "Excursus on Article 90: The Commission 'Iustitia et Pax'" in Vorgrimler, pp 382-83. Also consult Marjorie Keenan, "Pontifical Council for Justice and Peace," NDCST, pp. 754-755.

28. The two references to racism in *Populorum Progressio* are:

> 1. The struggle against destitution, though urgent and necessary, is not enough. It is a question rather, of building a world where every man, no matter what his race, religion or nationality, can live a fully human life, freed from servitude imposed on him by other men.... (47)

> Racism is not the exclusive lot of young nations, where sometimes it hides beneath the rivalries of clans and political parties, with heavy losses for justice and at the risk of civil war. ...It is still an obstacle to collaboration among disadvantaged nations and a cause of division and hatred within countries whenever individuals and families see the inviolable rights of the human person held in scorn, as they themselves are unjustly subjected to a regime of discrimination because of their race or their colour. (63).

29. NCCB, "The National Race Crisis," April 25, 1968, J. Brian Benestad & Francis Butler, eds., *Quest for Justice: A Compendium of Statements of the United States Catholic Bishops on Political and Social Order 1966-1980* (Washington, D.C.: USCC, 1981), p. 360.

30. John Harriott, "The Difficulty of Justice," *Month* 5 (January 1972): 15.

31. Cardinal Carberry's speech at the Synod, October 21, 1971 as quoted in William Callahan, S.J., "The Quest for Justice: Guidelines to a Creative Response by American Catholics to the 1971 Synod Statement, 'Justice in the World'" (Washington, D.C.: Center of Concern, 1972), p. 11.

32. Cyprian Davis, "Two Side of a Coin: The Black Presence in the History of the Catholic

Church in America," in Secretariat for Black Catholics, *Many Rains Ago: A Historical and Theological Reflection on the Role of the Episcopate in the Evangelization of African American Catholics* (Washington, D.C.: USCC, 1990), p. 49.

33. My description of racism is taken from James Jones, in *Prejudice and Racism* (Reading, MA: Addison-Wesley, 1972), pp. 114-167. On page 117 he offers this broad definition:

> Racism results from the transformation of race prejudice and/or ethnocentrism through the exercise of power against a racial group defined as inferior, by individuals, and institutions with the intentional or unintentional support of the entire culture.

He moves beyond other notions of racism which have seen racism as the attitude and belief in the superiority of one's own ethnic or racial group. Jones includes actions: "The significant factor of ingroup preference, whether racially of ethnically based, is the POWER that the ingroup has over an outgroup." (p. 117) Power is always defined in action terms: "possession of control, authority, of influence over others;... ability to act or produce and effect; ...physical might...." (Webster's Dictionary)

> By the above definitions, black people are oppressed for reasons of both race and culture. ...To understand racism in America is to understand more than the simple facts of slavery, segregation, discrimination, and prejudice. To understand racism is also to understand differences in cultural heritage, the categorical suppression of the subordinate culture as well as the imposition of the dominant culture's values on members of minority cultures.

Three levels of racism:

I. Individual

Two types of individual racism are described by Joel Kovel in his book, *White Racism*: dominative and aversive.

> a. The *Dominative racist* is the type who acts out bigoted beliefs. He or she is the open flame of racial hatred. "The true white bigot expresses a definitive ambition through all his activity: he openly seeks to keep the black man down, and is willing to use force to further his ends."

> b. The *Aversive racist* is the type who believes in white race superiority and is more or less aware of it but does nothing overt about it. He or she tries to ignore the existence of black people, tries to avoid contact with them, and at most tries to be polite, correct and cold in whatever dealings are necessary between the races.

II. Institutional racism "can be defined as those established laws, customs, and practices which systematically reflect and produce racial inequalities in American society." [p. 131 Jones] If racist consequences follow from our laws, customs, or practices, the *institution* is racist whether or not the *individual* maintaining those practices have racist intentions.

Institutional racism can be either overt or covert and either intentional or unintentional.

III. Cultural racism—working from the following definition of culture from the 1967 Funk and Wagnall's Dictionary—"The sum total of the attainments and activities of any specific period, race, or people, including their implements, handicrafts, agriculture, economics, music, art religious beliefs, traditions, language and story."

Cultural racism in the in the U.S. has two forms:

> 1) the belief in the inferiority of the implements, handicrafts, agriculture, economics, music, art, religious beliefs, traditions, language, and story of African peoples; and

2) a neo-racism which suggests that African Americans have no distinctive implements, handicrafts, agriculture, economics, music, art, religious beliefs, traditions, language, or story apart from those of mainstream white America and those deriving from the pathology of years of oppression in American society.

Cultural racism is closely related to ethnocentrism—the belief in the superiority of one's own ethnic group and the inferiority of other ethnic groups. The significant difference is the issue of power. The "power to significantly affect the lives of people who are ethnically and/or culturally different is the factor which transforms white ethnocentrism into white cultural racism." Jones, pp. 148-149.

34. Robert Robinson, "Black and Catholic—II," *America* 142 (March 29, 1980): 257-258.

35. Francesca Thompson, "Black and Catholic—III," *America* 142 (March 29, 1980): 261.

36. Jamie T. Phelps, "Caught Between Thunder and Lightning: A Historical and Theological Critique of the Episcopal Response to Slavery," Secretariat for Black Catholics, *Many Rains Ago*, p. 30.

37. Francis Maxwell, *Slavery and the Catholic Church* (Westminster, MD: Christian Classics, 1975), pp. 10-12.

38. Cyprian Davis, *The History of Black Catholics in the United States* (New York: Crossroad, 1990), pp. 36-37.

39. Phelps, p. 22.

40. Diana Hayes, *And Still We Rise: An Introduction to Black Liberation Theology* (New York: Paulist, 1996), p. 47. Hayes notes that "the first black Catholic priest ordained in the United States was Fr. Augustus Tolton in 1886. Today there are only approximately 300+ Black priests and religious in the United States" (p. 52).

41. Hayes, *And Still*, p. 162.

42. George Cummings, "Racism in the U.S. from 1492 to 1992: A Theological Critique of the Context of Contemporary Ministry," in T. Howland Sanks and John Coleman, eds., *Reading the Signs of the Times: Resources for Social and Cultural Analysis* (New York: Paulist Press, 1993), pp. 85-86 [emphasis mine].

43. Hayes, *And Still*, p. 165.

44. *The US Catholic Miscellany* (October 10, 1840) as quoted in Maria Genoino Caravaglios, *The American Catholic Church and the Negro Problem in the XVIII-XIX Centuries* (Rome: Tipografia delle Mantellate, 1974), p. 89; cited by Phelps, p. 24.

45. Phelps, p. 26.

46. Ibid., p. 26.

47. Ibid., p. 29.

48. Hennesey, p. 193.

49. Phelps, p. 29.

50. Davis, "Two Sides," p. 55.

51. Hennesey, *American Catholics*, p. 192.

52. *The National Black Catholic Pastoral Plan* is the culmination of the National Black Catholic Congress that was held in Washington, D.C., May 21-24, 1987. The National Conference of Catholic Bishops responded to the Pastoral Plan in a brief document entitled *Here I am Send Me*, November 8, 1989 (Washington, D.C.: USCC, 1989). In this response document, which includes the text of the Pastoral Plan in the Appendix we find the following information on the Pastoral Plan: "During the two years of planning for the congress, an extensive consultation process took place. U.S. dioceses with a significant number of African American

Catholics were requested to conduct a series of 'Reflection Days' to discuss issues relating to evangelization of African Americans on the local level. One hundred and seven dioceses participated in the process, developing particular evangelization goals and objectives for the local Church. The diocesan goals and objectives were collected from the participants and forwarded to the central planning committee of the congress, where common elements were transformed into a cohesive national evangelization plan. It can truly be said that *The National Black Catholic Pastoral Plan* is the result of a distillation of the dreams and aspirations of the African American community as a whole" (p. 1).

53. Vivian Rouson, "Black Catholics Share Pride, Renew Roots," *National Catholic Reporter*, September 19, 1997, p. 8.

54. Davis, *History*, p. 193 [emphasis mine].

55. Cyprian Rowe, "Black and Catholic—IV," *America* 142 (March 29, 1980): 262.

56. Davis, "Two Sides," p. 59.

57. Rowe, p. 262.

58. Davis, *History*, p. 220.

59. Rowe, p. 263 [emphasis mine].

60. Ibid.

61. Ibid., p. 263.

62. Michael Graham, "John LaFarge," NDCST, pp. 535-539.

63. Some argue that if the church had spoken out strongly against the Nov. 9-10 raiding of Jewish shops and beatings and killings of Jews, known as *Kristallnacht*, it might have altered Hitler's scapegoating of the Jews. Because of the silence of the churches after these atrocities Hitler felt he could attack the Jews with impunity. Michael Farrell, "Encyclical Might Have Changed Things: Book recalls Attempt to Decry '30's Racism," *National Catholic Reporter* (March 8, 1996): 13. The book which tells of this unpublished encyclical is written by two Belgian scholars, Georges Passelecq and Bernard Suchecky, *L'Encyclique Cachée de Pie XI: Une Occasion Manquée de l'Eglise face a l'Antisemitisme* (Editions La D'ecouverte, 1993). The English edition, *Pius XI's Hidden Encyclical: A Lost Opportunity for the Church vis-à-vis Anti-Semitism*, was published by Harcourt Brace/Harvest Books in 1997.

64. Dolan, *The American Catholic Experience*, p. 405.

65. Joel Kovel, *White Racism* (1970), p. 54; as quoted by Jones, in *Prejudice and Racism*, p. 121.

66. Copeland, p. 101.

67. Ibid., p. 101.

68. Jerome LeDoux, "Christian Pastoral Theology Looks at Black Experience," in *Theology: A Portrait in Black Theology*, Thaddeus Posey, ed. (Pittsburgh: Capuchin Press, 1980), p. 115.

69. Davis, *History*, p. 255.

70. Ibid., p. 256.

71. Ibid., p. 258.

72. Copeland, pp. 101-102 and "A Statement of the Black Catholic Clergy Caucus, April 18, 1968," in Gayraud Wilmore and James Cone, eds., *Black Theology: A Documentary History, 1966-1979* (Maryknoll, NY: Orbis Books, 1979), p. 322.

73. From Davis's summary, *History*, p. 258.

74. Ibid., pp. 258-9.

75. Clarence Williams, "A Black Catholic Perspective of Evangelization on the Occasion of

the 500th Anniversary of the Catholic Church in the New World," in *Our Roots and Gifts—Proceedings of the Rejoice! Seminar, Rome, Italy, November 1989*, sponsored by Office of Black Catholics Archdiocese of Washington, D.C. (Washington, D.C.: Archdiocese of Washington, 1990), p. 25.

76. Ibid., p. 25.

77. Copeland, p. 102.

78. Ibid., pp. 102-103.

79. Hayes, "Tracings," p. 71.

80. Cone, pp. 50-51.

81. Ibid., p. 51.

82. Copeland, p. 109.

83. *What We Have Seen and Heard: A Pastoral Letter on Evangelization from the Black Bishops of the United States, September 9, 1984* (Cincinnati: St. Anthony Messenger Press), pp. 8-11.

84. Hayes, "Tracings," p. 76.

85. Clarence Rivers, *The Spirit in Worship* (Cincinnati: Stimuli, Inc., 1978), p. 8.

86. Copeland, p. 103.

87. Ibid., p. 104.

88. Cyprian Rowe, "The Case for a Distinctive Black Culture," in *This Far by Faith: American Black Worship and Its African Roots* (Washington, D.C.: NOBC and the Liturgical Conference, 1977), p. 27; cited in Copeland, p. 104.

89. Hayes, "Tracings," p. 72.

90. Wilton Gregory, "African-American Catholics and the Summer of '89'" *Origins* 19 (September 7, 1989): 229.

91. NCCB, *Brothers and Sisters to Us: U.S. Bishops' Pastoral Letter on Racism in Our Day* (Washington, D.C.: USCC, 1979), p. 1.

92. Bishops' Committee on Black Catholics, NCCB, *For the Love of One Another: A Special Message on the Occasion of the Tenth Anniversary of Brothers and Sisters to Us* (Washington, D.C.: USCC, 1989), p. 6.

93. Ibid., p. 7.

94. "Study Finds Racist Attitudes in Catholic Diocese," *Democrat and Chronicle* (October 17, 1992), p. 1B.

95. Hayes, *And Still*, p. 167.

96. Cornel West, *Race Matters* (New York: Vintage Books, 1994), pp. 19-20.

97. Ibid., pp. 22-23.

98. Ibid., p. 24.

99. Ibid., pp. 24-25.

100. Ibid., pp. 26-27.

101. Ibid., p. 27.

102. Ibid., p. 28.

103. Ibid., p. 29.

CHAPTER 6

1. Heinrich Krauss, *"Populorum Progressio": Die Entwicklungsenenzyklika Pauls VI Mit Einfuhrung und Kommentar* (Freiburg: Herder, 1967), pp. 102-103.

2. Cardinal Joseph Schroeffer who had been the chairman of the subcommission of chapter five of *Gaudium et Spes* pointed out the unanimity of the two: "Even when there are no explicit references to the Council, the spirit and doctrine of the latter [*Gaudium et Spes*] are unmistakably apparent." Joseph Schroeffer, "Continuity of the Conciliar and Pontifical Magisterium from 'Gaudium et Spes' to 'Populorum Progressio,'" *L'Osservatore Romano* [English edition] (April 28, 1977): 6. Another commentator, Rene Laurentin, underscores that assessment: "In any event, *Populorum Progressio* is not a starting point. It is categorically and explicitly situated as a consequence of the Council." Rene Laurentin, *Liberation, Development and Salvation*, trans. C.U. Quinn (Maryknoll: Orbis Books, 1972), p. 25.

3. The reasons for the writing *Populorum Progressio* are from Rene Laurentin, ibid., pp. 108-109.

4. For descriptions of the various approaches see Charles Elliott, *The Development Debate* (London: SCM Press, 1971), pp. 15-69; Denis Goulet, *The Cruel Choice: A New Concept in the Theory of Development* (New York: Atheneum, 1977), pp. xiii- xiv; Richard Dickinson, *To Set at Liberty the Oppressed: Towards an Understanding of Christian Responsibilities of Development/Liberation* (Geneva: WCC, 1975), pp. 61-68.

5. In the margin referring to Lebret's thought, Pope Paul wrote, "Molto belle. Molto toccanti. Molto edificanti. Bisogna che il suo ideale di civilizazione si compia." [Very fine. Very touching. Very edifying. His ideal of civilization should be filled out.] Paul Poupard, "Genesi e carattere del documento," *Il Regno Attualita' Cattolica* (Bologna) 12 (May 1, 1967): 197.

6. John Pawlikowski, "Introduction to *Populorum Progressio* and *Octogesima Adveniens*, in *Justice in the Marketplace: Collected Statements of the Vatican and the United States Catholic Bishops on Economic Justice, 1891-1984*, David Byers, ed., (Washington, D.C.: USCC., 1985), p. 201.

7. The question emerged regarding which text was intended by the pope, the original text which was written in French or the official language which is the Latin text. The original French has a stronger condemnation of capitalism than the official Latin text. The controversy developed around the correct English translation—from the French or the Latin. The question was which version to follow and which was the intention of the pope. "Confusion over Latin," *America* 116 (May 20, 1967): 747-8.

8. "Businessmen Study Encyclical," *Tablet* 221 (July 8, 1967): 760.

9. *Insegnamenti dei Paolo VI 1967* (Vatican City: Polyglot, 1968), p. 970.

10. Reactions to the encyclical were mixed—depending on the commentator's political and economic philosophy. Conservatives like Milton Friedman called the pope's principles "warmed-over Marxism" in the article in *The Wall Street Journal*. The liberal press represented by the *New Republic* argued that "the Pope's agenda for 'a new humanism' is radical and reasonable. Radical, because it goes to the root of our affiliations and because the remedies it proposes, if understood, would jolt very many members of the U.S. Congress, reasonable, because it prescribes no more than what we are capable of doing." "Appeals to Reason," *New Republic* 156 (April 8, 1967): 7. *The New York Times* gave it a positive reading, noting that the economic philosophy "is sophisticated, comprehensive and penetrating, and it shows a profound grasp of the problems of developed versus underdeveloped countries in their technical as well as moral and religious aspects." Quoted in Benjamin L. Masse, "The Pope's Plea for Poor

Nations," *America* 117 (August 5, 1967): 129. Radicals, naturally found the letter wanting. Herve Chaigne complained that the pope merely presented the traditional "reformist" attitude of Catholic social thought in a new language. Cited by Pedro Altares, "Hacia un nuevo sentido del pensamiento social de la Iglesia?" in *Comentarios de Cuadernos para el Dialogo a la Populorum Progressio* (Madrid: Cuadernos, 1967), pp. 198-99. J. M. Setien Alberro criticized the encyclical for not being able to free itself from the sociopolitical conditioning which was revealed in its acceptance of capitalism. As a consequence the social teaching is "reformist" of the capitalistic system unable to provoke the "bold solutions" needed. J. M. Setien Alberro, "Profecia y doctrina social de la iglesia en la enc. 'Populorum Progressio,'" *Salamanticensis* 15 (1968):8.

11. See W. W. Rostow, *The Stages of Economic Growth* (Cambridge: Cambridge University Press, 1969).

12. Robert McAfee Brown, "Paul VI's Secular Ecumenism," *Commonweal* 86 (May 19, 1967): 264.

13. *NC News Service*, "'Populorum Progressio' Lives up to its Name for Families in Colombia" (March 19, 1979): 23-24.

14. Thomas Sieger Derr, *Barriers to Ecumenism: The Holy See and the World Council on Social Questions* (Maryknoll, NY: Orbis Books, 1983), pp. 1-2. While doing research for my doctoral dissertation I was privileged to live with the last director of Sodepax, John Lucal, S.J., in Geneva in the summer of 1978. From him and from my work at WCC I learned firsthand of the accomplishments of Sodepax and the uncooperative mood from the Roman Catholic side in its waning years.

15. Reinhold Niebuhr, *Moral Man and Immoral Society: A Study in Ethics and Politics* (New York: Charles Scribner's Sons, 1932, reprinted 1960), p. xii.

16. *La Croix* (April 19, 1967): 4; as quoted by Laurentin, pp. 112-13.

17. Charles Curran, see his chapter on "Saul D. Alinsky, Catholic Social Practice, and Catholic Theory," in idem, *Directions in Catholic Social Ethics* (Notre Dame: University of Notre Dame Press, 1985), p. 159.

18. Gregory Pierce, *Activism That Makes Sense: Congregations and Community Organizations* (New York: Paulist Press, 1984), p. 44.

19. Ronald Taylor, *Chavez and the Farm Workers* (Boston: Beacon Press, 1975), p. 81. [emphasis added.]

20. Sanford Horwitt, *Let Them Call Me Rebel: Saul Alinsky—His Life and Legacy* (New York: Alfred A. Knopf, 1989), p. 520.

21. This outline for Alinsky-style community organizing is taken from my own experience with the Industrial Areas Foundation (IAF) method. In 1975 I did a two-week training session at IAF in Chicago, and for three years I was a leader in a community organization in Milwaukee known as the Milwaukee Alliance of Concerned Citizens. For a fuller discussion of the thought and methodology of Saul Alinsky see: Saul Alinsky, *Reveille for Radicals* (New York: Random House, 1969); idem, *Rules for Radicals: A Practical Primer for Realistic Radicals* (New York: Random House, 1971); P. David Finks, *The Radical Vision of Saul Alinsky* (New York: Paulist Press, 1984); Harry Fagan, *Empowerment: Skills for Parish Social Action* (New Yortk: Paulist Press, 1979).

22. Jean Maddern Pitrone, *Chavez: Man of the Migrants, A Plea for Social Justice* (New York: Alba House, 1971), p. 53. Also see P. David Finks' discussion under the heading "Chavez Moves On" in idem, *The Radical Vision of Saul Alinsky*, pp. 170-173.

23. Sydney D. Smith, *Grapes of Conflict* (Pasedena, CA: Hope Pub. House, 1987), p. 80.

24. Horwitt, p. 521.

25. Smith, p. 83 ff.

26. Ibid., p. 89.

27. Ibid., p. 91. At the time of the second grape boycott and the lettuce boycott I was serving in a central city parish in Milwaukee and I organized a group of UFW supporters—parishioners, seminarians and seminary faculty. We picketed every Friday afternoon for six months in front of a grocery chain store that was selling California grapes and lettuce. The Priests' Senate of the Archdiocese of Milwaukee also debated a resolution supporting the Gallo boycott. I worked on this resolution with Father Michael Crosby, OFM.Cap., and the Peace and Justice Committee. Because the people of Wisconsin consumed so much brandy, two executives of the Gallo Wine Company flew out to the Priests' Senate meeting to present their side of the story. A UFW farm worker also addressed the Priests' Senate. The resolution which called upon the parishes and Catholics of the archdiocese to honor the UFW boycotts was approved by the Milwaukee Priests' Senate.

28. Ibid., pp. 95-96.

29. Pitrone, pp. 121-23.

30. Smith, p. 98.

31. Arthur Jones, "Million Reaped What Cesar Chavez Sowed," *National Catholic Reporter* (May 7, 1993): 7.

32. Smith, p. 98.

33. Leslie Wirpsa, "UFW targets strawberry fields: Catholic bishops' statements support farm workers' cause," *National Catholic Reporter* 34 (May 15, 1998): 4.

34. Ibid., pp. 3-4.

CHAPTER 7

1. Patrick McDermott, S.J., "A New 'Encyclical' on Social Justice," *The Christian Century* 88 (June 16, 1971): 748.

2. Bernard Evans identifies five new themes in his analysis of *Octogesima Adveniens* as found in his article, "*Octogesima Adveniens*," NDCST, pp. 686-692. I have added the sixth theme on methodology.

3. See Bartolomeo Sorge's discussion of this point in "L'Apporto Dottrinale della Lettera Apostolica 'Octogesima Adveniens,'" *La Civiltà Cattolica* 122 (1971): 420-22.

4. Walter Kerber, "*Octogesima Adveniens*: Ein Dokument der Freiheit," *Stimmen der Zeit* 188 (1971): 178.

5. Donal Dorr, *Option for the Poor*, p. 218, quoting Marie-Dominique Chenu, *La 'doctrina sociale' de l'Eglise comme ideologie* (Paris: Cerf, 1979), p. 80.

6. Ibid., p. 219.

7. Evans, p. 688.

8. Philip Land, "The Social Teaching of Pope Paul VI," *America* (May 12, 1979): 394.

9. I prefer Donal Dorr's translation of this sentence: "Yet it [economic activity] runs the risk of *unduly absorbing human energies and limiting people's freedom*." Dorr, p. 214.

10. John Krol, "CHD Policies," USCC Administrative Board, February 1972, quoted by Evans, pp. 691-692.

11. Dorr, p. 219.

12. J. Bryan Hehir, "Catholic Teaching on War and Peace: The Decade 1979-1989," Charles

E. Curran, ed., *Moral Theology: Challenges for the Future* (New York: Paulist Press, 1990), p. 365.

13. Ibid.

14. Ibid.

15. Mary Elsbernd, O.S.F., "What Ever Happened to *Octogesima Adveniens?*" *Theological Studies* 56 (1995): 39-60.

16. Ibid., p. 56.

17. Ibid., p. 40.

18. Ronald Hamel, "Justice in the World," NDCST, p. 495.

19. Ibid.

20. Ibid., p. 496.

21. John F. X. Harriott, S.J., "The Difficulty of Justice," *Month* 5 (new series) (January 1972): 9.

22. Francis X. Murphy, C.SS.R., "The Roman Synod of Bishops 1971," *American Ecclesiastical Review* 165 (October 1971): 76.

23. Joseph Gremillion, "The Context and Content of the Synodal Document," an unpublished lecture at the "Commemorative Conference on the Tenth Anniversary of *Justice in the World*" held at St. Francis Seminary, Milwaukee, Wisconsin, December 1, 1981, p. 3.

24. Harriot, pp. 10-11.

25. Gremillion, p. 3.

26. Harriot, pp. 11 and 16.

27. Hamel, p. 495.

28. Murphy, 153. Cosmao was associated with the Centre Foie et Developement founded by Louis Lebret, the first editor of *Populorum Progressio*.

29. Ibid., p. 161.

30. Hamel, p. 496.

31. Oral remarks made at a convocation on liberation theology held in Detroit in August, 1975 as quoted by John Coleman, *An American Strategic Theology* (New York: Paulist, 1982), p. 24.

32. See John Coleman's discussion of this, pp. 24-25.

33. Harriot, p. 18.

34. "Brief History of the Center of Concern," a two-page report from the Center of Concern, p. 1; reprinted in part in "Center of Concern's 25 Years Living Gospel of Justice," *National Catholic Reporter* (September 20, 1996): 24. Hereafter cited as "Brief History."

35. Sister Helen Prejean, *Dead Man Walking* (New York: Random House, 1993), p. 5.

36. "Soon after the dramatic deliberations of Synod '71, the Jesuit Order decided to hold its most formal kind of assembly, referred to as a General Congregation, the thirty-second such convocation held by it since the Order's beginning in the sixteenth century. In that formal consultation, held from December 1974 until March 1975, the Jesuit Order determined that the promotion of justice in the world was to become a major focus of its work in the future and a primary way of expressing the faith commitment of its membership." John Haughey, "Forward" in idem, *The Faith That Does Justice: Examining the Christian Sources for Social Change*, p. 3.

37. "Brief History," p. 1. Father Arrupe had asked Father Ryan in October of 1970 to begin planning for the Center of Concern.

38. Ibid.

39. Joe Holland and Peter Henriot, *Social Analysis: Linking Faith and Justice* (Maryknoll, NY: Orbis, 1993), p. 121.

40. "Brief History," p. 2.

41. "Center of Concern's 25 Years Living Gospel of Justice," *National Catholic Reporter* (September 20, 1996): 24.

42. Dorothy Vidulich, "The Network Story," *Sisters Today* 58 (April 1987): 473.

43. Ibid., p. 474.

44. Ibid., p., 476. The 1997 membership is taken from a NETWORK fund-raising letter dated May 1997.

45. From a NETWORK brochure entitled, "Your Voice in Washington for Social Change."

46. From May 1997 membership literature.

47. National Federation of Priests' Councils, Province of St. Paul-Minneapolis, *Exploitation or Liberation: Ethics for Investors,* 24-page pamphlet, 1972, p. 1.

48. Ibid., pp. 7-8.

49. Michael H. Crosby and Ginny Schauble, "NCCRI Organizational History," *National Catholic Coalition for Responsible Investment Directory, Winter 1978-79* (Milwaukee: NCCRI, 32-page booklet), p. 4.

50. Ibid., p. 4.

51. Protestant churches were organized as early as 1967 when five denominations used their combined $2.7 million in Eastman Kodak stock to demand the hiring of more unskilled African American workers. That effort was successful as Kodak "significantly increased its complement of black workers." Bevis Longstreth and H. David Rosenbloom, *Corporate Social Responsibility and the Institutional Investor* (New York: Praeger Publishers, 1973), p. 4. The five denominations were United Presbyterian USA, Reformed Church in America, Episcopal Church, United Church of Christ, and the United Methodist Church. Most other major denominations were also involved in social responsibility. See Michael Crosby, *Catholic Church Investments for Corporate Social Responsibility* (Milwaukee, WI: Justice and Peace Center, 1973), pp. 6-7.

52. Telephone conversation with Michael H. Crosby, January 27, 1998.

53. J. Andy Smith, III, "Religious Activism and Economic Power: Assessing 25 Years of the Interfaith Center on Corporate Responsibility." This paper was presented at the Annual Meeting of the Society of Christian Ethics, January 9-11, 1998; photocopy of the paper from the author, p. 9.

54. "Message from Executive Director Timothy Smith," *The Corporate Examiner* 25 (November 1, 1996), p. 3.

55. Ibid., p. 4.

56. *Woodstock Theological Center 1998 Annual Appeal and Report.*

57. Ibid.

CHAPTER 8

1. Margaret O'Brien Steinfels, "Consider the Seamless Garment," in Patricia Jung and Thomas Shannon, eds., *Abortion and Catholicism: the American Debate* (New York: Crossroad, 1988), p. 268; hereafter cited as *Abortion and Catholicism.*

2. Ibid.

3. Ibid.

4. In 1965 the Vatican Council fathers articulated the "seamless garment" ethic in a powerful way:

> In our times a special obligation binds us to make ourselves the neighbor of absolutely every person, and of actively helping him when he come across our path, whether he be an old person abandoned by all, a foreign laborer unjustly looked down upon, a refugee, a child born of an unlawful union and wrongly suffering for a sin he did not commit, or a hungry person who disturbs our conscience by recalling the voice of the Lord: "As long as you did it for one of these, the least of my brethren, you did it for me" (Mt. 25:40).
>
> Furthermore, whatever is opposed to life itself, such as any type of murder, genocide, abortion, euthanasia, or willful self-destruction, whatever violates the integrity of the human person, such as mutilation, torments inflicted on body or mind, attempts to coerce the will itself; whatever insults human dignity, such as subhuman living conditions, arbitrary imprisonment, deportation, slavery, prostitution, the selling of women and children; as well as disgraceful working conditions, where men are treated as mere tools for profit, rather than as free and responsible persons; all these things and others of their like are infamies indeed. They poison human society, but they do more harm to those who practice them than those who suffer from the injury. Moreover, they are a supreme dishonor to the Creator.

See *Gaudium et Spes*, paragraph 27, in Abbott, *The Documents of Vatican II*, pp. 226-227.

5. From the *Consistent Ethic of Life*, a videotape produced by the Seamless Garment Network, 1993.

6. Humberto Medeiros, "A Call to a Consistent Ethic of Life and the Law," *Pilot* (July 10, 1971) 7. McCormick's brief report on the address is found in "Notes on Moral Theology," *Theological Studies* 33 (1972): 118.

7. Rosemary Bottcher, "Celebrating 25 Years of Pro-Life Feminism," *The American Feminist* (Feminists for Life of America) 4 (Summer 1997): 8.

8. Bottcher, p. 8.

9. Feminists for Life of America, "Justice for All" November, 11, 1994, [an eleven-page Long Range Plan], p. 1; discussed in Mary Beth Frampton, "Feminists for Life of America Restructures," *The American Feminist* 2 (Winter 1995): 14.

10. Feminists for Life flyer, dated Sept. 1995.

11. Frampton, pp. 14-15.

12. Net Hentoff, "Yes, There Are Pro-Life Feminists," *The Washington Post* (October 29, 1994) reprinted in *The American Feminist* 2 (Winter 1995): 6.

13. FFLA flyer.

14. From a telephone conversation with the Washington office, August 25, 1997. I was told the membership is between 5,000 and 10,000. I used the conservative estimate.

15. Men are also part of the Feminist for Life movement. One of the most articulate is a writer for the *Village Voice* in New York City, Nat Hentoff. For an example of his writing see note 12 above.

16. Cecilia Voss Kock, "Reflecting As FFL Celebrates Its Tenth Birthday," in Gail Grenier Sweet, *Pro-Life Feminism: Different Voices* (Toronto: Life Cycle Books, 1985), p. 23.

17. Faye and Jeff Kunce, "The Seamless Garment Network," *Harmony: Voices for a Just Future* 1 (September-October, 1987): 14.

18. While the work is no doubt morally and spiritually rewarding, writing for *Harmony* does not appear to be a way of getting rich. In the third year of the periodical the editor reported that "*Harmony* is published at a loss. Our editors and writers are unpaid volunteers. Your help is appreciated." *Harmony* 3 (May 1992): 2.

19. *Harmony* 4 (December 1993): 11.

20. Carol Crossed, "What's Happening with the Seamless Garment Network?" *Harmony* 4 (December 1993): 11.

21. Crossed, p. 11.

22. Diocese of Rochester, *Strategic Plan*, "Synod Goal Two: To Advocate for a Consistent Life Ethic," (June 1997), p. 9.

23. Joseph Cardinal Bernardin, *Consistent Ethic of Life* (Kansas City: Sheed & Ward, 1988), p. 2. The first part of this text presents Cardinal Bernardin's ten talks on the topic and part two presents responses and evaluations from Richard McCormick, Frans Jozef van Beeck, John Finnis, James Walter, James Gustafson, Lisa Cahill, J. Bryan Hehir, and Sidney Callahan with a "response to the symposium" by Bernardin.

24. Ibid., p. 5.

25. Ibid., p. 7; emphasis mine.

26. Ibid., p. 10.

27. Ibid., p. 10; emphasis mine.

28. Ibid., pp. 16-17.

29. Ibid., p. 15.

30. Ibid., pp. 8-9 and quoted on p. 82.

31. Ibid., p. 83.

32. Ibid., p. 83.

33. Ibid., pp. 92-93.

34. Ibid., p. 93.

35. Ibid., p. 77.

36. Bernardin, "The Consistent Ethic After 'Webster': Opportunities and Dangers," *Commonweal* 117 (April 20, 1990): 248.

37. Ibid., 1990, p. 248.

38. Andre Frossard, *Portraits of John Paul II* (San Francisco: Ignatius Press, 1990), p. 9.

39. Wilton Wynn, *Keepers of the Keys: John XXIII, Paul VI and John Paul II—Three Who Changed the Church* (New York: Random House, 1988), pp. 63-64.

40. Ibid., p. 65.

41. Frossard, pp. 145-146.

42. Ibid., pp. 85-88.

43. This visit took place on December 27, 1984, Wynn, pp. 145-146.

44. See chapter 10.

45. Juan Arias, a Spanish journalist in the Vatican, calls Pope John Paul an enigma: "Karol Wojtyla... es sin duda, uno de los personajes mas relevantes del mundo actual; paradojico,

polierdrico, contradictorio. Pero es, tambien, un enigma. Y un enigma nada facil de descifrar." ["Karol Wojtyla is, without a doubt, one of the most relevant persons of the world today; paradoxical, polyhedral, contradictory. But he is also an enigma. And an enigma is never easy to decode." my translation] Juan Aria, *El Enigma Wojtyla* (Madrid: Edicione El Pais, 1985), p. 11.

46. Francis A. Sullivan, "The Doctrinal Weight of *Evangelium Vitae*," *Theological Studies* 56 (1995): 565. Sullivan used these words to clarify the question of the infallibility of contraception which was also condemned in *Evangelium Vitae*. He used the following phrasing for the abortion and euthanasia statements: "In view of the present uncertainty, I would fall back on a thesis which I defended in a previous note in this journal: that a doctrine should not be understood as having been infallibly taught by the ordinary magisterium, unless this fact is clearly established, and such a fact can hardly be said to be 'clearly established' unless there is a consensus of Catholic theologians about it" (p. 664).

47. James J. Megivern, *The Death Penalty: An Historical and Theological Survey* (New York: Paulist Press, 1997), p. 444.

48. "Revisions Alter Death Penalty, Homosexuality Views," *Catholic Courier* [Rochester, NY](September 11, 1997): 6. The paper reported the phrasing: "suppression of the offender." This was retranslated to read the "execution of the offender" according to the *Courier* reporter Lee Strong. Telephone conversation, September 15, 1997.

49. As late as 1969 the Vatican still had a statute that reserved the death penalty for anyone who tried to assassinate a pope within Vatican City. In 1969 Pope Paul VI quietly removed this statute because of the rethinking of the question. See Megivern, p. 261.

50. Richard A. McCormick, "The Gospel of Life," *America* 172 (April 29, 1995): 14.

51. Quoted by *The American Feminist* 2 (Summer 1995): 6; no date given for the *Chicago Tribune* editorial.

52. Curran, p. 4.

53. Ibid., p. 13.

54. Charles Curran, "Encyclical is Positive, Problematic," *National Catholic Reporter* (April 14, 1995): 5.

55. Richard Gula, *Reason Informed by Faith* (New York: Paulist Press, 1989), p. 237.

56. Ibid., pp. 237-238.

57. Christine Gudorf, "To Make a Seamless Garment, Use a Single Piece of Cloth," in *Abortion and Catholicism*, p. 283.

58. Ibid., p. 284.

59. The way to resolve this inconsistency is to recognize that all moral norms when applied to specific situations are limited and tentative. This means that exceptions to the norms are possible and that debate about "prudential judgments" is to be expected in all areas of moral reflection.

This resolution of the "inconsistency" will not be accepted by all moralists. Those who hold to a deontological methodology will give scant attention to arguments that give more weight to "consequences." Richard Gula also calls for a revised view of the natural law which "calls for an inductive method of moral argument which takes historical human experience seriously. It is sensitive to the ambiguity of moral experience and to the limitations of formulating absolute, universal, concrete moral norms." He is confident that "The use of natural law in Catholic morality today is becoming more open to the great complexity and ambiguity of human, personal reality. Its conclusions, while as accurate as the evidence will allow, are accurate enough to be reliable but must necessarily be tentative and open to revision." Ibid., 245-246.

60. See Patricia Beattie Jung and Ralph F. Smith, *Heterosexism: An Ethical Challenge* (Albany,

NY: State University of New York Press, 1993) and Richard Peddicord, *Gay and Lesbian Rights: A Question: Sexual Ethics or Social Justice* (Kansas City, MO: Sheed and Ward, 1996).

61. James Gustafson, "The Consistent Ethic of Life: A Protestant Perspective," in Bernardin, *Consistent Ethic of Life*, p. 199.

62. Gustafson, p. 208.

63. Ibid., emphasis mine.

64. The statistics are those available as of August 1994. Committee for Domestic Social Policy, NCCB, *Confronting a Culture of Violence: A Catholic Framework for Action, A Pastoral Message of the U.S. Catholic Bishops* (Washington, D.C., USCC, 1994), pp. 4-5.

65. Historians like Richard Brown and sociologists of religion like John Coleman are putting us in touch with the way violence is so evident in our history and in our attitudes. Drawing on Brown's work, *A Strain of Violence*, Father Coleman unpacks the deep cultural roots of violence as "the shadow-side" possibility of three American cultural realities:

> 1. our exalted sense of popular sovereignty—"Indeed, free and absolutely unfettered ownership and use of guns have come to be for many the litmus test of the continued validity and guarantee of popular sovereignty."

> 2. American racism—first the native Americans, e.g. the folk saying of the pioneer society, "the only good Indian is a dead Indian" and then the African American community, Asians, Latinos, etc.; and

> 3. American individualism—breeds isolation and the breakdown of social bonds of community which allows the spread of violence. See John Coleman, "Responding to Violence," *Origins* (1995): 180-184.

66. NCCB, *Confronting a Culture of Violence*, pp. 9-10.

67. Ibid., pp. 22-23.

68. Daryl P. Domning, "Pope's Cultural Critique Lacks Perspective: Deriding the West as a 'Culture of Death,'" *National Catholic Reporter* (September 19, 1997): 18.

CHAPTER 9

1. Alfred T. Hennelly, ed., *Liberation Theology: A Documentary History* (Maryknoll, NY: Orbis Books, 1990), p. xv.

2. Hubert Herring, *A History of Latin America* (New York: Alfred A. Knopf, 1956), p. 173; as quoted by Penny Lernoux, "The Long Path to Puebla," in John Eagleson and Philip Scharper, eds., *Puebla and Beyond* (Maryknoll, NY: Orbis Books, 1979), p. 3.

3. Enrique Dussel, *History and the Theology of Liberation: A Latin American Perspective.* (Maryknoll, NY: Orbis Books, 1976), p. 74.

4. Lernoux, p. 3.

5. Leslie Wirpsa, "After 25 Years Medellín Spirit Lives, No Thanks to Vatican," *National Catholic Reporter* (October 15, 1993): 11.

6. Lernoux, p. 11.

7. Segunda Conferencia General del Episcopado Latinoamericano, *La Iglesia en la Actual Transformacion de America Latina a la Luz del Concilio: Conclusiones* (Mexico City: Talleres de la Imprenta Mexicana, 1970), p. 16 [author's translation]. The selections of the Medellín documents are found in Gremillion, *The Gospel of Peace and Justice*, pp. 445-476; and in

Hennelly, *Liberation Theology: A Documentary History,* pp. 89-119. Quoted from Hennelly, the section entitled "Justice," par. 16, p. 110.

8. "Justice," par. 7.

9. Ibid., par. 14.

10. Ibid., par. 20; emphasis mine.

11. "Peace" par. 5, and 6, Hennelly, p. 107.

12. "Justice," par. 21 and 22, Hennelly, p. 104-5.

13. Lernoux, p. 12.

14. Ibid., p. 11.

15. Ibid., p. 12.

16. Hennelly, p. 89.

17. Vekemans received approximately $200,000 from the DeRance Foundation; Lernoux, p. 14 and footnote 65. Adveniat and Misereor are two aid agencies supported by the German Catholic church. Adveniat is specifically concerned with church projects in Latin America, such as the construction of chapels or seminaries and Misereor supports social development programs in the Third World, including health centers and schools.

18. Lernoux, pp. 21-22.

19. Synod of Bishops, "Justice in the World," in Gremillion, *The Gospel of Peace and Justice,* par. 6, p. 514.

20. Hennelly, p. 121.

21. Ibid., p. 121.

22. Ibid., p. 178.

23. Lernoux, pp. 23-24.

24. Joseph Comblin, "The Bishops' Conference at Puebla," *Theology Digest* 28 (Spring 1980): 9. For a translation and commentary on the Puebla document see Eagleson and Scharper, *Puebla and Beyond.*

25. Comblin, p. 10.

26. I am following Joseph Comblin's analysis of the Puebla documents.

27. Jon Sobrino, "Puebla: a Quiet Affirmation of Medellín," *Theology Digest* 28 (Spring, 1980): 14.

28. Alfred T. Hennelly, ed., *Santo Domingo and Beyond* (Maryknoll, NY: Orbis, 1993), p. 24; hereafter cited as Hennelly, *SD.*

29. "Pope John Paul II to CELAM: The Task of the Latin American Bishop," *Origins* 12 (March 24, 1983): 661.

30. Hennelly, *SD,* p. 26.

31. Ibid.

32. Guillermo Melendez, "Bishops Reaffirm Option for the Poor: CELAM IV Document Provokes Vatican Ire," *Latinamerica Press* 24 (July 9, 1992): 1.

33. Leslie Wirpsa, "Curia Ignites Angry Protest at CELAM IV," *National Catholic Reporter* (November 6, 1992): 12.

34. Hennelly, *SD,* p. 27.

35. Francis McDonagh, "Legacy of Santo Domingo," *Tablet* 246 (November 21, 1992): 1489.

36. This chronology is taken from Hennelly's report of the conference as presented in *SD,* pp. 26-28.

37. Peter Hebblethwaite, "CELAM: Final Report: 'Small But Substantial Changes,'" *National Catholic Reporter* (January 22, 1993): 12.

38. McDonagh, p. 1489.

39. Jon Sobrino, "The Winds in Santo Domingo and the Evangelization of Culture," in Hennelly, SD, p. 177.

40. Ibid., p. 177.

41. Ibid.

42. Tommie Sue Montgomery, "The Church in the Salvadoran Revolution," *Latin American Perspectives* 10 (Winter 1983): 81.

43. Sobrino, pp. 179-180.

44. Sobrino quotes the section on the martyrs from the Second Report; see pp. 169-170.

45. This is the judgment of Pablo Richard and Alfred Hennelly; see Pablo Richard, "La Iglesia Catolica despues de Santo Domingo," *Pastoral Popular*, nos. 224-25 (Nov.-Dec. 1992): 14-22; as quoted by Edward L. Cleary, "The Journey to Santo Domingo," in Hennelly, SD, p. 18; also see Hennelly's assessment in ibid., p. 31.

46. Ibid., p. 34.

47. Leslie Wirpsa, "Hints of Ecclesial Self-Criticism Disappear," *National Catholic Reporter* (January 22, 1993): 13.

48. Sobrino, "The Winds," in Hennelly, SD, p. 170.

49. William H. Shannon, "Stirrings of the Spirit" presented at the St. Bernard's Institute Women's Scholarship Awards Banquet, June 3, 1997.

50. Sobrino, p. 172.

51. Leslie Wirpsa, "After 25 Years Medellín Spirit Lives, No Thanks to Vatican," *National Catholic Reporter* (October 15, 1993): 11.

52. Ibid., p. 13.

53. Jose Marins, "Basic Christian Communities in Latin America," *LADOC [Latin American Documentation]* "Keyhole" Series VI (Washington, D.C.: USCC, 1976): 2.

54. Montgomery, p. 67. The threefold framework of this section is taken from Montgomery's article.

55. Hennelly, *Doc. History*, p. xiiiv-xix.

56. "By 1968 U.S. aid was contributing massively to the balance of payments, accounting for a $904 million surplus entry—the amount by which the $1.5 billion received by U.S. aid agencies in the form of interest in principal repayments on past U.S. aid exceeded the balance-of-payments cost of new aid, as *95% of this new aid was tied directly to purchases of U.S. goods and services.*" Denis Goulet and Michael Hudson, *The Myth of Aid: The Hidden Agenda of the Development Reports* (Maryknoll, NY: Orbis Books, 1971), p. 93.

57. For an introduction to his thought see: Alfred Hennelly, *Liberation Theologies: The Global Pursuit of Justice* (Mystic, CT: Twenty-Third Publications, 1995), pp. 10-26; Robert McAfee Brown, *Gustavo Gutiérrez: An Introduction to Liberation Theology* (Maryknoll, NY: Orbis Books, 1990); James Nickoloff, ed., *Gustavo Gutiérrez: Essential Writings* (Minneapolis: Fortress, 1996); and Curt Cadorette, *From the Heart of the People: the Theology of Gustavo Gutiérrez* (Oak Park, IL: Meyer-Stone, 1988).

58. Brown, pp. 23-24.

59. Gustavo Gutiérrez, *Teologia de la liberacion, Perspectivas* (Lima: CEP, 1971), the English translation, *A Theology of Liberation*, was published by Orbis Books in 1973.

60. Henri Nouwen, *¡Gracias!* (New York: Harper and Row, 1983), pp. 174-175.

61. Gustavo Gutiérrez, *Teologia de la liberacion: Perspectivas* (Salamanca: Ediciones Sigueme, 1972), p. 35. This is my translation of "Lo primero es el compromiso de caridad, de servicio. La teologia viene *despues*, es acto segundo." In the English version these two crucial sentences are translated simply as "Theology follows; it is the second step." The first sentence, "First is the commitment of charity, of service," is missing. See *A Theology of Liberation: History, Politics and Salvation*, translated and edited by Caridad Inda and John Eagleson (Maryknoll, NY: Orbis Books, 1973), p.11.

62 Leonardo and Clodovis Boff, *Introducing Liberation Theology* (Maryknoll, NY: Orbis Books, 1987), pp. 1-2. Hereafter Boffs.

63. Ibid., p. 4.

64. Gustavo Gutiérrez, *The Power of the Poor in History* (Maryknoll, NY: Orbis, 1983), p. 101.

65. Phillip Berryman, *Liberation Theology: The Essential Facts About the Revolutionary Movement in Latin America and Beyond* (New York: Pantheon Books, 1987), p. 205.

66. Boffs, pp. 16-17.

67. Ernesto Cardenal, *The Gospel in Solentiname*, Vol. 1 (Maryknoll, NY: Orbis, 1982).

68. Frances O'Gorman and the women from Rocinha and Santa Marta, *Hillside Woman* (Rio de Janeiro: Ecumenical Center for Action and Reflection, 1985), p. 10.

69. Jennifer Atlee, *A Popular Theology of Suffering and Liberation*, M.A. thesis at Colgate-Rochester Divinity School/Bexley Hall/Crozer Theological Seminary, Rochester, NY, 1992.

70. Boffs, p. 19.

71. Videotape: "Faces in Faith: Gustavo Gutiérrez" (Ecufilm, United Methodist Church, Nashville, TN).

72. From a 1976 film, *Excuse Me America*, which covered his speech at the 1976 Eucharistic Congress, held in Philadelphia. The film also included segments on Dorothy Day, Mother Teresa, and Cesar Chavez.

73. Berryman, p. 60.

74. Boffs, p. 3.

75. Jon Sobrino, "Spirituality and the Following of Jesus," in Ignacio Ellacuría and Jon Sobrino, eds., *Mysterium Liberationis: Fundamental Concepts of Liberation Theology* (Maryknoll, NY: Orbis Books, 1993), p. 679.

76. Ibid., pp. 681-686.

77. Congregation for the Doctrine of the Faith, "Instruction on Certain Aspects of the Theology of Liberation," *National Catholic Reporter* (September 21, 1984). These three summary points are taken from Arthur F. McGovern, *Liberation Theology and Its Critics: Toward an Assessment* (Maryknoll, NY: Orbis Books, 1989), pp. 15-16.

78. Congregation for the Doctrine of the Faith, "Instruction on Christian Freedom and Liberation," *National Catholic Reporter*, April 25, 1986.

79. Leonardo Boff, *Ecclesiogenesis: The Base Communities Reinvent the Church* (Maryknoll, NY: Orbis Books, 1986).

80. McGovern, pp. 17-18.

81. McGovern, "Chapter 3: The Critics: An Overview," pp. 47-61; Michael Novak, "The Case Against Liberation Theology," *New York Times Magazine* (Oct. 21, 1984): 51 ff.; Paul Sigmund, *Liberation Theology at the Crossroads: Democracy or Revolution?* (New York: Oxford University Press, 1990).

82. David Molineaux, "Women, Native People Challenge Theology," *National Catholic Reporter* (September 15, 1995): 13.

83. Leonardo Boff, *Ecology and Liberation: A New Paradigm* (Maryknoll, NY: Orbis Books, 1995).

84. Maria Pilar Aquino, *Our Cry for Life: Feminist Theology from Latin America* (Maryknoll, NY: Orbis Books, 1993); Elsa Tamez, ed., *Through Her Eyes: Women's Theology from Latin America* (Maryknoll, NY: Orbis Books, 1989); Virginia Fabella & Mercy Amba Oduyoye, eds., *With Passion and Compassion: Third World Women Doing Theology* (Maryknoll, NY: Orbis Books, 1988); John Pobee and Barbel von Wartenberg-Potter, *New Eyes for Reading: Biblical and Theological Reflections by Women from the Third World* (Oak Park, IL: Meyer-Stone, 1987).

85. Ivone Gebara, "Women Doing Theology in Latin America," in Fabella and Oduyoye, p. 134.

86. Also see Charles Bayer, *A Guide to Liberation Theology for Middle-Class Congregations* (St. Louis, MO: CBP Press, 1986).

87. (Maryknoll, NY: Orbis Books, 1981).

88. See note 57.

89. Juan Luis Segundo, *The Liberation of Theology* (Maryknoll, NY: Orbis Books, 1976), p. 3.

90. Berryman, p. 204.

91. Gebara, p. 134.

CHAPTER 10

1. The origins of the National Conference of Catholic Bishops are found in the Church's desire "to study, coordinate, unify and put in operation all Catholic activities incidental to the war [World War I]." Although the original executive committee was envisioned to include a lay and clerical appointee of each of the fourteen Archbishoprics, the heads of the American Federation of Catholic Societies, and Knights of Columbus, the bishops, thinking this broader structure would be unwieldy and inefficient, constituted themselves as the National Catholic War Council in November 1917. After the First World War the bishops realized the need for a long-range program of systematic teaching and study of social and economic issues, so they transformed the National Catholic War Council into a permanent peacetime agency, the National Catholic Welfare Conference. See Abell, *American Catholicism and Social Action*, p. 206.

At the end of 1966, after the Second Vatican Council, the bishops restructured the National Catholic Welfare Conference into two entities, the National Conference of Catholic Bishops (NCCB) and the United States Catholic Conference (USCC). Both of these organizations are under the control of the U.S. bishops. "Through these distinct but closely related organizations—one a canonical entity, the other a civil corporation—the bishops fulfill their responsibilities of leadership and service to Church and nation." The NCCB is a *canonical entity* established by Church law rooted in the Vatican II's Decree on Bishops' Pastoral Office in the Church. The membership of the NCCB includes all the bishops of the U.S. (approximately 375). The "NCCB enables the bishops to exchange ideas and information, deliberate on the Church's broad concerns, and respond as a body. The conference functions through a general assembly [which meets usually twice a year], an administrative committee of 48 members, several executive-level committees, and some 40 standing and ad hoc committees. NCCB committees deal with pastoral matters important to the Church as a whole."

The other episcopal organization is the USCC which as a public policy agency of the US

Catholic bishops is a *civil corporation.* "The USCC provides an organizational structure and assistance in the public, educational, and social concerns of the Church at the national or interdiocesan level." Unlike the NCCB, whose members are only bishops, the USCC includes lay, religious and priest members in its policy-making structures. The USCC shares several structures with the NCCB: the Administrative Board for both is the same, the same executive-level committees serve both conferences, the General Secretariat in Washington, D.C., handles both NCCB and USCC business. While some staff are assigned to one conference or the other, a significant number work for both. Descriptions are taken from Hugh J. Nolan, ed., *Pastoral Letter of the United States Catholic Bishops* (Washington, D.C.: USCC, 1983), p. 11.

2. J. Bryan Hehir, "Catholic Teaching on War and Peace: The Decade 1979-1989," in Charles Curran, ed., *Moral Theology: Challenges for the Future—Essays in Honor of Richard A. McCormick* (New York: Paulist, 1990), p. 365 [emphasis added].

3. Ibid., p. 356.

4. Bishop Matthew Clark of Rochester, New York has addressed these concerns from his perspective as a bishop; see his article "The Pastoral Exercise of Authority," *New Theology Review* 10 (August 1997): 6-17.

5. For instance, I attended a three-day hearing on the economics pastoral that was held at Notre Dame University in October, 1983. I still remember the symbolism of the five bishops sitting in the front row of the *audience,* listening to the analysis and advice of various moral theologians, economists, business and government leaders. It would be my hope that in the near future we would see the pope and the presidents of the various curial offices taking on the same kind of public *listening* stance.

6. Rembert G. Weakland, "The Economic Pastoral: Draft Two," *America* (September 21, 1985): 132.

7. A concise presentation of the history of the just war theory is found in *La Civiltà Cattolica,* "Conscienza cristiana e guerra moderna." v. 142 (1991):3-16, translated by William H. Shannon: "Modern War and Christian Conscience," *Origins* 21 (December 1991): 450-455. Also see: Roland Bainton, *Christian Attitudes Toward War and Peace: A Historical Survey and Critical Reevaluation* (Nashville, TN: Abingdon, 1960); Lisa Cahill, *Love Your Enemies: Discipleship, Pacifism, and Just War Theory* (Minneapolis, MN: Fortress Press, 1994); James Turner Johnson, *Just War Tradition and the Restraint of War: A Moral and Historical Inquiry* (New Haven, CT: Princeton University Press, 1981); David G. Hunter, "A Decade of Research on Early Christians and Military Service," *Religious Studies Review* 18 (April 1992): 87-94; and Ronald Musto, *The Catholic Peace Tradition* (Maryknoll, NY: Orbis Books, 1986).

8. Kenneth Himes, "War," NDCST, p. 978.

9. Pope Pius XII, "Christmas Message," 1956, *The Pope Speaks.*

10. Himes, ibid., p. 979.

11. Ibid.

12. Stephen Lammers, "Peace," NDCST, p. 721.

13. Jim Castelli, *The Bishops and the Bomb* (Garden City, NY: Doubleday, 1983), pp. 14-15.

14. Ibid., p. 15.

15. Ibid., pp. 85-6.

16. Juliana Casey, *Where is God Now? Nuclear Terror, Feminism and the Search for God* (Kansas City, MO: Sheed and Ward, 1987), p. 69.

17. Ibid., p. 106.

18. Castelli, p. 98.

19. Ibid., pp. 106-7.

20. Ibid., p. 138. The bishops of West Germany and France also wrote a pastoral letters on peace during this same time period. See James V. Schall, ed., *Out of Justice, Peace: Joint Pastoral Letter of the West German Bishops; Winning the Peace: Joint Pastoral Letter of the French Bishops* (San Francisco, CA: Ignatius Press, 1984). For a comparison of the German and American letters see Charles E. Curran, *Tensions in Moral Theology* (Notre Dame, IN: University of Notre Dame Press, 1988), pp. 138-161. Also see J. Bryan Hehir, "Catholic Teaching on War and Peace: The Decade 1979-1989," in Curran, *Moral Theology: Challenges for the Future*, pp. 366-69.

21. Castelli, pp. 166-7.

22. I am drawing upon Bryan Hehir's summary of the pastoral letter as found in his "Catholic Teaching on War and Peace: The Decade 1979-1989," in Curran, *Moral Theology: Challenges for the Future*, p. 366.

23. Kenneth R. Himes, OFM, "Pacifism and the Just War Tradition in Roman Catholic Social Teaching," John Coleman, S.J., ed., *One Hundred Years of Catholic Social Thought: Celebration and Challenge* (Maryknoll, NY: Orbis Books, 1991), p. 339-40.

24. Ibid., p. 338.

25. Ibid.

26. Ibid., pp. 341 and 340.

27. John Courtney Murray, *We Hold These Truths: Catholic Reflections on the American Proposition* (New York: Sheed and Ward, 1960), p. 271; cited by Hehir p. 374. George Weigel has argued his position for 475 pages with a separate section on Hehir pp. 314-24 in *Tranquillitas Ordinis: The Present Failure and Future Promise of American Catholic Thought on War and Peace* (New York: Oxford University Press, 1987).

28. Ibid., p. 379.

29. John Finnis, Joseph Boyle and Germain Grisez, *Nuclear Deterrence, Morality and Realism* (New York: Oxford University Press, 1987).

30. Hehir, p. 375.

31. Ibid., pp. 374-5.

32. Andrew M. Greeley, "Why the Peace Pastoral Didn't Bomb," *National Catholic Reporter* (April 12, 1985).

33. These documents were published by the National Conference of Catholic Bishops, June 1988 (Washington, D.C.: USCC). Cardinal Bernardin's summary of the Report is found in Joseph Cardinal Bernardin, "The Challenge of Peace Revisited," in Coleman, *One Hundred Years of Catholic Social Thought*, pp. 282–3.

34. Ibid., p. 284.

35. Gerard R. Powers, Drew Christiansen, and Robert Hennemeyer, eds., *Peacemaking: Moral and Policy Challenges for a New World* (Washington, D.C.: USCC, 1994).

36. National Conference of Catholic Bishops, *The Harvest of Justice Is Sown in Peace*, Origins 23 (December 9, 1993): 449; 451-464.

37. Powers, et al., p. 2.

38. "President Bush Defends War as Just," [the president's speech on January 28, 1991 to the National Religious Broadcasters' convention in Washington, D.C.] *Origins* 20 (February 7, 1991): 571.

39. Pope John Paul II, "War, A Decline for Humanity," *Origins* 20 (January 24, 1991): 525-531 and "The Pope's Letters to Bush and Hussein, " ibid., pp. 534-535.

40. At the Annual Meeting of the Society of Christian Ethics a resolution was adopted on January 13—three days before the allied counterattack—which worked through the just war criteria and concluded that "Given the above considerations, a majority of those of us assembled, as we ourselves seek to apply the above criteria, conclude that it would be unjustifiable for the United States, even in concert with other forces, to take offensive military action in the Gulf at this time." *Council of the Scientific Study of Religion Bulletin* 20 (April 1991): 44.

41. Distributed by Professor Joseph Martos, Allentown College, Center Valley, Pennsylvania.

42. Archbishop John Quinn, "Can There Be a Just War Today?" *Origins* 20 (February 28, 1991): 623-625; "Church Leaders React to the War," *Origins* 20 (February 7, 1991): 572-579; Tom Fox, *Iraq: Military Victory, Moral Defeat* (Kansas City, MO: Sheed and Ward, 1991); Michael Duffey, *Peacemaking Christians: The Future of Just Wars, Pacifism, and Nonviolent Resistance* (Kansas City, MO: Sheed and Ward, 1995); a political scientist at Notre Dame, George Lopez, "The Gulf War: Not So Clean," *Bulletin of the Atomic Scientists* 47 (1991): 32.

43. While not a "supporter" Father J. Bryan Hehir —who played a shaping role in the debate as an advisor both to the USCC and to many individual bishops and as a very well-informed and careful scholar— acknowledged that "I am not prepared to declare the entire war unjust purely and simply." "The Moral Calculus of War: Just But Unwise," *Commonweal* 118 (1991): 126; a philosopher from Emory University, Nicholas Fotion, "The Gulf War: Cleanly Fought, " *Bulletin of the Atomic Scientists* 47 (1991): 25.

44. Langan, pp. 99-106.

45. A Harvard study-team reported that "infant and child mortality will double and that at least 170,000 children under five will die during the coming year as a result of the delayed effects of the of the Gulf Crisis." Harvard Study Team Report, "Public Health in Iraq," (May 1991): 5. Also see the testimony of Lawrence Pezzullo, executive director of Catholic Relief Services, to the House Select Committee on Hunger, August 1, 1991, "The Worsening Humanitarian Picture in Iraq," *Origins* 21 (1991): 171-174.

46. Langan, p. 110.

47. William H. Shannon, "Christian Conscience and Modern Warfare," *America* 166 (February 15, 1992): 108.

48. Ibid., p. 108, emphasis mine.

49. *La Civiltà Cattolica,* "Coscienza cristiana e guerra moderna," 142 (1991): 3-16. Translated by William H. Shannon: "Modern War and Christian Conscience," *Origins* 21 (December 1991): 453; emphasis mine.

50. John R. Langan, "The Just War After the Gulf War," *Theological Studies* 53 (1992): 101.

51. Shannon, p. 108.

52. Brian Johnstone, "Abandoning the Just War Theory? The Development of B. Häring's Thought on Peace, 1945-1990," *Studia Moralia* 33 (1995): 289. Also see George Weigel and John Langan, eds., *The American Search for Peace: Moral Reasoning, Religious Hope, and National Security* (Washington, D.C., 1991), pp. 102-108.

53. Ronald Musto, *The Catholic Peace Tradition* (Maryknoll, NY: Orbis Books, 1986).

54. Ibid., pp. 240-254.

55. Ibid., p. 243.

56. A conservative and accommodating stance was taken by an organization founded by Msgr. John Ryan and Raymond McGowan in 1927. They formed the Catholic Association

for International Peace (CAIP), which was part of the National Catholic Welfare Conference. Over the years CAIP rejected pacifism and accommodated the just war theory to the nuclear age and the goals of U.S. military security. When the bishops' conference was reorganized in 1967 CAIP was dissolved, and its functions were absorbed by the Commission for World Justice and Peace of the United States Catholic Conference.

57. Musto, p. 253.

58. Himes, p. 336.

59. Musto, p. 253.

60. Ibid., p. 254.

61. Ibid., p. 259.

62. Mary Evelyn Jegen, S.N.D., "Peace and Pluralism: Church and Churches," in Coleman, *One Hundred Years*, p. 293.

63. Ibid., p. 293.

64. Ibid., p. 293.

65. Ibid., p. 294.

66. Ibid., p. 296.

67. Ibid., pp. 299-301.

68. Duffey, p. 118.

69. Mary Craig, *Lech Walesa and His Poland* (New York: Continuum, 1987), p. 114.

70. Rainer Hildebrandt, *From Gandhi to Walesa* (Berlin: Verlag Hausam Checkpoint Charlie, 1987), p. 15: quoted by Duffey, pp. 120-121.

71. Craig, p. 214.

72. Ibid., p. 195.

73. Ibid., p. 271.

74. Helmar Junghans, "The Christians' Contribution to the Non-violent Revolution in the GDR in the Fall of 1989," *Philosophy and Theology* 6 (Fall, 1991): 80.

75. In northern and eastern Germany the higher percentage of Christians are Lutheran, whereas, in southern Germany the higher percentage are Roman Catholic.

76. Junghans, p. 91.

77. Jorg Swoboda, *The Revolution of the Candles* (Wuppertal und Kassel: Oncken Verlag, 1990), p. 5; quoted in Duffey, p. 127; emphasis mine.

78. Duffey, p. 129.

79. Peggy Rosenthal, "The Precarious Road: Nonviolence in the Philippines," *Commonweal* 113 (June 20, 1986): 364; emphasis mine.

80. Ibid., p. 367.

81. Ibid., p. 365.

82. Ibid., p. 366.

83. Ibid., p. 366.

84. Bryan Johnson, *The Four Days of Courage* (New York: The Free Press, 1987), p. 46.

85. Duffey, p. 138.

86. Richard B. Miller "Christian Pacifism and Just-War Tenets: How Do They Converge?" *Theological Studies* 47 (1986): 448-472.

87. James Turner Johnson, "On Keeping Faith: The Use of History for Religious Ethics," *Journal of Religious Ethics* 7 (1979): 113.

88. Himes, "War," p. 981.

89. Jose Miguez Bonino, *Doing Theology in a Revolutionary Situation* (Philadelphia: Fortress, 1975).

90. Lammers, p. 720.

91. Drew Christiansen and Gerard Powers, "Send in the Peacekeepers: Sovereignty Isn't Sacred," *Commonweal* 124 (February 28, 1997): 16. Also see Kenneth Himes, "Just War, Pacifism and Humanitarian Intervention," *America* 169 (August 14, 1993): 10-15; 28-30 and idem "Catholic Social Thought and Humanitarian Intervention," in Gerard F. Powers, Drew Christiansen and Robert T. Hennemeyer, eds., *Peacemaking: Moral and Policy Challenge for a New World* (Washington, D.C.: USCC, 1994).

92. Lammers, p. 721.

CHAPTER 11

1. Eugene Kennedy, "America's Activist Bishops: Examining Capitalism," *The New York Times Magazine* (August 12, 1984): 14 & ff.

2. Phillip Berryman, *Our Unfinished Business: The U.S. Catholic Bishops' Letters on Peace and the Economy* (New York: Pantheon, 1989), p. 75.

3. National Conference of Catholic Bishops, *Pastoral Letter on Catholic Social Teaching and the U.S. Economy: First Draft*, November 11, 1984 (Washington, D.C.: USCC, 1984), Appendix I "Persons Who Have Presented Testimony," pp. 130-135.

4. Rembert Weakland, "The Economic Pastoral: Draft Two," *America* 153 (September 21, 1985): 132.

5. Richard McCormick, *The Critical Calling: Reflections on Moral Dilemmas Since Vatican II* (Washington, D.C.: Georgetown University Press, 1989), p. 38.

6. For a discussion of response to Charles Curran and the twenty-four women religious who signed an ad in *The New York Times* on the abortion issue see chapter four, "Contested Authority," in Anne E. Patrick, *Liberating Conscience: Feminist Explorations in Catholic Moral Theology* (New York: Continuum, 1996), pp. 102-133.

7. Milton Friedman, "Good Ends, Bad Means," in Thomas Gannon, ed., *The Catholic Challenge to the American Economy* (New York: Macmillan, 1987), p. 99.

8. Berryman, pp. 108-109.

9. From a fund-raising letter by the American Catholic Committee, quoted in *The Roundtable: A National Association of Catholic Diocesan Social Action Directors*, mimeographed material sent out in late September, 1984.

10. Lay Commission on Catholic Social Teaching and the U.S. Economy, *Toward the Future: Catholic Social Thought and the U.S. Economy: A Lay Letter* (New York: American Catholic Committee, 1984), p. 106.

11. William E. Simon and Michael Novak, "Liberty and Justice for All," in James Finn, ed., *Private Virtue and Public Policy: Catholic Thought and National Life* (New Brunswick, NJ: Transaction Publishers, 1990), pp. 1-28. Also see Berryman, pp. 115-116.

12. From a short statement that accompanied the Lay Commission's November 1986 document "Liberty and Justice for All," see Berryman, pp. 118-119.

13. Clodovis Boff and Leonardo Boff, "A Igreja Perante a Economia nos EUA: Un Olhar a Partir da Periferia," *Revista Eclesiatica Brasileira* 47 (June 1987): 356-77. For an edited

English version see "The Church and the Economy of the United States: A Look from the Point of View of the Periphery," trans. Joseph Rozansky, *National Catholic Reporter* (August 28, 1987): 14, 23-24. I am following Rembert Weakland's summary of the article as found in "Revisited" pp. 19-20. For a fuller summary of the Boffs article see Thomas L. Schubeck, *Liberation Ethics: Sources, Models and Norms* (Minneapolis, MN: Fortress Press, 1993), pp. 89-106. While the Boffs raise some important points about the pastoral letter, their criticisms are also subject to critique. Schubeck has responded to the Boffs' criticisms in his work, pp. 100-106.

14. For a further discussion of these three perspectives consult the following: Gregory Baum, *Theology and Society* (New York: Paulist, 1987), pp. 197-205; Leonardo and Clodovis Boff, *Introducing Liberation Theology* (Maryknoll NY: Orbis Books, 1987), pp. 25-27; and Joseph Holland and Peter Henriot, *Social Analysis: Linking Faith and Social Justice* (Maryknoll, NY: Orbis Books, 1980), pp. 32-40.

15. Baum, p. 197.

16. Ibid., p. 198.

17. Ibid., p. 199.

18. Ibid., pp. 202 and ff.

19. Cardinal Ratzinger's lecture is found in *L'Osservatore Romano*, German ed. (November 29, 1985); English ed. (December 23, 1985). I am using Archbishop Rembert G. Weakland's summary of it, from "The Economic Pastoral Letter Revisited," in Coleman, *One Hundred Years of Catholic Social Thought*, p. 203.

20. Weakland, "Letter Revisited," pp. 203-204.

21. David Hollenbach, "Liberalism, Communitarianism and Bishops' Pastoral Letter on the Economy," in *The Annual of the Society of Christian Ethics 1987*, Diane Yeager, ed., (Washington, D.C.: Georgetown University Press, 1987): 35. Hollenbach continued this discussion of communitarian and liberal social vision in "The Common Good Revisited," *Theological Studies* 50 (1989): 70-94.

22. Some commentaries and symposia on *Economic Justice for All* not previously mentioned are: Walter Block, *The U.S. Bishops and Their Critics: An Economic and Ethical Perspective* (Vancouver, B.C.: The Fraser Institute, 1986); R. Bruce Douglass, ed., *The Deeper Meaning of Economic Life: Critical Essays on the U.S. Catholic Bishops' Pastoral Letter on the Economy* (Washington, D.C.: Georgetown University Press, 1986); Thomas M. Gannon, ed., *The Catholic Challenge to the American Economy: Reflections on the U.S. Bishops' Pastoral Letter on Catholic Social Teaching and the U.S. Economy* (New York: Macmillan, 1987); George E. McCarthy & Royal W. Rhodes, eds., *Eclipse of Justice: Ethics, Economics, and the Lost Traditions of American Catholicism* (Maryknoll, NY: Orbis Books, 1992).

23. Rembert G. Weakland, "'Economic Justice for All' Ten Years Later," *America* 176 (March 22, 1997): 8-9.

24. National Conference of Catholic Bishops, *A Decade After Economic Justice for All: Continuing Principles, Changing Context, New Challenges* (Washington, D.C.: USCC, 1995).

25. "Bishops Issues Call to Justice" *Catholic Courier* [Rochester, NY] (November 21, 1996): 1.

26. Ibid., p. 1.

27. Willmar Thorkelson, "Weakland: 'Individualism Fights Economic Justice,'" *National Catholic Reporter* (January 29, 1988): 20.

28. Weakland, "Revisited," p. 209; also see Rembert Weakland, *Faith and the Human Enterprise: A Post-Vatican II Vision* (Maryknoll, NY: Orbis Books, 1992), pp. 123 & ff.

29. Ibid., p. 210.

30. William E. Murnion, "The 'Preferential Option for the Poor' in *Economic Justice for All: Theology or Ideology?*" in Bernard Prusak, ed., *Raising the Torch of Good News: Catholic Authority and Dialogue with the World* (Lanham, MD: University Press of America, 1988), p. 34.

31. "Catholic Charities and the Poor: An Interview with Fred Kammer," *America* 176 (August 16, 1997), p. 10; hereafter "Interview."

32. Ibid., p. 9.

33. Catholic Charities USA, *Cadre Study: Toward a Renewed Catholic Charities Movement* (Alexandria, VA: Catholic Charities USA, 1992), p. 63.

34. Anne Simpson, "Catholic Charities USA," NDCST, p. 124.

35. Ibid., p. 124.

36. *Cadre Study*, p. 18.

37. Ibid., p. 19.

38. "Catholic Charities and the Poor: An Interview with Fred Kammer," *America* 177 (August 16, 1997): 10; hereafter cited as "Interview."

39. Ibid., p. 14.

40. Simpson, p. 124.

41. "Interview," p. 12.

42. Campaign for Human Development, *Daring to Seek Justice: People Working Together: The Story of the Campaign for Human Development, Its Roots, Its Programs and Its Challenges* (Washington, D.C.: USCC, 1986), p. 1; hereafter cited as *Daring*.

43. Ibid., p. 4.

44. Ibid., p. 5.

45. Ibid., p. 14.

46. "Criteria and Guidelines for 1985 CHD Funding," in *Daring*, p. 71.

47. "Resolution on Crusade Against Poverty: A Resolution Adopted by the National Conference of Catholic Bishops, November 14, 1969," in *Daring*, p. 69.

48. Ibid., p. 72.

49. Ibid., p. 16.

50. Ibid., p. 21.

51. Campaign for Human Development, *For 25 Years We've Been Turning Lives Around— 1994-95 Annual Report.*

52. Campaign for Human Development, *Thanksgiving 1970 Appeal, Fact Sheet No. 1—The Campaign: Origin, Objectives, Organization, Education and Information Program* (Washington, D.C.: USCC, 1970), p. 1.

53. Campaign for Human Development, *Empowerment and Hope: 25 Years of Turning Lives Around* (Washington, D.C.: USCC, 1996), p. 19; hereafter cited as *Empowerment.*

54. William T. Poole & Thomas W. Pauken, *The Campaign for Human Development: Christian Charity or Political Activism?* (Washington, D.C.: Capital Research Center, 1988), p. iii.

55. *Empowerment*, p. 61.

56. The letter is dated May 1989 and is included with the CRC booklet.

57. Campaign for Human Development Committee, *The Cries of the Poor Are Still With Us: 25 Years of Working to Empower the Poor* (Washington, D.C.: USCC, 1997), p. 11.

58. *Empowerment*, p. 119. McCarthy and Castelli's study is entitled *Working for Justice: The*

Campaign for Human Development and Poor Empowerment Groups (Washington, D.C.: USCC, 1994).

59. *Empowerment*, p. 105.

60. Ibid., pp. 107-108.

61. Ibid., pp. 110-111.

62. Ibid., pp. 59-60.

CHAPTER 12

1. Dorr, *Option for the Poor:*, p. 372.

2. Anne E. Carr, *Transforming Grace: Christian Tradition and Women's Experience* (San Francisco: Harper and Row, 1988), p. 1.

3. Maria Riley, "Women," NDCST, p. 986.

4. Ibid., p. 987.

5. Pius XII, "Address to Girls of Catholic Action, April 24, 1943," *Acta apostolicae sedi* [AAS] 35 (1943) trans.: *Papal Teaching: The Woman in the Modern World* (Boston: Daughters of St. Paul, 1959), p. 109.

6. Pius XII, "Address to Italian Women," October 21, 1945, AAS 37 (1945), trans.: *Women in the Modern World*, pp. 128-129.

7. Christine E. Gudorf, "Sexism," NDCST, p. 878.

8. John XXIII, *Pacem in Terris*, par. 41.

9. Rosemary Radford Ruether, "The Place of Women in the Church," L. Adrian Hastings, ed., *Modern Catholicism: Aspects of Church Life Since the Council* (New York: Oxford University Press, 1991), p. 260.

10. Ibid., pp. 260-261.

11. Anne E. Patrick, "Toward Renewing 'The Life and Culture of Fallen Man': *Gaudium et Spes* as Catalyst for Catholic Feminist Theology," in Charles E. Curran, Margaret A. Farley & Richard A. McCormick, eds., *Feminist Ethics and the Catholic Moral Tradition: Readings in Moral Theology No. 9* (New York: Paulist, 1996), p. 485.

12. Ruether, p. 261.

13. Patrick, pp. 486 and 494.

14. Riley, p. 988.

15. Ibid., p. 989.

16. Gudorf, p. 878. This discussion calls to mind the insights of psychologist Sidney Callahan, in her book *In Good Conscience: Reason and Emotion in Moral Decision Making* (New York: HarperCollins, 1991). She discusses the question of male and female attributes. She maintains that the difference is not between men and women, but between "insiders" and "outsiders". Those outside the power structures are invested with the qualities that are not as evident in the those who have the power: "Most women have been relative outsiders and newcomers in the professional and public worlds of our culture. They may more often bring the view of the marginal person into the discussion; but men who are outsiders by class, race, or education can do the same. The moral resources of outsiders, whether women or men, can be invaluable." p. 197.

17. Riley, p. 989.

18. Ibid., 989.

19. John Paul II, *Familiaris Consortio, Origins* 11 (December 24, 1981): 107-109.

20. Pope John Paul II, "Chi troviamo." [Whom do we find], *The Pope Speaks* 24, p.166; quoted in Gudorf, p. 879.

21. Pope John Paul II, "All 'indirizzo," *The Pope Speaks* 24, pp. 181-82; Gudorf, p. 879.

22. Ibid., p. 879.

23. *Evangelization in Latin America's Present and Future, Final Document of the Third General Conference of Latin American Episcopate, Puebla de Los Angeles, Mexico, 27 January—13 February 1979*, par. 834; as reprinted in Eagleson and Scharper, *Puebla and Beyond*, p. 233; hereafter cited as *Puebla*.

24. *Puebla*, pars. 835-840, p. 233.

25. Riley, p. 990.

26. Ibid.

27. Catholic News Service, "Odyssey of a Failed Pastoral," *National Catholic Reporter*, (December 4, 1992) 3. The article does not specify the site on the West Coast.

28. Thomas J. Reese, "Women's Pastoral Fails," *America* 167 (December 5, 1992): 443.

29. Ibid..

30. "Odyssey," p. 3.

31. Catholic News Service report by Laurie Hansen, dated April 9, 1992 and reprinted in the margin of *Origins* 21 (April 23, 1992): 763.

32. Lee Strong, "Draft of Women's Pastoral Criticizes Sexism," *The Catholic Courier* [Rochester, NY] (April, 16, 1992): 3.

33. Jim Bowman, "The First Ten Years: Pastoral on Women's Concerns—What Do These Men Want?" *Commonweal* 119 (July 17, 1992): 6.

34. Ibid., p. 6. My research revealed four departures from the committee by April of 1990 (Brabeck, Eugene, Perkins, and Carr), *Origins* 19 (April 5, 1990): 721. I am not sure who the other three departees were.

35. Ibid., p. 6-7. Also see Tim McCarthy's summary of the debate, "Bishops Hear Clawing at the Castle Walls," *National Catholic Reporter* (July 3, 1992): 4-5.

36. Bowman, p. 6.

37. Dorothy Vidulich, "Women's Pastoral Buried After 10 Years," *National Catholic Reporter*, (December 4, 1992): 3.

38. Dorothy Vidulich and Thomas Fox, "Women's Letter Draft Moves Sharply Right," *National Catholic Reporter*, (September 11, 1992): 3.

39. Ibid.

40. Reese, p. 443.

41. Vidulich, Dec. 4, 1992, p. 4.

42. Ibid., pp. 3-4.

43. Ibid., p. 3.

44. From the introductory note by Robert Lynch, the General Secretary of the NCCB, on the inside of the cover page, Ad Hoc Committee for a Pastoral Response to Women's Concerns, National Conference of Catholic Bishops, Committee Report, November 1992, *One In Christ Jesus: Toward a Pastoral Response to the Concerns of Women for Church and Society* (Washington, D.C.: USCC, 1992).

45. Jack Wintz, "What's Happening to the Women's Pastoral: Some Candid Answers from Bishop Joseph L. Imesch," *St Anthony Messenger* 97 (October 1989): 10.

46. The committee devised and sent out the following questionnaire which really focused in on women's experience:

> 1. As you reflect upon your experiences as a Catholic woman, what stands out for you?
>
> 2. In what ways do you feel appreciated as a woman in the Church? In society?
>
> 3. In what ways do you feel oppressed/discriminated against in the Church? In society?
>
> 4. As you reflect upon your personal experiences, what do you find contributes the most to the reconciliation (harmony, affirmation, dignity, healing) of women in the Church? Of women in society?
>
> 5. As you reflect upon your personal experiences, what do you find contributed the most to the alienation (abuse, divisiveness, dehumanization) of women in the Church? In society?
>
> 6. As you reflect upon your personal experiences, what issues/themes emerge as the most important for the development of the bishops' pastoral letter on women in the Church and in society?

Partners in the Mystery of Redemption, First Draft, "Appendix III," p. 87.

47. The letter was dated June 1, 1992, see marginal notes, *Origins* 21 (1992): 91-92.

48. P. Francis Murphy, "Let's Start Over: A Bishop Appraises the Pastoral on Women," *Commonweal* 119 (September 25, 1992):12.

49. Ibid.

50. Ibid., p. 11.

51. Wintz, pp. 9-10.

52. Marginal notes, *Origins* 20 (August 30, 1990): 187.

53. Leadership Conference of Women Religious Executive Committee, "Critiquing the Women's Pastoral Draft," *Origins* 20 (August 30, 1990): 187.

54. Catherine Spretnak, *States of Grace* (San Francisco:Harper, 1991), as quoted by Murphy, p. 13.

55. Murphy, p. 13.

56. Ibid.; emphasis mine.

57. Michael Rogness, "Lutheran Confessional Identity and Human Sexuality," *Word and World* 14 (Summer 1994): 330.

58. Committee on Women in Society and in the Church, *Strengthening the Bonds of Peace: A Pastoral Reflection on Women in the Church and in Society* (Washington, D.C.: USCC, 1995), pp. 12-13.

59. Vidulich, Dec. 4, 1992, p. 5.

60. Barbara Hogan, "Feminism and Catholic Social Thought," in NDCST, p. 394ff.

61. Ibid., p. 394.

62. Ibid..

63. Ibid.

64. Rosemary Radford Ruether, "Ecofeminism: First and Third World Women," in Mary

John Mananzan, et. al., eds., *Women Resisting Violence: Spirituality for Life* (Maryknoll, NY: Orbis Books, 1996), p. 27; emphasis mine.

65. I am following feminist theologian Barbara Hogan's explanation of the three schools of feminist thought, as presented in NDCST, p. 394 ff.

66. Hogan, p. 395.

67. Rosemary Radford Ruether, "Feminist Theology," in Joseph A. Komanchak, et al. eds., *The New Dictionary of Theology* (Wilmington, DE: Michael Glazier, 1987), p. 392. Hereafter NDT.

68. Ibid., p. 391.

69. Ibid., p. 392.

70. Carr, p. 7.

71. Ibid.

72. Giorgio Otranto, "Note sul sacerdozio femminile nell'antichita in margine a una testimonianza di Gelasio I," *Vetera Christianorum* 19 (1982): 341-60; translated with an introduction by Mary Ann Rossi, "Priesthood, Precedent, and Prejudice: On Recovering the Women Priests of Early Christianity," *Journal of Feminist Studies in Religion* 7 (Spring 1991): 73-94.

73. Ruether reports, "One expression of Quaker feminist theology is the tract by Margaret Fell, co-founder of the Society of Friends with George Fox, 'Women's Speaking Justified, Approved and Allowed by the Scripture,' written in 1667"; NDT, p. 392.

74. Ibid., p.394

75. Ibid., p. 394.

76. Rosemary Radford Ruether, *Sexism and God-Talk: Toward a Feminist Theology* (Boston: Beacon Press, 1983), pp. 18-19.

77. Susan L. Secker, "Women's Experience in Feminist Theology: The "Problem" or "Truth" of Difference," *Journal of Hispanic/Latino Theology* 1 (November 1993): 57.

78. Sally B. Purvis, "Lines and Textures; Authoritative Sources for Contemporary Christian Feminist Ethics," *The Annual of the Society of Christian Ethics* (1994): 264.

79. Sallie McFague, *Models of God: Theology for an Ecological, Nuclear Age* (Philadelphia: Fortress, 1987).

80. Sallie McFague, *Body of God: An Ecological Theology* (Minneapolis: Fortress, 1993).

81. Elizabeth A. Johnson, *Women, Earth, and Creator Spirit* (New York: Paulist, 1993); *She Who Is: The Mystery of God in Feminist Theological Discourse* (New York: Crossroad, 1993); and a lecture "How do we Name God? Female and Cosmic Images of God," at St. Bernard's Institute, Rochester, NY, October 23, 1996.

82. Ruether, NDT, p. 392.

83. Delores S. Williams, "Womanist Theology: Black Women's Voices," Judith Plaskow and Carol P. Christ, eds., *Weaving the Visions: New Patterns in Feminist Spirituality* (San Francisco: Harper & Row, 1989), p.179.

84. Ibid., pp. 180-181.

85. Ibid., p. 182.

86. Ibid., p. 184-185.

87. Delores S. Williams, *Sisters in the Wilderness: The Challenge of Womanist God-Talk* (Maryknoll, NY: Orbis Books, 1993).

88. Diana L. Hayes, "Feminist Theology, Womanist Theology: a Black Catholic Perspective,"

in James Cone and Gayraud Wilmore, eds., *Black Theology: A Documentary History,* Volume II (Maryknoll, NY: Orbis, 1993), pp. 332-333. Also see her work, *And Still We Rise: An Introduction to Black Theology.*

89. Williams, *Weaving the Visions,* p. 186.

90. Virgilio Elizondo, *The Future is Mestizo: Life Where Cultures Meet* (Bloomington, IN: Meyer-Stone Books, 1988), p. 40.

91. Gloria Anzaldua, *Borderlands: The New Mestiza* (San Francisco: Aunt Lute Book Co., 1987), pp. 78-81 as quoted by Jeanette Rodriguez, "Experience as a Resource for Feminist Thought," *Journal of Hispanic/Latino Theology* 1 (November 1993), p. 71.

92. Ada María Isasi-Díaz, *En la Lucha—in the Struggle: Elaborating a Mujeristia Theology* (Minneapolis, MN: Augsburg Fortress, 1993), p. 16.

93. Ibid., pp. 132-133.

94. Ibid., p. 134.

95. Ada María Isasi-Díaz and Yolanda Tarango, *Hispanic Women: Prophetic Voice in the Church* (San Francisco: Harper & Row, 1988), p. xii.

96. Isasi-Díaz, *En la Lucha,* p. 3.

97. Secker and Rodriguez wrote about their dialogue: Susan L. Secker, "Women's Experience in Feminist Theology: The 'Problem' or the 'Truth' of Difference," *Journal of Hispanic/Latino Theology* 1 (November 1993): 56-67. Also see Jeanette Rodriguez, "Experience as a Resource for Feminist Thought," *Journal of Hispanic/Latino Theology* 1 (November 1993): 68-76. Their work was also presented at the 1992 meeting of the Catholic Theological Society held in Pittsburgh. It was a very engaging workshop to be part of. See the next note for a report on the session.

98. Ellen Leonard, "Experience as a Resource for Feminist Thought," *CTSA Proceedings* 47 (1992): 125.

99. Isasi-Díaz, *En la Lucha,* p. 179.

CHAPTER 13

1. Rachel Carson, *Silent Spring* (Cambridge, MA: The Riverside Press, 1962).

2. Sean McDonagh reports that there was a symposium on animal rights sponsored by the Vatican held in October of 1962. This symposium was in response to a request by the National Catholic Society for Animal Welfare in the USA. The aim of the conference, held under the direction of the Archbishop Pietro Palazzine, the secretary of the Sacred Congregation of the Council, was to compile church teaching on animals and the need for laws to protect them. See Sean Mc Donagh, *The Greening of the Church* (Maryknoll, NY: Orbis Books, 1990), p. 176.

3. Abbott, *The Documents of Vatican II,* par. 33, p. 231.

4. *Octogesima Adveniens,* par. 21 in O'Brien and Shannon, *Catholic Social Thought,* p. 273.

5. McDonagh, p. 178.

6. Thomas M. Landy, "Environmentalism and Catholic Social Thought: Some Background, Challenges, and Opportunities," *New Theology Review* 9 (May 1996): 24.

7. *Justice in the World,* par. 11, in O'Brien and Shannon, p. 290, emphasis mine.

8. McDonagh, p. 178.

9. Barbara Ward, *A New Creation? Reflections on the Environmental Issue* (Vatican City: Tipografria Poliglotta Vaticana, 1973), p. 10

10. Pontifical Commission "Iustitia et Pax," *The Universal Purpose of Created Things: on the Conference on the Law of the Sea* (Vatican City: Tipografia Poliglotta Vaticana, 1977).

11. *Redemptor Hominis,* par. 14, *Origins* 8 (1979): 625 ff.

12. *The Holy Bible: New Revised Standard Version* (New York: Oxford University Press, 1989).

13. McDonagh, p. 180.

14. See Gregory Baum's helpful analysis of the letter: *The Priority of Labor* (New York: Paulist, 1982).

15. *L'Osservatore Romano,* October 10, 1983, as quoted in McDonagh, p. 180.

16. Ibid., p. 189.

17. John Paul II, "World Day of Peace: Peace With All Creation," *Origins* 19 (December 14, 1989): 465-468.

18. McDonagh, p. 191.

19. Landy, p. 26.

20. Pope John Paul II, *Evangelium Vitae, Origins* 24 (April 6, 1995): 689; 691-730.

21. McDonagh, p.191.

22. See Drew Christiansen and Walter Grazier, eds., *"And God Saw That It Was Good": Catholic Theology and the Environment* (Washington, D.C: USCC, 1996) for copies of these statements. Hereafter cited as *And God Saw.*

The editors note (on p. 16, footnote 4) that by 1996 there were 48 known statements on ecology or the environment issued by bishops' conferences of individual dioceses around the world including Australia, Belgium/Walloon, a joint statement by Brazil/Bolivia, Brazil, Burundi, CELAM, Canada, Chile, Dominican Republic, Ecuador, England and Wales, Federation of Asian Bishops' Conferences, Germany, Haiti, Indonesia, Ireland, Italy, Kenya, Korea, the Pacific Region, the Philippines, Portugal, Spain, Thailand, the United States, and Zaire.

23. Landy, p. 28.

24. Ibid., p. 28.

25. Lynn White, Jr.,"The Historical Roots of Our Ecological Crisis," *Science* 155 (March 1967): 1207.

26. Ian McHarg [landscape architect], *Design with Nature* (Philadelphia: Falcon, 1969); C. Amery, *Das Ende der Vorsehung: Die gnadenlosen Folgen des Christentums,* (Reinbek, 1972); E. Drewermann, *Der todliche Fortschritt* (Rengensburg, 1981). These last two references are discussed in "Che E Responsabile Dell'Attuale Degrado Ecologica?" *Civiltà Cattolica* 141 (January 20, 1990): 110.

27. Drew Christiansen, "Ecology, Justice, and Development," *Theological Studies* 51 (March 1990): 71, footnote 22.

28. Anne M. Clifford, "Foundations for a Catholic Ecological Theology of God," in *And God Saw,* p. 24.

29. Cf. Clifford, pp. 24-36; other references given in Christiansen, p. 71, footnote 22.

30. Counterpoint: Christian and Jewish asceticism, rightly understood, can be an antidote to the compulsive consumerism and desire for immediate gratification that are so obvious in our culture. "The intention of the ascetic practices associated with *Lent, Yom Kippur* and *Ramadan* is to sharpen a believer's focus on God and to consider God's requirement that people of faith live upright lives." Christian asceticism can be translated into life-styles that strive to live in less consumptive ways such as walking, bicycles, carpooling, and mass transportation; making the effort to recycle and reuse—there thousands of ways to live

and do business in ways that are less destructive of nature. Christian asceticism is not a somber undertaking, rather it brings a sense of peace, simplicity, and joy. Coupled with the value of asceticism is the value of developing an aesthetic sense—a sense that enables people to be open to and aware of the beauty, order, and loveliness in all areas of nature. The Judeo-Christian tradition has long encouraged the development of this sense of the beauty of God's creation in all its myriad expressions. See Flynn, pp. 83-85.

31. Flynn, p. 77.

32. Bishop James Malone, "Environmental Degradation and Social Injustice," *Origins* 22 (March 18, 1993): 691.

33. Archbishop John Quinn reported that "a study at Princeton University concluded that 76.5 percent of American Catholic women ... were using some form of birth regulation, and that *94 percent of these Catholic women were using methods condemned by the encyclical.*" See "'New Context' for Contraceptive Teaching," *Origins* 10 (October, 9, 1980): 263; emphasis mine.

34. Mother Teresa argued that the women of India learn the natural birth control methods easily and effectively because they are in touch with nature and the cycles of their own bodies. (From a discussion with her in Calcutta in October, 1978.) At the same time, a Father Rex Mansmann, who has worked for 27 years in the province of South Cotabato in southwest Mindanao in the Philippines, argues that "... the fact remains that not a single family, even those with whom the sister had daily contact, was able to effectively apply the natural birth control system. ...This experience throws a shadow of serious doubt on the effectiveness of natural birth control methods in the tribal setting." Rex Mansmann, "Insights into the Population Issue: Tablo," an unpublished paper of research conducted in the latter part of 1987 by the fieldworkers in Tabo and the health personnel of the Santa Cruz Mission under the supervision of Sister Cecilia Lorayes; quoted by McDonagh, pp. 43-44.

35. McDonagh, p. 65.

36. Ibid., p. 182.

37. Charles Lee, "Toxic Pollution and Race," *The Egg: Ecojustice Newsletter* (Summer, 1988): 7.

38. U.S. General Accounting Office, *Siting of Hazardous Waste Landfill and Their Correlation with Racial and Socioeconomic Status of Surrounding Communities* (Washington, D.C.: Government Printing Office, 1983).

39. United Church of Christ Commission for Racial Justice, *Toxic Wastes and Race in the United States: A National Report on the Racial and Socio-Economic Characteristics of Communities with Hazardous Waste Sites* (New York, 1987) as reported by Charles Lee, p. 9.

40. Quoted by Laura Westra and Peter S. Wenz, eds., *Faces of Environmental Racism: Confronting Issues of Global Justice* (Lanham, MD: Rowman & Littlefield Publishers, 1995), p. xvi.

41. Bunyon Bryant and Paul Mohai, eds., *Race and the Incidence of Environmental Hazards: A Time for Discourse* (Boulder, CO: Westview Press, 1992); and Robert D. Bullard, *Dumping in Dixie: Race, Class, and Environmental Quality* (Boulder, CO: Westview Press, 1990).

42. Aaron Gallegos, "A Partnership for the Earth: Churches and the Environmental Movement," *Sojourners* 26 (March-April, 1997): 14.

43. Richard Hofrichter, ed., *Toxic Struggles: The Theory and Practice of Environmental Justice* (Philadelphia, PA: New Society Publishers, 1993), p. 1.

44. United States Catholic Conference, *Renewing the Earth: An Invitation to Reflection and Action on Environment in Light of Catholic Social Teaching* (Washington, D.C.: USCC, 1992), pp. 5-6; also see Bishop James Malone, "Environmental Degradation and Social Injustice," *Origins* 22 (March 18, 1993): 689.

45. Kenneth and Michael Himes, "The Sacrament of Creation," *Commonweal* 117 (Jan. 26, 1990): 45 [emphasis added].

46. See Kevin W. Irwin, "The Sacramentality of Creation and the Role of Creation in Liturgy and Sacraments," in idem, and Edmund D. Pellegrino, eds., *Preserving the Creation: Environmental Theology and Ethics* (Washington, D.C.: Georgetown University Press, 1994), pp. 67-111.

47. Bishop Anthony Pilla, "Christian Faith and the Environment," *Origins* 20 (November 1, 1990): 338.

48. Yet, even here we have a mistrust of creation for we limit our understanding of "sacred space" to church buildings—for instance in the Canon Law restriction that weddings are not to be held outdoors. Hints of dualism are present in our liturgical and canonical disciplines.

49. Thomas Merton, *New Seeds of Contemplation* (New York: New Directions Books, 1961), pp. 30-31.

50. *Summa Theologica* I.8.1; see Josef Pieper, *Guide to Thomas Aquinas* (New York: New American Library, 1964), p.125.

51. *Summa Theologica* Part I Q. 47, Art. 1.

52. Jaime Ehegartner Schaefer, *Ethical Implications of Applying Aquinas' Notions of the Unity and Diversity of Creation to Functioning in Ecosystems,* Ph.D. dissertation, Marquette University, 1994 and Pamela A. Smith, *Aquinas and Today's Environmental Ethics: An Exploration of How Vision and the Virtue Ethic of "Ecothomism" Might Inform a Viable Eco-Ethic,* Ph.D. dissertation, Duquesne University, 1995.

53. Presented at the annual meeting of the Society of Christian Ethics, January 10, 1997, Pamela A Smith, "Toward 'Ecothomism'? Applying Aquinas to Issues in Environmental Ethics." Smith excerpted these twelve points from her Ph.D dissertation.

54. Albert Gore, *Earth in the Balance* (Boston: Houghton Mifflin, 1992), p. 345.

55 Tom Hayden, *The Lost Gospel: A Call for Renewing Nature, Spirit, and Politics* (San Francisco, CA: Sierra Club Books, 1996), pp. 237-238.

56. Noted by Drew Christiansen, "Christian Theology and Ecological Responsibility," *America* 166 (1992): 451.

57. Leonardo Boff, *St. Francis, a Model for Human Liberation* (New York: Crossroad Publishing, 1982), p. 39; also see Michael and Kenneth Himes, *Fullness of Faith: The Public Significance of Theology* (New York: Paulist, 1993), p. 119.

58. Gallegos, p. 14.

59. The budget for the Partnership's excellent educational and outreach programs during its first three years was also $4 million. Most of this money came from *secular* sources such as Nathan Cummings, Pew, and Rockefeller foundations. This signals "negligible investments in environmental programming." See Hayden, p. 69.

60. Hayden, pp.106-115.

61. Ibid., p. 173.

62. The Buddhist, Hindu, Jewish, Muslim and Christian "Declarations" on Nature can be found in Susan J. Clark, *Celebrating Earth Holy Days: A Resource Guide for Faith Communities* (New York: Crossroad, 1992), pp. 142-154.

63. William K. Reilly, "Theology and Ecology: A Confluence of Interests," *New Theology Review* 4 (May, 1991): 20.

64. Quoted by Bishop John McRaith of Owensboro, KY, "Giving Justice a Family Base," *Origins* 22 (1993): 397.

65. Chief Oren Lyons, Faithkeeper of the Onondaga Nation, which is part of the Haudenosaunee Confederacy of Northeastern North America, gave this figure on November 5, 1992. Reported by John A. Grim, "Native North American Worldviews and Ecology," in Mary Evelyn Tucker & John A. Grim, eds., *Worldviews and Ecology: Religion, Philosophy, and the Environment* (Maryknoll, NY: Orbis, 1994), p. 53.

66. Akwesasne Notes, *Basic Call to Consciousness* (Roosevelttown, NY: Akwesasne Notes, Mohawk Nation, Revised Ed., 1986), pp. 49, 53, and 78.

67. George E. Tinker, "An American Indian Theological Response to Ecojustice," in Jace Weaver, ed., *Defending Mother Earth: Native American Perspectives on Environmental Justice* (Maryknoll, NY: Orbis Books, 1996), pp. 160-162.

68. National Conference of Catholic Bishops, *1992: A Time of Remembering, Reconciling, and Recommitting Ourselves as a People—Pastoral Reflections on the Fifth Centenary and Native Americans* (Washington, D.C.: USCC, 1992), p.1.

69. John Paul II, "Meeting with Native Americans," in *Unity in the Work of Service* (Washington, D.C.: USCC, 1987), pp. 110-111.

70. *Renewing the Earth*, p. 6.

CONCLUSION

1. John Coleman, "Development of Church Social Teaching," *Origins* 11 (June 4, 1981): 41.

Index

Of Related Interest

Beyond Violence
*In the Spirit of
the Nonviolent Christ*
Gerard Vanderhaar
Offers suggestions for incorporating peace, compassion, and justice into our homes, at work, with difficult people, and as part of the political process. Demonstrates how we can become active and responsible citizens of the world, working together to build a compassionate commonwealth that will spread throughout the globe.
ISBN: 0-89622-739-1, 176 pp, $12.95

Christian Ethics
Shaping Values, Vision, Decisions
Judith Caron
Details how contemporary Christian ethics and personal moral decision-making are affected and shaped by complex social, environmental, personal, physical, mental, and emotional forces—as well as spiritual and religious beliefs and practices.
ISBN: 0-89622-658-1, 256 pp, $14.95

Liberation Theologies
The Global Pursuit of Justice
Alfred T. Hennelly, S.J.
Surveys the ideas and ideals of the major players in the field of liberation theology, demonstrating the far-reaching implications of the principles involved.
ISBN: 0-89622-647-6, 392 pp, $19.95

Tomorrow's Catholic
*Understanding God and Jesus
in a New Millennium*
Michael Morwood, MSC
Foreword by Dr. Thomas Groome
Challenges an outdated worldview that has influenced our images and ideas of God to the present day. Will inspire and encourage readers with its positive presentation of a religious worldview and spirituality relevant to a new millennium. Includes questions for discussion, an extensive bibliography, and a comprehensive index.
ISBN: 0-89622-724-3, 160 pp, $9.95

Befriending the Earth
*A Theology of Reconciliation
Between Humans and the Earth*
Edited by Anne Lonergan
and Stephen Dunn
In this challenging book, Thomas Berry and Thomas Clarke discuss a range of theological topics, including the Trinity, creation, redemption, evil, grace, sacrifice, and spirituality, among others. Thomas Berry then develops his ideas, while Thomas Clarke critiques and expands on them. Questions for discussion and reflection end each chapter.
ISBN: 0-89622-471-6, 168 pp, $9.95

Available at religious bookstores or from:

 **TWENTY-THIRD PUBLICATIONS**
XXIII P.O. Box 180 • Mystic, CT 06355
1-800-321-0411 • E-Mail:ttpubs@aol.com